PATERNOSTER THEOLOGICAL MONOGRAPHS

On Being a Christian in the Academy

Nicholas Wolterstorff and the Practice of Christian Scholarship

PATERNOSTER THEOLOGICAL MONOGRAPHS

A full listing of titles in both Paternoster
Biblical and Theological Monographs
will be found at the close of this book

PATERNOSTER THEOLOGICAL MONOGRAPHS

On Being a Christian in the Academy

Nicholas Wolterstorff and the Practice of Christian Scholarship

Andrew Sloane

Foreword by Nicholas Wolterstorff

Wipf & Stock
PUBLISHERS
Eugene, Oregon

Wipf and Stock Publishers
199 W 8th Ave, Suite 3
Eugene, OR 97401

On Being a Christian in the Academy
Nicholas Wolterstorff and the Practice Christian Scholarship
By Sloane, Andrew
Copyright©2003 Paternoster
ISBN: 1-59752-771-8
Publication date 6/10/2006
Previously published by Paternoster, 2003

This Edition Published by Wipf and Stock Publishers
by arrangement with Paternoster

Paternoster
9 Holdom Avenue
Bletchley
Milton Keyes, MK1 1QR
Great Britain

PATERNOSTER THEOLOGICAL MONOGRAPHS

Series Preface

In the West the churches may be declining, but theology—serious, academic (mostly doctoral level) and mainstream orthodox in evaluative commitment—shows no sign of withering on the vine. This series of *Paternoster Theological Monographs* extends the expertise of the Press especially to first-time authors whose work stands broadly within the parameters created by fidelity to Scripture and has satisfied the critical scrutiny of respected assessors in the academy. Such theology may come in several distinct intellectual disciplines—historical, dogmatic, pastoral, apologetic, missional, aesthetic and no doubt others also. The series will be particularly hospitable to promising constructive theology within an evangelical frame, for it is of this that the church's need seems to be greatest. Quality writing will be published across the confessions—Anabaptist, Episcopalian, Reformed, Arminian and Orthodox—across the ages—patristic, medieval, reformation, modern and counter-modern—and across the continents. The aim of the series is theology written in the twofold conviction that the church needs theology and theology needs the church—which in reality means theology done for the glory of God.

Series Editors

David F. Wright, Emeritus Professor of Patristic and Reformed Christianity, University of Edinburgh, Scotland, UK

Trevor A. Hart, Head of School and Principal of St Mary's College School of Divinity, University of St Andrews, Scotland, UK

Anthony N.S. Lane, Professor of Historical Theology and Director of Research, London School of Theology, UK

Anthony C. Thiselton, Emeritus Professor of Christian Theology, University of Nottingham, Research Professor in Christian Theology, University College Chester, and Canon Theologian of Leicester Cathedral and Southwell Minster, UK

Kevin J. Vanhoozer, Research Professor of Systematic Theology, Trinity Evangelical Divinity School, Deerfield, Illinois, USA

To Alison,
"bone of my bones, and flesh of my flesh"

Contents

Foreword xiii

Acknowledgements xv

Introduction 1

PART ONE
A Justification of the Adoption of
Wolterstorff's Defeasible, Situated Rationality

Introduction to Part One 9

Chapter 1: Wolterstorff and Foundationalism 11
A. Wolterstorff's Construal of Foundationalism 11
B. Wolterstorff's Critique of Foundationalism 20
   B.1. Wolterstorff's rejection of classical foundationalist
   notions of justification 20
   B.2. Wolterstorff's rejection of classical foundationalist
   notions of a foundation of certitudes 28
   B.3. Further arguments against classical foundationalism ... 34

Chapter 2: Wolterstorff and Relativism 43
A. Kuhnian Relativism 44
   A.1. An outline of cognitive relativism 46
   A.2. Kuhnian radicalism 48
   A.3. Kuhn and relativism 51
B. A Critique of Kuhnian Relativism 60
   B.1. The history and sociology of science and relativism ... 60
   B.2. Paradigms and relativism 65
   B.3. The incoherence of cognitive relativism 70

Conclusion to Part One 73

PART TWO
Wolterstorff's Theories of Rationality and *Wissenschaft*

Introduction to Part Two 77

Chapter 3: Wolterstorff's Situated Rationality 79
A. Wolterstorff's Notion of Rationality 79
   A.1. Innocent until proven guilty 79
   A.2. Rational justification of belief 83
   A.3. Obligation and justification 84
   A.4. Non-innocent beliefs and the noetic effects of sin 89
   A.5. Ceasing to believe and entitled belief 95
B. The Main Features of Wolterstorff's Rationality 97
   B.1. It is empirically rooted 98
   B.2. It is situated and non-absolutist 102
   B.3. It is rational and non-relativist 109

Chapter 4: Wolterstorff's Meta-theory 111
A. Wolterstorff and Neo-Calvinist Meta-Theories 111
   A.1. Kuyper's two sciences 113
   A.2. Dooyeweerd and the reductionism of idolatry 118
   A.3. Wolterstorff's rejection of Neo-Calvinist meta-theories 123
B. Wolterstorff's Meta-Theory 127
   B.1. Beliefs and theories 128
   B.2. Authentic Christian commitment and the function of control beliefs .. 132
C. Wolterstorff's Heuristics of *Shalom* 148
   C.1. Heuristics and shalom 148
   C.2. Shalom and pure versus praxis-oriented theory 151

PART THREE
A Critical Analysis of Wolterstorff's Meta-Theory

Introduction to Part Three 163

**Chapter 5: An Articulation and Defence
of Wolterstorff's Meta-Theory** 165
A. Wolterstorff's Meta-Theory and his Situated Rationality 165
   A.1. Empirical and situated 165
   A.2. Entitled theory-choice and his criterion of rationality 180
B. Wolterstorff's Meta-Theory is Rational and Non-Relativist 191
   B.1. Realism and relativism 192
   B.2. Heuristics of shalom, historicism and relativism 200

Chapter 6: The Structure of Wolterstorff's Meta-Theory 203
A. Wolterstorff's Meta-Theory is Non-Foundationalist 203
B. Wolterstorff and other Non-Foundationalist Meta-Theories 215
C. A Dynamic Model of Wolterstorff's Meta-Theory 223

Conclusion to Part Three 233

Conclusion 235
Retrospect and Prospect 235
Summary and Conclusions 250

Bibliography 255
Abbreviations 255
Primary Sources 255
Secondary Sources 257

Index 271

Foreword

Reading a discussion of what one has oneself written, while somewhat flattering if it's done with sympathy, can also be rather boring: "Nothing new here; I've heard it all before"! My experience of reading Andrew Sloane's discussion of my epistemology and reflections on Christian learning has been, instead, not only interesting but illuminating.
Andrew has meticulously researched everything that I have written on these topics; I have been reminded of things I had forgotten. The illumination went deeper than that, though. Rather than putting everything I had to say on these topics in one volume and then moving on to something else, I have discussed different aspects of the topic in different books, chapters, and essays; furthermore, my thinking on certain matters has developed over the years. Andrew has done what I myself have never done: traced the development and shown how the pieces fit together into a larger whole.

It would be possible to discuss an author by, in effect, stringing together quotations and near-quotations; there are familiar commentaries of that sort on some of the great figures from the philosophical tradition. In former years I was disdainful of such commentaries; I have come to see that they have some utility. Suppose, for example, that one wants to know what Aquinas had to say about human agency. Though Aquinas had a good deal to say on the topic, he never wrote a sustained treatise on the matter; his comments occur scattered about in his discussion of other issues. It's useful to have someone bring them all together.

But though I now concede the utility of such discussions, I hold that their utility lies in the service they render to the other sort of commentary: the commentary in which, from his own perspective, the commentator engages the author in a philosophical discussion. What emerges from such a discussion is what H.-G. Gadamer, in a now-famous metaphor, called a "fusion of horizons." When the author being discussed himself reads a commentary of this sort, he finds that it casts on his own thought a fresh and interesting light. That was my experience upon reading Andrew's discussion of my epistemology and reflections on Christian learning. Every now and then I found myself saying: "I hadn't thought of what I said quite like that; but yes, that's right."

Gadamer disagrees with a well-known passage in Schleiermacher, in which Schleiermacher says that the goal of the interpreter is to understand the author better than the author understood himself; the goal, Gadamer insists, is instead a fusion of horizons. I concede that Schleiermacher's goal can be used, and probably has been used, to justify arrogant mis-interpretation; nonetheless, I think Schleiermacher was on to something. In my own book on John Locke, and even more in my book on Thomas Reid, I saw myself as engaged in that sort of interpretation.

How can an interpreter understand an author better than the author understood himself? Philosophizing, if there is any creativity in it, is always a struggle to arrive at understanding: a struggle to break free from inherited patterns of thought, a struggle to bring to clarity certain vague intuitions, a struggle to discern and articulate the ramifications and implications of the positions one has staked out, a struggle to spell out the ways in which one's own position differs from that of others. The struggle is often only partially successful. Thus it is that rather often a philosopher only sees later see what it was that he was struggling to think and say at an earlier stage of his career; and thus it is that a gifted commentator may understand better than the author himself what the author was struggling to think and say overall. At some points, Andrew has understood me better than I had understood myself.

It was for all these reasons that I found Andrew's commentary not only interesting but illuminating. And a pleasure to read; for his discussion throughout is accurate, meticulously researched, lucidly presented, and critically sympathetic.

Nicholas Wolterstorff

Acknowledgements

This book began its life as a ThD thesis, arising out of my initial explorations in anthropology in Genesis 1–3. Noticing the wide range of interpretations of these texts led me to think further about the practice of scholarship – hence the turn to epistemology and its application to OT scholarship. The title of my original thesis, *Wolterstorff, Exegetical Theorising and Interpersonal Relationships in Genesis 1–3* reflects these interests. For a number of practical reasons, when it came to revising it for publication it seemed wisest to restrict its scope to the philosophical material. Hence, I have not included the final section in which I applied the meta-theory developed in the first three to the exegetical theories of Genesis 1–3 developed by Claus Westermann, Phyllis Trible and James Kennedy. I have focussed instead on revising and updating the other three sections. The result is a book that deals with the epistemology of Nicholas Wolterstorff and its application to the practice of Christian scholarship. Nonetheless, my interest in biblical and theological scholarship persists, as is evident throughout the book. I hope it will be of value for people working in these fields.

A work like this depends on the support and encouragement of many people – too many to mention here. However the contribution of some is too great to ignore. First, to those who contributed to the production of the doctoral thesis of which this book is a revision. Morling College provided the intellectual and spiritual environment that nourished me and my work. I extend my thanks to this community, and particularly to Rev Bill Leng and Rev Dr Vic Eldridge for their support, and their comments on the latter parts of the thesis. While that material does not form part of this book, my debt to them remains. My supervisor, Dr Bill Andersen, not only guided my research and helpfully critiqued the results, but also provided me with a model of what it means to be a Christian and a scholar. I can't see how I could have done it without him.

Second, to the many who contributed to the transformation of thesis into book. The examiners of my thesis, Professors Kelly Clark, Vern Poythress and Nicholas Wolterstorff, who by their challenging and encouraging comments have contributed significantly to this book. Jeremy Mudditt of Paternoster Press has been both helpful and understanding of delays in the production of this book. Ridley Theological College enhanced my intellectual and spiritual development in ways too many to enumerate. I extend my thanks to this community, especially the Principal, Dr Graham Cole, the faculty, library and administrative staff. Thanks, too, to Andrew Malone for his valuable assistance in the preparation and correction of the proofs. I am also indebted to the Council of Ridley College for their generous provision of sabbatical leave and to the Delegates of the Australian College of Theology for the faculty research scholarship, enabling me to undertake further research at Yale Divinity School with Prof Nicholas Wolterstorff. Prof Wolterstorff has demonstrated extraordinary grace and generosity over many years, extending to the writing of a Foreword to this book. I am grateful for all his help, especially the time and energy he gave to discussing matters philosophical and theological, both in person and by email, and for providing me with material otherwise unavailable to me, including unpublished manuscripts.

Finally, to my family, who contributed to every stage of this work, but more importantly, to me as a person. My gratitude is beyond words. I am deeply indebted to my parents David and Avril Sloane for their invaluable help and support. Much as they were puzzled by what I was doing and why I was doing it, they supported me unstintingly. I can only wish that Dad had lived to see the publication of this book. To my wife, Alison, and daughters Elanor, Laura and Alexandra, first let me extend my apologies for many absences – physical and mental – due to this work. Along with them, I offer thanks that it is done, and now I can be home. Elanor, Laura and Alexandra provided me with an enriching and joyful – if somewhat taxing – escape from the rigours of philosophy and theology. I thank them for reminding me of the joys and responsibilities of living in God's world, not just thinking about it. Alison, well it's hard to say enough without waxing lyrical and sentimental (neither of which I do well). So, in grateful, and loving thanks for all her patience, love and companionship, this thesis is dedicated to her.

Introduction

It is almost a truism to assert that theological and exegetical scholarship are pluralistic practices, and that a scholar's starting point, assumptions, methodology and so on greatly influence or even control her conclusions. Such is certainly the case in the interpretation of the early chapters of Genesis, as a survey of recent commentaries demonstrates.[1] However, it is one thing to make such assertions or observations, it is quite another to understand how and why this is the case, and to determine how theological scholars, and in particular Christians working in the field, should respond to this pluralism.

Two classical responses to this situation have been proposed. The first is to argue that this is an unjustified plurality of scholarship, due to a defect in methodology or religious commitment. If scholars were to govern their scholarly practice as they ought, and for the reasons they ought to have, then consensus would result and theological truth would be established. The alternative is to assert that this plurality of scholarship is justified, for all theories, particularly theological theories, are rational from within a particular conceptual framework. There is no arbitrating between such frameworks and their theories: rationality, if such exists, can only be determined from within conceptual systems. These are two typical responses to the current plurality of theological and exegetical scholarship.

---

1 This work grew out of my engagement in OT studies, particularly the interpretation of Genesis 1–3. My 1994 doctoral dissertation, *Wolterstorff, Exegetical Theorising and Interpersonal Relationships in Genesis 1–3* (ThD thesis; Kingsford: Australian College of Theology, 1994) of which this is a revision, dealt with Wolterstorff's epistemology and its specific application to exegetical studies of Genesis 1–3. For various practical reasons I have removed the final section of my thesis, which dealt with a Wolterstorffian analysis of three exegetical theories of Genesis 1–3. Hence, while this book deals only with epistemological issues, evidence of my interest in biblical and theological scholarship will be found throughout this work, particularly in relation to the examples I use and implications I draw for Christian scholarship.

In this book I attempt to develop an alternative explanation of this phenomenon, and a corresponding alternative prescription for how we should respond to it. This description and prescription is guided by Nicholas Wolterstorff's theory of rationality and *Wissenschaft*, and informed by recent studies in epistemology and philosophy of science. The inevitable questions are: Why use Wolterstorff's theory? and How can the use of epistemology and philosophy of science be justified in the analysis of theological theorising?

The choice of Wolterstorff's model of rationality and *Wissenschaft* is easy to understand, as he is one of the leaders in the loose school of Christian philosophers who champion "Reformed Epistemology". The use of insights from philosophy of science and their application to the practice of theological scholarship, on the other hand, requires justification. A *prima facie* case for this can be made on the grounds of the character of Wolterstorff's meta-theory. He claims that it is an epistemic strategy that can be applied to all *Wissenschaft*, indeed to all human knowing. Thus, for his model to be valid, it must conform to the observed pattern(s) of scientific rationality, and in turn be clearly applicable to theological methodology.

Further justification for the use of the philosophy of science can be derived from the recent history of epistemology. Increasingly through the last century the physical sciences were seen as paradigm cases or exemplars of rational knowledge, because they are evidently productive of explanations and techniques to control our environment. While it is inappropriate to force all scholarship into the mould of (a particular construal of) scientific practice, nonetheless, epistemological theories ought to be cognisant of and responsive to findings in philosophy of science. Wolterstorff has noted some of these connections in his meta-theory, but has not drawn out their significance, nor related his model in detail to the findings of recent philosophy of science. This study will attempt to fill this gap and thereby show the value of Wolterstorff's meta-theory to science in particular, and indeed to rationality in general.

However, this does not necessarily justify applying insights from the physical sciences, and theories of *Wissenschaft* developed in relation to them, to theological theorising. It could be claimed that theology and exegesis differ so much in subject matter and methodology from the physical sciences that there could be no substantive or methodological contact between them. A preliminary rationale for my methodology can be found, however, in recent studies in the interaction between faith, theology and science. Such people as Torrance, Mitchell, Polkinghorne, Barbour and Murphy, while recognising the particularity of the content and methodology of science and theology, have identified significant similarities in theological and scientific method.[2] From such a perspective Wolterstorff's development of a meta-theory which can be applied to all *Wissenschaft* would seem to be justified, as would its application to theological theorising. This does not mean that theological and scientific method are assimilated, for each has its own distinctive form and content: rather general patterns of rationality can be inferred from science and applied, *mutatis mutandis* to theological scholarship. Further justification of my method must occur in the context of the argument itself. If, as I will argue is the case, Wolterstorff's meta-theory provides a defensible and cogent explanation of general scholarly practice, including the existence and arbitration of a plurality of truth-claims within a particular discipline, then this would be an indicator that the proposed methodology is valid.

I should note a caveat here: in this work I will not directly engage postmodern theory or postliberal theology in a sustained sense. There are a number of reasons for this. First, postmodern theory and postliberal theology are protean terms, and defining the nature and scope of these movements (or perhaps, constellations of movements) and determining who is or is not an exponent of these views would take me too far afield. Indeed, on some analyses Wolterstorff himself would fit these categories, which seems an inappropriate designation. Second, on a more pragmatic note, in my original thesis, of which this is a revision, I did not engage in such a clearly thematic discussion. To do so at this stage would make this book much larger than it already is, and significantly change the nature of the project, which seems inappropriate to me. I will at times address thinkers such as Rorty, Feyerabend and Murphy who are generally associated with postmodern theory. This will, however, be done in a piecemeal way, as it is germane to my broader thesis, rather than systematically. Which brings me to my final, and deepest reason: that the project, as I develop it here, effectively deals with the relevant philosophical issues associated with postmodern and postliberal thought. Postmodern theory, where it addresses epistemology, is generally seen as anti-realist and either relativist or radically pluralist. And, where it is in fact rather than mere perception anti-realist and relativist, frequently the work of Thomas Kuhn is appealed to in support of such claims. If my argument

---

2   T. F. Torrance, *Theological Science* (Oxford: Oxford University Press, 1969) 286–312; B. Mitchell, *The Justification of Religious Belief* (London: Macmillan, 1973) 59–95, 117–156; J. Polkinghorne, *One World: the interaction of science and theology* (London: SPCK, 1986) 6–42; I. Barbour, *Religion in an Age of Science* (London: SCM, 1990) 3–92; N. Murphy, *Theology in the Age of Scientific Reasoning* (Ithaca: Cornell University Press, 1990) esp 1–18, 51–87.

against Kuhnian relativism is sound, then postmodern relativism is equally flawed.³ In regards to postliberal theology the situation is more complex, for it is an open question as to whether it is anti-realist and radically pluralist, or a complex, perhaps at times confused, holist expression of critical realism and particularism or perspectivalism.⁴ Adjudicating such questions is clearly beyond the scope of my thesis and would be, I believe, largely irrelevant. For if postliberal theology is anti-realist and pluralist and, further, if it either depends upon or is allied with Kuhnian views, then, once again, my argument against Kuhnian relativism applies equally to this aspect of postliberal theology. If, on the other hand, it should be taken as a version of realism, then its claims are consistent with the Wolterstorffian perspective I develop in this work.

This book has three main aims. First, I endeavour to indicate the need for a defeasible and situated theory of rationality and *Wissenschaft* such as Wolterstorff develops. Second, I aim to outline Wolterstorff's theory of rationality and his meta-theory in relation to their conceptual roots. Third, I attempt to critically evaluate his meta-theory in light of specific criticisms and general issues in epistemology and philosophy of science, where necessary modifying it in order to deal with them effectively.

The structure of the argument corresponds to these three aims. In Part One I attempt to show the need for a Wolterstorffian defeasible, person- and situation-specific theory of rationality and *Wissenschaft*. In order to do this I need to outline and critique the main alternatives to Wolterstorff's approach to epistemology. In Chapter 1 I outline, therefore, the absolutist, value-neutral meta-theory of classical foundationalism and its allies. I then present Wolterstorff's arguments against its claims to provide a firm foundation for incorrigible theories. Arguments from epistemology and philosophy of science that support his position are adduced in an attempt to show that classical foundationalism is an implausible theory of *Wissenschaft*. If successful, this discussion will justify Wolterstorff's rejection of classical foundationalist meta-theories.

Chapter 2 explores the relativist alternative to defeasible, situated theories of rationality. While he clearly rejects relativist theories of ration-

---

[3] For Kuhnian philosophy of science and its association with relativist versions of postmodern theory, see J. Taylor, "Science, Christianity and the Post-Modern Agenda", *Science and Christian Belief* 10 (1998) 163–178.

[4] The classical presentation of postliberal theology is G. Lindbeck, *The Nature of Doctrine: Religion and Theology in a Postliberal Age* (London: SPCK, 1984) which itself seems allow for different views on this matter (see, e.g., pp. 63–69). For contrasting assessments of whether Lindbeck and other postliberals are anti-realist and radically pluralist, see the essays in *The Nature of Confession: Evangelicals and Postliberals in Conversation*, ed. T. R. Phillips and D. L. Okholm (Downers Grove: IVP, 1996).

ality and *Wissenschaft*, Wolterstorff does not specifically critique them, as he does foundationalist theories. In order to fill this gap, I therefore outline cognitive relativism, paying particular attention to Kuhn's theory of science, which has been used extensively in recent attempts to justify relativism. I then identify the main arguments that have been used to justify these perspectives, and attempt to show that they are conceptually and empirically suspect. The aim is to show that Wolterstorff's rejection of cognitive relativism and related views is justified. In thus analysing classical foundationalist and relativist meta-theories I do not break any new ground. Rather, I seek to provide the context of Wolterstorff's meta-theory, and show that his adoption of a defeasible, situation- and person-specific approach to rationality and science is justified.

Before they can be assessed and applied, Wolterstorff's theories of rationality and *Wissenschaft* need to be expounded and comprehended. In Part Two, therefore, I outline them and identify their main features. Chapter 3 comprises an exposition of Wolterstorff's theory of rationality. This is undertaken primarily to illustrate the general context of his meta-theory, as well as providing tools for its analysis and development. I examine his criterion of rationality, and identify the main tenets of his notion of rational justification or entitlement, noting its relationship to other theories, notably that of Thomas Reid. In Chapter 4 I outline his meta-theory, and discuss its relationship to its Neo-Calvinist forebears, indicating the reasons Wolterstorff gives for taking it to be superior to them. In examining the nature of his meta-theory I focus on his notion of *control beliefs*, and the role he presents for the belief-content of authentic Christian commitment functioning as a control on a Christian scholar's devising and weighing of theories. This seeks to indicate that Wolterstorff's is a defeasible, person- and situation-specific theory of *Wissenschaft* in which there is no algorithm of theory choice or heuristics. The basis of a Christian scholar's heuristic decisions is discussed, and Wolterstorff's notion of *shalom* as the overriding governing principle in those decisions is outlined.

For Wolterstorff's meta-theory to be seen to be adequate, it needs to deal with specific criticisms that have been levelled against it, and creatively to interact with its rivals. Part Three consists of a critical analysis of Wolterstorff's meta-theory. In Chapter 5 I draw conceptual links between his theories of rationality and of *Wissenschaft*. I attempt to deal with specific criticisms that have been directed against his meta-theory, indicating that Wolterstorff presents adequate counter-arguments to them. A criterion of rational or entitled theory choice is devised which directly relates his person- and situation-specific criterion of rationality to his meta-theory. I seek to show that he avoids relativism by means of his adoption of a critical-realist perspective on theoretical entities and by his separation of the contexts of theory-choice and heuristics. In this chapter, where relevant, I attempt to articulate his meta-theory, thereby extending its scope and enabling it to more effectively deal with its rivals.

In Chapter 6 I seek to present a meta-epistemological analysis of Wolterstorff's theories of rationality and *Wissenschaft*. This aims to show that Wolterstorff adopts a dynamic model of human belief systems that is neither broadly foundationalist nor coherentist. This dynamic theory is contrasted with Plantinga's broad foundationalism, concentrating on their respective notions of control beliefs and properly basic beliefs, in an attempt to show that Wolterstorff's theory avoids some of the infelicities of Plantinga's. I also draw connections between Wolterstorff's and other non-foundationalist meta-theories, thereby seeking to indicate ways in which Wolterstorff's is preferable to its alternatives. I conclude the chapter by offering a dynamic epistemological metaphor which aims to do justice to the nature of Wolterstorff's meta-theory and human belief systems. At appropriate points in the argument throughout Parts One Two and Three I note examples of various meta-theories from theological and exegetical scholarship in order to indicate that these general epistemological concerns are directly relevant to theological theorising.

This book, then seeks to understand the nature of the devising and weighing of theories through the lens of Wolterstorff's meta-theory. It contends that he provides a cogent explanation for this scholarly practice, including why it is an irremediably pluralistic enterprise. In so doing it endeavours to provide a more cogent explanation than the classical foundationalist and relativist alternatives. In expounding and critically analysing his meta-theory I attempt to defeat counter-arguments to his position, and modify his theory to cope with its rivals more successfully. I also seek to show that his meta-theory provides a challenging and fruitful means of appraising theories, including theological theories. The claim that Wolterstorff's is a cogent and fruitful meta-theory, which holds the potential to faithfully transform Christian scholarship, will, I believe, be justified in its exposition and articulation in this book.

PART ONE

A Justification of the Adoption of Wolterstorff's Defeasible, Situated Rationality

Introduction to Part One

Nicholas Wolterstorff has claimed that his version of Reformed epistemology provides a model of rationality that is relevant to all *Wissenschaft*, indeed to all human knowledge. Part One aims to demonstrate that such an epistemology is a viable alternative to objectivist and subjectivist views.

An essential component of Wolterstorff's argument is his critique of classical foundationalism and the models of rationality, especially scientific rationality, affiliated with it. He proposes his model as a viable alternative to classical foundationalism. Chapter 1 aims to examine his critique of classical foundationalism and provide supporting arguments for it from the philosophy of science and epistemology. This will entail a brief outline of the salient features of classical foundationalism, paying particular attention to logical positivism, the most influential ally of classic foundationalist rationality in recent times. Wolterstorff's critique will be presented in detail, noting supporting arguments where appropriate from other sources, as well as possible problems with it. Further arguments that support his thesis that classical foundationalism is a non-viable epistemic strategy will be presented.

Chapter 2 will present an outline and critique of one of the most influential recent epistemologies of science, namely that of Thomas Kuhn. This is a necessary task as, with the demise of foundationalist objectivity, there has been a concomitant rise in non-rational, subjectivist views of science in particular and knowledge in general. While Kuhn does not avow an irrational and subjective view of science, his arguments provide some of the most cogent support for such a position. In order to justify Wolterstorff's *rational* epistemology it will be necessary, therefore, to demonstrate the inadequacy of Kuhnian views. This will entail a detailed outline of Kuhn's model of science, paying particular attention to the role that "paradigms" play in his notion of scientific knowledge. The ways in which his arguments support relativist epistemologies will be identified, and a detailed critique offered which demonstrates that they do not justify irrationalist and relativist conclusions. Indeed, to the extent that Kuhn endorses such conclusions it will be shown that he is inconsistent with his own disavowal of relativism and the arguments that he presents in favour of limited rationality. This critique will thereby demonstrate that while there is much of value in Kuhn's work, his tendency to accept irrationalist conclusions is unnecessary and invalid. This will in turn justify the use of some of Kuhn's insights in the development of defeasible, person- and situation-specific theories of rationality and *Wissenschaft*, such as those presented by Wolterstorff.

CHAPTER 1

Wolterstorff and Foundationalism

Nicholas Wolterstorff develops his theories of rationality and *Wissenschaft* as specific alternatives to traditional foundationalist models. In order, then, to understand his meta-theory, it is important to understand his construal of foundationalism and his reasons for rejecting it as a suitable model of rationality or *Wissenschaft*. A further reason to study his anti-foundationalist arguments is that a *prima facie* justification for his alternative epistemology is that its chief rival – foundationalism – is untenable. I will therefore outline Wolterstorff's concept of foundationalism and determine whether it is an accurate portrayal of this epistemic position.[1] I will then present his critique of foundationalism, in the process identifying and analysing counter-arguments and supporting evidence for his approach.

A. Wolterstorff's Construal of Foundationalism

Wolterstorff identifies foundationalism as the classical theory of theorising in the Western world since the Middle Ages, it having been embraced by Aquinas, Descartes, Leibniz, Berkeley and the logical positivists.[2]

---

[1] Throughout this book I utilise two deliberate linguistic conventions. I will not avoid the use of the first person singular, as such avoidance is allied with value-neutral views of scholarly practice that comport poorly with the argument of the book. I will also specifically use third person feminine pronouns when referring to indefinite agents. This is an attempt to counter-balance the preponderance of masculine and androcentric language in academic literature that has prevailed until recently. I consistently use feminine pronouns because I find the use of "him/her", "him or her" or "they" (and cognates) cumbersome. I have avoided alternating "her" and "him" in different sections of the book because it may give rise to the misapprehension that I am claiming that a particular way of thought or epistemology is typical of males or females.

[2] N. Wolterstorff, *Reason Within the Bounds of Religion* (2nd ed; Grand Rapids: Eerdmans, 1984) [from here on *RWBR*], 28, 30; "Commitment and Theory" *Christian Higher Education: The Contemporary Challenge* (Potchesfstroom: Institute for the Advancement of Calvinism, 1976) [from here on *C&T*], 117.

Foundationalism of various kinds is, indeed, fundamental to the "Grand Project" of the Western academy, which was characterised by the quest for generic knowledge, knowledge from which all the particularities of the human noetic agent had been removed.[3] This, in turn, would result in a body of knowledge that would be accepted by all fully rational agents: it would lead to a rational consensus in the academy. "When learning, *Wissenschaft*, is rightly conducted, pluralism in the academy is an accidental and temporary phenomenon."[4] Strictly speaking, "foundationalism" is a meta-epistemological rather than an epistemological category: it describes the *structure* of epistemological theories rather than their content.[5] It is the recent rise of meta-epistemology that has resulted in the recognition of the predominance of foundationalism amongst western theories of knowledge.[6] Essential to foundationalist epistemologies is the distinction between mediate beliefs, which are held on the basis of other beliefs, and immediate beliefs, which are not held on the basis of other beliefs.[7]

The foundationalist claims that there must be a set of beliefs which are directly induced in a person, say by perception and mental states, on which she can base other beliefs.[8] This is not merely conceptually so, it is the case in the belief practices of any given person.[9] This "quasi-psychological distinction" between immediate and mediate beliefs is the basis for foundationalist epistemologies.[10] Both mediate and immediate beliefs may be held rationally, the former being justified by the fact that they are

---

[3] N. Wolterstorff, "Does the Truth Still Matter? Reflections on the Crisis of the Postmodern University", *Crux* 31/3 (Sept 1995) 17–28, reprinted as "Suffering, Power, and Privileged Cognitive Access: The Revenge of the Particular", *Christianity and Culture in the Crossfire*, ed. D. A. Hoekema and B. Fong (Grand Rapids: Eerdmans, 1997) 79–89; "The Travail of Theology in the Modern Academy", *The Future of Theology: Essays in Honour of Jürgen Moltmann*, ed. M. Volf, *et al* (Grand Rapids: Eerdmans, 1996) 35–46; "Theology and Science: Listening to Each Other", *Religion and Science: History, Method, Dialogue*, ed. W. M. Richardson and W. J. Wildman (New York: Routledge, 1996) 95–104; "Can Scholarship and Christian Conviction Mix? A New Look at the Integration of Knowledge", *Journal of Education and Christian Belief* 3/1 (1999) 35–50.
[4] Wolterstorff, "Scholarship and Conviction", 36.
[5] N. Wolterstorff, "Introduction", *Faith and Rationality: Reason and Belief in God*, ed. A. Plantinga and N. Wolterstorff (Notre Dame: University of Notre Dame Press, 1983) 1.
[6] Ibid.
[7] Wolterstorff, "Introduction", 2; "Scholarship and Conviction", 37.
[8] Ibid.
[9] Wolterstorff, "Introduction", 2.
[10] Ibid.

supported by the latter.[11] While there are varieties of foundationalist stances,[12] all foundationalists agree that if a mediate belief is justified, one must be able to trace a chain of beliefs that lead, more or less directly, to a foundation of rational immediate beliefs.[13] The differences amongst foundationalists are the result of disagreements about the content rather than the structure of rational belief systems.[14] These differences particularly relate to which beliefs are rational foundational beliefs, and how propositions must be related to each other in order for one belief to provide evidence for another: that is, they disagree with respect to the content of the foundation, and how the superstructure is supported by it.[15]

Within the camp of foundationalist epistemologies, Wolterstorff has identified what he calls "classical foundationalism", which asserts that only two sorts of beliefs are properly foundational for any person: propositions which are self evident to that person, and propositions which are incorrigible for that person.[16] This version of foundationalism was a close ally of modernist versions of the "Grand Project" of the western academy.[17] The goal of *Wissenschaft*, according to classical foundationalism, is "to form a body of theories from which all prejudice, bias, and unjustified conjecture has been eliminated".[18] In classical foundationalist

---

11   Ibid., 2–3.
12   Wolterstorff, *RWBR*, 30–33, "Scholarship and Conviction", 37.
13   Wolterstorff, "Introduction", 3.
14   Ibid.
15   Ibid.
16   Wolterstorff, "Introduction", 3. He notes that what he labels "Classical Foundationalism" is termed "Modern Foundationalism" by Plantinga: see A. Plantinga "Reason and Belief in God", *Faith and Rationality: Reason and Belief in God*, ed. A. Plantinga and N. Wolterstorff (Notre Dame: University of Notre Dame Press, 1983) [from here on *R&BG*], 16–93. For a detailed discussion of the distinctions between medieval foundationalists and classical foundationalism as typified by Aquinas and Locke respectively, see N. Wolterstorff, "The Migration of the Theistic Arguments: From Natural Theology to Evidentialist Apologetics", *Rationality, Religious Belief, and Moral Commitment: New Essays in the Philosophy of Religion*, ed. R Audi and W. J. Wainwright (London: Cornell University Press, 1986) esp 78–81. He argues that Descartes is a transitional figure between medieval and modern epistemology. His famous sceptical foundationalism relates only to the project of developing a body of *scientia* characterised by certitude, and not to general matters of belief. See N. Wolterstorff, "What is Cartesian Doubt?", *American Catholic Philosophical Quarterly*, 67/4 (1993) 467–495. For a detailed exposition and critique of Locke's foundationalism, see N. Wolterstorff, *John Locke and the Ethics of Belief* (Cambridge: Cambridge University Press, 1996).
17   Wolterstorff, "Privileged Access", 81.
18   Wolterstorff, *RWBR*, 28. For this as characterising the Cartesian project, see Wolterstorff, "Cartesian Doubt", 467–470, 472–476, 486–488. Throughout this discussion I shall use the term *Wissenschaft* to refer to what Wolterstorff calls "science", or "*scientia*".

versions of modern learning, this goal is achieved by basing all knowledge on a foundation of certitudes, and structuring theories using methods whose reliability is certain.[19] Classical foundationalism had a rigid criterion for warranted theory acceptance:

> A person is warranted in accepting a theory at a certain time if and only if he is then warranted in believing that that theory belongs to genuine science (*scientia*).[20]

Further,
> A theory belongs to genuine science if and only if it is justified by some foundational proposition and some human being could know with certitude that it is thus justified.[21]

And,
> A proposition is foundational if and only if it is true and some human being could know noninferentially and with certitude that it is true.[22]

It is to this version of foundationalism, particularly as embraced by the logical positivists, that Wolterstorff addresses most of his arguments.[23]

The question naturally arises as to whether his construal is an accurate one. Wolterstorff's assertion that *all* logical positivists were classic foundationalists is open to question, as some developed specifically coherentist models of truth.[24] However it is beyond doubt that the program

---

Wolterstorff makes that identification in *RWBR*, 11. I shall use this terminology to avoid ambiguity: except in quotes, I shall use *Wissenschaft* to refer to the scholarly enterprise in general, reserving *science* for the narrower disciplines of the physical and biological sciences.

19   Wolterstorff, *RWBR*, 28. For his discussion of the first formulation of this strategy in the work of Locke, see "The Migration of the Theistic Arguments", 50; for this strategy in Descartes' methodology of *scientia*, see "Cartesian Doubt", 470–472.

20   Wolterstorff, *RWBR*, 28; *C&T*, 116.

21   Wolterstorff, *RWBR*, 29; cf. *C&T*, 116–117.

22   Wolterstorff, *RWBR*, 29; *C&T*, 117.

23   Wolterstorff, *RWBR*, 37.

24   T. Triplett, "Recent Work on Foundationalism", *American Philosophical Quarterly* 27/2 (April 1990) 94. However, for the correctness of Reformed epistemology's construal of classical foundationalism, its close association with logical positivism, specifically the verificationist program, and its associated collapse along with verificationism, see J. Duran, "Reliabilism, Foundationalism, and Naturalized Epistemic Justification Theory", *Metaphilosophy* 19/2 (April 1988) 114–115; D. Hatcher, "Plantinga and Reformed Epistemology: A Critique", *Philosophy and Theology* 1/1 (Fall 1986) 87; V. M. Cooke, "Current Theology: The New Calvinist Epistemology", *TS* 47/2 (1986) 275–277. For the failure of verificationism, see D. Ratsch, *Philosophy of Science* (Downers Grove: IVP, 1986) 37–38;

of logical positivism aimed to develop criteria for indubitable knowledge.[25] Thus, while some of Wolterstorff's specific arguments are not strictly relevant to all logical positivists, they are generally relevant in as much as they comprise a refutation of the possibility of indubitable knowledge.[26] This contention can be supported by a brief outline of the characteristics of logical positivism.[27]

Logical positivism was an essentially normative epistemic system; it sought to specify the kind of statements that qualify as being scientific and thus meaningful.[28] For a statement to have the possibility of being right or wrong it had to be meaningful within the confines of the logical empiricist or positivist canon of meaning.[29] Thus logical empiricism was not

---

for its logical flaws, see W. V. O. Quine, "Two Dogmas of Empiricism", *From a Logical Point of View* (Cambridge Mass: Harvard University Press, 1964) 20–42. For a brief introduction to the character and development of "Reformed Epistemology" and its critique of foundationalism, see, N. Wolterstorff, "What Reformed Epistemology is Not", *Perspectives* 7/9 (Nov 1992) 14–16; "The reformed tradition", *A Companion to Philosophy of Religion*, ed. P. Quinn and C. Taliaferro (Oxford: Blackwell, 1997) 165–170; M. Westphal, "A Reader's Guide to 'Reformed Epistemology'", *Perspectives* 7/9 (Nov 1992) 10–13; A. Plantinga, "Reformed Epistemology", *A Companion to Philosophy of Religion*, ed. P. Quinn and C. Taliaferro (Oxford: Blackwell, 1997) 383–389.

25 For examples of this, and the use of foundationalist categories see M. Schlick, "The Foundation of Knowledge", *Logical Positivism*, ed. A. J. Ayer (Glencoe: The Free Press, 1963) 209–227; A. J. Ayer, "Verification and Experience", *Logical Positivism*, 228–243.

26 If logical positivists or empiricists are non-classical foundationalists then they must identify a set of infallible propositions, and a set of relationships that must obtain between a proposition and the foundation, in order to have indubitable knowledge. In this case Wolterstorff's arguments are directly relevant. If they are coherentists, then they have no guarantee of indubitable knowledge without a clear notion of coherence and how it provides certitude. This is notoriously lacking in such theories, thus they cannot provide infallible knowledge. See A. Plantinga "Coherentism and the Evidentialist Objection to Belief in God", *Rationality, Religious Belief, and Moral Commitment: New Essays in the Philosophy of Religion*, ed. R Audi and W. J. Wainwright (London: Cornell University Press, 1986) 113, 127–133, 138.

27 A detailed outline of its history, development and permutations is beyond the scope of this study. For this see H. Feigh, "The origin and development of logical positivism" *The Legacy of Logical Positivism*, ed. P. Achinstein and S. F. Barker (Baltimore: John Hopkins, 1969) 3–23; L. Kolakowski *Positivist Philosophy* (Harmondsworth: Penguin, 1972), esp 203–240 for the recent history of the movement.

28 Ratsch, 32–36; D. Shapere "Modern Science and the Philosophical Tradition", *Reason and the Search for Knowledge* (Dordrecht: D. Reidel, 1984) 410; Wolterstorff, *RWBR*, 34; Kolakowski, 10–11. Strictly speaking, logical positivism was a normative philosophy of language, identifying proper and improper uses of language. However these linguistic claims had clear epistemological entailments and so the movement can be identified as a normative epistemology as well as a philosophy of language. I am indebted to Kelly Clark for these observations.

29 Kolakowski, 11.

concerned with how people actually attain knowledge, but how they should attain it, thereby establishing a demarcation between meaningful and meaningless statements.[30]

The limitations placed upon meaningful statements were rigorous. Only empirical statements were allowed, any assertion about unobservable entities was illegitimate.[31] This phenomenalist approach was extended to include the nature of theories, which were seen in strictly nominalist, or instrumentalist terms: theoretical abstractions have no bearing on hidden structures of reality, but are merely conceptual tools enabling researchers to more adequately order and thus understand concrete entities.[32] This radical empiricism was not limited to the natural sciences, for all legitimate knowledge had the same structure.[33] Philosophy, Theology and Ethics were all included under this banner and, given the essentially non-empirical nature of the latter two disciplines, they were labelled meaningless word-games.[34] Thus logical empiricism's normative program deliberately aimed to exclude everything of a metaphysical nature from philosophical and scientific assertions.[35]

This rigorous anti-metaphysical stance was not purely negative: it sought to establish a means for arriving at indubitable, infallible, or inviolable knowledge. The aim was "to form a body of theories from which all prejudice, bias, and unjustified conjecture has been eliminated".[36] Underlying the quest for indubitability is an idea that Shapere has termed "The Inviolability Thesis".[37] This consists of the claim that

> there is something, whatever its precise character, which is presupposed by, or is essential to, or is necessary to, the knowledge seeking enterprise... and that that presupposed or essential or necessary ingredient

---

30 Ibid., 10–11.
31 C. G. Hempel, "The Empiricist Criterion on Meaning", *Logical Positivism*, ed. A. J. Ayer (Glencoe: The Free Press, 1969) 108–129; Kolakowski, 11–13; Ratsch, 33–34.
32 Kolakowski, 13–15; Ratsch, 35–37.
33 Kolakowski, 17–18; Ratsch, 36.
34 Kolakowski, 16–17, 19; Ratsch, 36. It is intriguing to note that on positivist grounds all normative statements are ruled illegitimate, thus negating the positivist's normative program of epistemology.
35 R. Carnap, "The Elimination of Metaphysics Through Logical Analysis of Language", *Logical Positivism*, ed. A. J. Ayer (Glencoe: The Free Press, 1969) 60–81; Kolakowski, 13, 19.
36 Wolterstorff, *RWBR*, 28; cf. J. Dancy *Introduction to Contemporary Epistemology* (Oxford: Basil Blackwell, 1985) 53–54.
37 Shapere, "Modern Science", 410.

cannot be revised or rejected in the light of any new scientific knowledge or beliefs at which we may arrive.[38]

While the search for infallible knowledge is common to a number of epistemologies, it is most characteristic of positivist philosophies, most notably the baconian scientific method, and logical empiricism.[39]

In foundationalist theories the means of attaining the goal of indubitable knowledge was to base all knowledge on a foundation of certitudes, ensuring that all theories are reliably grounded on those foundations.[40] There are two key notions in this formulation, the first of which is that of a foundational proposition.[41] "A proposition is foundational if and only if it is true and some human being could know non-inferentially and with certitude it is true."[42] The usual candidates for such foundations are observation statements, that is, singular propositions about observed physical entities.[43] The assumption is that data is gathered without prior theories influencing the processes of observation or the scope of the data which is to be assessed, and thus observation statements are objective. The second concept is that of the existence of an indubitable connection between theories and the foundations which justify those theories by the transfer of the certitude of the foundations to them.[44] This connection has classically been identified as induction, the process by which generalisations are made about the qualities of all existing entities on the basis of observed qualities of observed entities.[45] This notion of discovery received its most popular and influential form in the "baconian method".[46] It is by means of this structure of theories that foundationalism in general, and logical empiricism in particular, classically base their claims to infallible objective knowledge.[47]

---

38   Ibid., 409. This is similar to Wolterstorff's notion of the "Grand Project" of the (modern) Western academy, for which see above.

39   Ibid., 408–409.

40   Dancy, 53–54; K. J. Clarke, *Return to Reason* (Grand Rapids: Eerdmans, 1990) 132–133; Wolterstorff, *RWBR*, 28–29.

41   Wolterstorff, *RWBR*, 28–29, 47; A. F. Chalmers, *What is this thing called science?* (St Lucia: University of Queensland Press, 1976) 10.

42   Wolterstorff, *RWBR*, 29.

43   Wolterstorff, *RWBR*, 47; Chalmers, 10.

44   Wolterstorff, *RWBR*, 36–37; K. Clark, 133.

45   Chalmers, 2. The inductive method is so important to classical views of science in particular that he has labelled these views as "Inductivist".

46   V. S. Poythress, *Science and Hermeneutics* (Leicester: Apollos, 1987) 32–33.

47   K. Clark, 132.

The quest for infallibility was in part inspired by the desire to avoid relativism, which legitimises any and all claims to knowledge, and scepticism, which denies the very possibility of knowledge.[48] Despite this, the quest failed, both on philosophical and historical grounds.[49] The philosophical critique of foundationalist certitude focuses on the two central tenets of the theory: the existence of a foundation of certitudes, and the development of veridical links between the foundations and theoretical structures. The historical critique focuses on the actual structure of science and the way it develops and tests theories. This can be expanded in relation to knowledge in general in order to determine whether normal human believings conform to foundationalist canons. Each of these criticisms will be examined in turn.

The conclusion, in brief is this: while classical foundationalism has been the most influential epistemic strategy in recent Western scholarship, it has been dealt "a series of deadly blows", so that to many working in epistemology and philosophy "it now looks all but dead".[50] "On close scrutiny they have found classical foundationalism untenable. And it makes no difference now whether it is construed as a theory of rational acceptance, or of knowledge, or of scientia. It has seemed unacceptable as any of these."[51] This judgement is one which Wolterstorff heartily endorses,[52] and is of profound significance for the constitution of Christian epistemology in general and meta-theories in particular. For classical foundationalism is a normative theory, which thus says not just how things *are* done, but prescribes how they *should be* done.[53] Despite the fact that not even its proponents did, or could, follow its epistemic procedure, classical foundationalism has had a great impact upon the practice of all western *Wissenschaft*, including Christian scholarship.[54]

This influence of classical foundationalism upon the practice of Christian scholarship is not limited to the natural sciences, but has significantly shaped nineteenth and twentieth century biblical scholarship in two main ways. It is firstly seen in the claims made by dogmatic and

---

48 Shapere, "Modern Science", 412; cf. Wolterstorff, "The Migration of the Theistic Arguments", 55–56.
49 Shapere, "Modern Science", 410–411.
50 Wolterstorff, *RWBR*, 33.
51 Wolterstorff, "Introduction", 4.
52 Wolterstorff, *RWBR*, 33; *C&T*, 117; "Introduction", 4.
53 Wolterstorff, *RWBR*, 34.
54 Wolterstorff, *RWBR*, 34; "Thomas Reid on Rationality", *Rationality in the Calvinian Tradition*, ed. H. Hart, *et al* (Boston: University Press of America, 1983) [from here on *TRR*], 53–55; "Scholarship and Conviction", 38.

biblical theologians that their scholarship is, and all scholarship should be, free from confessional and dogmatic presuppositions or biases.[55] While such claims have never been justified by the actual practice of theology or exegesis,[56] they have been very influential on the practice of biblical scholarship.[57] Thus, while Wolterstorff's earlier assertion that the (Neo-Calvinist) rejection of the neutrality of *Wissenschaft* is controversial only with respect to non-theological scholarship, for "no one would claim that *theology* is religiously neutral",[58] may be philosophically and normatively sound, it does not, unfortunately, reflect the history of biblical interpretation, as he now acknowledges.[59] Secondly, it is apparent in the adoption of the (generally baconian) "scientific method" in the practice of exegetical and theological theorising, with all its attendant problems for the resulting theories.[60] Given its impact on theological and non-theological scholarship,

---

55   E. Troeltsch, "Religion and the Science of Religion", *Ernst Troeltsch: Writings on Theology and Religion*, ed. R. Morgan and M. Pye (London: Duckworth, 1977) 82–123; "Historical and Dogmatic Method in Theology", *Religion in History*, (ed. J. L. Adams and W. F. Bense; Edinburgh: T&T Clark, 1991) 11–32; M. Noth, "The Laws in the Pentateuch: Their Assumptions and Meaning", *The Laws in the Pentateuch and Other Essays* (Edinburgh: Oliver and Boyd, 1966) 1; *Numbers* (London: SCM, 1968) 4–11; *The History of Israel* (2nd ed; London: SCM, 1960); cf. R. G. Gruenler, *Meaning and Understanding: The Philosophical framework for understanding biblical interpretation* (Grand Rapids: Zondervan, 1991) 48–49, 61–64; Poythress, 18–19.

56   For the non-neutrality of Noth and other OT scholars who make claim to neutrality, see J. Bright, *Early Israel in Recent History Writing* (London: SCM, 1956), esp Ch. 4, pp. 79–110; G. Hasel *Old Testament Theology: Basic Issues in the Current Debate* (4th ed; Grand Rapids: Eerdmans, 1991); E. Jacob, *Theology of the Old Testament* (London: Hodder and Stoughton, 1964) 11–33.

57   See P. Davies, "Do Old Testament Studies Need a Dictionary?", *The Bible in Three Dimensions* (Sheffield: JSOT, 1990) 321–335, for a contemporary proponent of neutrality in OT scholarship. Note especially his claim that the confessional and academic use of the Bible are inevitably and necessarily incompatible, and that true biblical scholarship ought to be conducted using a neutral observation language. It is intriguing, and more than a little ironic, to realise that this vision of scholarly neutrality in the academy has survived the demise of the modernist project – for Davies is avowedly post-modern in his scholarly practice.

58   N. Wolterstorff, "On Christian Learning", *Worldview and Social Theory*, ed. P. Marshall, S. Griffioen and R. Mouw (Lanham: University Press of America, 1986) 56.

59   Wolterstorff, "Travail of Theology", 35–46.

60   e.g. C. Hodge, *Systematic Theology* (ed. E. N. Gross; Grand Rapids: Baker, 1992) 23–31; F. Schleiermacher, *The Christian Faith* (2nd ed; Edinburgh: T&T Clark, 1928) II,ii,27–31; Troeltsch, "Historical and Dogmatic Method in Theology"; cf. G. Marsden, "The Collapse of American Evangelical Academia", *Faith and Rationality: Reason and Belief in God*, ed. A. Plantinga and N. Wolterstorff (Notre Dame: University of Notre Dame Press, 1983) 230–242; Poythress, 32–37. For further discussion of the role of foundationalism in both liberal and conservative theology and its attendant problems, see N. Murphy, *Beyond Liberalism and Fundamentalism: How Modern and Postmodern*

it is imperative to show why classical foundationalism is dead in order to free Christian scholarship from its impossible constraints.[61] This is what Wolterstorff seeks to do in his critique of classical foundationalism.

B. Wolterstorff's Critique of Foundationalism

Wolterstorff's most detailed and systematic argument against foundationalism is found in his *Reason Within the Bounds of Religion*. His argument there is two-pronged, focusing on the relationship that must exist between propositions and their foundations if they are to be rational,[62] and the criteria that a proposition must meet in order to belong to the set of rational foundational beliefs.[63] I shall examine this anti-foundationalist argument before moving on to subsidiary supporting arguments presented in his other works. At each stage of this analysis I will adduce relevant supporting arguments from philosophy of science and epistemology.

B.1. WOLTERSTORFF'S REJECTION OF CLASSICAL FOUNDATIONALIST NOTIONS OF JUSTIFICATION

In the first part of the argument, he identifies two main elements in the foundationalist thesis: the notion of a theory belonging to genuine science (*Wissenschaft*), and the notion of warranted belief.[64] For the sake of this argument, he leaves the notion of warranted belief unchallenged, arguing that there is no need to define it, nor to outline a specific criterion of warrant, for if such a definition or criterion is valid for one epistemic system, it can be taken to be valid for foundationalism as well.[65] What is needed in the context of a critique of foundationalism is an explanation of exactly what is required for a theory to belong to genuine *Wissenschaft*.[66] This, in foundationalist terms, is the issue of the justifying relationship that a theory must have with its foundation in order to be an acceptable

---

Philosophy Set the Theological Agenda (Valley Forge, Pennsylvania: Trinity, 1996) esp 11–35; B. Marshall, *Trinity and Truth* (Cambridge: Cambridge University Press, 2000) 50–107.

61 Wolterstorff, *RWBR*, 34.

62 Wolterstorff, *RWBR*, chapter 5, 35–45. This he entitles "Difficulties in explaining what constitutes justification of theory by foundation".

63 Ibid., Ch. 6, 46–55. This chapter he entitles "Difficulties in finding enough propositions to belong to the foundation".

64 Ibid., 35.

65 Ibid., 35–36. He addresses this issue elsewhere, for which see my discussion of his situated rationality in Chapter 3 below.

66 Ibid., 36.

theory.[67] To pre-empt his argument, his claim is that: "No one has yet offered a satisfactory explanation of what it is for a theory to be *justified* by what the scientist takes as data, and I think it most unlikely that anyone ever will".[68] Let us examine this claim.

The classical relationship that was believed to exist between a theory and its foundations is that of deduction. "A theory belongs to genuine science just in case it is deducible from its foundations."[69] This view is particularly appealing to foundationalists in light of their desire to remove all bias and conjecture from *Wissenschaft*, thus making it a matter of certain knowledge.[70] Deduction does this because it "always and necessarily transmits truth from premises to conclusions".[71] Thus, if theories are deductively derived from a foundation of certitudes, then they will necessarily be certain.[72]

Deduction has, however, "all but collapsed", because "many theories which seem warranted of acceptance are not deducible from any foundation."[73] This is the case for nearly all theories about physical objects which make general or universal claims.[74] The most acceptable candidates for foundational propositions for such theories are propositions concerning the observation of singular instances of a given entity.[75] One cannot, however, generalise from those instances unless one is able to claim with certainty that one has examined every single instance of the entity in question.[76] But this is almost never possible.[77] Thus general or universal theories about physical entities, even such a simple theory as: "All swans have wings", are not deducible from foundational propositions.[78] Yet many such theories are warranted of acceptance.[79] Thus deduction is not a suitable candidate for the relationship of theory and foundation.

---

67   Wolterstorff, *RWBR*, 36–37.
68   Wolterstorff, *C&T*, 117.
69   Wolterstorff, *RWBR*, 35.
70   Ibid., 37.
71   Ibid., 37.
72   Ibid. He cites Rudolph Carnap as stating that this is what he saw as the goal of the physical sciences in the twenties.
73   Ibid.
74   Ibid.
75   Ibid., 38.
76   Ibid.
77   Ibid.
78   Ibid.
79   Ibid.

An alternative to deduction arose: namely, what Wolterstorff calls "probabilism". "On this view a theory belongs to genuine science [*Wissenschaft*] just in case it is *probable* with respect to the foundation."[80] Wolterstorff sees this shift as a "radical lowering of standards as to what constitutes genuine *scientia*", since appeal to probability necessarily involves the abandoning of certitude and the introduction of some degree of conjecture, both of which were unacceptable to the original foundationalist ideal.[81] However the shift from deductivism to probabilism resulted in the acceptance of an important and necessary option for linking theory and foundation, that of induction.[82] An inductive argument has the following structure:

> The relative frequency of observed B's among observed A's is m/n.
> Therefore, it is probable that the relative frequency of B's among all A's is m/n.[83]

The problem of all such arguments from induction is that they assume that nature is uniform between observed and unobserved instances of any given entity.[84] This, however, is something that needs to be demonstrated to be so; otherwise the foundationalist has violated her own anti-conjectural criterion of justified knowledge. Now, there are just two ways that induction can be included amongst the set of justified beliefs: if it is inferentially or noninferentially certain that nature is uniform, or; if it can be demonstrated that it is probably uniform on the basis of evidence.[85] However it is self-evident, by the very nature of the case, that no one can say with certitude that nature is uniform between what has been observed and what has not.[86] Nor is it possible to argue for the uniformity of nature

---

80   Ibid.
81   Ibid.
82   Ibid., 39.
83   Ibid.
84   Ibid.
85   Ibid., 40.
86   Wolterstorff, *RWBR*, 39–40, citing David Hume's argument in *A Treatise on Human Nature* (Oxford: The Clarendon Press, 1888) Book I, Part II, Section VI, esp pp. 89–92. The argument is worth outlining briefly: unless an entity has been observed one can not know its character, for it is at least conceivable that there is non-uniformity in nature. But if it has been observed, then it has been transferred from the set of unobserved entities to the set of observed entities, and thus the relationship between observed and unobserved entities can not be established by reference to that evidence. It is logically impossible to compare unobserved entities with observed entities in order to determine whether there are uniform relationships among them: all one can do is increase the set of observed entities. Given that the set of observed entities is finite, whereas the set of unobserved entities is at least

on the basis of its probability with respect to evidence, for such an argument assumes the validity of induction – the very thing that is open to question.[87] Thus:

> as far as foundationalism is concerned, all probabilistic inductive arguments are equally untenable, for they all use a rule of inference that is neither known with certitude to be satisfactory nor known to be probably satisfactory. But this leaves us without any acceptable explanation of the relation that theories bear to the foundation just in case they belong to genuine science [*Wissenschaft*].[88]

While this does not constitute a rigorous refutation of foundationalism, for there is the possibility that someone may propose a satisfactory alternative to deductivism and probabilism, it does make classical foundationalism seem "an extremely unpromising theory".[89]

The philosophy of science supports Wolterstorff's critique of these methods of establishing indubitable connections between "facts" and theories.[90] Induction was generally proposed as the way in which scientists generalise on the basis of observation, and was thus considered to be the most appropriate way of developing theories.[91] The inductive method, however, has been shown to be wanting at just the points where logical empiricism needs it to be strongest. On logical empiricist grounds, all propositions must be either empirically based, or logically sound.[92] The inductive principle cannot be empirically based, for underlying the inductive argument is the assumption of the uniformity of nature: for only if nature is uniform will the observed cases of an entity be any guide to

---

conceptually infinite, then the probability of any inductive theory is always zero.

[87] Wolterstorff, *RWBR*, 40; cf. I. Lakatos, "Falsification and the Methodology of Scientific Research Programmes", *Criticism and the Growth of Knowledge*, ed. I. Lakatos and A. Musgrave (Cambridge: Cambridge University Press, 1970) 94–95.

[88] Wolterstorff, *RWBR*, 40.

[89] Ibid., 40–41. Wolterstorff particularly has in mind those forms of classical foundationalism propounded by the positivists. An alternative to these views has been developed which bears striking similarities to the program of classical foundationalism, namely *reliabilism*. For an outline of this theory, and a detailed critique of it which supports Wolterstorff's contention, see Duran, 113–127.

[90] That the actual methods of scientific research can provide evidence against positivism can be supported by the recognition that their criterion of meaning is not self-justifying, but is based upon its being an explanation of how science actually operates. See Hempel, 108–129.

[91] Chalmers, 1; Ratsch, 22. The question of the accuracy of Inductivism as a *description* of scientific theorising will be dealt with later.

[92] Chalmers, 13–14; cf. Kolakowski, 10–19.

unobserved cases.[93] This assumption, however, cannot be established on foundationalist grounds, for in order to demonstrate it, both the inductive method, and the uniformity of nature need to be assumed.[94] Indeed, the nature of human observation necessarily assumes the uniformity principle, for as observers we tend to watch for regularities and thus impose uniformity on nature.[95] Nor can the principle of induction be shown to be logically sound, for "valid logical arguments are characterised by the fact that, if the premise of the argument is true, then the conclusion must be true".[96] But this is not the form of inductive arguments, for there is no *logical* reason to suppose that just because all previous ravens have been black the next one cannot be pink.[97] This conclusion can only be based on experience, which, while useful, does not *prove* the inductive method to be correct.[98] Inductivism also suffers from the problem of vagueness: the number of observations that suffice to warrant a given conclusion seems to vary with the nature of the observation and/or conclusion.[99] The attempt to retreat to a probabilist stance also fails, for not only does it assume the validity of the principle of induction, it is impossible to establish a valid basis for inductive conclusions on the grounds of probability.[100] The number of *possible* observations of a given entity is always infinite, but the number of *actual* entities observed is always finite.[101] The probability, therefore, of the inductive conclusion is always zero.[102]

There is an alternative remaining which, while not a classical foundationalist theory, nonetheless embraces an appeal to foundations: *viz, falsificationism*.[103] This theory recognises that we cannot on foundationalist grounds give both necessary and sufficient criteria for a theory's belonging to genuine *Wissenschaft*, but claims that we can present a

---

93 See above, 28–31, and Wolterstorff, *RWBR*, 39.
94 Chalmers, 14; cf. Wolterstorff, *RWBR*, 40.
95 K. R. Popper, *Conjectures and Refutations* (London: Routledge and Keagan Paul, 1974) 49.
96 Chalmers, 12.
97 Ibid., 13.
98 Ibid., 14.
99 Ibid., 15.
100 Wolterstorff, *RWBR*, 40; Ratsch, 34–35.
101 Chalmers, 16–17.
102 Chalmers, 17–18; Lakatos, "Falsification and the Method of Scientific Research Programmes" [from here on *MSRP*], 95.
103 Wolterstorff, *RWBR*, 41.

necessary condition for theory acceptance, or better, a sufficient condition for the rejection of a theory on such grounds.[104] This condition is:

> A theory does not belong to genuine science [*Wissenschaft*] if it is inconsistent with the foundation and someone could know with certitude that it is inconsistent.[105]

This means, however, that there is no *criterion* (necessary and sufficient condition) for warranted theory acceptance, but only a sufficient condition for warranted theory rejection,[106] thus:

> A person is warranted in rejecting a theory at a given time if at that time he is warranted in believing that that theory does not belong to genuine science [*Wissenschaft*].[107]

Falsificationists claim that work in the physical sciences aims not at *confirmation* of theories, but attempted *refutation* of their theories.[108] The idea is that they deduce certain consequences of a given theory and then devise experiments which test those consequences. If the theory fails the tests then it is refuted and discarded.[109]

The falsificationist theory of *Wissenschaft* states that theories of science are never proven, but that they can be refuted.[110] The justification of a theory is not and cannot be a matter of the identification of the origins of the ideas, for that is both logically and practically impossible.[111] The justification of a theory, or better, the demonstration of its not being unjustified, consists in rigorously testing it in relation to its conformity to the "facts".[112] As soon as it fails a critical test, the theory is unjustified and

---

104 Ibid., 41.
105 Ibid., 41. In n. 15 he notes that other relationships than inconsistency may be envisaged, but this then means the theory is a mixed rather than pure foundationalist theory. Such a quasi-foundationalist criterion is thereby a diminished criterion in foundationalist terms.
106 Ibid., 41–42.
107 Ibid., 42.
108 Wolterstorff, *RWBR*, 42; Lakatos, *MSRP*, 96.
109 Wolterstorff, *RWBR*, 42; Lakatos, *MSRP*, 96–97.
110 Popper, *Conjectures and Refutations*, 28; cf. Chalmers, 35.
111 Popper, *Conjectures and Refutations*, 21–25, 27; cf. K. R. Popper, *The Logic of Scientific Discovery* (rev; London: Hutchinson, 1980) 31.
112 Popper, *Conjectures and Refutations*, 27; *The Logic of Scientific Discovery*, 32–33, 86–87, 109–111. This idea of the rigorous testing of theories by the "facts" means that naive falsificationism is vulnerable to the theory dependence of observation statements, for there are no neutral "facts" by which a theory may be rigorously tested (Chalmers, 57–58;

is to be rejected.[113] It also claims that the better a theory is, the more falsifiable it will be: i.e. the more specific and inclusive it is in its predictions and explanations, thus providing more possibility for its failing the test of its own predictions and explanations.[114] Later "sophisticated" falsificationism modified the basic "naive" falsificationist position so as to rule out *ad hoc* modifications of a theory which might enable it to escape legitimate falsification, and to allow for confirmations of theories in relation to crucial experiments.[115] This latter move enabled it to establish a basis for scientific progress by means of the falsification of a conservative conjecture, which falsifies an established theory, or the confirmation of a bold conjecture, which confirms (but does not prove) a bold new theory.[116]

However, there is a crucial problem with falsificationism: rarely does it in fact result in the rejection of a given theory, "for seldom are theories shown to be inconsistent with what is taken as the foundation".[117] There are always multiple reasons for an anomaly occurring between the predictions of a theory and observed data, reasons such as equipment failure, unknown factors which influence the data, and so on.[118] The falsification test rarely instructs one to reject a theory:

Lakatos, *MSRP*, 98–99). It is interesting that Popper clearly recognises the theory dependence of "facts", but not its implications for his theory (*Conjectures and Refutations*, 46–49). For the notion of the theory dependence of "facts", see below.

[113] Popper, *Conjectures and Refutations*, 26, 28; *The Logic of Scientific Discovery*, 33; cf. Chalmers, 35, 40.

[114] Popper, *Conjectures and Refutations*, 28, 36–37; *The Logic of Scientific Discovery*, 112–135; *Objective Knowledge: An Evolutionary Approach* (Oxford: Clarendon, 1972) 13–17; cf. Chalmers, 36–39.

[115] Popper, *Conjectures and Refutations*, 36, 215–230; Chalmers, 47–50. The basic stance of falsificationism was maintained in its "sophisticated" form, as can be seen by the affirmation of many of the ideas of "naive" falsification in such late works as *Conjectures and Refutations*, and K. R. Popper, "Normal Science and its Dangers", *Criticism and the Growth of Knowledge*, ed. I. Lakatos and A. Musgrave (Cambridge: Cambridge University Press, 1970) 56–57.

[116] Chalmers, 51–54.

[117] Wolterstorff, *RWBR*, 42; cf. Chalmers, 63–71, where he shows that in the early phase of theory development, a new theory is *always* inferior to its older rival, and should thereby be rejected on falsificationist lines. Thus falsificationism is falsified by reference to the history of science it sought to explain.

[118] Wolterstorff, *RWBR*, 43–45. Here he quotes Imre Lakatos' "little tale" from *MSRP*, 100–101. Lakatos has a lengthy section in which he demonstrates the inadequacy of dogmatic falsification in the light of the history of science, 93–103, (cf. Chalmers, 61–62) and another in which he demonstrates the inadequacy of naive methodological falsificationism, 112–116.

> For no theory ever stands alone. Every theorist confronts the world with a whole web of theoretical and non-theoretical beliefs. And seldom will there be a direct contradiction between his theory and what he takes as indisputably known. Rather, there will be at best a contradiction between *the whole web* of his beliefs and what he takes as indisputably known. It is then up to him to decide which of his beliefs to surrender.[119]

It may be that the theory is discarded, it may be that the evidence is ignored, or it may be that some subsidiary belief is modified of discarded.[120] But which of these takes place cannot be determined by the falsification rule.[121]

From these criticisms of the deductivist, inductivist and falsificationist strategies, it can be seen that Wolterstorff's contention that there is no satisfactory explanation of what it means for a theory to be justified by foundational propositions has *prima facie* justification. Thus:

> even if there is a set of foundational propositions, no one has yet succeeded in stating what relation theories that we are warranted in accepting or rejecting bear to the members of that set. Even if there is a set of foundational propositions, we are without a general logic of the sciences [*Wissenschaften*], and hence without a general rule for warranted theory acceptance and rejection.[122]

If this is deemed an inadequate reason for the rejection of foundationalism, Wolterstorff has another claim that, if justified, would provide compelling reasons to reject it:

> even if we did know what constitutes justification, the body of propositions that we know noninferentially and with certitude to be true constitutes far too slender a base for the justification of all acceptable theories.[123]

I will proceed to examine this claim.

---

119 Wolterstorff, *RWBR*, 43; cf. Lakatos, *MSRP*, 115.
120 Indeed Chalmers, 60, demonstrates that erroneous falsifications of acceptable theories may occur due to the acceptance of data which is false; cf. Lakatos, *MSRP*, 114–115.
121 Wolterstorff, *RWBR*, 43; Lakatos, *MSRP*, 115.
122 Wolterstorff, *RWBR*, 45.
123 Wolterstorff, *C&T*, 117–118.

B.2. Wolterstorff's Rejection of Classical Foundationalist Notions of a Foundation of Certitudes

Essential to the foundationalist position is the existence of foundational propositions "which are not only true but can be known noninferentially and with certitude to be true".[124] The question that Wolterstorff seeks to answer is whether there are sufficient propositions of that kind to serve as the basis for theory acceptance and rejection.[125] No sooner is the question raised, however, than Wolterstorff raises a caveat about the validity of this question, for without a clear notion of what it means for a proposition to be justified with respect to foundational statements we have no clear notion of what will constitute an adequate base for theorising.[126] However, having raised the question he sets it aside, giving the foundationalist the benefit of the doubt by examining the status of singular propositions about physical entities.[127] The question then becomes: "Are there singular propositions about physical objects which we can know noninferentially and with certitude to be true?"[128]

Two points of clarification need to be addressed in dealing with this issue. The first is: what constitutes certitude? For the sake of the argument, Wolterstorff adopts a definition which he perceives to be most conducive to the foundationalist position, one which is as expansive as possible, without including propositions which would violate the basic intent of foundationalism.[129] This he takes to be the notion of "indubitability":

> A proposition known with certitude to be true by someone at a given time is one which is indubitable for him at that time.[130]

This notion needs further clarification in order to limit it to warranted inability to disbelieve, rather than a causal phenomenon or psychological disposition. Thus:

> x knows p indubitably $=_{df}$ x believes p; p is true; and it is impossible that p should be true and that x should have reasons for not believing p which,

---

124 Wolterstorff, *RWBR*, 46.
125 Ibid.
126 Ibid.
127 Ibid., 47.
128 Ibid., 46.
129 Ibid., 47.
130 Ibid., 48.

in conjunction with those he has for believing *p*, warrant him in not believing *p*.[131]

"So our question becomes: Are there singular propositions about physical objects which we can know noninferentially and indubitably?"[132]

This raises the second issue of clarification: just what is noninferential knowledge?[133] In foundationalist theories of knowledge, for a theory to be of genuine *Wissenschaft* it must be inferred from foundational certitudes. These foundational certitudes must, in turn, not be inferred from anything else, lest we be led into an endless, and for a foundationalist a vicious, circle. Wolterstorff phrases it thus:

> *x* knows *p* noninferentially =$_{df}$ *x* knows *p*; and there is no other proposition *q* which *x* knows from which *p* can be inferred by satisfactory rules of inference, and which is such that if *x* didn't know *q* he wouldn't know *p*.[134]

The question of the existence of properly foundational singular propositions about physical objects now needs to be asked in the light of the understanding of "noninferential" and "indubitable" given above. Now most of these propositions are such that if they are known, then they are known by way of observation of some sort.[135] Thus the question now becomes: "can we, by the use of our perceptual capacities, acquire a noninferential indubitable knowledge of singular propositions about physical objects?"[136]

The burden of proof, according to Wolterstorff, falls upon the notion of indubitable, for that of noninferential knowledge is one that follows on the requirement of indubitability in knowledge.[137] This is, however, a difficult criterion to meet, for it is well known that particular conditions result in an ineluctable distortion of perception; for example lighting conditions, ingestion of alcohol or hallucinogens, and so on.[138] In order to have indubitable knowledge of perceived entities we would, therefore, need to know all the conditions under which perception is distorted, and

---

[131] Ibid., 48 n. 23.
[132] Ibid., 48.
[133] Ibid.
[134] Ibid., 48 n. 24.
[135] Ibid., 48–49.
[136] Ibid., 49.
[137] Ibid.
[138] Ibid.

that none of those conditions pertain to this case of perceiving.[139] However, this is impossible of knowing, for the only way of determining the presence of such a distorting factor is by way of one's perceptual faculties.[140] Thus, "if I am to come to the indubitable knowledge that my perceptual capacities are in the normal state by the use of my perceptual capacities, I must already have indubitable knowledge that my perceptual capacities are in their normal state".[141]

For the argument against foundationalism there is yet another, and more persuasive factor that undermines the possibility of indubitable perceptual knowledge. This is the well documented effect that expectations and prior beliefs about a given entity have upon our perceiving of that entity.[142] This means, as Wolterstorff states, that "to an alarming degree things appear to us as we believe they are rather than as they are, and fail to appear to us as they are when we do not expect them thus to appear."[143] Thus: "Only if our beliefs about the nature of what we are experiencing are already fully accurate will that which we experience appear to us as it really is.[144] This observation is "obviously devastating to foundationalism", for perception does not provide a certain foundation on which we can build our theories.[145] "Rather our theories must already be accurate if our perceptions are to be veridical. Perception is not insulated from theory. Theories cart along their own confirmations."[146] As we shall see, it is this latter point that has proven to be the death-blow to foundationalist philosophies of science.

There is another gap between experience and reality which further weakens the case for foundationalism: not only can we not say with certitude that our perceptions of physical entities are accurate, we can not even say indubitably that the entities we believe that we are perceiving actually exist.[147] Cases of delusions and hallucinations demonstrate that there is the possibility that when we believe we are perceiving an entity, there is in fact nothing there that we are perceiving.[148] Given we cannot

---

[139] Ibid., 50–51.
[140] Ibid., 51–52.
[141] Ibid., 52.
[142] Ibid., where he specifically mentions the influence of expectations upon artistic representations of reality.
[143] Ibid.
[144] Ibid.
[145] Ibid., 52–53.
[146] Ibid., 53.
[147] Ibid.
[148] Ibid.

indubitably demonstrate that we are not suffering from some such delusional state, the only beliefs which we can hold indubitably are those relating to our own states of consciousness.[149] These states of consciousness cannot, however, provide a foundation for theorising; in order for to do so we would need to be able to prove indubitably that our perceptions directly correlate with reality.[150] But that, as we have seen, is just what we cannot do. Thus our states of consciousness do not provide us with access to singular propositions about physical entities.[151] Given that science deals with theories about physical entities rather than one's own states of consciousness,[152] there is no adequate foundation of indubitables on which we can erect the structure of science.[153]

The philosophy of science supports Wolterstorff's challenge to the existence of foundational "facts" upon which theories can be built with its notion of the *theory dependence (or ladenness) of observation statements*. Traditionally observation has been considered to be prior to, and independent of, the theories it supports, thus providing a secure foundation for theorising.[154] This notion is in turn based on a common-sense view of observation in science and everyday life, which believes that different observers share a common *object* of observation, and a common *experience* of the sensations produced as a result of perceiving that object.[155] Both of these propositions depend in turn upon the idea that perceptual experiences are determined directly and solely by neural stimuli from the perceptual organs.[156] As we shall see, these claims are unjustified, being inconsistent with everyday experience, and incompatible with the processes of scientific data-collection.[157]

---

149 Ibid., 53–54.

150 Ibid., 54.

151 Ibid.

152 This is the case even for the psychological sciences, for they deal not with the researcher's states of consciousness alone, but with other entities, be they human or animal, and their observed behaviours, reported states of consciousness, and so on.

153 Wolterstorff, *RWBR*, 54–55. For arguments against Scripture as such a foundation for Christian scholars, see *RWBR*, 58–62, and below (Chapter 6, B.).

154 Chalmers, 20.

155 Chalmers, 21; cf. W. V. O. Quine and J. S. Ullian *The Web of Belief* (New York: Random House, 1970) 12–20, who, while not foundationalists, accept this concept of observation statements.

156 Chalmers, 21.

157 M. Polanyi, *Science, Faith and Society* (2nd ed; Chicago: The University of Chicago Press, 1964) 10–11; *Personal Knowledge: Towards a Post-critical Philosophy* (London: Routledge and Keagan Paul, 1962) vii, 63–64. This latter point, dealing with the actual nature of scientific theorising, will be dealt with in the next section.

A number of recent experiments in perception have demonstrated that everyday perception is not as clear-cut as is usually imagined.[158] Presuppositions about the nature of the object observed, previous experiences of similar objects and observation conditions, the conditions under which an object is observed, all dramatically influence the observation statements of different subjects.[159] This indicates that the commonsense notion of perceptual experiences is wrong: they are not determined directly and solely by neural stimuli, but are influenced by the subject's pre-existing beliefs, "knowledge", expectations and other mental events.[160] Thus Wolterstorff's contention is seen to be true: "Only if our beliefs about the nature of what we are experiencing are already fully accurate will that which we experience appear to us as it really is."[161]

These effects, far from being minimised by the processes of scientific observation, are in fact exacerbated by them. Scientific theories, to a greater extent than everyday theories, are built upon publicly shared statements of observations.[162] These observation statements are not equivalent to "brute facts", for once perceptual experiences are transferred from the subject's own internal world to the external world of shared language and propositions they come to carry a considerable load of theoretical assumptions.[163] Scientific language is theoretical language, in which terms and concepts are endowed with a certain meaning because of, and in the context of, the theories which they express.[164] Since all statements must be framed linguistically, including observation statements, they come to share the assumptions and limitations of the theories the language supports.[165] Every statement of science, be it of a "factual" or a "theoretical" nature, must be made in the language of a theory, and is only

---

[158] Some of these are discussed in detail by Chalmers, 22–23; cf. the "thought experiment" of Wolterstorff, *RWBR*, 50–54.

[159] Chalmers, 23–24; Polanyi, *Science, Faith and Society*, 10, *Personal Knowledge*, vii, 63–64.

[160] Chalmers, 23–24; Popper, *Conjectures and Refutations*, 46–48. Wolterstorff, *RWBR*, 52–53.

[161] Wolterstorff, *RWBR*, 52.

[162] Chalmers, 26; cf. Wolterstorff, *RWBR*, 54.

[163] T. S. Kuhn, "Reflections on my Critics", *Criticism and the Growth of Knowledge*, ed. I. Lakatos and A. Musgrave (Cambridge: Cambridge University Press, 1970) 270–274; P. K. Feyerabend, "Philosophy of Science: A Subject with a Great Past" *Historical and Philosophical Perspectives on Science* ed. H. Stuewer (Minnesota Studies in the Philosophy of Science, vol V; Minneapolis: University of Minnesota Press, 1970) 182–183.

[164] Kuhn, "Reflections", 274.

[165] Chalmers, 26–27; Kuhn, "Reflections", 275.

as precise as that theory.[166] Thus prior experience and existing theories necessarily influence the way an observation is reported.[167]

The influence of theory extends beyond the reporting of observations to the very perceptual process itself, which demonstrates in turn the influence of prior experience upon perception.[168] Indeed, to a great extent, until an observer learns the common language of a given discipline, and participates in the shared experiences of observation events with a more experienced colleague, the observation experiences of that discipline are closed to her.[169] This "apprenticeship" experience is a necessary concomitant of all scientific investigation, and means that all observation is coloured by "tacit knowledge".[170] Observation and experience are thus guided by theoretical constraints: the scope of relevant data, what counts as data, how that data is to influence the theory, all depend upon the theoretical project that underlies the investigative process, whether that theory is at the stage of construction or testing.[171] Thus Wolterstorff's contention is clearly supported: "Perception is not insulated from theory. Theories carry along their own confirmation."[172] Consequently Wolterstorff's critique of classical foundationalism, and indeed all analogous attempts to develop a system of indubitable knowledge by reference to "hard data" is justified. Empirical observation, even at the most basic level of singular propositions about physical objects, is not properly foundational, for since they are influenced by language and theoretical assumptions, such propositions are not known, and cannot be known, to be true

---

166   Chalmers, 26–27.

167   This is in part what Polanyi means by the "tacit co-efficient" of all scientific (and other) knowing (*Science, Faith and Society*, 10, 13, *Personal Knowledge*, 160–171). As we shall see, experience and theoretical presuppositions also influence the very process of observation in science.

168   The use of the history of science to explain the philosophy of science, and hence of knowledge in general, which underlies this argument, has come under attack. I will deal with this issue later (Chapter 2, B.1.).

169   P. J. Riggs, *Whys and Ways of Science* (Carlton: Melbourne University Press, 1992) 20–21. This has certainly been my experience in medical observations, including the interpretation of radiographic images. The actual perception of the object of observation (e.g. an X-ray of a broken limb, or a diseased lung) is dependent upon the knowledge of both the observation process and the expected possible outcomes of the investigative technique.

170   This is argued forcefully by Polanyi (*Science, Faith and Society*, 42–62). He argues that this tacit co-efficient is not acquired prior to the pursuit of scientific investigation, but in the very process of it, especially in the "apprenticeship" period (*Personal Knowledge*, 171).

171   Chalmers, 31–33; T. S. Kuhn, *The Structure of Scientific Revolutions* (Chicago: The University of Chicago Press, 1962) [from here on *SSR*], 144–146.

172   Wolterstorff, *RWBR*, 53.

non-inferentially and with certitude.[173] "Theorising is without a foundation of indubitables."[174]

B.3. FURTHER ARGUMENTS AGAINST CLASSICAL FOUNDATIONALISM

Wolterstorff presents further arguments against foundationalism in his endorsement of Reidian epistemology. In order to accurately construe Reid's critique of scepticism, it is necessary to understand what it is that he rejects: who is the "Reidian sceptic". According to Wolterstorff:

> Reid's sceptic is the person who holds that we are justified in believing something only if we hold it on the basis of other beliefs which constitute adequate evidence for it. In particular, we must not accept the 'testimony' of some noetic faculty until we can infer on the basis of good reasons that this testimony is reliable.[175]

While Reid never uses the term, Wolterstorff believes his critique of the "Way of Ideas" in relation to warranted belief constituted a critique of classical foundationalism.[176] "Reid's significance lies in the fact that he is the first great critic of what in recent years has come to be called 'classical foundationalism.'"[177] The particular form of foundationalism that Reid had in mind was that of "objectivist foundationalism with respect to justified (warranted) belief – with the concept of justified belief in question being a purely evaluative concept".[178] While not all classical foundationalists hold to this version of the theory,[179] "most if not all his arguments do apply to all of his predecessors *mutatis mutandis.*"[180]

Reid presents three lines of argument against foundationalist sceptics such as Hume.[181] The first is the *ad hominem* observation that the sceptics

---

[173] Chalmers, 28; Dancy, 55–61; Wolterstorff, *RWBR*, 47–48, 54.

[174] Wolterstorff, *RWBR*, 56.

[175] Wolterstorff, *TRR*, 53; It must be noted that "the deliverances of the faculties of reflection, self-evidence and reasoning" are exempt from this criterion (N. Wolterstorff, "Hume and Reid", *The Monist* 70/4 (Oct 1987) [from here on *H&R*], 408).

[176] Wolterstorff, *H&R*, 406. Strictly speaking, he critiques classically modern foundationalism, for which see, N. Wolterstorff, *Thomas Reid and the Story of Epistemology* (Cambridge: Cambridge University Press, 2001) [from here on *Reid*], 186–192, 216.

[177] Ibid.

[178] Ibid. Objectivism is contrasted with subjectivism; evaluative with deontic.

[179] Ibid. Wolterstorff suggests that perhaps Hume did hold it – or at least something like it.

[180] Ibid.

[181] Wolterstorff, *TRR*, 53–57. Wolterstorff there identifies two points of argument, apparently including my third line of argument in his first. In addition, see Wolterstorff,

violate their own principle of scepticism with respect to their philosophising and their living: the first because they accept, without first establishing its reliability, the testimony of states of consciousness; the second because they fail to treat the testimony of the senses with the scepticism that they apparently deserve.[182] The second line of argument is closely related to the first: the sceptic's inability to live and think in a manner consistent with her theory is no accident, or singular instance, but an inevitability. For "all normal human beings are so constructed that they *cannot* follow the advice of the sceptic".[183] While the sceptic may suggest that we ought to discard all beliefs not founded on adequate evidence, Reid claims that we are simply unable to do this.[184] This does not consist of a proof of the truth of those ineluctable beliefs that we hold without evidence: it is a justification of those beliefs, for "one is never obliged to do what one *cannot* do".[185] Indeed, Reid believed that our noetic faculties and the beliefs they engender are sufficiently reliable as they are. If a philosophical theory calls them into question, this questioning comprises a most cogent argument against that theory, rather than against the faculties.[186]

This argument is supported by recent work in "reformed epistemology" which criticises classical foundationalism's notion of justified knowledge with respect to the nature of normal human knowing. Positivism entailed normative epistemic claims:[187] as such it could theoretically afford to ignore the way in which people actually acquire justified knowledge. It claimed that "*a belief is rational for a person only if that person has sufficient evidence or arguments or reasons for that belief*".[188] This, however, would exclude the majority of beliefs that people

---

Reid, 45–95, for Reid's critique of the "Way of Ideas" and its associated theory of perception, which he sees as fundamental to the foundationalism he rejects. Wolterstorff there identifies three main arguments, which he identifies as "we couldn't do it if we tried" (what I identify as Reid's second argument), "the skeptic's injunction is arbitrarily discriminatory" (my third argument below), and "the skeptic plunges into absurdity" (roughly akin to my first argument below).

182 Wolterstorff, *TRR*, 53–55; c/f *Reid*, 206–212, where he speaks of the sceptic plunging into absurdity; T. Reid, *An Inquiry into the Human Mind*, ed. T. Duggan; Chicago: University of Chicago Press, 1970) V,7; VII,7; VI,20.

183 Wolterstorff, *TRR*, 55; Reid, *Inquiry*, VI,20.

184 Wolterstorff, *TRR*, 55, *Reid*, 194–197. Reid makes this point particularly in relation to sensory beliefs, but as we shall see, it holds equally for our other noetic faculties.

185 Ibid. For an explication and defence of this ethics of belief, see Chapter 3 below.

186 Wolterstorff, *H&R*, 407; Reid, *Inquiry*, I,4.

187 Plantinga, *R&BG*, 48.

188 K. Clark, 3, emphasis in the original.

have in normal life, beliefs which have at least *prima facie* rationality.[189] As Plantinga states: "relative to propositions that are self-evident and incorrigible, most of the beliefs that form the stock in trade of ordinary everyday life are not probable – at any rate there is no reason to think they are probable."[190] However, given that people seem to have much more knowledge than they can justifiably have on positivist grounds, the question must be asked: Is positivism right, in which case we do not know many things that in fact we seem justified in claiming that we know, or are we right, and positivism wrong? It seems in fact that positivism, and classical foundationalism in general, unreasonably exclude many beliefs that are clearly justified, such as memory, knowledge of other minds and persons, the reality of the external world (i.e. we are not "brains in a vat") because they fail to attain its normative standards of justified belief.[191] Classical foundationalism should therefore be rejected on the grounds that "any philosophical principle that excludes cases of obviously rational belief ought to be rejected".[192] This charge is not relevant to normal knowing alone; it is also applicable to scientific knowing since the two are parallel in many ways.[193]

His third line of argument is that the sceptical position is "completely arbitrary".[194] The sceptic assumes that the deliverances of inference are trustworthy without having demonstrated that inference is a reliable belief-forming mechanism, but that we are not justified in accepting the deliverances of other noetic faculties.[195] According to Reid, "this is an unjustifiable, arbitrary, singling out of reason".[196] Instead, we should afford all our belief-forming mechanisms the same epistemic status as that ascribed by the sceptic to reason.[197] A possible reply is that since all such mechanisms are liable to error we should not accept the testimony of

---

189   This is discussed in detail by K. Clark, 97–122, cf. Plantinga, *R&BG*, 59–60.
190   Plantinga, *R&BG*, 59.
191   Plantinga, *R&BG*, 59–60; K. Clark, 138.
192   K. Clark, 138; cf. Plantinga *R&BG*, 60. This is supported by V. M. Cooke, 277–278.
193   Polanyi, *Science, Faith and Society*, 10. This line of argument depends upon a common-sense view of rationality. This notion is valid for normal knowing, but may not be for academic rationality, in particular scientific rationality, for different rules may legitimately apply to these different categories of knowing. This seems to be acknowledged by Clark, 102–112, and Polanyi, 10.
194   Wolterstorff, *TRR*, 55; *Reid*, 197–206.
195   Ibid., 55–56.
196   Wolterstorff, *TRR*, 56; Reid, *Inquiry*, VI,20.
197   Wolterstorff, *TRR*, 56; *H&R*, 406; *Reid*, 198–199.

reason unless we can infer its reliability from other beliefs.[198] This position inevitably leads to the abandonment of all possibility of justified belief, for we cannot prove the reliability of inference without recourse to inference itself, the very thing under question.[199] There is no point in arguing with a person who affirms such a position – the best thing is to walk away and leave him to his scepticism.[200]

However, Wolterstorff and Reid do not claim that our noetic faculties are without error: they are limited and imperfect.[201] The reason that inference was afforded the privileged status it had along with reflection and self-evidence in this form of classical foundationalism was the promise of certainty that they proffered.[202] And in relation to this, Reid did not count them altogether foolish for preferring reason over other belief forming mechanisms, for he saw it as "the least mysterious and most perfectly comprehended" of them all.[203] His response is not to reject the value of reason, but to reject the possibility of certainty with respect to any of our noetic faculties and the beliefs they engender in us.[204] "Reid refuses to bite at that most ancient of all philosophical lures: the lure of grounding all our beliefs in certitude."[205] Thus Reid's critique of classical foundationalism reinforces the conclusion that foundationalism is an untenable meta-theory, and that indubitable knowledge is a chimera.

A number of supporting arguments may be presented for Wolterstorff's critique of classical foundationalism, some of which he specifically refers to in his writings. The first of these is the anti-foundationalist argument of Alvin Plantinga. Wolterstorff endorses Plantinga's argument in the context of his own critique of the "evidentialist challenge" to belief in God.[206] According to Wolterstorff, the evidentialist challenge comprises two primary claims: "if it is not rational to accept some proposition about God then one ought not to accept it"; and "it is not rational to accept

---

198 Wolterstorff, *TRR*, 56; *H&R*, 409.

199 Wolterstorff, *TRR*, 56; *H&R*, 409; *Reid*, 205–206; cf. pp. 28–33 above.

200 Wolterstorff, *TRR*, 56–57; *Reid*, 246–249; T. Reid, *Essays on the Intellectual Powers of Man* (Glasgow: Richmond Griffin, 1854) VI,5.

201 Wolterstorff, *H&R*, 408. This point is clearer in Wolterstorff than in Reid, but needs further articulation in the former as well, see below (Chapter 3, A.4.).

202 Ibid.

203 Wolterstorff, *H&R*, 408; *TRR*, 56; Reid, *Inquiry*, II,20.

204 Wolterstorff, *H&R*, 408; *Reid*, 206.

205 Ibid., 409.

206 N. Wolterstorff, "Can Belief in God be Rational If It Has No Foundations?" *Faith and Rationality: Reason and Belief in God*, ed. A. Plantinga and N. Wolterstorff (Notre Dame: University of Notre Dame Press, 1983) [from here on *CBGR?*], 135–186.

propositions about God unless one does so on the basis of others of one's beliefs which provide adequate evidence for them, and with a firmness not exceeding that warranted by the strength of that evidence".[207] Elsewhere he has defined evidentialism in more general terms:

> Given a thesis, one first collects adequate evidence pro and con; one then adequately scrutinizes the relation of the thesis to the evidence so as to determine the probability of the former as to the latter; and finally one believes or disbelieves the thesis with a firmness proportional to the probability one has determined it to have on the evidence. For the sake of convenience, let me call this complex activity the *evidential* activity.[208]

In *Can Belief In God Be Rational If It Has No Foundations?* he does not specifically refute the evidentialist position, but rather presents an alternative view of rationality by which he judges the evidentialist challenge to be a false one.[209] He does, however, note that Plantinga directly challenges evidentialist epistemology in "Reason and Belief in God",[210] and endorses that challenge:

> He [Plantinga] there suggests that common to all, or almost all, evidentialists is a certain 'model' of rationality, a certain criterion for the application of the concept *rational* – the criterion being that of classical foundationalism. Plantinga then goes on to argue that that criterion is unacceptable. I judge Plantinga to be correct in both these contentions. Almost always when you lift an evidentialist you find a foundationalist. But the careful formulation of classical foundationalism by a number of philosophers in recent years has been accompanied by a growing consensus that it is not a plausible criterion of rational belief... His [Plantinga's] discussion puts us in the position of seeing that the most common and powerful argument for evidentialism is classical foundationalism, and of seeing that classical foundationalism is unacceptable.[211]

---

207 Wolterstorff, *CBGR?*, 136; cf. "The Migration of the Theistic Arguments", 41, 49–50.
208 Wolterstorff, "Evidence, Entitled Belief and the Gospels" *Faith and Philosophy* 6/4 (Oct 1989) [from here on *EB&G*], 429.
209 Wolterstorff, *CBGR?*, 142.
210 Plantinga, *R&BG*, 16–93.
211 Wolterstorff, *CBGR?*, 142. It must be noted that Wolterstorff's endorsement of Plantinga's critique of classical foundationalism does not entail the endorsement of the broad foundationalism that Plantinga proposes as an alternative. Indeed, Wolterstorff specifically states that he does not see foundationalism as a particularly fruitful epistemic structure. See *CBGR?*, 172. It is also important to note that Plantinga acknowledges that not all evidentialists are classic foundationalists – indeed some may be coherentist – and that he adduces counter-arguments to coherentist versions of the evidentialist objection. See Plantinga, "Coherentism and the Evidentialist Objection", 109–138.

Thus I will outline Plantinga's critique of classical foundationalism as further support for Wolterstorff's rejection of classical foundationalism.

His most important criticism is that classical foundationalism is internally inconsistent.[212] The argument is a simple one: classical foundationalism is neither a properly basic nor a properly non-basic belief in terms of classical foundationalist canons, and is therefore a meaningless assertion.[213] Indeed, when one examines it on foundationalist principles, it seems that it is just the kind of normative and metaphysical statement most vigorously impugned by foundationalists. This argument needs, of course, some expansion. It is not a properly basic belief, for it does not conform to their canons of properly basic beliefs: it is not an empirical statement, for it is not something which is evident to one's senses; it is not self-evidently true since one can understand it and still reject it, as indeed I, and a great many philosophers do; it is not incorrigible, for there is at least the possibility that one can be mistaken about its truth claims.[214] It is not a properly non-basic belief, for no one has yet presented an argument that establishes its truth with respect to the foundations of knowledge, and it is hard to imagine that this could in fact be done.[215] This means, however, that classical foundationalism's criterion of rationality can only be maintained by denying that criterion, and thus it ought to be rejected on classical foundationalism's own terms.[216] "CF [classical foundationalism] is therefore *self-referentially inconsistent*."[217]

---

212 Plantinga, *R&BG*, 60–61; cf. K. Clark, 137–138.
213 Plantinga, *R&BG*, 60–62; K. Clark, 137–138.
214 Plantinga, *R&BG*, 60; cf. K. Clark, 137.
215 Plantinga, *R&BG*, 60; K. Clark, 137–138.
216 This is true of every conceivable formulation of the criterion. Plantinga, *R&BG*, 61–62.
217 K. Clark, 138, emphasis in original; cf. Plantinga, *R&BG*, 60–61. This conclusion has been denied by P. Quinn ("In Search of the Foundations of Theism", *Faith and Philosophy* 2/4 (Oct 1985) 468–486). The argument is that no classic foundationalist would assert that the foundationalist criterion is properly basic, and that the failure to demonstrate how it can be justified as a properly non-basic belief does not mean that the theory is wrong – only that it is not yet fully articulated (Hatcher, 84–95; W. P. Alston, "Plantinga's Epistemology of Religious Belief", *Alvin Plantinga*, ed. J. E. Tomberlin and P. van Inwagen (Dordrecht: Reidel, 1985) 297–298). He does state that unless and until classical foundationalists articulate this criterion we are not obliged to accept it. Quinn (473–476) and J. Runzo ("World-views and the Epistemic Foundations of Theism", *RelS* 25/1 (March 1989) 38) claim that the classical foundationalist criterion can be justified in terms of Plantinga's inductive method for determining proper basicality. But that is just the point: it is not a criterion which has been, or can be reasonably expected to be, justified by the canons of classic foundationalism itself, and thus the criterion is bankrupt, whether or not Plantinga's own epistemology is a viable alternative. So J. Malino, "Comments on Quinn", *Faith and Philosophy* 2/4 (Oct 1985) 487–491; V. M. Cooke, 273–285; cf. A. Plantinga, "Replies to my Colleagues", *Alvin Plantinga*, ed. J. E. Tomberlin and P. van Ingwagen (Dordrecht:

Recent studies in the history and philosophy of science also support Wolterstorff's contentions, in that they have shown that the nature of science as it is actually practised bears no relation to the logical empiricist ideal, and in fact that it cannot.[218] The actual character of scientific theorising negates the empiricist concept of the processes of theory development and testing. Even if the inductive method could be shown to establish the certitude of theories, it could not be used to support the objectivity of science, for theories are not developed by a system of induction from a mass of evidence.[219] In fact unless the theory exists, at least in tentative form, prior to the collection of data, there will be no means of determining what counts as data, or how it is to be collected in such a way as to ensure it meets necessary initial conditions.[220] "Every established proposition of science enters into the current premises of science and affects the scientist's decision to accept an observation as fact or to disregard it as probably unsound."[221] Indeed, Sir Arthur Eddington is quoted as stating, "It is a good rule not to put too much confidence in observational results that are put forward until they are confirmed by theory."[222] Thus theories cannot be developed by the inductive method since they already exist prior to the collection of the data upon which they are supposedly founded: as Popper has said, "without waiting for premises we [scientists] jump to conclusions".[223] Just how theories do come into being is a matter of some debate.[224] They are not, however, developed using the "objective" tool of the inductive method. Foundationalist objectivism has thus been shown to be fatally flawed.

Thus there are many reasons to conclude that classical foundationalism, and the allied positivist position, are implausible. This demonstrates the need for an alternative view of the epistemic process which is cognisant of the realities of human knowing in general, and scientific

---

Reidel, 1985) 392–393. This argument is supported by Quine's assertion that the separation of synthetic and analytic statements, and the attempt to reduce all the factual components of science to confirming experiences are in fact *metaphysical dogmas* of positivism, and thereby illegitimate according to positivism's own criterion (Quine, "Two Dogmas", 20–42).

[218] Wolterstorff, "Scholarship and Conviction", 38–41.
[219] Polanyi, *Science, Faith and Society*, 13–14.
[220] Popper, *Conjectures and Refutations*, 28.
[221] Polanyi, *Science, Faith and Society*, 11.
[222] cited in V. H. Fiddes, *Science and the Gospel* (Edinburgh: Scottish Academic Press, 1987) 37.
[223] Popper, *Conjectures and Refutations*, 46.
[224] This will be discussed in detail later.

knowing in particular. One alternative that has received a great deal of attention, and which has become popular in the light of the collapse of foundationalism, is that of relativism, to which I will now turn.

CHAPTER 2

Wolterstorff and Relativism

Wolterstorff's rejection of classical foundationalism does not lead him to reject the notions of rationality, truth, or knowledge, even though he recognises that the collapse of foundationalism has led many of his philosophical colleagues to do so.[1] It is worth quoting him in some detail on this:

> In saying this [that theorising is without a foundation of indubitables] I do not mean at all to deny that there is an objective reality with a nature independent of what we all conceive and believe. Nothing I have said requires the affirmation that man is the creator of that which is.
>
> Nor do I mean to deny that you and I can attain true belief of that objective reality. Nothing I have said requires the repudiation of truth as a legitimate and attainable goal of inquiry.
>
> Nor do I mean to deny that we are warranted in accepting some from among the thicket of human beliefs and rejecting others. Nothing I have said requires the profession of "anything goes".
>
> I mean just to affirm that the proposed rule for warranted theory acceptance is untenable. It is not the case that one is warranted in accepting some theory if and only if one is warranted in believing that it is justified by propositions knowable noninferentially and with certitude... All that follows is that theorising is without a foundation of indubitables.
>
> Our future theories of theorising will have to be nonfoundationalist ones.[2]

---

1   Wolterstorff, *RWBR*, 56–57; *C&T*, 118; "Introduction", 4–5, *TRR*, 64; "Between the Pincers of Increased Diversity and Supposed Irrationality", *God, Philosophy and Academic Culture*, ed. W. Wainwright (Atlanta: Scholars, 1996) 12–20.
2   Wolterstorff, *RWBR*, 56–57.

A. Kuhnian Relativism

Wolterstorff nowhere presents a detailed critique of epistemological relativism, although he does present reasons for its rejection from a Christian perspective.[3] It is important to analyse relativist views, however, as the validity of Wolterstorff's rationality and meta-theory depends in part on the plausibility of his rejection of relativism and foundationalism. So too, the recent rise of relativist theories of theology[4] and biblical interpretation[5] following the collapse of (foundationalist) absolutist epistemology warrants an analysis of the relativist epistemology which they exemplify. I will therefore briefly outline the basic stance of relativism, drawing upon the work of Goodman and Rorty, before passing on to a discussion of Kuhn and Kuhnian relativism.

Before I discuss relativism, I need to defend my identification of Rorty as a relativist, since he claims his epistemological pragmatism is not a relativist theory.[6] He claims that the charges of irrationalism and relativism levelled against this position are "merely the mindless defensive reflexes" of traditional philosophy which have no weight if the abolition of the false idea of "mirroring nature" is abandoned.[7] He argues that such an identification is illegitimate since notions such as relativism and irration-

---

[3] See below, Chapter 3, B.3., in relation to his theory of rationality; Chapter 5, B.1., in relation to his meta-theory.

[4] e.g. G. D. Kaufman, *In Face of Mystery: A Constructive Theology* (Cambridge, Ma: Harvard University Press, 1993) esp 3–69.

[5] See, e.g., S. E. Fowl, "The Ethics of Interpretation: or What's Left After the Elimination of Meaning", *The Bible in Three Dimensions*, ed. D. J. A. Clines, *et al* (Sheffield: JSOT, 1990) 379–398; D. G. Gunn, "Reading Right: Reliable and Omniscient Narrator, Omniscient God, and Foolproof Composition in the Hebrew Bible", *The Bible in Three Dimensions*, ed. D. J. A. Clines, *et al* (Sheffield: JSOT, 1990) 53–64; G. Kennedy, "'Truth' and 'Rhetoric' in the Pauline Epistles", *The Bible as Rhetoric: Studies in Biblical Persuasion and Credibility*, ed. M. Warner (Routledge: London, 1990) 195–202; E. V. McKnight, *Post-Modern Use of the Bible: The Emergence of Reader-Oriented Criticism* (Nashville: Abingdon, 1988) esp 167–177, 217–267.

[6] R. Rorty, *Philosophy and the Mirror of Nature* (Oxford: Basil Blackwell, 1979) 13; "Pragmatism, Relativism and Irrationalism", *Consequences of Pragmatism* (Minneapolis: University of Minnesota Press, 1982) 166–174; "Introduction: Antirepresentationalism, ethnocentrism and liberalism", *Objectivity, relativism and truth: Philosophical Papers, Vol One* (Cambridge: Cambridge University Press, 1991) 9; "Is Natural Science a Natural Kind?", *Objectivity, relativism and truth: Philosophical Papers, Vol One* (Cambridge: Cambridge University Press, 1991) 49–51. Wolterstorff, "Introduction", 4, is perhaps more circumspect in calling him an epistemic agnostic, one who has abandoned the very idea of knowledge. However, as I hope to demonstrate, my bolder ascription of relativism to Rorty is legitimate. See H. Siegel *Relativism Refuted: A Critique of Contemporary Epistemological Relativism* (Dordrecht: D. Reidel, 1987) 32.

[7] Rorty, *Philosophy*, 13.

alism are relevant only to the representationalist philosophy he rejects.[8] He identifies relativism as the view that any belief is as good as any other.[9] Rorty suspects that no one seriously holds to this view, and claims he is not a relativist, as he believes that some beliefs are better than others.[10] He further identifies irrationalism as the view that there are no workable rules for discourse.[11] Rorty again denies that pragmatism is irrationalist, for he believes in rules for discourse. While they are established solely by a given community on the basis of their utility and are relevant only to that community at that time, they are nonetheless real guidelines.[12]

Rorty acknowledges that his discussion of relativism "may seem to have ducked the real issues".[13] That, I believe, is just what it has done. Indeed, his repudiation of relativism rests more upon philosophical "tricks" than upon argumentation. This may be appropriate in the context of "edifying philosophy", but it is not suitable in the establishing or defending of his position.[14] He claims that justification and truth are purely social notions, relative to a given intellectual community at a given time,[15] that truth is "what is better for us to believe", what is more useful for us, rather than an accurate representation of reality,[16] and that truth is "what

---

[8] Rorty, "Introduction", *Objectivity, relativism and truth*, 9; "Is Natural Science a Natural Kind?" 49–51.

[9] This is a tendentious and misleading definition, given that N. Goodman "The Fabrication of Facts", *Relativism: Cognitive and Moral* ed. J. W. Meiland and M. Kraus (Notre Dame: University of Notre Dame Press, 1982) 20, who is avowedly relativist, claims that relativism does not entail this.

[10] Rorty, "Pragmatism, Relativism and Irrationalism", 166–169.

[11] This he does not specifically state, but clearly implies when he talks of irrationalists proposing "such rubbishy pseudo-epistemological notions as 'intuition' or 'an articulate sense of tradition' or 'thinking with the blood' or 'expressing the will of the oppressed classes'" (Rorty, "Pragmatism, Relativism and Irrationalism" 171).

[12] Rorty, "Pragmatism, Relativism and Irrationalism", 173–174.

[13] Ibid.

[14] Note the argument in Rorty, *Philosophy*, 13, where his rejection of relativist charges depends upon the legitimacy of his critique of traditional philosophy, which in turn rests largely upon his pragmatist claims. cf. G. Vision, "Veritable Reflections", *Reading Rorty*, ed. A. R. Malachowski (Oxford: Basil Blackwell, 1990) 78–79, 97–98, in the context of Rorty's critique of representationalism. A similar judgement is made in relation to Rorty's rejection of relativism by B. Williams ("Auto-da-Fé: Consequences of Pragmatism", *Reading Rorty*, ed. A. R. Malachowski (Oxford: Basil Blackwell, 1990) 28–29) who states that while Rorty may not be a relativist, he cannot simply dismiss relativism and the problems associated with it.

[15] Rorty, *Philosophy*, 9–10, 170–171, 176, 210; "Pragmatism, Relativism and Irrationalism", 165.

[16] Rorty, *Philosophy*, 10; "Introduction", *Essays on Heidegger and others: Philosophical Papers, Vol Two* (Cambridge: Cambridge University Press, 1991) 3, 5.

our peers will, *ceteris paribus*, let us get away with saying".[17] When these claims are taken into account, his pragmatism is seen to be effectively indistinguishable from relativism.[18]

A.1. AN OUTLINE OF COGNITIVE RELATIVISM

Relativism as an epistemological stance argues from a perceived plurality of interpretations of the world, and their dependence upon conceptual categories framed by communities, to the claim that there can be no knowledge of the world which is free from bias, and nor should there be.[19] Relativists assert that while the world has an existence independent of our observation of it, this is epistemologically irrelevant, for we have no access to the world except via our theories (versions) of the world.[20] Since all facts are theory-laden, what counts as a fact is an intellectual construction: "facts are small theories, and true theories are big facts".[21] Thus in the context of human knowledge there is no World, no Reality, understood as something that has an existence independent of human observation, there

---

17   Rorty, *Philosophy*, 176. Elsewhere Rorty argues that this claim, and others like it, should not be taken as a *definition* of truth, for truth is a "primitive predicate", not subject to definition (see S. Louthan, "On Religion: A Discussion with Richard Rorty, Alvin Plantinga and Nicholas Wolterstorff", *Christian Scholar's Review* 26/2 (Wint 1996) 177–183, 180). I take it, then, that Rorty is not defining "truth", but describing its pragmatic value in intellectual conversation, and so "true" is equivalent to "justified" or "entitled". Truth, then, is not a goal of our inquiry, but a way of speaking of the pragmatic value of ideas in the life of a particular community. (see Richard Rorty, "Introduction", *Philosophical Papers, vol 3: Truth and Progress*, (Cambridge: Cambridge University Press, 1998) 1–15; "Is Truth a Goal of Inquiry? Donald Davidson versus Crispin Wright", *Philosophical Papers, vol 3*, 19–42.) Given, then, his explicitly pragmatist view of such notions as justification, entitlement, and so on, as being relative to a community's interests, what is useful for the members of that community in its life in the world, my appraisal of his views as an example of framework relativism stands.

18   cf. Siegel, 32. For an attempt to rescue Rorty's "rationality" from the relativist dilemma, see S. E. Rosenbaum ("Rortian Rationality", *Metaphilosophy*, 17/2&3 (Ap/Jul 1986) 93–101). His attempt to moderate some of Rorty's more extreme statements, and to develop a non-relativist historicist position is, I believe, unsuccessful. This is because the arguments against objective truth based on the world-view dependence of all knowledge which he raises in support of his position are invalid in much the same way as I believe Kuhn's arguments are invalid.

19   Goodman, 18–20; cf. Rorty, *Philosophy*, 10, 13, 210, 315–320.

20   Goodman, 21–22. This largely depends upon an identification of representationalist with foundationalist and absolutist views of truth, and the rejection of absolutism on the grounds of the world-view dependent nature of all human knowing. See Rorty, *Philosophy*, 3, 6, 8–10, 11, 131–164, 165–212, 315–320; Rosenbaum, 93–95. For the illegitimacy of many of these arguments, see Vision, 74–100.

21   Goodman, 23; cf. Rorty, *Philosophy*, 315–342.

are only worlds, or realities, which are the product of human perceptions.[22] It is only these "versions" that have epistemic value: there is no one "true" way of looking at the world.[23] It is claimed that this does not mean that "anything goes" in the field of knowledge, or that truth and falsehood are meaningless concepts.[24] Rather it means that "truth must be otherwise conceived than as correspondence with a ready-made world".[25] True versions are not limited to science, for since versions are active constructs of perceived reality anything that constructively shapes the way we look at "the world" is a valid version.[26] Thus the arts, music, literature are all valid versions, because they encourage us to look at the world in new ways.[27] Standards for assessing versions must be extended beyond "truth' and "falsehood" in order to embrace the worlds created by artists, musicians and poets which have no referents for the concept of "truth", for no assertions are made.[28] From this perspective only internal factors, such as coherence and consistency, or the judgement of the relevant community, determine whether a version is valid.[29] Analogous claims have been made in relation to (Christian) belief and the interpretation of biblical texts, using identical arguments.[30]

This view of the nature of the human epistemic task has received significant impetus from the work of T. S. Kuhn.[31] While he categorically

---

22   Goodman, 18–20; Rorty, "Introduction", *Essays on Heidegger and others*, 4.

23   Goodman, 18–22.

24   Goodman, 20; Rorty, *Philosophy*, 13; "Pragmatism, Relativism and Irrationalism, 166–174; "Introduction", *Objectivity, relativism and truth*, 9; "Is Natural Science a Natural Kind?", 49–51. But note that Feyerabend asserts just that position in his plea for "Epistemological Anarchy" (P. K. Feyerabend, "Consolations for the Specialist", *Criticism and the Growth of Knowledge*, ed. I. Lakatos and A. Musgrave (Cambridge: Cambridge University Press, 1970) 214, 228–230).

25   Goodman, 20; cf. Rorty, *Philosophy*, 3.

26   Goodman, 24–25.

27   Ibid., 25–26.

28   Ibid., 27–28.

29   Ibid., 27–28; cf. J. W. Meiland and M. Kraus "Introduction to the 'Fabrication of Facts'", *Relativism: Cognitive and Moral* ed. J. W. Meiland and M. Kraus (Notre Dame: University of Notre Dame Press, 1982) 14; Rorty, *Philosophy*, 333–342.

30   Gunn, 53–64; Fowl, 379–398; Kaufman, 3–69; Kennedy, "'Truth' and 'Rhetoric'", 195–202; McKnight, 167–177, 217–267; cf. the exposition and critique of these views in J. Goldingay, "How far do readers make sense? Interpreting biblical narrative", *Themelios* 18/2 (Jan 1993) 5–10; H. A. Netland, *Dissonant Voices: Religious Pluralism and the Question of Truth* (Leicester: Apollos, 1991) 112–233.

31   See Rorty, *Philosophy*, 11, 315–320, 322–333, for his specific endorsement of Kuhn's views, although it must be noted that he criticises what he perceives as Kuhn's tacit idealism; cf. *Philosophy*, 324–325.

rejects the label of relativism and irrationalism in relation to his epistemic program,[32] many aspects of his work foster relativist epistemologies.[33] Indeed, in some ways his position is indistinguishable from relativism, at least in the sense that he has so far failed to demonstrate adequately how his position can avoid cognitive relativism.[34] In order to assess the claims of relativism it will therefore be necessary to examine the work of Kuhn in some detail. This analysis will focus on those aspects of his thought that most directly relate to relativist epistemologies. I will, therefore, ignore those aspects that deal more directly with the history and sociology of science, except when they have bearing on the overall epistemology that derives from his work.

A.2. KUHNIAN RADICALISM

Kuhn's analysis of the nature of science depends in large part upon his interpretation of the history of science.[35] Central to Kuhn's analysis of the history, and hence philosophy, of science is the notion that science is typified by an open-ended pattern of normal science–crisis–revolution–(new pattern of) normal science, which is repeated more or less frequently.[36] Normal science, as the name suggests, is the typical state of the scientific enterprise, in which the assumptions, tools, techniques and tasks of a given discipline are uncritically accepted by a given scientific community.[37] This stage of science is characterised by "puzzle-solving" research which aims at sharpening the accepted theory by increasing its theoretical range and scope, and the accuracy and scope of the experimen-

---

32   Kuhn, *SSR*, 192–200; "Reflections", 260–265.

33   This is seen most clearly in T. S. Kuhn "Logic of Discovery or Psychology of Research?", *Criticism and the Growth of Knowledge* ed. I. Lakatos and A. Musgrave (Cambridge: Cambridge University Press, 1970) 1–22; "Objectivity, Value Judgement, and Theory Choice", *The Essential Tension* (Chicago: University of Chicago Press, 1977) 320–339; cf. M. C. Banner, *The Justification of Science and the Rationality of Religious Belief* (Oxford: Clarendon, 1990) 8–13; G. Doppelt "Kuhn's Epistemological Relativism: An Interpretation and Defence" *Relativism: Cognitive and Moral*, ed. J. W. Meiland and M. Kraus (Notre Dame: University of Notre Dame Press, 1982) 113–146; W. H. Newton-Smith, *The Rationality of Science* (Boston: Routledge and Keagan Paul, 1981) 35, 102–124.

34   Siegel, 55–68. It must be noted that, while many of Kuhn's claims foster cognitive relativist conclusions, his theory is also open to non-relativist construals (or, perhaps, non-relativist rational reconstructions). For this, see M. Stenmark, *Rationality in Science, Religion and Everyday Life: A Critical Evaluation of Four Models of Rationality* (Notre Dame: University of Notre Dame Press, 1995) 115–139.

35   Kuhn, *SSR*, 1–9; cf. Chalmers, 85.

36   Chalmers, 86.

37   Kuhn, *SSR*, 10–22.

tal data which supports it.³⁸ This uncritical, puzzle-solving activity is not, he believes, the result of inadequate, dogmatic education, but is essential to the nature of science, and necessary for its progress.³⁹

In the very puzzle-solving nature of normal science according to Kuhn lie the seeds of its own demise, for inevitably some puzzles resist solution. These failures are usually ascribed to a flaw in the investigators or their methodology rather than to a problem in the underlying theory.⁴⁰ They are experimental *anomalies* not falsifications of the theory.⁴¹ The existence of such anomalies, even in great number, does not necessarily lead to the demise of the theory and the period of normal science it supports.⁴² This only occurs if the anomalies are considered to be significant enough to warrant such a major change in the concept of the relevant discipline. This in turn depends upon a number of factors, including the centrality of the anomalies in relation to crucial assumptions of the theory, their number, their persistence and their social relevance.⁴³ When they are significant enough, then an increasing number of scientists lose confidence in the adequacy of the current theory and shift their allegiance to a new theory.⁴⁴ Once this process has progressed to the point that the majority of scientists have adopted the new theory it constitutes a "scientific revolution".⁴⁵ This revolution engenders a new period of normal science, for the new theory becomes the accepted standard by which all related research is assessed.⁴⁶

Central to this analysis of the history of science is the concept of "paradigm", for according to Kuhn scientific paradigms play a crucial role in both normal and revolutionary science.⁴⁷ Both the term itself, and the way it was used in his original work have been the object of much criticism, largely because it was used in so many different ways, covering a number of discrete functional entities.⁴⁸ As a result of this critique, in

---

38 Ibid., 23, 34.
39 Kuhn, "Reflections", 242–245; contra Popper, "Normal Science", 52–55.
40 Kuhn, *SSR*, 80.
41 Ibid., 52, 80–82.
42 Ibid., 64.
43 Kuhn, *SSR*, 81–82; cf. Banner, 9–10; Chalmers, 90.
44 Kuhn, *SSR*, 89–90, 158–159; cf. Chalmers, 91, 93.
45 This is more a psychological and sociological event than a philosophical one, Kuhn, *SSR*, 86, 144–159; cf. Banner, 10–11.
46 Kuhn, *SSR*, 92, 109–110, for examples see 111–126.
47 See Ibid., 52–65, 111–126 for normal and revolutionary science respectively.
48 Banner, 8–9; M. Masterman "The Nature of a Paradigm", *Criticism and the Growth of Knowledge*, ed. I. Lakatos and A. Musgrave (Cambridge: Cambridge University Press, 1970) 59–89; D. Shapere "The Structure of Scientific Revolutions", *Reason and the Search*

particular the detailed work of Masterman, Kuhn has clarified his terminology, replacing the all-embracing "paradigm" with the more specific terms "disciplinary matrix" and "exemplar".[49] A disciplinary matrix is "the entire constellation of beliefs, values, techniques and so on shared by members of a given community".[50] It is made up of a number of components, including symbolic generalisations, metaphysical beliefs, values and exemplars.[51] Exemplars are "the concrete puzzle-solutions which, employed as models or examples, can replace specific rules for the solution of the remaining problems of normal science".[52] They involve both rational elements, such as theories and rules for their application, and non-rational elements, such as intuition and the ability to draw parallels between seemingly unrelated types of problems.[53] The latter must not be seen, Kuhn believes, as irrational, but as irreducible to rigid rules or laws which can be propounded without reference to the exemplar itself.[54] This tacit element is valid in scientific research in part *because* it is so imprecise, thus providing a model for further research, and pointing to issues that need to be clarified by that research.[55]

Normal science is characterised by a single disciplinary matrix with its associated exemplars, which is shared by all the members of a given scientific community.[56] This commitment to a given disciplinary matrix is inculcated via the processes of apprenticeship and didactic scientific education.[57] The task of normal science is that of "articulating" the paradigm or disciplinary matrix, via the processes of puzzle solving.[58] During this stage of science the disciplinary matrix is accepted uncritically, which results in the characteristic features of normal science.[59] Indeed it is that uncritical acceptance of a disciplinary matrix that distinguishes mature science from immature science.[60] This pattern changes dramatically during

---

for Knowledge (Dordrecht: D. Reidel, 1984) 38–39, 48; "The Paradigm Concept" *Reason and the Search for Knowledge*, 50–51.

[49] Kuhn, *SSR*, 175–189.
[50] Ibid., 175.
[51] Ibid., 182–187.
[52] Ibid., 175.
[53] Ibid., 187–189.
[54] Ibid., 192.
[55] Kuhn, "Logic", 19.
[56] Kuhn, *SSR*, 10–22.
[57] Kuhn, *SSR*, 46–47; "Reflections", 242.
[58] Kuhn, *SSR*, 24–34; "Logic", 7–10.
[59] Kuhn, *SSR*, 23, 34, 80–82.
[60] Kuhn, *SSR*, 10–22; "Logic", 6–10.

periods of revolution: in fact the return to questions of methodology and basic theoretical principles which characterised the stage of pre-science is typical of the uncertainty which accompanies incipient revolution.[61] The result of this fundamental change in the nature and purpose of science is the emergence of a new disciplinary matrix which is incompatible with the old one.[62] The centrality of disciplinary matrices is thus a feature of revolutionary science as much as it is for normal science, for the former deals with the inadequacies of the old system, and its replacement with the new.[63] Once a new phase of normal science begins, the disciplinary matrix again functions as the (new) assumed basis of all research:[64] at no stage can science operate without a disciplinary matrix, without ceasing to *be* science.[65] It is this paradigm-, or matrix-dependence which characterises Kuhn's vision of the nature of science. As we shall see in the following section, it is this which opens Kuhn to the charge of relativism.[66]

A.3. KUHN AND RELATIVISM

Central to the charge of relativism that has been levelled at Kuhn is the issue of what he calls the "incommensurability of paradigms", by which he means that the change from one paradigm or disciplinary matrix to another is an all-or-nothing event rather than a step-wise logical progression.[67] The underlying reason for this is that scientists operating in different disciplinary matrices see the world in fundamentally different ways, being guided in their perception by different paradigms.[68] Thus, although all scientists live in the same world, in the sense that they inhabit a common Reality, they live in different worlds, for they see fundamentally different things when they observe Reality.[69]

---

61   Kuhn, *SSR*, 86.
62   Ibid., 92.
63   Ibid., 89–90: indeed, the new paradigm generally arrives "all of a sudden" to one immersed in the problems of the old paradigm.
64   Ibid., 111–126.
65   Ibid., 79.
66   It must be noted that Kuhn specifically repudiates relativism, and argues that his conclusions are not relativistic or irrational with regard to scientific knowledge (Kuhn, *SSR*, 206). As I shall point out in the next section, however, this disavowal is not compelling.
67   Kuhn, *SSR*, 103, 150.
68   Ibid., 111–126.
69   Ibid., 111–126. I will use the following linguistic convention: *Reality* refers to the world-as-it-is: *reality* refers to the world-as-we-see-it.

This is a complex notion which depends upon two subsidiary claims: the determining role that metaphysical beliefs play in observation, and the role of language in theory development and testing. According to the first, when scientists from different paradigms assess data and rival theories, the fundamental questions they ask, the fundamental entities they see, and the investigative methods that are deemed suitable are all different.[70] This results in a radically different perception of the data, for observation statements can only function in the context of a framework, because they depend upon these underlying assumptions.[71] So too, the validity of rival theories is automatically suspect since they operate under different rules, with different assumptions.[72] With respect to the second, Kuhn challenges the oft-held assumption that proponents of rival theories share a "neutral language" which can be used to compare rival observation statements.[73] He argues that since the observation statements made in the context of a given theory are made using the language of that theory, there is no linguistic convention that can be used to test rival theories.[74] The language of a theory embodies a way of looking at the world, since underlying the language are theoretical assumptions about the connections that exist between the terms and Reality.[75] Language conditions the way we perceive Reality, and so learning a theoretical language involves tacitly learning to see Reality in a new way.[76]

This problem of communicating across linguistic barriers is complicated further by the way in which terms form a coherent network, and so similar terms in rival theories have different relationships with other terms in the theory, the theory as a whole, and Reality itself.[77] Thus proponents of rival theories cannot communicate with each other across the linguistic barriers their respective theories generate, for while their languages describe the same Reality, they generate a different reality, both conceptually and perceptually.[78] The only way rival theorists can communicate is to learn to see reality in the terms of their rivals, thus, at least provisionally, adopting the rival disciplinary matrix.[79] This means that while it is possible

---

[70] Ibid., 111–126.
[71] Ibid.
[72] Ibid., 109–110.
[73] Kuhn, "Reflections", 265–266.
[74] Ibid., 266–270.
[75] Ibid., 270–274.
[76] Ibid., 274–275.
[77] Ibid., 276.
[78] Ibid.
[79] Ibid., 277.

to weigh theories, this is not done in terms of a neutral language, or even conceptual scheme, but from within the confines of a given disciplinary matrix.[80] Given, then, that rival theories have fundamentally incompatible metaphysical systems, and share no common language with which they might communicate, different disciplinary matrices are incommensurable.[81]

Kuhn's conclusions on the incommensurability of disciplinary matrices lead him to conclude that theory choice, or theory weighing or testing, is not a strictly rational process.[82] The underlying reason for this claim is that theories do not function as independent entities but as components of a larger disciplinary-matrix, and so a change in a theory constitutes a more-or-less serious change in the matrix itself.[83] Thus, given the theory-dependence of observation statements, empirical data cannot be used to test rival theories, because different theories assess "facts" differently: what counts as a fact, how facts are derived from observation, and how they relate to the theories under scrutiny all vary with varying theories.[84] There is no single criterion, or even collection of criteria, by which rival theories or disciplinary matrices can be assessed, for all criteria function necessarily in the context of a disciplinary matrix, and thus are internal to the entities being assessed.[85] Thus the change from one disciplinary matrix to another, or even from one theory to another, is not the result of a step-wise logical progression, but is an all-or-nothing event, parallelling religious conversion.[86]

From these arguments it might seem that he believed theory choice was *irrational*, and there certainly are passages which can be read in such a light, as Kuhn himself acknowledges.[87] This, he claimed, however, was a *misreading* of his views by philosophers who read too much into isolated statements.[88] It may well be that his later views are a departure from his more rigorous earlier irrationalism.[89] However, it is important to recognise

---

80 Ibid., 277.
81 Kuhn, *SSR*, 103; "Reflections", 276.
82 Kuhn, *SSR*, 198–200; "Logic", 19; "Reflections", 160–161.
83 This, while not stated, seems to be the underlying premise of much of Kuhn's argument in "Objectivity", cf. 324–325, 330–331.
84 Kuhn, *SSR*, 144–146.
85 Ibid., 155–157. This is part of a longer discussion on pp. 144–159 in which he presents a number of examples of the process. cf. Kuhn, "Objectivity", 338–339; "Logic", 19.
86 Kuhn, *SSR*, 150; "Objectivity", 338–339.
87 Kuhn, *SSR*, 5, 151.
88 Kuhn, "Reflections", 260.
89 So Shapere, "The Paradigm Concept", 52–54. He claims, in fact, that this departure results in a less consistent position than Kuhn's earlier strong relativism.

that overall Kuhn does not claim that theory choice is *irrational*, but rather, that it is not a purely rational enterprise.[90] Reasons are not the only factors involved in the change from one disciplinary-matrix to another, nor are they sufficient grounds for that change; but they are important factors nonetheless.[91] They are not and cannot be the only factors at work, for logic involves arguing from the basis of accepted premises to clearly justified conclusions: but in any discussion between adherents to rival matrices, accepted premises are just what do not exist, and so attempts to persuade an opponent to accept different premises comprise a considerable part of the discussion.[92]

His most developed and well integrated discussion of this issue is found in "Objectivity, Value Judgement, and Theory Choice", and so this will form the basis of this description of his mature views. He identifies five main criteria that function as determiners of a good scientific theory: accuracy – a theory should comport as well as possible with existing observation statements; consistency – it should not contradict existing theories or itself; scope – it must relate to a wider body of data than those which it was devised to explain; simplicity – it should order otherwise unrelated data; fruitfulness – it should disclose new phenomena or unrecognised relationships between existing phenomena and open up new options for research.[93] What is revolutionary in his view is not the identification of the criteria, which are common to most philosophers of science, but the way in which they are seen to operate in theory choice.[94] Scientists with shared criteria of theory choice may, and in fact often do, differ in their assessment of rival theories because of different concepts, and hierarchies of the various criteria.[95] These differences are largely the result of aspects of tacit knowledge resulting from differing experiences, training, social background, and even personality.[96] These "subjective" factors need to be recognised as having as significant and valid a role as the "objective" factors of the criteria, rules of logic, and so on.[97] Indeed, Kuhn believes that the very categories of "subjectivity" and "objectivity" are illegitimate in general, and even more so with respect to theory choice, for they interact in such a way that these distinctions become arbitrary, and

---

[90] Kuhn, *SSR*, 198–200; "Logic", 19; "Reflections", 160–161.
[91] Kuhn, *SSR*, 198–199; "Logic", 19.
[92] Kuhn, *SSR*, 199–200; "Logic", 19; "Reflections", 260–261.
[93] Kuhn, "Objectivity", 321–322; "Reflections", 261.
[94] Kuhn, "Objectivity", 322.
[95] Kuhn, "Objectivity", 323–324; "Reflections", 262.
[96] Kuhn, "Objectivity", 325; "Logic", 21.
[97] Kuhn, "Objectivity", 325–326.

actually obscure the nature of theorising.[98] Thus the shared criteria function not as rules or axioms that can be used to construct an "algorithm of theory choice", but as *values* which cannot and should not be clearly and unambiguously articulated, for they interact with the tacit components of knowledge, resulting in the varying decisions of different scientists.[99] This, he believes, describes not only how scientists actually *make decisions*, but also how they *ought to make them*: it is a prescriptive meta-theory.[100] Such a view recognises that theory choice is not an objective, risk-free decision, but is a risky commitment on the basis of partial evidence.[101] It is only such commitments, when balanced out over the scientific community as a whole, that keep science both vital and true to its task.[102] The quest for so-called impersonal, value-free knowledge is not only a myth; it is a mistake, in both the construction and evaluation of theories.[103]

The personal and matrix-dependent nature of all knowledge, and of theory weighing raises significant questions about the truth-value of scientific explanations. Kuhn maintains the matrix-dependent nature of scientific knowledge, recognising that judgements about scientific theories are in large part a product of a scientist's allegiance to a given community.[104] This holds also for judgements concerning a given theory's relative worth: the notion of what constitutes progress is determined in the light of the current disciplinary matrix.[105] This, as Kuhn acknowledges, raises the spectre of Orwellian revisionist history: all previous matrices will be assessed, and found to be obviously wanting, because they do not conform to the new pattern of science.[106] While there is a degree of truth in this fear, Kuhn believes it should not be a source of concern, for the community that judges the value of different theories is the same one that acknowledged the anomalies which led to the revolution.[107] Thus the power to judge progress not only is in the hands of the relevant scientific community, but

---

98   Ibid., 336–338.
99   Kuhn, "Objectivity", 330–331; "Logic", 21–22; "Reflections", 261–262.
100 Kuhn, "Objectivity", 325–326.
101 Kuhn, "Reflections", 262.
102 Ibid.
103 Kuhn, "Objectivity", 326–329. This construal of the nature and function of values in theory-choice can be fruitfully applied to Wolterstorff's meta-theory, for which see below (Chapter 5, A.2.).
104 Kuhn, *SSR*, 94.
105 Ibid., 166–167.
106 Ibid., 167.
107 Ibid., 167–169.

also that is where it belongs.[108] The important question with respect to scientific progress is not, then, how to determine which is a more successful paradigm, but "what are the essential characteristics of these [the determining] communities?"[109] It is the existence of the right kind of community, and only that, which will determine that the scope and specificity of problem solutions will grow.[110]

Many critics charge Kuhn with relativism on this point, arguing that he leaves himself with no grounds on which to claim that one explanation is better than another.[111] This charge Kuhn vigorously denies.[112] The basis of that denial is a particular view of the nature of scientific theories, and the resultant redefinition of the notion of scientific progress. He holds to an instrumentalist notion of theories and matrices: the entities they describe do not exist in Reality: the only existence they have is in the context of the theory.[113] Theories are simply tools to enable scientists to explain and relate observable entities: their only truth value is in relation to their relative ability to solve problems.[114] It is because successive matrices provide better explanations of Reality, and more effective solutions to scientific puzzles, that they can be seen as improvements upon earlier ones.[115] This value is increased, especially in the eyes of the relevant community, if the new matrix is not only able to explain the phenomena explained by the old one, but also *why* it was able to provide such explanations.[116] This means, however, that the idea of science progressing toward an end point of objective truth, at which time the theories of science will truly describe Reality, is a myth.[117] It does not mean that there is no such thing as scientific progress, or that successive theories are no better than their precursors. Rather it means that progress must be seen in non-teleological terms: it does not consist of progress *towards* an ideal of objective truth, but of progress *away from* primitive ignorance.[118] Thus

---

[108] Ibid.

[109] Ibid., 168.

[110] Ibid., 170.

[111] For these arguments, and my evaluation of them, see below (this chapter, B.).

[112] Kuhn, *SSR*, 206.

[113] Kuhn, *SSR*, 170–171; "Reflections", 265.

[114] Kuhn, *SSR*, 172. Indeed he criticises Popper's Falsificationism on the grounds that it makes theories *too rigorous*, thus limiting their explanatory capacity, Kuhn, "Logic", 13–19.

[115] Kuhn, *SSR*, 172, 205–207.

[116] Ibid., 102. He specifically cites the Einsteinian matrix, and the way it explained the value of the Newtonian matrix *in terms of the new matrix*.

[117] Ibid., 170–171.

[118] Ibid. He specifically draws parallels between this notion of noetic evolution and contemporary non-teleological views of biological evolution.

when we examine the idea of "progress" we must "substitute evolution-from-what-we-know for evolution-toward-what-we-wish-to-know".[119]

While Kuhn disavows the relativism his position tends towards, others have employed his views in support of their relativist positions. Doppelt identifies four grounds for the incommensurability of paradigms in Kuhn's perspective: different paradigms have no common linguistic or conceptual system; they do not address, acknowledge or perceive the same data; they do not address the same questions; they have no shared notion of what counts as an adequate, or even a legitimate explanation of data and the problems they generate.[120] Of these four grounds, he sees the incompatibility of fundamental questions as that which is central to Kuhn's relativism: the other grounds for incommensurability are derived from it.[121] He believes, in fact, that it is only the disparity between fundamental questions that results in the incommensurability of different paradigms, for there are always areas of overlap in the language, data, and standards of different paradigms. It is only when they are examined in relation to basic questions that their incommensurability is manifest.[122] He attempts to show on this basis that Kuhn supports this particular form of relativism.[123]

I believe, however, that he is mistaken regarding what Kuhn sees as crucial to the incommensurability of paradigms. It is true in the passages he cites from *The Structure of Scientific Revolutions* that Kuhn sees fundamental questions as contributing to the incommensurability of paradigms.[124] However, when he comes to elucidate the exact extent of incommensurability, and the grounds on which that *relative* incommensurability is founded, Kuhn identifies the linguistic problem as that which is most important.[125] The grounds for incommensurability he identifies are a helpful analysis of Kuhn's position,[126] but he is mistaken, I believe, in ascribing centrality to disparity of questions: if anything is crucial to Kuhn's view of the incommensurability of paradigms, it is language.[127] This does not mean, however, that Doppelt's work is of no

---

119 Ibid., 171. As I will later demonstrate (Chapter 5, B.1.), Wolterstorff specifically rejects this view, which is one of the factors that enable him to adopt a non-relativist stance.
120 Doppelt, 114.
121 Doppelt, 118–124.
122 Doppelt, 124.
123 Doppelt, 124–140.
124 Doppelt, 119–120; see e.g. Kuhn, *SSR*, 111–126 for supporting passages.
125 Kuhn, "Reflections" 265–277.
126 cf. Chalmers, 91–93.
127 Banner, 13–17; cf. Newton-Smith, 9–13, 150–156, where he notes that Kuhn's later "softer" views on this matter require the abandonment of radical meaning variance thesis regarding terms and their translation across disciplinary matrices.

value, for he has identified a number of areas that need to be explored in relation to Kuhn's work: the relativism that is implicit (though denied) in Kuhn; the ways his arguments can be used to support relativism; the need for modification of Kuhn's meta-theory if it is to avoid relativism, as he seeks to do. These will be explored later.

The work of Feyerabend is potentially more interesting and challenging, because while he supports many of Kuhn's contentions, he consciously departs from Kuhn in a specifically relativist direction.[128] Feyerabend criticises Kuhn on a number of grounds, including his claim that puzzle-solving is *the* characteristic feature of scientific investigation,[129] and that normal science and revolutionary science are consecutive rather than contemporaneous.[130] His most radical critique, however, is his rejection of the elements of rationality that exist in Kuhn's theory of science.[131] Reason, while it is a factor in theory choice, is not the only factor, nor is it the decisive factor.[132] Science is, and should be, fundamentally irrational.[133] Theory choice is and should be based on issues that are fundamental to human existence, not on supposedly objective grounds.[134] The goals of science should conform to the goals of society as a whole, and so matters of taste, style, preference and so on *should be* determinative for theory choice, just because they will tend to produce more human and humane science.[135]

---

[128] P. K. Feyerabend, *Science in a Free Society* (London: New Left Books, 1978) 28; *Against Method* (rev; London: Verso, 1988) 244.

[129] In fact, he claims there is *no one methodology which characterises successful science*, Feyerabend, "Consolations", 199–201; *Against Method*, 1–3, 9–12, 14–19.

[130] Feyerabend, "Consolations" 201–214. These criticisms will be discussed in detail later.

[131] Ibid., 214.

[132] Feyerabend, "Consolations", 214; *Science in a Free Society*, 40.

[133] Feyerabend, "Consolations", 214; "Philosophy of Science", 173–174; *Science in a Free Society*, 13–15, 37–39. Indeed he argues that science and rationality are merely traditions of thought which are not clearly superior to other rival traditions and which should be given no priority in education and so on in a "free society" (*Against Method*, 231–247; *Science in a Free Society*, 27–28, 30–31).

[134] Feyerabend, "Consolations", 228–229.

[135] Feyerabend, "Consolations", 228–229; *Science in a Free Society*, 16–17. This so-called principle of "anything goes" is not, according to Feyerabend, a principle at all, "but the terrified exclamation of a rationalist who takes a closer look at history", for principles are irrelevant to anything but concrete research projects (*Against Method*, vii; cf. *Science in a Free Society*, 39–40). It entails that any and all types of knowledge may be utilised in the quest for the humanisation of our existence (*Against Method*, 33–36; 256–259). Indeed, he argues that a subjective, irrational, intellectually anarchic approach is more productive of results in science itself, and thus that the pragmatic philosophy it engenders is an ideal for all intellectual endeavours (*Science in a Free Society*, 19–20, 29).

The arguments he adduces in support of this thesis ultimately depend upon his version of the *Incommensurability Thesis*.[136] He uses one of Kuhn's favourite examples, that of Einstein's Special Relativity and Newton's Celestial Mechanics, arguing that they are absolutely incomparable, for even such a fundamental concept as that of length is different in the two systems.[137] In Celestial Mechanics, length is a fixed property irrespective of the conditions of the object or the observer, while in Special Relativity it is absolutely dependent upon relative relationships of velocity and so on.[138] Thus, while different theories may use common terms, the meanings of the terms are radically different in the two theories, for the entities to which they relate are fundamentally different. It is, therefore, a translation error for a new theory to use the terms of an older one: it should rather create a new terminology *de novo*.[139] This, he believes, does not mean that incommensurable theories cannot be assessed with respect to "facts": they can be assessed *internally* in relation to observation statements made in the context of that theory.[140] Observations framed in the terms of one theory, say Special Relativity, support it, but when they are translated into terms of another theory, say Celestial Mechanics, they refute it.[141] However it does mean that rival theories cannot be compared on rational grounds, for there is no common terminology by which they can be compared, and no neutral stance from which they can be assessed.[142] When choices need to be made between rival theories, therefore, rational factors are irrelevant, for they refer only to the *internal structure* of the rival theories: only aesthetic choices between rival theories remain.[143]

---

[136] This is asserted in Feyerabend, "Consolations", 219, and argued on pp. 219–229; cf. *Against Method*, 20–24.
[137] Feyerabend, "Consolations", 219–221.
[138] Ibid.
[139] Ibid., 222–225.
[140] Ibid., 227–228.
[141] Ibid., 226.
[142] Feyerabend, "Consolations", 227–228. A similar line of argument is developed in *Against Method*, 171–230.
[143] Feyerabend, "Consolations", 228–229.

B. A Critique of Kuhnian Relativism

B.1. THE HISTORY AND SOCIOLOGY OF SCIENCE AND RELATIVISM

Essential to Kuhn's analysis of scientific theorising is the requirement that philosophical accounts of science should be consistent with, and controlled by, the observed nature of science rather than a rational reconstruction of science based on an ideal of how it should be done.[144] This, as Suppe has noted, involves the rejection of a central tenet of classical philosophy of science, namely that the context of discovery and the context of justification of theories must be kept separate, only the latter being a valid object of philosophical inquiry.[145] This aspect of Kuhn's theory of science has understandably been the object of stringent criticism, largely on the grounds that he fails to observe the necessary division between the contexts of discovery and justification.[146] However, the conjunction of the contexts of the developing and the weighing of theories is supported by the observation that testing a theory is not the end point of its development, as if it either passes or fails the test, and that is the end of the matter.[147] Rather, testing becomes a spur to further development of the theory, as Kuhn has demonstrated for a number of "paradigm shifts" in science.[148] Thus the justification of a theory is necessarily caught up with theory development, and so "the context of discovery was held to be a legitimate and essential concern of epistemology".[149] It is this requirement that prompted the stance that research into the actual pattern of discovery is central to the philosophy of science.[150]

Kuhn, however, goes too far when he claims that there is no such thing as a "logic of discovery" in science, there is only the "psychology of research".[151] It is this assertion which fosters the impression that Kuhn's

---

[144] Kuhn, *SSR*, 1–9; "Reflections", 233–241; "Objectivity", 325–329; cf. Chalmers, 85; F. Suppe, "Critical Introduction", *The Structure of Scientific Theories*, ed. F. Suppe; Urbana: University of Illinois Press, 1974) 126–127.

[145] Suppe, "Introduction", 126. The separation of theory development and testing is vigorously endorsed by Popper, *Conjectures and Refutations*, 21–27.

[146] Chalmers, 86; Popper, "Normal Science", 57, cf. *Conjectures and Refutations*, 21–27.

[147] Kuhn, *SSR*, 80–82; cf. Suppe, "Introduction", 126. For a proponent of that view, see Popper, *Conjectures and Refutations*, 46.

[148] Kuhn, *SSR*, 52–65.

[149] Suppe, "Introduction", 126.

[150] Kuhn, "Logic", 21–22; "Objectivity", 326–329.

[151] Kuhn, "Logic", 21. The difficulty here is, not that Kuhn rejects an algorithm of scientific rationality, nor that he recognises the many factors that give rise to theories. These points seem clear. The difficulty is that, perhaps due to rhetorical excess, he gives the impression that scientific practice is to be subject to sociological *rather than* rational

view of science is irrational and relativist. He claims, on the basis of the importance of personal factors in the devising and weighing of theories, that there is no sense in which theories increase in "objective" content as they decrease in "subjective" elements through the process of testing.[152] There is indeed a growing sense of consensus, even unanimity, in the community's support of a given theory, but this is the result of that community's growing commitment to common values, rather than a recognition of growth in the rational status of the theory itself.[153] This, he later asserts, does not mean that there is psychological unanimity amongst a given community, but rather that there is a fundamental unity that transcends individual diversity.[154] However it does mean that questions of advance in scientific knowledge are determined solely by the community concerned.[155] The focus, therefore, for the philosophy of science is not to be on the logic, or rationality of acceptable *theories*, but on the psychology or sociology of *the communities that give rise to such theories*.[156] "It must, that is, be a description of a value system, an ideology, together with an analysis of the institutions through which that value system is transmitted and enforced."[157] That is primary. Questions of logical structure of theories are secondary to that primary concern.[158]

Despite his frequent disavowals of relativism, it is easy to see how these claims can be taken in support of relativism.[159] Chalmers believes that these (potentially at least) relativist assertions are the result of a category confusion in his thought.[160] This consists of a failure to recognise that there are three compatible models of science: the subjective, which focuses on the beliefs held by an individual scientist (e.g. Polanyi); the consensus, which sees science as those beliefs that are accepted by relevant communities; and the objective, which sees that science, or better, its

---

appraisal, as the discussion below shows. I am indebted to Kelly Clark and Vern Poythress for this, and other clarifications in this section.

152 Kuhn, "Objectivity", 328–329.
153 Kuhn, "Objectivity", 328–329.
154 Kuhn, "Reflections", 241. This does seem to be not so much a clarification of an area of possible confusion, as a retreat from his earlier more consistent position: cf. similar criticisms made by Shapere, "The Paradigm Concept", 51–52.
155 Kuhn, "Logic", 21.
156 Ibid., 20–21.
157 Ibid., 21.
158 Ibid., 22.
159 This conclusion is supported by Stenmark's discussion of Kuhnian theories as versions of social evidentialsim, for which see Stenmark, 141–165.
160 Chalmers, 101–104.

practices and deliverances, has an existence independent of the beliefs of individuals or communities.[161] While I agree with Chalmers' identification of the three models of science, I differ regarding the diagnosis of the cause of Kuhn's relativism. I believe his problem is not so much the indiscriminate confusion of these models of science,[162] as the granting of priority to the consensus model, with its focus on sociological analysis over-against the others.[163] However, I agree with Chalmers in recognising the *value*, but not the *priority* of psychological and sociological analysis to the philosophy of science.[164] The objective model legitimately has priority in the philosophy of science, for without a recognition of the objective reality of the practices and deliverances of the scientific enterprise, there is no object for psychological or sociological analysis.[165] So too, historically there are examples of communities that falsely claimed scientific status, such as Soviet science under Stalin.[166] It is only when investigators have some vision of what constitutes the *genius* of science that such decisions can be made. They cannot rest on nothingness, or the self-understanding of scientific communities, for those communities often consider themselves to be scientific.[167] Thus science has an objective, real existence which is independent of its practitioners and which is the object of sociological analysis, or sociological analysis of science is itself groundless.[168]

This brings us to an important point where again Kuhn's analysis is flawed: his adoption of a purely instrumentalist view of scientific theories.[169] Just as he denies any ontological existence for scientific

---

161   Ibid., 98–100.
162   Ibid., 100–104.
163   Kuhn, "Logic", 22.
164   Chalmers, 101, 104.
165   Ibid.
166   Chalmers, 106–107; Polanyi, *Science, Faith and Society*, 7–8.
167   Chalmers, 106–107; cf. Kuhn, "Logic", 7–10, where he refuses to allow the scientific claims of astrology on the grounds of its failure to meet an objective requirement.
168   Chalmers, 107. Let me clarify what I am and am not claiming here. I am not claiming that science exists without reference to its practitioners, or that it has an eternal, immutable essence or method. I take it that Kuhn, and others, have refuted that mistaken view of the scientific enterprise, for which see Wolterstorff, "Scholarship and Conviction", 38–41. Nor am I here making (critical) realist claims about the referents of scientific theories. Critical realism will be discussed below. Rather, I am claiming that once a scientific theory is produced, however that happens, it exists as an "intellectual entity" that can be appraised by others, including those who operate in different contexts or disciplinary matrices – and, indeed, that it must be so appraised. And it is that (limited) objectivity of science and its deliverances that Kuhn neglects in favour of sociological analyses of the producing and appraising communities, with associated relativist implications.
169   See above for an outline of his approach. Note also its obvious similarities to Rorty's pragmatist view of theories, Rorty, *Philosophy*, 10.

communities, favouring a purely functional approach, so he adopts a purely functional view of the theoretical products of those communities. He specifically defines the scientific value of a discipline or theory as dependent upon an increase in its explanatory capacity as opposed to its truth content.[170] The status of theories is a complex and controversial area in the philosophy of science, which will need to be addressed separately.[171] However I believe that in order to avoid an irrational and relativistic view of science, some form of realism needs to be adopted.[172] It is not possible, as Kuhn and many others have shown, to "rise above" a theoretical framework in order to have direct contact with the Reality that is addressed in the theory. Thus there is no possibility of a non-question-begging ascription of truth-content to a theory on the basis of its correlation with Reality. Nonetheless, the very explanatory value of "better" theories, and the way that they characteristically give rise to novel explanations, and even novel and useful theoretical entities, suggests that there is some correlation between good theories and the Reality they describe.[173] Thus, even though assessments of truth-content can only be made on the basis of the explanatory power of theories, this does not invalidate the notion of theories drawing closer (or even at times further away from) a true picture of Reality.[174] Such a concept of theories would, I believe, go a long way

---

170   Kuhn, *SSR*, 172. Indeed he criticises Popper's Falsificationism on the grounds that it makes theories *too rigorous*, thus limiting their explanatory capacity, Kuhn, "Logic", 13–19.

171   What follows is necessarily brief. See below (Chapter 5, B.1.) for a fuller discussion of this issue.

172   For a critical-realist and non-relativist application of Kuhn's meta-theory to biblical interpretation, see Poythress, *Science and Hermeneutics*. For anti-realism as an argument for relativist theories of theology and interpretation, see Kaufman, 3–69; Fowl, 379–398; Gunn, 53–64; McKnight, 167–177, 217–267. For the critique and limitation of such views from a "critical realist" perspective, which asserts that there is a determinative meaning encoded in a text, no matter how multi-faceted it is, see M. Davies, "Reader-Response Criticism", *A Dictionary of Biblical Interpretation*, ed. R. J. Coggins and J. L. Houlden (London: SCM, 1990) 578–580; Goldingay, "How far do readers make sense?", 5–10; Netland, *Dissonant Voices*, 151–195; B. F. Meyer, "The Challenge of Text and Reader to the Historical-Critical Method", *The Bible and its Readers*, ed. W. Beuken, *et al* (*Concilium*, 1991/1; London: SCM, 1991) 3–12.

173   Banner, 24–32; Chalmers, 116–117, Newton-Smith, *The Rationality of Science*, esp 185–192, 195–207; Ratsch, 57–58, 60; Williams, 29–32, 36.

174   Chalmers, 113–134, has an extended discussion of this issue, at the end of which he comes to a position which he calls *Radical Instrumentalism*, or *Pluralistic Realism*. While he rejects my conclusion that there is some correlation between theoretical and real entities, he does avoid the problems of relativism. For non-realist rejections of relativism and their relevance to Christian theology, see S. Grenz and J. Franke, *Beyond Foundationalism: Shaping Theology in a Postmodern Context* (Louisville: Westminster John Knox, 2001); Marshall, *Trinity and Truth*. For support of the critical-realist position here endorsed, see

towards mitigating the relativist and irrationalist conclusions that have been drawn from Kuhn's vision of science.[175]

Major criticisms have also been levelled against the interpretation of the history of science upon which Kuhn bases his conclusions. The first of these is the clear distinction he draws between normal and revolutionary science. From the very structure of Kuhn's major work, *The Structure of Scientific Revolutions*, it is clear that this distinction is in fact central to his argument.[176] The empirical soundness of this interpretation of the historical development of science and its theories has been questioned largely on the basis that it ignores the gradations that are apparent in the history of science between normal and revolutionary science.[177] It also falsely generalises the pattern of Astronomy, which more or less follows Kuhn's pattern, to other disciplines.[178] For example even in Physics, in relation to the theory of matter, rival theories have co-existed throughout the history of the discipline.[179] Even when "revolutions" do occur, however, they are not the rare all-or-nothing phenomena that Kuhn claims. They are more numerous, frequent and less radical than the clear distinction between normal and revolutionary science would imply.[180] There is, therefore, no clear empirical distinction between normal and revolutionary science.[181]

Shapere goes further, arguing that Kuhn's interpretive framework distorts his assessment of the historical evidence, resulting in the suppression of the commonalities that exist between different theories, and even different historical periods in science, and overemphasising the differ-

---

Banner, 24–32; Newton-Smith, *The Rationality of Science*, esp 223–236; Taylor, 163–178. For a similar position in relation to theological theorising, see J. W. Van Huyssteen, "Is the Postmodernist Always a Postfoundationalist?", *TToday* 50/3 (Oct 1993) 385–386.

175 This sort of model is developed by Wolterstorff, for which see below (Chapters 3–6).

176 Note especially the chapter divisions.

177 Popper, "Normal Science", 54. J. Watkins, "Against 'Normal Science'", *Criticism and the Growth of Knowledge*, ed. I. Lakatos and A. Musgrave (Cambridge: Cambridge University Press, 1970) 35–37, notes the way that Newton's supposed paradigm-shift actually developed over a course of years.

178 Popper, "Normal Science", 54–55.

179 Popper, "Normal Science", 54–55; Watkins, 34.

180 S. Toulmin, "Does the Distinction Between Normal and Revolutionary Science Hold Water?", *Criticism and the Growth of Knowledge*, ed. I. Lakatos and A. Musgrave (Cambridge: Cambridge University Press, 1970) 45–47.

181 Popper, "Normal Science", 55. The existence of multiple rival paradigms in theological and hermeneutical scholarship, and their persistence after a "revolution" in the field has been seen as a clear distinction between the natural sciences and these disciplines. See, D. J. Bosch, *Transforming Mission: Paradigm Shifts in the Theology of Mission* (Maryknoll: Orbis, 1991) 185–186; Poythress, 51–72. However, in the light of this criticism of Kuhn's history of science, this becomes a difference of degree, rather than of kind.

ences.[182] This observation provides an interesting insight into the way Kuhn's view of the inescapable paradigm-dependence of all knowledge distorts the knowledge that is produced with such an epistemology. This in turn highlights the pragmatic need for the development of an epistemology that recognises both the unavoidable theory-dependence of observation statements and the need for critical reflection upon theoretical pre-understanding in the quest for a critically committed objectivism.[183] Popper makes similar observations about the *danger* of Kuhn's notion of uncritical normal science.[184] He asserts that normal science exists, but only as an aberration of the scientific enterprise. Those who uncritically adopt a given exemplar or disciplinary matrix are poorly taught *applied scientists*, not ideal models of normal pure scientific methodology.[185] If they are seen in the latter light, it is not only empirically misleading, it is socially dangerous to science and society, potentially leading to the aberrations of state-driven uncritically dogmatic research.[186]

B.2. Paradigms and Relativism

This point raises the issue of the role of paradigms or disciplinary matrices in normal science. Kuhn has claimed that during a period of normal science a common disciplinary matrix is used by all practitioners of a given discipline.[187] Watkins has argued that this perception of the uncritical nature of normal science is the result of Kuhn drawing illegitimate parallels between scientific and religious communities.[188] Not only is it false to say that there is no criticism of the matrix in normal science, it is

---

182 Shapere, "Structure", 45; cf. Popper, "Normal Science", 52.

183 Ratsch, 61. This observation undergirds my attempt to justify Wolterstorff's version of such an epistemology.

184 Popper, "Normal Science and its Dangers", 51–58. comprises a lengthy exposition of the dangers he sees inherent in that position. Many of his criticisms are weak or invalid, but some have weight.

185 Ibid., 52–53.

186 Ibid., 53.

187 Kuhn, *SSR*, 47, 165, 135, 157.

188 Watkins, 33. The validity of this argument ultimately depends upon detailed sociological analyses of scientific and religious communities. Some recent research into the nature of Science and Theology raises questions about the legitimacy of clear-cut distinctions between the natures of the two communities. This research, however, far from invalidating the criticisms of Watkins in fact supports them, for neither scientific nor religious (especially theological) communities are uncritical of the traditions that guide them. See A. Thomson, *Tradition and Authority in Science and Theology* (Edinburgh: Scottish Academic Press, 1987) especially 98–106; similarly, Poythress, 51–89.

wrong to suggest that normal science is characterised by a single dominant matrix, for as shown above, matrices evolve over time, and multiple matrices or theories can co-exist in a given discipline.[189] Paradigms, or disciplinary matrices, are not monolithic entities common to all practitioners of a given science which determine the way they see Reality.[190] If this claim is justified, it calls into question the determinative nature of any *Weltanschauung* seen as a world-view which is necessarily associated with a given theoretical structure.[191]

This in turn has broader ramifications for Kuhn's theory of scientific theories, for if matrices can evolve over time, if multiple matrices can co-exist, and if progress can be discerned through a process of linear development combined with relatively small theoretical "jumps", then Kuhn's Incommensurability Thesis is empirically suspect.[192] Toulmin argues that the conceptual changes following the introduction of a new matrix are not so great that they result in profound conceptual incongruities between the old and the new systems as Kuhn suggests.[193] If Kuhn's incommensurability thesis is correct, then it should be possible to document massive conceptual disruption from the experiences of, say, physicists involved in the transition to Special Relativity.[194] However, "if the conceptual change involved in the transition was as deep as Kuhn claims, these physicists at any rate appeared curiously unaware of the fact."[195] In fact many of them were able to give *reasons* as to why they changed from classical to relativity physics.[196] Thus their "paradigm shift" was not purely the result of persuasion.[197]

Now this does not by itself disprove Kuhn's later notion of incommensurability, for he recognises that reasons do play a role in theory choice, but insists that they are not the only factor involved. Toulmin acknowledges that there are areas of conceptual discontinuity between rival conceptual systems, involving incongruous principles and maxims,

---

[189] Popper, "Normal Science", 55; Shapere, "Structure", 39–43; Watkins, 35–37.
[190] Shapere, "The Paradigm Concept", 53. He believes, in fact, that the use of "disciplinary matrix" as opposed to "paradigm" in Kuhn's later work betrays a retreat from his original view of the monolithic nature of *Weltanschauungen*. For the co-existence of multiple disciplinary matrices in biblical interpretation, see Poythress, 52–55, 72, 73–75.
[191] Shapere, 53; Suppe, "Introduction", 217–221.
[192] Toulmin, 43–44.
[193] Ibid., 43.
[194] Ibid., 44.
[195] Ibid.
[196] Ibid.
[197] Ibid.

but believes that they are neither as great nor as incapacitating as Kuhn claims.[198] "For the displacement of one system of concepts by another is itself something that happens for perfectly good reasons, even though these 'reasons' cannot be formalised into still broader concepts, or still more general axioms."[199] This may not seem far from Kuhn's position, especially as formulated in his later work.[200] However there remains a major difference: whereas Kuhn believes that the incongruities between different frameworks are so great as to preclude effective communication *across* the boundaries of the theories, Toulmin does not.[201] There is a good deal of continuity between rival conceptual systems, based upon shared selection rules for decisions between rival theories or systems, thus allowing for communication.[202] Theories and paradigms are not incommensurable.[203]

The empirical questions raised concerning the incommensurability of disciplinary matrices are matched by philosophical questions concerning his theoretical rationale for that notion. The very fact that theories are rivals shows they are logically incompatible and hence comparable, and if comparable, then commensurable.[204] For if rival paradigms are, strictly speaking *incommensurable*, then there can be no basis to decide between them.[205] Indeed, if they are truly incommensurable then two rival theories can be held simultaneously, for they do not deal with the same things, and thus there is no need, and no possibility of, rejecting one in favour of another.[206] However, if there are ways of determining which theory is better, however that is understood, then strictly speaking they are no longer incommensurable.[207] This in turn means that there is no reason to doubt that logic, while not the only factor in theory choice, is a legitimate concern, thus saving the whole notion of theory *choice* from Kuhn's radical demurs.

There are two aspects of *Weltanschauungen* which are used as further arguments in favour of the incommensurability of theories and world-

---

198 Ibid.
199 Ibid.
200 Especially Kuhn, "Objectivity", 320–339; "Reflections", 261–262. See detailed discussion above.
201 Kuhn, *SSR*, 111–126; 150; "Reflections", 265–277; cf. Toulmin, 45–47.
202 Toulmin, 44.
203 Toulmin, 45. This argument is supported by Ratsch, 58–60 and Riggs, 46.
204 Watkins, 36–37.
205 Shapere, "Structure", 45–46.
206 Watkins, 36.
207 Ibid.

views: the theory-ladenness of observations statements, and the incomprehensibility of terms in different systems. The first argues that since what constitutes data, how it is to be discovered and related to theoretical structures and so on are predetermined by theory, there can be no empirical testing of rival theories except from within the theory itself. While the role of data is problematic in science, the theory-ladenness of observation being a well established notion, this does not mean that it is a non-empirical discipline.[208] For the latter to follow, it is necessary not only to establish the theory-ladenness of observation, but the determinative role of *Weltanschauungen* in investigation.[209]

Having established the theory-dependence of "facts", most *Weltanschauungen* theorists assume that it establishes the incommensurability of theories.[210] This, however, depends on the assumption that *Weltanschauungen* are determined by the theories that one holds, and thus that there are no criteria outside a theory that can be used to test it.[211] This latter assumption is dubious, for there is no evidence that theories determine *Weltanschauungen*, nor are there convincing arguments which support that assertion.[212] Thus, while *Weltanschauungen* determine the relevance of facts and so on in such a way that there are no criteria outside an investigator's *Weltanschauungen* by which a theory is to be judged, theories themselves are not incommensurable, for in the context of the *Weltanschauung* itself facts retain their ability to empirically test the adequacy of a given theory.[213]

This then opens up the possibility of critical analysis of *Weltanschauungen* themselves. This does not occur via neutral facts or rules of assessment,[214] but from within the *Weltanschauung* itself. While a given theory does not carry a particular *Weltanschauung* along with it, *Weltanschauungen* are nonetheless made up of a network of theories, experiences, assumptions and so on. These subsidiary components can be individually identified and then analysed in relation to the facts as they are perceived within a given *Weltanschauung* to determine their empirical adequacy, as well as their relationship to the other theories that comprise the investiga-

---

[208] Suppe, "Introduction", 198–199.
[209] Ibid., 192–199.
[210] Kuhn, *SSR*, 111–126, 144–146; "Logic", 19.
[211] Suppe, "Introduction", 199.
[212] Ibid., 209–217.
[213] Ibid., 216–217.
[214] contra Popper, "Normal Science", 56, where he argues that we are trapped by paradigms in a purely "Pickwickian" sense, in that we can transcend the framework at any time.

tor's *Weltanschauung*. Thus, while the criteria of accuracy, consistency, scope, simplicity, and fruitfulness do not function as an algorithm of theory-choice,[215] the notion of theory *choice* is a valid one, for the *Weltanschauung* of the person making the choice provides an adequate context for reasonable choices between rival theories.[216]

The second line of argument for the incommensurability of theories is the notion of the incomprehensibility of terms in rival theories. Suppe identifies two forms of the incomprehensibility thesis, which he identifies as "strong" and "weak" forms.[217] The "strong" form of the thesis states that all the principles in a theory influence the meaning of all the terms associated with that theory, thus any change in the theory results in a change in the meaning of all related terms.[218] This particular formulation of the thesis has been shown by Suppe to be in error, as he demonstrates that it is not only logically, but empirically possible for some terms in a theory to be unaffected by changes in the theory.[219] The "weak" form of the thesis states that the meaning of terms in a theory is *partially* determined by the principles of the theory in such a way that only *some* changes in the theory may lead to alterations in the meaning of related terms.[220] This, as Suppe states, is a much weaker form of the thesis, and is supportable in a way that the strong form is not, but it does not demonstrate the claim that theories are thereby incommensurable.[221] It must first be noted that, strictly speaking, it is not theories themselves that are linguistic phenomena, for a theory is the same whether it is expressed in French, or English, or even mathematical or logical terms. Rather it is only their specific formulations, whatever language it is expressed in, that can be classified as strictly linguistic entities.[222] Thus, if there is a problem with the meaning of a term in a *specific formulation of a theory*, that problem can potentially be overcome by a different formulation of the same theory using language that an adherent to a rival theory can comprehend.[223] This demonstrates that theories are not incommensurable,

---

215 So Kuhn, "Objectivity", 330–331, and the discussion above.
216 cf. Suppe, "Introduction", 217.
217 Ibid., 199–206.
218 Ibid., 199; this "strong gestalt" view is espoused by Feyerabend, "Consolations", 219–225.
219 Suppe, "Introduction", 200–202.
220 Ibid., 201–202; this "weak gestalt" form of the thesis is supported by Kuhn, "Reflections", 265–277.
221 Suppe, "Introduction", 206–207.
222 Ibid.
223 Ibid. cf. Shapere's notion of different *application* rather than different *meaning* of

for there is the possibility that the theory can be formulated, not in terms of a neutral, theory-independent language, but in terms that are common to another theory.[224] This allows for communication between proponents of rival theories on grounds that permit at least a partially rational appraisal of the claims of rival theories.

As demonstrated above, once the incommensurability of theories is shown to be a questionable notion, the way is opened up for the return of rationality to theory choice. This rationality is not the simple, neutral, indefeasible rationality of positivist epistemologies, but it is nonetheless rationality. "For the displacement of one system of concepts by another is itself something that happens for perfectly good *reasons*, even though these 'reasons' cannot be formalised into still broader concepts, or still more general axioms."[225] Indeed, Toulmin uses Kuhn's notion of shared selection rules as a specific basis for the rationality of theory choice, showing that this aspect of Kuhn's irrationality thesis is erroneous.[226] This receives further empirical support when it is recognised that there is a certain amount of "rhetorical exaggeration" in Kuhn's description of the radical differences that exist between rival paradigms,[227] which as Shapere notes, results in the obscuring of the reasons that do exist for investigator's changing theories.[228] Thus while there are both rational and irrational factors at work in the process of theory choice, the end result is not irrationality, but fallible rationality, for rational factors can and often do, control choices between rival theories. Thus the notion of theory *choice* as a conceivably rational process is valid.[229]

B.3. The Incoherence of Cognitive Relativism

A further line of criticism of Kuhnian views of scientific theorising focuses on the fundamental incoherence of all relativistic theories.[230] In order to

---

terms in rival theories, "Structure", 44–45. Suppe's analysis adheres more to the concepts and formulations of Kuhn himself, and thus his critique is the more powerful and relevant of the two.

224 Suppe, "Introduction", 207, Ratsch, 59. cf. Shapere, "Structure", 45, where he makes a similar statement in terms of his notion of different application of identical terms.

225 Toulmin, 44, emphasis mine.

226 Ibid.

227 Ibid., 43.

228 Shapere, "Structure", 45, 47.

229 Ratsch, 61; Riggs, 53. contra Kuhn, "Objectivity", 338–339.

230 Cf. Wolterstorff, "Between the Pincers", 20, where he states that he expects that "the anti-realist, interpretation-universalist branch of post-foundationalism will shortly dry up, principally, I would guess, because of its self-referential incoherence and its

argue for relativism, whether of the framework (*Weltanschauung*) variety or not, relativists have to assume a non-relativistic stance.[231] For "the recognition of the equal epistemological status of alternative frameworks, which is necessary for framework relativism, necessitates as well the rejection of framework-boundedness, which is a central component of the framework relativist position".[232] This is necessarily so because if truth is framework-bound then the framework relativist ought to see her own framework-bound truth as absolute from within the context of that framework.[233] But if she argues that other frameworks are true, or have some elements of truth, then she must adopt some sort of framework-transcendent category of truth, or at least transcend the limits of her own framework.[234] "Thus framework relativism can not proclaim itself, or even recognise itself, without defeating itself".[235] Now these criticisms may not appear to be relevant to a discussion of the validity of Kuhnian models of scientific theorising, however framework relativism, despite all his demurs, is the context in which Kuhn develops his meta-theory of science.

---

inability to answer the charge of moral relativism".

231 Siegel, 3–31, 44.

232 Ibid., 43.

233 Ibid.

234 Ibid.

235 Ibid. in relation to framework relativism; Williams, 31–32, in relation to pragmatism. Similar arguments are levelled against religious pluralistic relativism by A. McGrath, "The Challenge of Pluralism for the Contemporary Christian Church", *Journal of the Evangelical Theological Society* 35/3 (Sept 1992) 361–373. These, and similar claims that relativism is self-refuting have been challenged by Meiland, who argues that it is not necessarily true of carefully constructed framework relativism (J. W. Meiland, "On the paradox of cognitive relativism", *Metaphilosophy* 11/2 (April 1980) 115–126). This has been effectively countered by Beach and Wainwright, who argue, respectively, that it is in fact self-refuting, and that it may not be *necessarily* self-refuting, but if not then it must necessarily become irrational and subjective in order to avoid the fallacy of self-exception or pragmatic self-contradiction (E. Beach, "The paradox of cognitive relativism revisited: a reply to Jack W. Meiland", *Metaphilosophy*, 15/3&4 (Jul/Oct 1984) 157–171; W. J. Wainwright "Meiland and the coherence of cognitive relativism", *Metaphilosophy* 17/1 (Jan 1986) 61–69). This is accepted by Bearn, who uses it to argue for Feyerabendian radical subjectivism and irrationalism, and claims that relativism need not even assert itself, but need only, by means of polemic, description and exemplification, commend itself to others (G. C. F. Bearn, "Nietzsche, Feyerabend, and the voices of relativism", *Metaphilosophy* 17/2&3 (Ap/Jul 1986) 135–152). But this is so far from the rational framework relativism of Meiland, and the non-irrational framework relativism implied in Kuhn's theory, as to be unrecognisable. Indeed, the recourse of relativism to such presentations comprises a strong counter to all but the most extreme forms of the position. It would perhaps be best, if confronted by such an extreme relativist, to follow Reid's advice in relation to extreme sceptics and simply walk away. cf. Wolterstorff, *TRR*, 56–57.

His meta-theory, and the related accounts of theorising developed by those I have termed "Kuhnian Relativists" clearly are allied with an overall irrationalist and relativist epistemology. Their models of scientific irrationality are therefore inadequate, since "the account of theories is no more adequate than the epistemology to which it belongs".[236]

This general philosophical critique of framework relativism is reinforced by the recognition of tensions and even contradictions within Kuhn's theory, thus demonstrating that those aspects of his theory that support framework relativism are incoherent.[237] This is especially clear in relation to his notion of the incommensurability of paradigms, which he seems to simultaneously, or at least successively, reject and endorse, resulting in irresolvable ambiguities in his position.[238] These ambiguities are as apparent in the later Kuhn as they are in earlier versions of his position. "His position remains both confusing and confused".[239] As Siegel tellingly states,

> Kuhn seems to want to have it both ways: he wants to maintain incommensurability (and so irrationality), yet deny irrationality and allow for communication between proponents of competing paradigms (thus giving up incommensurability). It is clear, I hope, that Kuhn cannot have it both ways. His maintenance of incommensurability vitiates his denial of the irrationality thesis of relativism.[240]

This discussion demonstrates that Wolterstorff's rejection of cognitive relativism is justified. There are crucial empirical and philosophical problems with Kuhn's theory, and so a significant body of evidence that is used to justify the adoption of cognitive relativism is seen to be implausible. Equally, cognitive relativism is self-referentially inconsistent, and so there exist no good reasons to adopt such a view, and many to reject it. An alternative to it must therefore be found.

---

[236] Suppe, "Introduction", 150.

[237] See Shapere, "Paradigm", 54–55. This is especially apparent in Kuhn's attempts to salvage rationality, or at least avoid irrationality, in scientific investigation. The tension, or perhaps contradiction, can be best seen by comparing his argument in "Logic" with those in "Objectivity".

[238] Siegel, 56–59.

[239] Siegel, 68, and his discussion on pp. 59–68.

[240] Siegel, 59.

Conclusion to Part One

Recent work in philosophy of science has demonstrated that traditional notions of scientific rationality are naive and ultimately misleading. This has resulted in the development of a number of irrational and relativist views of the scientific process, many of which depend on the work of Kuhn. A number of his insights are of profound significance, notably the theory-dependence of observation statements, the paradigm centred nature of investigative procedures, and the role of non-rational factors in the attainment of knowledge. However, a number of flaws have been identified in his views, most of which are equally relevant to those relativistic views associated with his work. These centre on the refutation of the incommensurability thesis and the irrationalism and relativism with which it is necessarily associated. Thus, while relativistic theories of knowledge highlight the problems that are associated with all epistemic enterprises, they do not demonstrate that all knowledge is essentially relativist.[1] This in turn points the way to a mediating position between infallible objectivism/absolutism and relativism.[2] Such a position will be developed in the next section, in which I outline Wolterstorff's situated rationality and situation- and person-specific meta-theory.

---

1   It is interesting that some relativists effectively deny the validity of relativists proving, or even asserting, anything from a relativist position; see Bearn, 135–152.
2   Ratsch, 61. Stenmark, 193–234, draws on the work of Kuhn and the insights of what he calls "social evidentialist" theories of science in developing such a view.

PART TWO

Wolterstorff's Theories of Rationality and *Wissenschaft*

Introduction to Part Two

An important component in the analysis of Wolterstorff's meta-theory is its relationship to his general theory of rationality. Indeed it is impossible to adequately assess his meta-theory without reference to his broader theory of rationality, for the former is an articulation of the latter.[1] His meta-theory is thus best seen as a paradigm case or exemplar of his general theory of rationality, in which the theory is applied, modified, extended and made more rigorous.[2] Therefore, in order to analyse satisfactorily his meta-theory, I must outline Wolterstorff's theory of rationality before turning more specifically to his discussion of the devising and weighing of theories. In so doing I will not rehearse the supporting arguments for his theory of rationality in detail – that is beyond my scope. Instead I will present his notion of rationality, together with an outline of his theory of rationality. I will then proceed to identify and discuss the main features of that model, and rehearse the arguments and counter-arguments which relate to my thesis.

---

1   This is clearly seen in his discussion of theory-choice for scholars in N. Wolterstorff, *Until Justice and Peace Embrace* (Grand Rapids: Eerdmans, 1983) [from here on *J&P*], 167–171, where he specifically refers to the general epistemology he develops in "Can Belief in God Be Rational If It Has No Foundations?"; see *J&P*, 167 n. 1.
2   I am here drawing upon the ideas of Kuhn in relation to the articulation of scientific paradigms, and applying it to Wolterstorff's theories of rationality and *Wissenschaft*.

CHAPTER 3

Wolterstorff's Situated Rationality

A. Wolterstorff's Notion of Rationality

A.1. INNOCENT UNTIL PROVEN GUILTY

The central notion in Wolterstorff's theory of rationality is that of a belief's being *innocent until proven guilty*. He puts it thus:

> A person is rationally justified in believing a certain proposition which he does believe unless he has adequate reason to cease from believing it. Our beliefs are rational unless we have reason for refraining; they are not nonrational unless we have reason *for* believing. They are innocent until proven guilty, not guilty until proven innocent.[1]

This position is in stark contrast to the evidentialist approach, in which beliefs are guilty until proven innocent by the evidence.[2] This "guilty until innocent" stance is typical not only of anti-Christian evidentialism, but also of evangelical evidentialist apologetics and post-Enlightenment theology.[3] In contrast to the evidentialist contention that propositions are not to be believed until one has good grounds for believing them,[4] Wolterstorff contends that beliefs are justified unless there exist good

---

[1] Wolterstorff, *CBGR?*, 163. This stance is adopted also by R. Chisholm, *The Problem of the Criterion* (Milwaukee: Marquette University Press, 1973) 33.
[2] Wolterstorff, "The Migration of the Theistic Arguments", 38.
[3] See Wolterstorff, "Is Reason Enough?", 21, in relation to evangelical apologetics with particular reference to Clark Pinnock, and "The Migration of the Theistic Arguments", 44 nn. 6 and 7, on Pannenberg's theological method. See also D. Holwerda, "Faith, Reason and the Resurrection", *Faith and Rationality: Reason and Belief in God*, ed. A. Plantinga and N. Wolterstorff (Notre Dame: University of Notre Dame Press, 1983) 265–316, for a detailed discussion of Pannenberg's theological methodology.
[4] cf. Wolterstorff, "Is Reason Enough?", 21.

reason why we should not believe them; if, on the other hand, we do have "*adequate reason to cease believing*", then we are not justified in believing them.[5]

Here we need to recognise the distinction between the *justifying* of a belief and its *being justified*.[6] The former is an action which is performed upon a belief, while the latter is its epistemic status.[7] It is vital, Wolterstorff contends, that we clearly distinguish these two phenomena, and recognise that a belief may have the status of *being justified* without having had the *justifying* action performed upon it.[8] Otherwise we must relinquish the rationality of most of our beliefs, many of which we may be justified in holding. "Most of the beliefs we are justified in holding are such that we never justify them – never even attempt to do so."[9] And their rationality is by no means thereby impaired, for their being justified is independent of our justifying them, necessarily so given that they are "innocent until proven guilty".

The central reason for Wolterstorff taking beliefs to be "innocent until proven guilty" is that our beliefs are the product of belief-dispositions,[10] and that it is only by means of these dispositions that we can have any knowledge at all.[11] As argued in an earlier section, we do not need to establish the veracity of these dispositions – indeed we cannot.[12] Instead, we should ascribe equal epistemic status to all our belief forming mechanisms and grant that their deliverances are trustworthy unless we

---

[5] Wolterstorff, *CBGR?*, 162.

[6] Wolterstorff, *CBGR?*, 157. W. P. Alston, *Epistemic Justification* (Ithaca: Cornell University Press, 1989) 55; R. Chisholm, *Theory of Knowledge* (3rd ed: Englewood Cliffs: Prentice Hall, 1989) 100–101 make similar statements, with similar epistemic consequences.

[7] Wolterstorff, *CBGR?*, 157.

[8] Ibid. Of course, other beliefs may need to have at least some justifying action performed upon them in order for them to be justified. Such would be the case, for instance, for a physician's belief that she is giving a patient a certain dose of a toxic drug. In such a circumstance the physician would be obliged to check carefully the nature and dosage of the drug before being satisfied that her belief that she is giving such-and-such a dose of such-and-such a drug is justified.

[9] Ibid.

[10] For a discussion of these dispositions, see below (this chapter, B.1.).

[11] Wolterstorff, *TRR*, 52; *H&R*, 414; *EB&G*, 454, *Reid*, 213. As I will discuss below, this idea, along with many others in his epistemology, are drawn from the work of Thomas Reid; cf. *Essays*, I,2; II,20; VI,5; *Inquiry*, II,6; V,7.

[12] See above (Chapter 1, B.3.) and Wolterstorff, *CBGR?*, 174–175; *TRR*, 56; *H&R*, 409; *Divine Discourse* (Cambridge: Cambridge University Press, 1995) 278–279; *Reid*, 241–249; cf. K. Lehrer, "Beyond Impressions and Ideas: Hume vs Reid", *The Monist* 70/4 (Oct 1987) 394.

have good reasons to believe otherwise.[13] The reason that we can so trust our native faculties is that they were created by God, and thus they are reliable.[14] Nor can we do otherwise, for they are the only means we have of gaining knowledge or beliefs, and therefore at some point we simply have to depend upon them and the beliefs they produce, unless we embrace radical scepticism or agnosticism.[15] However, this does not mean we have no choice but to accept the products of unreliable dispositions with no recourse to their correction; for the same God who gave us these dispositions, we trust, will ensure that their unreliability will become apparent.[16] Thus our beliefs are innocent until proven guilty, for they are the product of dispositions which are justifiably taken to be inherently dependable.

This stance, in which beliefs are "innocent until proven guilty" is refined and expressed in the criterion of rational (intellectually justified) belief which Wolterstorff proposes in "Can Belief in God be Rational If It Has No Foundations?".[17] The criterion is this:

> A person S is rational in his eluctable and innocently produced belief Bp if and only if S does believe p and either:
> (i) S neither has nor ought to have adequate reason to cease from believing p, and is not rationally obliged to believe that he *does* have adequate reason to cease; or

---

[13] Wolterstorff, *TRR*, 56; *H&R*, 406; *Reid*, 213–214. A similar argument is found in Alston, "Plantinga's Epistemology", 303–305.

[14] Wolterstorff, *CBGR?*, 174; *TRR*, 57–58; *H&R*, 414–415; *Reid*, 241–244, 260–261; cf. Reid, *Essays*, II,20; *Inquiry*, V,7; VI,20; VI,24. Thus Reid does use the existence and work of God to justify the reliability of commonsense beliefs, contra Lehrer, "Hume vs Reid", 394. Indeed, essential to Reid's epistemology is what Wolterstorff calls his "epistemological piety", characterised by trusting God and, with thanks, humility and confidence, taking for granted his good gifts of our noetic consitution (see *Reid*, 260–261). For Wolterstorff this is not an uncritical trust, however, for we are not only created but also fallen beings. Thus our faculties may be distorted by sin, and the deliverances of undistorted faculties may be put to corrupt ends. These distortions need to be guarded against. For this, see below (this chapter, A.4.).

[15] Wolterstorff, *EB&G*, 453–454; *Reid*, 243–244; cf. Reid, *Essays*, II,20; *Inquiry*, VI,20. This is, of course, a different kind of argument to the first. The first is an eminently theological argument, while this second is an essentially pragmatic one. A third, broadly inductive argument is presented by Alston, *Epistemic Justification*, 319–349.

[16] Wolterstorff, *CBGR?*, 174. This may perhaps be seen as the triumph of redemption over sin in the self-critically renewed mind, or of the workings of general grace. For this, see below (this chapter, A.4., B.3.).

[17] Wolterstorff, *CBGR?*, 164–169.

(ii) *S* does have adequate reason to cease from believing *p* but does not realise that he does, and is rationally justified in that.[18]

A later version of this criterion is found in *Divine Discourse*, which, while framed in terms of *entitlement* and the operation of *doxastic practices* rather than of justification and belief, is consistent with this earlier criterion, and indeed comprises an articulation of it.[19] It is:

A person *S* is *entitled* to his belief that *p* just in case *S* believes *p*, and there's no doxastic practice *D* pertaining to *p* such that *S* ought to have implemented *D* and *S* did not, or *S* ought to have implemented *D* better than *S* did.[20]

In line with the core contention that beliefs are innocent until proven guilty, the criterion is one which focuses on that which *removes* justification from a belief, rather than on that which *confers* justification on it.[21] There are a number of features of this criterion which require elucidation, namely: a belief's being eluctable and innocently produced; a person having or not having adequate reason to cease from believing; justified ignorance. I will proceed to examine each of these features in turn, presenting Wolterstorff's reasons for their inclusion in the criterion of situated rationality. Before I do so, however, it is vital to explore the issue

---

18   Ibid., 168. Compare the "negative version" of this criterion on p. 169 in relation to rationally *not* believing a proposition, in which exactly the same rules apply, thus:

(V) A person *S* is rational in an eluctable and innocently produced case of not believing *p* if and only if *S* does not believe *p*, and either:

(i) *S* neither has nor ought to have adequate reason to believe *p*, and is not rationally obliged to believe that he *does* have adequate reason to believe *p*, or;

(ii) *S* does have adequate reason to believe *p* but does not realise that he does, and is rationally justified in that.

19   For the inter-connection of entitlement, doxastic practices and belief-dispositions, see below (this chapter, A.4., A.5.) and *Divine Discourse*, 266–273. It is worth noting here the *active* nature of this epistemology: humans are not passive receptors of impressions that force themselves onto our awareness; rather beliefs are the product of our active engagement in the world, including the implementing of appropriate doxastic practices. On the active nature of human believings, see Wolterstorff, *Divine Discourse*, 266–273; *Reid*, 76, and my discussion of social practices below, Chapter 5, A.1.

20   Wolterstorff, *Divine Discourse*, 272. An earlier "crude approximation' of this criterion is found in Wolterstorff, "Once Again, Evidentialism – This Time, Social", *Philosophical Topics* 16/2 (Fall 1988) 55.

21   Wolterstorff, *CBGR?*, 171–172. This is not only clearly entailed in the formulation of the criterion in *Divine Discourse*, it is also the tenor of the chapter in which it is found, for which see *Divine Discourse*, 261.

of epistemic obligation and permission, for this is at the core of Wolterstorff's theory of rational belief.

A.2. RATIONAL JUSTIFICATION OF BELIEF

According to Wolterstorff, central to the idea of rationality is the question of *justification*, for he considers that rationality is intellectually justified belief.[22] In Wolterstorff's view justification is an essentially normative concept related to one's duties and responsibilities.[23] In this he largely follows Locke, and develops ideas from him.[24] Such duties are relevant to our believings as much as they are to our actions: "It is not true that 'anything goes' in our actions regarding other persons; neither is it true that 'anything goes' in our believings."[25] This being the case, to be justified in a belief is to be in accord with the norms for believing, which means "doing as well in one's believings as can rightly be demanded of a person".[26] This notion of *justified belief* needs to be carefully distinguished from that of *rational belief*: the two are not to be equated.[27] For a belief which a person is justified in holding may not be necessarily a rational belief: and a rational belief may not be one that she is justified in believing overall.[28]

Intellectual justification is thus a "species of justification in beliefs" which relates specifically to our "attempting to get in touch with reality".[29] The goal of our intellectual life is to attain truth and avoid falsehood, thus conforming our beliefs more completely with reality.[30] It is in relation to this goal that we have noetic obligations. Locke contended that we also have obligations with respect to firmness of belief: we must hold our

---

22 Wolterstorff, *TRR*, 45.
23 Wolterstorff, *TRR*, 45.
24 Wolterstorff, *CBGR?*, 143–145; *Divine Discourse*, 261–263, 267–268; cf. J. Locke, *An Essay Concerning Human Understanding* (2 vol; ed. A. C. Fraser; vol 2; New York: Dover, 1959) IV, xvii, 24. In particular he draws upon Locke's discussion of reality-possession obligations in this passage, from which he quotes at length.
25 Wolterstorff, *TRR*, 46.
26 Wolterstorff, *TRR*, 46; *CBGR?*, 144.
27 Wolterstorff, *TRR*, 44.
28 Ibid.
29 Wolterstorff, *TRR*, 46; *CBGR?*, 143–144. In these papers he only discusses the first issue, which in itself is a controversial claim. The second issue, that of getting in touch with reality as a goal in human believings, is equally controversial in that it assumes a realist position with respect to the entities described by theories. This latter point needs further elucidation, for which see below (Chapter 5, B.1., B.2.).
30 Wolterstorff, *TRR*, 46.

beliefs with no more or less firmness than is warranted.[31] Wolterstorff denies this contention, thereby restricting obligation to the reality component of our believings.[32] With respect to the goal of getting more amply in touch with reality, we need to both seek truth and seek to avoid error: if we only seek to maximise our store of true beliefs, then we may come to believe things which are false, while if we only seek not to believe those things which are false, then we will not believe many things that are true.[33] In either case we will not have as good a grasp on reality as we ought to have. At times, however, these two goals will conflict, in which case we need to determine in each instance whether attaining truth or avoiding error is the more important goal.[34]

A.3. OBLIGATION AND JUSTIFICATION

These noetic obligations, however, pertain only to those propositions that we do in fact believe and that are related to others of our obligations, not to all propositions, or all beliefs, or even all beliefs we *consider*.[35] For it may well be that a matter we consider is trivial, or that we do not consider

---

[31] Wolterstorff, "The Assurance of Faith", *Faith and Philosophy* 7/4 (Oct 1990) 403; cf. Locke, *Essay*, IV, xix, 1. For a detailed discussion of this feature of Locke's thought, see Wolterstorff, *Locke*, 60–118.

[32] Wolterstorff, "The Assurance of Faith", 401–410 His argument, in brief, is that firmness as an obligation only refers to what is subjectively obligatory, not what is "objectively obligatory": but the subjective notion is not an obligation, for if we believe we have good evidence for a non-immediate belief, we just *will* believe it with proportional firmness – if we don't then we really don't believe we have good evidence. cf. "The Migration of the Theistic Arguments", 41, on firmness obligations in Locke, and pp. 43–44 on Locke's notion of the social evils which follow their being ignored.

[33] Wolterstorff, *CBGR?*, 146.

[34] Ibid.

[35] Ibid., 146–147, *pace* R. Chisholm, *Theory of Knowledge* (2nd ed; Englewood Cliffs: Prentice Hall, 1977) 14–15; R. Feldman, "Epistemic Obligations", *Philosophical Perspectives, no.2: Epistemology* (1988) 248–252. Wolterstorff's widening of epistemic obligation beyond those things we consider to those we ought to consider, or evidence we ought to examine, and so on, is rejected by Feldman on the grounds that these are pragmatic or prudential or moral obligations, not epistemic ones. But this is to reject them before their claim to epistemic significance has been assessed. Feldman's rejection of them as epistemic obligations is an arbitrary restriction of such obligations, which legitimately include all those obligations which have bearing on our believings, not just those in relation to what we ought to believe now. It is interesting to note that in the 3rd edition of *Theory of Knowledge* Chisholm does not mention the limitation of obligations to those things we consider in his discussion of norms of believing. Whether this is a deliberate retreat from his earlier stance, or due to the exigencies of space, it indicates that this limitation is not central to his understanding of noetic obligations.

something we ought to consider, or that we ought to believe something we have not, and may not ever, consider.[36] Rather, "our noetic obligations arise from the whole diversity of obligations that we have in our concrete situations."[37] This means that rationality is both situation- and person-specific, and also generalised, for every individual's obligations-in-general have features that are unique to that individual as well as some that are common to all people.[38] It is because our general obligations require us to get more amply in touch with some relevant segment of reality that we are obliged to do so.[39] Thus our obligations with respect to our responsibilities in life determine the extent of our noetic obligations, be that in relation to the matters we are obliged to investigate, or the extent to which we are obliged to investigate them.[40] In general we have noetic obligations in those areas of our beliefs which are connected with some aspect of our praxis.[41] Moreover, our obligations even in respect of those beliefs are limited, for if we attempted to believe a proposition if and only if it were true, it may well interfere with others of our obligations.[42] Thus, in relation to relevant propositions, our noetic obligation is *"to do as well as can rightly be demanded* of us so as to bring it about that we believe them if they are true and disbelieve them if they are false".[43]

Once the existence of these obligations is assumed, the theist, in particular the Christian theist, must fulfil them, for otherwise she is acting in defiance of the will of God.[44] However, what reason is there to believe that there are such obligations in relation to our believings? For Wolterstorff, the very notion of *justification* requires that there be norms for believing, for the semantic range of the English words *justification, justify*, and its cognates necessarily entails the idea of conformity to norms.[45] Rationality may refer to a purely evaluative criterion, in which only the relative merits or demerits of a belief enter into the picture, with no

---

36   Wolterstorff, *CBGR?*, 147.
37   Wolterstorff, *CBGR?*, 148; cf. *Divine Discourse*, 272–273.
38   Wolterstorff, *CBGR?*, 147–148.
39   Ibid., 148.
40   Wolterstorff, *CBGR?*, 148; *Divine Discourse*, 273.
41   Wolterstorff, *CBGR?*, 148.
42   Ibid.
43   Ibid.
44   Ibid., 156.
45   Ibid., 161 n. 12, p. 161. It may be argued that there is no relevant application of these words to the issue of rationality. This, of course, is the position taken by epistemological anarchists, antinomians and relativists. This issue has received specific treatment Chapter 2 above.

reference being made to a person's control over her belief-dispositions.[46] While this may have validity as a notion of *rationality*, it has no validity as a criterion of *rational justification*, for *justification* entails the use of normative criteria.[47]

It may be argued, however, that there is no need for a criterion of *rational justification* in order to have a criterion of *rationality*, and further, that the use of a concept of justification in relation to rationality is question-begging.[48] Wolterstorff's aim, however, was not to prove that such a concept should be adopted, but to develop a criterion for its application: in such an enterprise the use of the notion in the formulation of the criterion is not only appropriate, it is necessary.[49] Indeed, a partial defence of his method is simply this: the major criteria of rationality that have hitherto been devised have made use of the concept of justification, whether they acknowledged it or not.[50]

A further possible objection to the way Wolterstorff uses norms in the development of his criterion is that a distinction must be made between *objective* and *subjective* justification or obligations in rationality.[51]

---

[46] Wolterstorff, *CBGR?*, 161 n. 12; *Divine Discourse*, 268. Such a criterion is presented by Alston, *Epistemic Justification*, 172–176.

[47] At least that is the case for the normal English use of the word, Wolterstorff, *CBGR?*, 161 n. 12. This normative approach to justification is rejected by Alston, *Epistemic Justification*, 81–97, 172–174. His argument is that a normative criterion assumes: a) that all beliefs are eluctable; b) a rational, self-aware, reflective epistemic agent. However, Wolterstorff's normative criterion is clearly one which takes note of ineluctable beliefs and limitations on a believing subject's rational capabilities, and Alston's problems are specifically countered by the justification-removing criterion Wolterstorff develops. See Wolterstorff, *CBGR?*, 162, 171; *Divine Discourse*, 268–273. It is interesting that in "Plantinga's Epistemology", 301–303, and "Christian Experience and Christian Belief", *Faith and Rationality: Reason and Belief in God*, ed. A. Plantinga and N. Wolterstorff (Notre Dame: University of Notre Dame Press, 1983) 116–120, Alston adopts a notion of rationality remarkably similar to Wolterstorff's.

[48] Wolterstorff, *CBGR?*, 169.

[49] Ibid., 169–170.

[50] Ibid., 170, in specific reference to reliabilism and classic foundationalism. Again, the question of the denial of the notion of rationality, or of its applicability to human believings, has been dealt with in a previous section, and so will not be discussed here. cf. Chisholm's discussion in *Criterion*, 37–38, that any development of a criterion of rationality or truth is necessarily question-begging at some point or other.

[51] Wolterstorff, *CBGR?*, 178. Such a distinction is made by Feldman, 235–237, who talks of epistemic obligation as "the propriety of a disinterested believer in Jones' situation having that belief", p. 236. Chisholm, *Criterion*, 7, 25, also draws a distinction between subjective and objective noetic justification. His usage is significantly different from Wolterstorff's: he takes *subjective justification* to be a statement of what an epistemic agent *believes* to be epistemically right or wrong, whereas *objective justification* refers to what is really right or wrong for that person to believe at that point in time under those conditions. Thus his

Wolterstorff's counter-argument uses an analogy with the idea of moral obligation to defeat this contention.[52] There is no valid use of the word "ought" in English in which someone could be subjectively obliged to act in a certain way, and yet be held culpable for objective reasons for so acting.[53] The only conditions in which the criterion of "what the fully knowledgeable person would do" can be applied to an individual are those in which that person is or ought to be fully knowledgeable.[54] Thus:

> The so-called subjective concept of obligation is the only concept of obligation there is... There is no difference between acting in accord with one's obligation and doing as well as can be rightly expected of one.[55]

What is true of moral obligations is true *mutatis mutandis* of noetic obligations: the only context in which so-called *objective* justification is applicable to an epistemic agent is one in which that agent is in fact fully knowledgeable.[56] But we are not fully knowledgeable epistemic agents, thus we are frequently justified in holding false beliefs, or in relinquishing "objectively" justified beliefs for what we take to be adequate reasons but are not, or in holding "objectively" unjustified beliefs for what we take to be adequate reasons but which are not.[57] Therefore the only criterion of noetic obligation which is applicable to us is one which takes note of our epistemic imperfection, and applies norms of believings to our fallible condition.[58] Wolterstorff states:

> I conclude that any satisfactory criterion for rational belief will have to be not only a *noetic* criterion, making explicit or tacit reference to beliefs of the person but also a *normative* noetic criterion, making explicit or tacit

---

advocating the adoption of an objective normative criterion is in this instance identical to Wolterstorff's advocating subjective obligation.

52 Wolterstorff, *CBGR?*, 178–181. It may be thought that the distinction Feldman, 236–237, makes between moral and epistemic obligations may defeat Wolterstorff's analogy. However, Wolterstorff makes a similar distinction with respect to *prima facie* versus *ultima facie* obligations to believe, in which moral and other obligations may override noetic obligations in some cases. Equally, Wolterstorff's argument depends, not upon the identification of moral and noetic obligations, but upon a relevant analogy between them.

53 Wolterstorff, *CBGR?*, 178–179, *pace* R. B. Brandt, *Ethical Theory: The Problems of Normative and Critical Ethics* (Englewood Cliffs: Prentice Hall, 1959) 357–367 who argues for just such a distinction.

54 Wolterstorff, *CBGR?*, 179–180.
55 Wolterstorff, *CBGR?*, 179.
56 Wolterstorff, *CBGR?*, 181.
57 Wolterstorff, *CBGR?*, 181.
58 Wolterstorff, *CBGR?*, 181.

use of some such normative concept as that of justification or obligation. In recognition of these facts the criterion I have offered not only takes the phenomenon of *not having adequate reason to surrender one's belief* as the key phenomenon determining rationality; it adds to this an explicitly noetic-normative component.[59]

The notion of a belief's being eluctable is integrally related to that of epistemic obligation, in particular to the intuitively significant idea of "ought implies can".[60] Some beliefs, he claims, are such that we are unable to refrain from believing them. Although this concept is difficult to formulate, Wolterstorff assumes that there may be such *ineluctable* beliefs.[61] And if there are such, and we are only obliged to do that which we can in fact do, then epistemic obligation applies only to those beliefs which are *eluctable*.[62] This point is more radical than it appears at first glance, for in formulating our obligations in this way Wolterstorff is downplaying the idea that we can decide to believe certain propositions.[63]

Ineluctable beliefs are the product of dispositions which we are unable to influence in such a way as to change the beliefs they produce.[64] And if we are unable to influence the mechanisms which produce these beliefs, and thus are unable to alter our believing or not believing certain propositions, then we have not transgressed our noetic obligations in that regard.[65] It is only in relation to our directing the attention of, or impairing or improving our noetic faculties, or in the level of consciousness of

---

[59] Ibid., 170.

[60] Ibid., 162.

[61] Wolterstorff, *CBGR?*, 162; *Divine Discourse*, 268–279. On the existence of ineluctable beliefs, see J. Heal, "Pragmatism and Choosing to Believe", *Reading Rorty*, ed. A. R. Malachowski (Oxford: Basil Blackwell, 1990) 101–114.

[62] Wolterstorff, *CBGR?*, 162. I think it is here important to note that while we may be unable to do something, we ought to be able to do it, and that our inability to do it is due to a culpable failure in some area of life. Thus we may still have an obligation to do something, or in this case to believe something, even though we are currently unable to do so, if that inability is due to some failure of ours in some area of obligation.

[63] Wolterstorff, *EG&G* 452; "Once Again, Evidentialism", 54; *Divine Discourse*, 268–273.

[64] Ibid. Wolterstorff is dependent here upon the existence and functioning of Reidian belief-dispositions, as is clear when he states "Beliefs are not the outcome of decisions but of dispositions".

[65] Here it is worth noting that Wolterstorff believes that very often in the case of our believing that there is conflict between certain of our beliefs we do not, and cannot, *decide* not to believe one or other of them. Rather one of the beliefs is held more firmly than the other, and this, along with the firmness of our belief that they conflict simply oust it from our set of beliefs. See *Divine Discourse*, 270.

certain of our beliefs, rather than in relation to the beliefs themselves, that we have the obligation to do as well as we can in the attempt to get in touch with reality.[66] It is this "steering of one's doxastic constitution" which Wolterstorff terms a *doxastic practice*.[67] While, as noted below, our belief-dispositions evolve over time and with experience, by and large "mostly we do and must accept our constitution, as we come to know it, and then steer it".[68] These doxastic practices "*recommend* themselves to us" as ways of gaining new beliefs, of removing defective beliefs, or of more reliably forming beliefs about something.[69] These beliefs that we have about our doxastic practices then become the basis for our obligations in directing them so as to do better in our attempt to get in touch with reality.[70]

A.4. NON-INNOCENT BELIEFS AND THE NOETIC EFFECTS OF SIN

However, the justification that is produced by the governing of our dispositions is only applicable to those beliefs which are produced by innocent belief-forming mechanisms.[71] It is possible for someone to cultivate or resist a given belief-disposition for reasons other than getting

---

[66] Wolterstorff, *EB&G* 452; "Once Again, Evidentialism", 54–55; *Divine Discourse*, 270–272. This argument is rejected by Feldman, 235–256, who argues that we can have epistemic obligations even if we have no control over our believings at all. His argument is flawed, however, in that he mistakenly restricts the idea of control to direct control over our believings, pp. 238–240, rather than allowing that we may have control of belief-dispositions, even if we have no direct control over our beliefs, and thus we have obligations in relation to their governance. He also presents a number of examples to support his contention that we can have obligations that we are nonetheless unable to fulfil, see pp. 239–243. Each of these inabilities to fulfil obligations depend, however, on the subject's delinquency in either making unfulfillable commitments, or failing to implement appropriate plans to fulfil conditional obligations, and thus is strictly irrelevant to the argument. Paul Helm discuss noetic obligations in relation to what he calls "belief policies", arguing, in a manner similar to Wolterstorff, that our beliefs are not subject to direct voluntary control, but are controlled by way of our adopting belief policies. See P. Helm, *Belief Policies* (Cambridge: Cambridge University Press, 1996) esp 32–84. While Helm's notion of rationality is significantly different to Wolterstorff's, given the role that evidence plays in his theory, and his rejection of Wolterstorff's central notion of beliefs being innocent until proven guilty (for these points see Helm, *Belief Policies*, 106–112, 189–216), the general point stands.

[67] Wolterstorff, *Divine Discourse*, 270.
[68] Ibid.
[69] Ibid.
[70] Ibid., 270–271.
[71] Wolterstorff, *CBGR?*, 163.

in touch with reality, or even for frankly perverse reasons.[72] These are rationally unjustified reasons for modifying a belief-disposition, for only if the goal of revision is to get more amply in touch with reality, and the disposition is seen to be unreliable as a means for doing so, is such revision justified.[73] The beliefs produced by such non-innocent belief-dispositions lie outside the "innocent until proven guilty" principle of rationality in believing.[74]

In this respect there is a lacuna in Wolterstorff's epistemology, for while he here acknowledges the influence of sin upon one's noetic faculties, he does not develop this into a comprehensive, systematic feature of human believings in his theory of rationality.[75] Rather, he simply briefly notes the "insightful" discussions of Calvin and Kuyper on the noetic effects of sin.[76] This is surprising given that he specifically chides Reid for failing to deal with the effects of sin on human believings in the face of clear pointers to do so.[77] I will address this gap in his epistemology with specific reference to Calvin and Kuyper in order to gain a more comprehensive understanding of the role of sin in human believings before proceeding further.

Calvin does not develop an epistemology as such, however his discussion of the effects of sin on the human apprehension of the knowledge of God has general epistemological significance.[78] For Calvin, God has revealed himself to humans in two primary ways: in the intrinsic, self-renewing knowledge of his divinity;[79] and in the testimony of the

---

72   Ibid.

73   Ibid., 164.

74   Ibid.

75   For the acknowledgment, see Wolterstorff, *CBGR?*, 149; *TRR*, 66–67. It must be noted that Wolterstorff obviously does not ignore the effects of sin in human believings, for he not only notes the gap in Reid's thought and points to those who can fill it, he has an extensive discussion of these effects in the context of his meta-theory. See Wolterstorff, *RWBR*, 145–146; *J&P*, 173–176. This should be seen as a gap rather than a flaw in his epistemology, *pace* M. Westphal, "Taking St. Paul Seriously: Sin as an Epistemological Category", *Christian Philosophy*, ed. T. P. Flint (Notre Dame: University of Notre Dame Press, 1990) 212–200, who fails to note Wolterstorff's treatment of this matter in his meta-theory. For he does not ignore or reject the idea of sinful distortion of noetic faculties: he simply does not expound it in detail in the context of his general epistemology. What follows is, in part, an articulation of his epistemology in light of his treatment of this issue in his meta-theory.

76   Wolterstorff, *TRR*, 66–67.

77   Wolterstorff, *TRR*, 66; cf. Reid, *Essays*, VI,6, in relation to a person's being hardened against belief in God.

78   So Wolterstorff, *TRR*, 66; cf. A. Plantinga, "The Reformed Objection to Natural Theology", *Christian Scholar's Review* 11/3 (1982) 187–198.

79   J. Calvin, *Institutes of the Christian Religion* (Grand Rapids: Eerdmans, 1983) I,iii,1;

natural order.[80] This revelation is clearly coupled with a natural epistemic capacity to respond to God's self-revelation, indeed an innate tendency to believe in God,[81] which itself ensures human culpability for the "impious" rejection of God.[82] Thus, as humans created in the image of God, we have been given both the objective revelation and the subjective noetic faculties we need in order to know God, but due to sin we culpably fail to use them to their proper ends.[83] There is, indeed, a systematic distortion of our created noetic faculties, inasmuch as the very dispositions and triggering factors which are intended to lead us to the knowledge of God instead lead us to idolatry.[84] Indeed, so great is this sinful distortion of our native faculties, that there is no possibility of Natural Theology, understood as an unaided human enterprise leading to a true apprehension of God himself.[85] This, while not developed by Calvin into an overall epistemology, clearly has implications for a general epistemology. Sin has distorted our intellects in such a way that we are unable to respond unambiguously by means of our innate created belief-dispositions to created reality. This global noetic distortion which is the enduring legacy of human sinfulness needs to be kept in mind, and compensated for, in all human noetic enterprises.[86]

The universal impact of sin upon our noetic faculties is affirmed and explored by Kuyper in his discussion of "Science and Sin" in his *Principles of Sacred Theology*:

> But of necessity we must accept this hard reality, and in every theory of knowledge which is not to deceive itself, the fact of sin must henceforth claim a more serious consideration... it is in place here to state definitely

---

The Gospel According to St. John, 1–10 (London: Oliver and Boyd, 1959) 11.

80   Calvin, *Institutes*, I,v,1.

81   Calvin, *Institutes*, I,v,4; cf. E. A. Dowey, *The Knowledge of God in Calvin's Theology* (New York: Columbia University Press, 1952) 51–52; Plantinga, "Natural Theology", 189.

82   Calvin, *Institutes*, I,iv,1 & 2; I,iv,14 & 15; *Commentary on the Epistle to the Romans*, ed. H. Beveridge (Edinburgh: The Calvin Translation Society, 1884) 26–27, commenting on Rom. 1:20–21.

83   W. Niesel, *The Theology of John Calvin* (Philadelphia: Westminster Press, 1956) 44–45; Dowey, 73.

84   Calvin, *Institutes*, I,v,12 & 13. For the systematic disordering of our rational faculties, along with the rest of our created nature, see Calvin, *Institutes*, II,i,5; *John*, 12.

85   Dowey, 85; Niesel, 49; T. F. Torrance, *Theology in Reconstruction* (Grand Rapids: Eerdmans, 1965) 109–110, *pace* G. J. Postema, "Calvin's alleged rejection of Natural Theology", *SJT* 24/4 (Nov 1971) 432–433.

86   These generalising conclusions drawn from Calvin's thought are supported by J. Klapwijk, "Rationality in the Dutch Neo-Calvinist Tradition", *Rationality in the Calvinian Tradition*, H. Hart, *et al*, ed. (Boston: University Press of America, 1983) 95–96; Westphal, "Taking St. Paul Seriously", 200–226.

that sin works its fatal effects also in the domain of our science [*Wissenschaft*], and is by no means restricted to what is thelematic (i.e. to the sphere of volition).[87]

He sees sin at work in the human knowing enterprise in five general areas.[88] It has a formal impact upon our investigative activities, resulting in intentional falsehood, unintentional errors, self-delusion and deception, over-active imagination, the negative impact of socialisation and experience upon our beliefs, physical disorders, and fallacious core beliefs, all of which result in noetic distortion.[89] Sin also influences the moral motives in our consciousness, resulting in perceptions and theories being influenced by personal interests.[90] Further, it impacts upon our nature in that our unloving alienation from the objects of our knowledge darkens our understanding, erecting a barrier to our truly apprehending reality.[91] It even affects our very selves, leading to an inward alienation amongst our faculties, distorting what we come to know.[92] Finally sin obstructs our knowledge of God, which in turn results in an inability to know the cosmos as a whole, for to do so requires a transcendent knowledge of the generic and teleological relationships that obtain amongst the various elements of the cosmos, and of the cosmos as a whole, a perspective which is effectively denied us by sin.[93] Kuyper's conclusion regarding the effects of sin upon human believings is clear:

---

[87] A. Kuyper, *Principles of Sacred Theology* (Grand Rapids: Baker, 1980) II,ii,43. It is clear from his discussion of the nature of science that Kuyper uses the term in reference to all *Wissenschaft*, including theology. See Kuyper, *Principles*, II,i,37, 41, 42. It is equally apparent from his repeated references to the general theory of knowledge that his comments are not restricted to the *Wissenschaft*, but are applicable to epistemology in general.

[88] Kuyper, *Principles*, II,ii,43.

[89] Ibid.

[90] Ibid.

[91] Ibid.

[92] Ibid.

[93] Ibid. A similar point is made in O. O'Donovan, *Resurrection and Moral Order: An Outline for Evangelical Ethics* (Leicester: IVP, 1986) 76–91, with the exception of the need of a transcendent perspective. O'Donovan's argument is more insightful than Kuyper's in that respect: he recognises that even from a time-bound human perspective, the knowledge of God is required for a true knowledge of the cosmos. For only with a knowledge of God and his inter-relationships with created entities can we have a true understanding from within the cosmos of the generic and teleological relationships of the created order in its parts and as a whole. Nonetheless, Kuyper's basic claim that the knowledge of God is required for a true knowledge of reality is clearly reinforced by O'Donovan's argument.

> From which [the above argument] it by no means follows, that you should sceptically doubt all science [*Wissenschaft*], but simply that it will not do to omit the fact of sin from your theory of knowledge. This would not be warranted if sin were only a thelematic conception and therefore purely ethic; how much less now, since immediately as well as mediately, sin modifies so largely all those data with which you have to deal in the intellectual domain and in the building up of your *science*. Ignorance wrought by sin is the most difficult obstacle in the way of all true science.[94]

Such a view mitigates the overly optimistic appraisal of human rationality in Reid's thought, in that it recognises that sin also plays a determinative role in human noetic enterprises.[95] This is not to say that it is a thoroughly pessimistic view, for there is still considerable scope for the operation of God-given belief-forming mechanisms.[96] It was, however, a more balanced position than Reid's in the way that it recognised the epistemological significance of divinely ordained noetic faculties and their distortion by sin.[97] The incorporation of these insights into Wolterstorff's

---

94 Kuyper, *Principles*, II,ii,43, emphasis in the original.
95 This is argued in detail by Marsden, "The Collapse of American Evangelical Academia", 219–264. Indeed he argues that the American evangelical dependence upon optimistic Reidian common-sense rationality was a major factor in its collapse in the mid-twentieth century, as opposed to the vitality of the Dutch Reformed academic movement with its more pessimistic view of human reason. cf. Westphal, "Taking St. Paul Seriously", 200–202, 212–220.
96 Kuyper, *Principles*, II,ii,46, p. 136; cf. Marsden, 248. However, it must be noted that in the articulation of this model in the realm of science, with his notion of "two sciences" corresponding to two different kinds of people (*viz* pagan and Christian) Kuyper does become overly pessimistic. See *Principles*, II,iii,48–51, pp. 150–182, and my discussion below (Chapter 4, A.1., A.3.). This pessimistic view of scientific noetic capabilities is taken further by Van Til, for which see C. Van Til, *A Christian Theory of Knowledge* (Grand Rapids: Baker, 1969) 288–309, esp p. 294. For a critique of Reformed presuppositionalist pessimistic epistemology, from an evidentialist view point see, for example, R. C. Sproul, J. Gerstner and A. Lindsley, *Classical Apologetics* (Grand Rapids: Academie, 1984) 241–252; J. W. Montgomery, "Once upon an A Priori: Van Til in Light of Three Fables", *Faith Founded on Fact* (Nashville: Thomas Nelson, 1978) 107–127. For a critique from a Calvinist perspective, see Klapwijk, "Rationality", 97–110. For a more nuanced version of the Neo-Calvinist perspective which, while rejecting a rigid epistemological demarcation between Christians and non-Christians nonetheless denies Wolterstorff's innocent-until-proven-guilty stance, see Westphal, "Taking St. Paul Seriously", 200–226.
97 Marsden, 253–256. My identification of this as a "more balanced position", as Marsden notes, is not uncontested. That sin affects us as believing and knowing beings is generally accepted in Christian theology; how it does so, and to what extent, is more controversial. See, e.g., Sproul, *et al*, 241–243; J. W. Montgomery, "The Place of Reason in Christian Witness", *Faith Founded on Fact* (Nashville: Thomas Nelson, 1978) 27–42, who argue that it does not distort the perception of facts, but only their interpretation. Indeed,

epistemology would take the following form. Sin results in a systematic epistemic distortion by means of the disordering and suppression of data, the improper functioning of innate belief-dispositions, the operation of ignoble belief-dispositions such as self-interest, the improper influence of previously held beliefs on potential new beliefs, the unhealthy interactions of different belief-dispositions and triggering mechanisms upon each other, and the presence of false beliefs due to socialisation and life experiences illegitimately influencing our governance of belief-dispositions.[98] All of these effects need to be overcome to the best of our ability if we are to be rational in our believings. This means that a belief ceases to be rational if S either knows or ought to know that it is the function of the epistemic distortions outlined above.[99] However, we are only obliged to modify our belief-dispositions to the best of our ability, which then means that some of these influences of sin will not, indeed can not, be overcome. This in turn provides a partial explanation for the phenomena of rational false beliefs and of a belief's being potentially rational for one person but not another.[100]

Sproul, *et al*, argue that the noetic effects of sin operate only indirectly through the totally depraved heart and not directly through a depraved mind. In this they adopt a Thomist line on the nature and extent of the noetic effects of sin, seeing it as having a primarily thelematic effect; see Thomas Aquinas, *The Summa Theologica* (rev ed. D. J. Sullivan; 2 vol; vol 1 and 2; Chicago: Chicago University Press, 1952) I,xii,12; I,xii,13; I,xvii,3; I,lxxxv,6; IIA,lxxxiii,3; IIA,lxxxiii,4; IIA,lxxxiii,5, and esp I,iciv,4. I think that Wolterstorff is here suggesting that, following Kuyper's general epistemology, sin influences the mind directly through disordered belief-forming mechanisms, as well as indirectly through the thelematic influence of self-interest and so on.

[98] Wolterstorff, *J&P*, 173, notes some of these effects drawn from Kuyper's epistemology. See also S. Moroney, "How Sin Affects Scholarship: A New Model", *Christian Scholar's Review* 28/3 (Spring 1999) 432–451, for an interesting preliminary account of these matters.

[99] This notion of someone being aware or being obliged to be aware of the distorting effects of sin needs some elucidation. Sometimes it happens that a person, S, becomes aware through the normal course of events that a belief, p, is the result of the noetic influence of sin. It is clear then that, all things being equal, S's belief that p is no longer rational for her at that time. This does not always happen however, and so in matters of sufficient importance – a notion which can not be exactly quantified or defined, but which can be ascertained in the light of S's general obligations – S has a duty to examine herself and her store of beliefs carefully for evidence of these distorting factors, as well as for anything else which may compromise the rationality of her belief that p.

[100] This is what Kuyper, *Principles*, II,i,41 and II,ii,43, pp. 90 and 106, sees as the fragmentation of subjectivity which is caused by sin.

A.5. Ceasing to Believe and Entitled Belief

Noetic obligations are also important in relation to the idea of "adequate reason for ceasing to believe". Reasons according to Wolterstorff are those beliefs which are the result of the "reasoning disposition", and which are seen to provide good evidence for another belief.[101] A particular person, S, has adequate reason believe that p, if S believes p for the reason q, and q does in fact provide good evidence for p.[102] In relation to ceasing to believe, q is an adequate reason for S to cease believing p only in relation to the totality of S's beliefs; for there may well be others amongst S's beliefs which show that q is a false belief, or does not in fact count as good evidence against p.[103] However, "adequate reason to cease from believing" needs to be understood in relation to noetic obligations, for while S may not have a reason q to cease from believing p, it may be that if she had governed her noetic faculties as she should have then she would have the belief that q, and thus her belief that p is unjustified.[104] It may also be that she does in fact have such a reason q, but does not recognise the significance of q for her belief that p.[105] This failure to perceive the relevant connections amongst her beliefs may or may not be the result of a failure to govern her noetic faculties: it is only in the case where such a breach of obligations occurs that justification for p is removed.[106] A further complication is that she may believe she has good reason q to cease from believing p, but her belief that q is mistaken. Again, it is not the truth or falsehood of her belief which confers justification or removes it, but only whether she has performed her duties with respect to her believings.[107] It is not the attainment of truth, but the adherence to governance obligations, which confers or removes justification on a belief.[108]

A later development of this model is the notion of *entitlement*, which is taken to be a type of justification distinct from *warrant*. The latter is an alternate version of a Reidian *doxastic practice* approach to epistemology,

---

[101] Wolterstorff, *CBGR?*, 164; "Once Again, Evidentialism", 56.

[102] Wolterstorff, *CBGR?*, 165.

[103] Ibid.

[104] Wolterstorff, *CBGR?*, 165; *Divine Discourse*, 272–272. It must be noted that this works the other way too, so that if she does believe q, but ought not to, then she is still justified in believing p, for her belief that she is not so justified is the result of a failure of her governance obligations; see *CBGR?*, 166.

[105] Wolterstorff, *CBGR?*, 167.

[106] Ibid.

[107] Ibid., 167–168.

[108] Ibid., 145.

which focuses on the appropriate use of such practices.¹⁰⁹ Wolterstorff's notion of *entitlement* is clearly distinct from this notion of warrant, for it deals with *obligations* with respect to both the factors that give rise to a belief, and those which maintain or defeat it – i.e., all the governance obligations which we have in relation to that belief.¹¹⁰ "Let us say that someone is *fully entitled* to some belief of theirs if it represents no failure of governance obligations on their behalf."¹¹¹ This, in fact, is simply a clarification of his prior criterion of *rationally justified belief* which avoids the potentially misleading words *rational* and *justification*, without substantially altering its central tenets.¹¹² Because *rational justification* is

---

109   Wolterstorff, *EB&G*, 453; *Divine Discourse*, 266–267. This is the notion developed by A. Plantinga, "Positive Epistemic Status and Proper Function" *Philosophical Perspectives, no.2: Epistemology* (1988) 1–50; *Warrant: The Current Debate* (New York: Oxford University Press, 1993); *Warrant and Proper Function* (New York: Oxford University Press, 1993); *Warranted Christian Belief* (New York: Oxford University Press, 2000) which concerns itself with the proper functioning of *doxastic practices* (what Wolterstorff usually terms belief-dispositions or belief forming mechanisms) in the environment for which they were devised. This idea receives some attention in *CBGR?*, e.g. 171–172, but is largely irrelevant to Wolterstorff's rationality, focussing as it does on an externalist account of knowledge rather than an internalist account of rational belief. Wolterstorff uses the term "warrant" extensively in *Reason Within the Bounds of Religion*, but does so in a manner distinct from that of Plantinga: in particular, Wolterstorff uses it with reference to an *internalist*, *normative* account of *rationality*; Plantinga uses it with reference to an *externalist*, *non-normative* account of *knowledge*.

110   Wolterstorff clearly includes the governance of belief-forming mechanisms within the idea of entitlement, and thus for him the sources of a belief are of epistemological significance ("Once Again, Evidentialism", 54–55; *Divine Discourse*, 269–272). The validity of sources of belief for the broader notion of entitlement can be rescued from Popperian demurs along the following lines. Many non-rational factors, such as hunch, intuition, social pressures and so on, give rise to acceptable theories, as Wolterstorff acknowledges in *RWBR*, 102–104. Some or all of them may be granted positive epistemic status by including them amongst the body of reliable belief-forming mechanisms for certain kinds of beliefs under certain conditions. A non-exclusive alternative is to draw a distinction between the mechanisms which give rise to an idea, hypothesis, or notion, and those which give rise to it *as a belief*. For example, an idea or possible line of investigation may spring into a research physicist's mind by way of a dream, intuition, or some other mechanism deemed to be unreliable. This idea may be accepted with more or less firmness, but at this stage it is not granted the status of a *belief*. It is only after reasoning, empirical observation and so on that the idea gains the status of a belief. When that belief is then examined with respect to its rational status, it is those mechanisms which converted it from an idea to a belief that need to be assessed, not those which first gave rise to the idea. Such moves rescue the role of belief-forming mechanisms in the origin of beliefs from Popperian demurs (for which see Popper, *Conjectures and Refutations*, 21–27) and enable them to be incorporated into Wolterstorff's notion of entitlement.

111   Wolterstorff, *EB&G*, 453; cf. *Divine Discourse*, 271–272, and the criterion on p. 272 quoted above, this chapter, A.1.

112   Wolterstorff, *EB&G*, 453, where he argues that *justification* should be avoided because

the terminology he uses in his earlier and most extensive published treatments of this issue, I shall continue to use that term, reserving, *entitlement* for Wolterstorff's later treatments of this issue.[113]

B. The Main Features of Wolterstorff's Rationality

Having discussed Wolterstorff's criterion of rationality, and the model of rationality it exemplifies, I now turn to the major features of this model which are relevant to the elucidation of his meta-theory. I will identify three main features of his model: its being integrally related to empirical observation of the nature of human beliefings; its situated, non-absolutist character; its rational, non-relativist character. It is interesting that Wolterstorff identifies these same features as the most significant aspects of Reid's account of rationality, a model which provides him with the starting point for his own reflections.[114] Reid is a particularly appropriate philosopher for Wolterstorff to use in this regard, for not only was he a Christian philosopher, he also opposed the classical foundationalists of his day, in much the same way that Wolterstorff opposes recent foundationalist thought. Indeed, Reid's epistemology was devised as a specific alternative to the foundationalist evidentialism that characterised the sceptics of his day.[115] It is this non-classical foundationalist theory of rationality which Wolterstorff identifies as "one of the most important things Reid offers us in our present philosophical situation".[116] The reason this is so important now is that with the demise of foundationalist theories

---

it is ambiguous between warrant and entitlement, and that *rational* should be avoided because it connotes reasons, which may or may not be part of entitlement in belief. Such broader notions may be valid, enabling the incorporation of a wider range of epistemic desiderata, such as epistemic virtue and even warrant, into the appraisal of a person and her beliefs. However, the articulation of such a theory lies beyond the scope of my thesis. For an interesting account of virtue epistemology, see W. J. Wood, *Epistemology: Becoming Intellectually Virtuous* (Downers Grove: IVP, 1998).

113 I should here note that Wolterstorff has an extensive discussion of the notion of entitlement in contrast to other epistemic desiderata in his Gifford Lectures for 1994–1995. See the section on "Entitlement", in N. Wolterstorff, *From Presence to Practice: Mind, World and Entitlement to Believe* (forthcoming).

114 Wolterstorff, *TRR*, 64–65. Wolterstorff notes, however, two major flaws in Reid's epistemology, namely his previously noted failure to discuss non-innocent belief-dispositions (*TRR*, 66–67; *CBGR?*, 149) and the lack of a criterion of rational belief (*TRR*, 58–60; *H&R*, 409–410, 413–414). In these matters he consciously goes beyond Reid.

115 Wolterstorff, *TRR*, 44–45.

116 Wolterstorff, *TRR*, 64. For the continuing validity of Reid's epistemological thought today, see E. H. Madden, "Did Reid's Metaphilosophy survive Kant, Hamilton and Mill?", *Metaphilosophy* 18/1 (Jan 1987) 31–48.

of rationality, some philosophers have abandoned rationality as a valid epistemic option.[117] There are three features of Reid's epistemology which Wolterstorff sees as being especially valuable. First, Reid's is a theory of *situated rationality*, in as much as a belief which is rational for one person may not be rational for another person.[118]

> Thus in general we cannot inquire into the rationality of some belief by asking whether *one* would be rational in holding that belief. We must ask whether it would be rational for *this particular person* to hold it, or whether it would be rational for *a person of this type in this situation* to hold it... Although our native belief-dispositions are shared in common, different "evidences" trigger these dispositions in different persons, and different justified beliefs emerge.[119]

Second, Reid's rationality was one which was set within a framework of a psychology of human being and believing, to an extent that makes his epistemology particularly significant.[120] Third, Reid's non-classical foundationalist theory is a non-sceptical theory in which true knowledge of the world-as-it-is is possible.[121] As we shall see, these three features of Reid's epistemology are characteristic of Wolterstorff. In my discussion of these features in relation to Wolterstorff's epistemology, I shall reverse the order of the first two, discussing the empirical nature of his model of rationality before proceeding to its non-absolutist and non-relativist qualities.

B.1. IT IS EMPIRICALLY ROOTED

As we have seen, Wolterstorff's model of situated rationality entails the notion of governing our assent to certain propositions so as to get more amply in touch with reality.[122] This, he suggests, in turn requires that there be certain belief-forming mechanisms, or belief-dispositions, which are to be governed so as to attain this goal.[123] It is in relation to these dispositions that Wolterstorff turns to the thought of Reid as one of the few places

---

[117] Wolterstorff, *TRR*, 64, where he notes that Rorty in *Philosophy and the Mirror of Nature* adopts that line.

[118] Ibid., 64–65.

[119] Ibid., 65, emphasis in the original.

[120] Ibid.

[121] Ibid.

[122] Wolterstorff, *CBGR?*, 148.

[123] Ibid.

where the existence of such dispositions is elucidated. Most notions of rationality are the product of abstract reflection upon the relations that obtain between propositions in an ideal belief-system, with the result that they "prove limited and myopic in application".[124] They have also tended to ignore the *active* nature of human belief formation: for rather than recognising that we engage in practices in order to develop new beliefs or correct problematic existing ones, they tend to portray human beings as "immobile solitary reactors".[125] Reid, on the other hand, develops a model of rationality which is rooted in the realities of human psychology, accounts for the role of testimony and practices in belief formation, and thus is broadly applicable to the full range of human believings.[126] As we have seen, such a concern with the empirical realities of human believings, while controversial, is nonetheless a necessary component of an adequate model of rationality.[127]

The foundation of Reid's rationality is his discussion of human belief-dispositions.[128] These are the dispositions, inclinations and propensities to believe which, when triggered by some appropriate stimulus, result in our believing something.[129] This accounts for the majority of our beliefs, and include such dispositions as memory, sensory and credulity dispositions, which produce their effects immediately.[130] Mediate beliefs are those which are produced by the *reasoning disposition*, by means of which we

---

124 Wolterstorff, *CBGR?*, 149; cf. "Privileged Access", 86–87, where he speaks of this as a "myopic focus on our cognitive constitution at the expense of reflecting on the practices whereby that constitution is employed".

125 Wolterstorff, "Privileged Access", 86, where he notes the need to develop a more active model of epistemology. Wolterstorff develops these ideas further in *From Presence to Practice*, in the chapter entitled "Practices of Acquaintance and Inquiry".

126 Wolterstorff, *CBGR?*, 149. It is interesting to note here that Reid bridged the traditional gap between psychology and epistemology. Indeed, "for Reid the two were closely intertwined", Lehrer, "Hume vs Reid", 394.

127 In this regard see the extensive discussions of the empirical adequacy of foundationalism and Kuhn's model of science in Chapters 1 and 2 above. Chisholm, *Criterion*, 12–23, adopts this broadly inductive or "particularist" approach, which works from rational everyday beliefs to a notion of rationality in direct opposition to the abstract or "methodist" approach of classical epistemology as found, for example in Locke, which works from an abstractly devised criterion of rationality to the justifiability of everyday beliefs.

128 Wolterstorff, *TRR*, 47; *CBGR?*, 149. Here it may be noted that while Reid's was not a *classic foundationalist* epistemology, it was a *broadly foundationalist* one.

129 Wolterstorff, *TRR*, 47; *Divine Discourse*, 269. As discussed in the section on classical foundationalism, these beliefs are justified without the need for the justifying action being performed on them. See above, and Lehrer, "Hume vs Reid", 394–396.

130 Wolterstorff, *TRR*, 47, *CBGR?*, 149; *Divine Discourse*, 269; Reid, *Essays*, I,2; II,20; *Inquiry*, II,3.

come to believe a proposition because we believe that others of our beliefs constitute good evidence for it.[131]

Reid discusses not only the identity of these dispositions, but also their origin.[132] Some of these dispositions, amongst which he included the *credulity disposition*,[133] are innate, "endowed by our Creator" rather than the product of some form of conditioning.[134] They are not necessarily present or operant at birth; many of them emerge at different stages of maturation.[135] However their emergence is not the result of conditioning, but of a natural disposition to acquire such dispositions.[136] In contrast, others of our dispositions are the result of conditioning of one type or another, including the induction into a social belief-dispositional practice.[137] The *inductive principle* is an innate, non-conditioned disposition for the acquisition of belief-dispositions, whereby two phenomena are associated in our experience in such a way that the experience of one leads us to believe in the presence of the other.[138] This acquisition of new belief-dispositions by means of the inductive principle is identified by Wolterstorff as a type of classical conditioning.[139]

The majority of our noninnate belief-dispositions, however, are formed by means of operant conditioning modifying our native belief-

---

[131] Wolterstorff, *TRR*, 47; *CBGR?*, 150; Reid, *Inquiry*, V,7.

[132] Wolterstorff, *TRR*, 48; *CBGR?*, 150.

[133] The credulity principle is the innate tendency to believe human testimony on trust, without having first assured ourselves by independent means that the information is reliable. In young children this disposition operates almost without restraint, and while it, like other dispositions, is modified in the light of experience, the tendency to believe the things we are told is restrained, rather than destroyed. Reid, *Inquiry*, V,7; VI,5; VI,24. For a discussion of this disposition in relation to believing on say-so, see Wolterstorff, *EB&G*, 445–449; *Reid*, 163–184.

[134] Wolterstorff, *TRR*, 48; *CBGR?*, 150.

[135] Ibid.

[136] Ibid; cf. "Privileged Access", 87, where he introduces a model based on the workings of computers. There he speaks of our being " dispositionally hard-wired in such as a way that, upon such-and-such things happening to us, we become aware of such-and-such entities; and upon becoming aware of such-and-such entities, we believe thus-and-so." For a more extensive articulation of this metaphor, see the chapter in Wolterstorff, *Presence to Practice*, entitled "Programmed with Belief".

[137] Wolterstorff, *TRR*, 48, *CBGR?*, 150; *Divine Discourse*, 270–271; cf. "Privileged Access", 87, where he extends the computing metaphor, stating: "In addition, we are all dispositionally hard-wired in such a way that upon such-and-such things happening to us, we acquire new awareness-dispositions and new belief-dispositions."

[138] Wolterstorff, *TRR*, 48; *CBGR?*, 150–151; Reid, *Inquiry*, II,9; VI,24; IV,1.

[139] Wolterstorff, *TRR*, 48–49; *CBGR?*, 150–151.

dispositions, rather than by means of classical conditioning.[140] This is the case with the credulity, memory and sensory dispositions.[141] We begin with an unmodified disposition which prompts us to believe variously sayso, memory or perceptual evidence.[142] Experience, however, shows us that under certain conditions and for certain deliverances of the disposition, the resulting beliefs are erroneous, whereas under other conditions and for other deliverances the resulting beliefs are veracious.[143] This results in the belief-disposition being modified and restrained, with certain conditions acting as aversive influences on the disposition, and others as reinforcing influences.[144] Thus "Our native belief-dispositions all go through stages of increasing articulation, as we experience how some beliefs produced by these dispositions are false, and others are true."[145]

Wolterstorff discusses these influences, which he terms *inhibitors* and *abetters* of a given belief-disposition.[146] These *inhibitors* and *abetters* are not primarily the result of the principle of induction, as Reid thought, since the operation of induction on the deliverances of a given disposition in order to determine whether they are veridical or not requires that we have reasons independent of the operation of induction for so determining their value.[147] Rather, they are the product of our framework of beliefs, for certain of our currently accepted beliefs function as abetters or inhibitors of

---

140 Wolterstorff, *TRR*, 49; *CBGR?*, 151.
141 Wolterstorff, *TRR*, 49–50; *CBGR?*, 151–152. For a detailed discussion of what is "believing on sayso" and its relation to the credulity principle, see *EB&G*, 445–448.
142 Wolterstorff, *TRR*, 49–50; *CBGR?*, 151–152, though Wolterstorff notes with surprise that Reid only deals with its influence on the credulity disposition, and fails to recognise its role in the articulation of other dispositions. It is worth noting the empirical evidence for this view adduced by Reid and Wolterstorff: the credulity disposition is most strongly operant in young children, and tends to diminish, or at least be modified, with age. See Reid, *Essays*, VI,5; *Inquiry*, VI,24; Wolterstorff, *EB&G*, 447–448.
143 Wolterstorff, *TRR*, 49–50; *CBGR?*, 151–152.
144 Wolterstorff, *TRR*, 49–50; *CBGR?*, 151–152.
145 Wolterstorff, *TRR*, 50. Reid has a detailed discussion of this process in relation to perception and testimony; For which see Reid, *Inquiry*, VI,20; VI,24; Wolterstorff, *Reid*, 96–184. Wolterstorff also discusses Reid's idea of the "first principles of common-sense" and the confusions in his thought relating to them, for which see *TRR*, 51–53; *Reid*, 215–249; cf. J. Somerville, "Reid's Conception of Common Sense", *The Monist* 70/4 (Oct 1987) 423–427. Wolterstorff provides a solution to the problems Somerville raises with his articulation of the role of belief-dispositions in believing.
146 Wolterstorff, *EB&G*, 450; cf. "Privileged Access", 87–88, where, extending his computing metaphor further, he speaks of the acquisition of cognitive programming which abets and inhibits the functioning of our hard-wiring in the acquisition of new beliefs.
147 Wolterstorff, *EB&G*, 449; cf. Reid, *Inquiry*, VI,24.

the operation of the disposition which suggests a certain belief to us.[148] This they do by instructing us that the belief is consistent or inconsistent with what we already believe, and thus more likely to be true or false.[149] This does not mean that we will only come to believe things which are consistent with our currently held beliefs, but that we will be more or less likely to believe a new proposition depending on its relation to our currently held beliefs.[150] How powerful these *abetters* and *inhibitors* are depends upon, amongst other factors, the importance of the relevant belief to our belief system, and the manner in which the belief was attained.[151]

B.2. It is Situated and Non-Absolutist

The first thing to be noted here is that Wolterstorff's notion of rationality is essentially person- and context-specific. This is evident in his assertion that rationality is a matter of the relation between a person and her believings, rather than the relations which exist amongst those beliefs.[152] It is also inherent in the idea of *abettors* and *inhibitors* of beliefs which he develops in relation to entitled belief, for these *abetters* and *inhibitors* are by their very nature beliefs that we already hold and which determine whether a proposition we examine, or a potential belief evoked by our doxastic practices, is acceptable or not.[153] Such a situational notion of rationality is

---

[148] Wolterstorff, *EB&G*, 450.

[149] Ibid.

[150] This matter is discussed in detail in relation to the function of control beliefs in Wolterstorff's meta-theory. See below (Chapter 4, B.).

[151] Wolterstorff, *EB&G*, 450.

[152] Wolterstorff, *CBGR?*, 158. This notion of rationality consisting in a relationship between persons and their believings clearly distinguishes Wolterstorff's model of rationality from coherentist ones. This is an important point to note, in as much as it may seem from the discussion of abettors and inhibitors of beliefs that his is a coherentist view. That it is not coherentist, be it pure or impure (for this distinction, see Plantinga "Coherentism and the Evidentialist Objection", 123–126) is also seen in his ascribing privileged epistemic status to belief-dispositions and in his rejection of the foundationalist/coherentist distinction as being "otiose", and the addition of a normative component to the possibly "negative coherence" criterion of rationality which he develops. See Wolterstorff, *CBGR?*, 172. As I will argue below, Wolterstorff's rationality, and his associated meta-theory, are neither foundationalist nor coherentist in their meta-epistemic structure. In as much as a clearly defined "structure" exists at all, which is doubtful given the dynamic nature of his theory, it departs from these traditional categories (see Chapter 6).

[153] See previous section, and Wolterstorff, *EB&G* 450–451; "Privileged Access", 88, 90–91. This idea has important links with the function of control beliefs in theorising. Indeed, such abettors and inhibitors here function as types of controls on the status of the deliverances of certain belief-dispositions. For the nature and function of control beliefs in Wolterstorff's meta-theory, see below (Chapter 4, B.2.).

a necessary corollary of his central contention that rationality is a matter of being permitted or entitled to hold certain beliefs, those beliefs being innocent until proven guilty.[154] This becomes apparent when the implications of this view are spelled out with respect to specific cases of belief.[155] According to Wolterstorff the same belief may be rational for one person to hold, but irrational for another, or even rational for the same person under certain conditions but irrational under others.[156] The irrationality or rationality of the belief is determined by the starting beliefs of those people at those times, and is thus inherently situation- and person-specific. Thus:

> Whether a given person is in fact rational in such belief cannot be answered in general and in the abstract, however. It can only be answered by scrutinising the belief system of the individual believer, and the ways in which that believer has used his noetic capacities.[157]

This person- and situation-specific nature of his epistemology is seen most clearly, perhaps, in his discussion of the contextual nature of our noetic obligations. "Our noetic obligations arise from the whole diversity of obligations that we have in our concrete situations."[158] This means that rationality is both situation and person specific, and also generalised, for every individual's obligations-in-general have features that are unique to that individual as well as those that are common to all people.[159] It is because our general obligations require us to become more closely in touch with some relevant aspect of reality that we are obliged to do so.[160] Thus

---

[154] Wolterstorff, *CBGR?*, 162–163.

[155] See, for example, Wolterstorff's discussion of apologetic strategies, in *Is Reason Enough?* 24.

[156] Wolterstorff, *CBGR?*, 166 n. 14; *Divine Discourse*, 272, 279–280. His argument can be summarised thus: If S already holds the belief that p, and finds that the evidence for p and *not p* is equal in weight, then she can either continue to believe that p, or give up her belief that p and believe neither p nor *not p*. What she cannot do is renounce her belief that p in favour of *not p*. However, if she believes that *not p* prior to her appraisal of the evidence, then exactly the reverse is true. Further, if she believes neither p nor *not p* at that time, then she must continue to do so, while if she believes both propositions, then she can continue to do so (if she is able, which is unlikely), or renounce her belief in both p and *not p*.

[157] Wolterstorff, *CBGR?*, 176. This comment is made specifically in relation to belief in God, but is also relevant to, and a reflection of his broader epistemic stance. cf. *Divine Discourse*, 272–273.

[158] Wolterstorff, *CBGR?*, 148. It is interesting to note that Wolterstorff sees the ignoring of this link as a characteristic flaw of traditional epistemology.

[159] Wolterstorff, *CBGR?*, 147–148.

[160] Wolterstorff, *CBGR?*, 148. This has specific application to scholarly rationality, a matter which will be dealt with later. It suffices here to note that in as much as a person

our obligations with respect to our general responsibilities in life determine the extent of our noetic obligations, be that in relation to the matters we are obliged to investigate, or the extent to which we are obliged to investigate them.[161] In general we have noetic obligations to those areas of our beliefs which are connected with some aspect of our praxis.[162] However, our obligations even in reference to those beliefs are limited, for if we attempted to believe a proposition if and only if it were true, it may well interfere with others of our obligations.[163] Thus, in relation to relevant propositions, our noetic obligation is *"to do as well as can rightly be demanded* of us so as to bring it about that we believe them if they are true and disbelieve them if they are false".[164]

This "doing as well as can rightly be demanded of us" means that there are situations in which truth is not our primary concern, and so rationality may need to be sacrificed for the sake of a higher obligation.[165] Rationality provides only *prima facie*, not *ultima facie* justification for a belief.[166] Here it is important to note Wolterstorff's discussion of the priority of belief in God over rationality in belief.[167]

> From the fact that it is not rational for some person to believe that God exists it does not follow that he ought to give up that belief. Rationality is only *prima facie* justification; lack of rationality only *prima facie* impermissibility. Perhaps, in spite of its irrationality for him, the person ought to continue believing that God exists. Perhaps it is our duty to believe more firmly that God exists than any proposition which conflicts with this, and/or more firmly than we believe that a certain proposition *does* conflict with it. Of course, for a believer who is a member of the modern Western intelligentsia to have his theistic convictions prove nonrational is to be put into a deeply troubling situation. There is a biblical category

---

enters into the task of scholarship, be it in a professional capacity or not, she is obliged to take extraordinary care in the exercise of her noetic faculties. This is due to a number of factors, including: the very scholarly enterprise is predicated upon rigorous intellectual discipline, and thus to fail to be as careful as possible is to be in conflict with the adoption of this form of life; as a scholar she is in part responsible for the beliefs that are formed by others as a result of her research, and thus she has a responsibility to her students/readers; in relation to praxis-oriented scholarship, she has a responsibility for the techniques which are proposed in, or developed from, her research and their consequences.

161 Wolterstorff, *CBGR?*, 148.
162 Ibid.
163 Wolterstorff, *CBGR?*, 148; *Divine Discourse*, 273, 278.
164 Wolterstorff, *CBGR?*, 148, emphasis in the original.
165 Wolterstorff, *CBGR?*, 157; "The Assurance of Faith", 416.
166 Wolterstorff, *CBGR?*, 157.
167 Ibid., 176–177.

which applies to such a situation. It is a *trial*, which the believer is called to endure. Sometimes suffering is a trial. May it not also be that sometimes the irrationality of one's conviction that God exists is a trial, to be endured?[168]

Thus, while in general we have an obligation to be rational in our believings because we are obliged to respond to God's claims upon us, this does not mean that God will never call upon us to believe something that is irrational, for the truth-obligation may be overridden by other obligations.[169] And what greater obligation is there for the Christian believer than to be faithful to God? Thus "Christians are obligated to hold the faith tenaciously, with steadfastness, with perseverance".[170]

In relation to this matter, although Wolterstorff does not specifically say so, I believe he is best seen as asserting that *shalom* has primacy in belief as well as in life.[171] *Shalom*, understood as harmonious relationships between God, each other, ourselves and the world, is the highest norm for all of Christian life, thereby supplying the norms required for the governing of all aspects of life.[172] *Shalom* provides the ultimate justification of all our actions and believings.[173] Truth is an aspect of the ultimate goal of *shalom* – but it is only a part, not the whole of *shalom*, and nor is it even the most important aspect of the whole.[174] Therefore, wherever obligations to truth and to other more important aspects of *shalom* conflict,

---

168 Wolterstorff, *CBGR?*, 177; cf. "Is Reason Enough?", 23.

169 Wolterstorff, "Is Reason Enough?", 23. In fact it may be that there is no real conflict between the claims of truth and the claims of God, assuming, of course, the Christian belief that belief in God, and other core beliefs of Christian commitment, are true. This then means that there may be a conflict between a given notion of truth, or a given criterion of rationality, and belief in God, rather than an actual conflict between the claims of truth and the claims of God. Belief in God may also be seen here as a central control belief for Christians, which thus legitimately limits the beliefs and logical connections amongst beliefs which are acceptable for a Christian. For the nature and function of control beliefs, see below (Chapter 4, B.2.).

170 Wolterstorff, "The Assurance of Faith", 412. This comment is an interpretation of Calvin's notion that in spite of doubts, whereby we are less than certain in a belief (ie hold the belief with less than maximal firmness), we can hold it with absolute confidence. See "The Assurance of Faith", 410–413 for this discussion, and pp. 414–415 for his assertion that such tenacious faith does not necessarily entail intolerance in belief: this is true only of certain *strategies* for maintaining belief.

171 This, of course, is related to his understanding of our obligations to God, and thus is an illustration of his epistemology at work.

172 Wolterstorff, *J&P*, 69–72.

173 Wolterstorff, *RWBR*, 111–116.

174 Wolterstorff, *RWBR*, 117–127; *J&P*, 162–176. For more on this, see below (Chapter 4, C.).

truth must give way. If truth or rationality is required for *shalom* in a particular instance, then it takes priority over other obligations: if not, then it is to be set aside. Love of God, it must be understood, is always the highest obligation in *shalom*, although of course it is not the only one. Thus tenacity of belief in God, which is necessary if we are to love God at all, takes precedence over rationality in that belief, or indeed, anything else we may do or believe. It is to be noted that Wolterstorff regards such a conflict as an exception rather than a norm in our believing and living, and a relatively rare one at that.

A related, but distinct matter is Wolterstorff's relativising of the role of reasons and reasoning in belief, and his disavowal of the possibility of the formulation of an algorithm of rationality. Believers, he claims, do not have to believe for reasons, although they are allowed to, thus:

> I have not contended that it is *wrong* for believers to believe for reasons. Neither have I denied that there are some projects for which even something like the evidential activity is the required or appropriate implementation. I have only contended that it is *not in general obligatory* for Christian believers to believe the identity-narrative of the gospels for reasons. Christian belief does not have to be rationally grounded.[175]

This does not mean that Christian belief in the gospels, or for that matter anything else,[176] is dogmatic, for there are objections to belief which must be considered, lest we lose entitlement in that belief.[177] What it does mean is that there is no algorithm of rationality which is applicable to all circumstances, people, or even intellectual communities.[178] Rationality is

---

[175] Wolterstorff, *EB&G*, 455; cf. *CBGR?*, 171–172.

[176] His argument in relation to the identity narrative of the gospels can be applied *mutatis mutandis* to any aspect of a Christian's belief system, be it a specifically *Christian* belief or not.

[177] Wolterstorff, *EB&G*, 455. cf. his discussion of the seeming paradox in diminishing the role of reason as a mechanism for rational belief, while holding that reasons are central to the criterion of rationality, *CBGR?*, 173. Note also Wolterstorff's acceptance of reasons and reasoning in Christian faith and apologetics, "Is Reason Enough?", 22, 23, 24, *pace* Pinnock's misconstrual of his epistemic and apologetic stance: "Response by Clark Pinnock", *The Reformed Journal* 31/4 (April 1981) 25–26. Note especially Pinnock's comment on p. 25 "It seems that while we may reason *from* God, we are forbidden to reason *to* him.", an obviously erroneous reading of Wolterstorff. In my view he is correct, however, in discerning that he and Wolterstorff "operate out of different perspectives as to the nature of human epistemology" ("Response by Clark Pinnock", 26). Pinnock's misreading of Wolterstorff is the result, I believe, of a conflict of paradigms for which Pinnock is unable or unwilling to compensate, something which I believe is typical of the anti/presuppositionalist debate in apologetics.

[178] Wolterstorff, *EB&G*, 455, and in relation to apologetics, "Is Reason Enough", 24.

person and even community specific, and so Wolterstorff suggests that we need a new model of thought about rationality.[179] Thus:

> Perhaps every community operates with a whole texture of rules for proper governance which it then teaches to its young members… And perhaps a given society's rules must be appraised not by reference to some "eternal" rules but by reference to how well the rules in question serve the flourishing, the shalom, of that community.[180]

What this then means is that believing, and even scholarship, are pluralistic enterprises conducted from within, and specifically related to, the life of a particular community.[181] The ideal of developing rules of rationality which are applicable to all people, which would ensure that diverse people with diverse beliefs could converse on common epistemic foundations and freely relinquish those beliefs that are not justified by those foundations is impossible of fulfilment.[182] At times rather than epistemology prising people from their world-view or religion, "their world-view or religion prises them loose from a certain epistemology".[183] If people are going to live and learn in this pluralistic environment, they need, not the Enlightenment myth of rational consensus, but the liberal ideal "of a society in which persons of diverse traditions live together in justice and friendship, conversing with each other and slowly altering their traditions in response to their conversation – to that, there is no viable alternative."[184]

---

179 Wolterstorff, *EB&G*, 455.

180 Ibid. Just what these rules may be, and how the *shalom* of a given community and communities in general may be determined he leaves "for some other occasion".

181 Wolterstorff, "The mission of the Christian college at the end of the 20th century" *The Reformed Journal* 33/6 (June 1983) 15; *EB&G*, 456; "Privileged Access", 86–92; "Scholarship and Conviction", 41–42.

182 Wolterstorff, *EB&G*, 456; "Privileged Access", 89–91; "Scholarship and Conviction", 42. Here Wolterstorff agrees with Siegel that this futile search for a common, certain foundation of knowledge, was at the heart of the Enlightenment, and positivist, vision.

183 Wolterstorff, *EB&G*, 456.

184 Wolterstorff, *EB&G*, 456; cf. "The mission of the Christian college", 15. Note that this is the liberal *political* or *social* ideal, not the liberal *intellectual* ideal which entails the adoption of a supposedly neutral and objective rationality, the very Enlightenment ideal which Wolterstorff has said is impossible of fulfilment. Further, it is the goal, or "animating vision" liberal politics, not its *polity* to which we must look. Liberal polity, allied as it is with liberal epistemology, is firmly repudiated by Wolterstorff in favour of his *consocial* alternative, for which see, N. Wolterstorff, "From Liberal to Plural", *Christian Philosophy at the close of the twentieth century*, ed. S. Griffioen and B. Balk (Kampen: Uitgeverij Kok, 1995) 201–215; and his engagement with the liberal alternative of Robert Audi in, R. Audi and N. Wolterstorff, *Religion in the Public Square: The Place*

What clearly follows from this is that Wolterstorff's notion of rationality is non-absolutist and defeasible. Rationality and truth in believing are connected but not identical concepts. While truth is the goal of all human believing enterprises, one has no obligation to actually attain truth; nor is there any blame in failing to attain it. Obligation and blame relate solely to doing one's best to attain truth and avoid error.[185] When one does so, the beliefs which result are rational. Such rational beliefs do not, however, constitute *knowledge*, for while one can never know something that is false, one may be intellectually justified in believing something false.[186] Truth is our epistemic goal, but it is neither guaranteed nor obligatory.[187] Thus, Wolterstorff's notion of rationality is non-absolutist, for a justified belief may be false without affecting its status as a rational belief,[188] and further, even if a belief is irrational, one may still be obliged to hold it.[189] It is defeasible in as much as a belief which is justified under certain conditions may not be under others, without affecting its status as a rational belief under the original conditions.[190]

---

of Religious Convictions in Political Debate (Lanham: Rowman & Littlefield, 1997). Strictly speaking, then, it is not to liberalism to which he appeals, but an alternative vision, the *consocial*, which he describes as an open conversation within a pluralistic community in which participants speak and critically listen from their particular traditions. For this, see, Wolterstorff, "Travail of Theology", 45–46; "Between the Pincers", 20; "Privileged Access", 92–94; "Scholarship and Conviction", 45–46. The alternative would be a cacophony of conflicting power claims in which true community would be impossible. The focus on *shalom* in Wolterstorff's vision of community and scholarly practice indicates that it is not relativistic, despite its clearly situational character. For the goal which the different criteria of rationality are meant to further is the *shalom* of a particular community, and Wolterstorff takes *shalom* to be an absolute, even if there are different visions of what it entails. His notion, however, of the *shalom* of scholarship requires the expression of specifically Christian virtues of repentance, forgiveness and the redemptive owning of suffering (Wolterstorff, "Privileged Access", 93). Similar points are made by A. McGrath, "The Christian Church's Response to Pluralism" *Journal of the Evangelical Theological Society* 35/4 (Dec 1992) 490–491; 498, in relation to religious dialogue in a pluralistic society. These notions have bearing on Wolterstorff's meta-theory, especially in relation to his rejection of the consensus view of science. See N. Wolterstorff, "Integration of Faith and Science – The Very Idea", *Journal of Psychology and Christianity* 3/2 (Summer 1984) 18–19; and below (Chapter 4, esp A., B.2.).

185 Wolterstorff, *CBGR?*, 145; *Divine Discourse*, 267–269.
186 Wolterstorff, *TRR*, 47.
187 Wolterstorff, *CBGR?*, 145.
188 Ibid., 167–168.
189 See above, 154–157.
190 Wolterstorff, *CBGR?*, 166 n. 14.

B.3. IT IS RATIONAL AND NON-RELATIVIST

Some would assert that such a situated rationality, which is relative to persons, time, situations, even communities, is necessarily tacitly or explicitly relativist or historicist.[191] This is not the case: it merely means that it is non-absolutist.[192] Indeed, the position that Wolterstorff adopts is necessary, if for no other reason than that the two alternatives of absolutism and relativism have been shown to be untenable.[193] His central reason for rejecting epistemological anarchy, relativism and antinomianism is this: God exists: he has created a real world which exists independently of our observing it: he has created us with the capacity to come to know this world.[194] The latter point receives particular attention in his discussions of Reidian belief-dispositions.[195] It is possible, given that there is no certain basis from which the veracity of our dispositions can be proven, that all of our belief-dispositions are misleading.[196] To assert this, however, is pointless, because the best we can do is trust those faculties which we have, as they are in fact the only means whereby we can come to know anything.[197] However his point goes well beyond that, for he acknowledges the existence of God, and his goodness as Creator. This means that, while sin has distorted our noetic faculties, if we are humble and open to correction, we can trust that God will enable us to recognise these effects and compensate for them to the best of our ability.[198] For these reasons we are able to trust our belief-forming mechanisms, for they are in part

---

[191] This charge will be discussed in detail in relation to Wolterstorff's meta-theory. For this, see below (Chapter 5, A.2., B.).

[192] To claim that it is relativist if it is non-absolutist is an example of "philosophical ping-pong". For this term in relation to theology, see B. Mitchell "How to Play Theological Ping-Pong" *How to Play Theological Ping-Pong: And Other Essays on Faith and Reason*, ed. W. J. Abraham and R. W. Prevost (London: Hodder & Stoughton, 1990) 166–183.

[193] See above (Part One, Chapters 1 and 2), and Siegel, *Relativism Refuted*, 161–167.

[194] This the clear implication of Wolterstorff, *RWBR*, 56–57, though it is nowhere stated outright.

[195] Wolterstorff, *TRR*, 60; *H&R*, 405, 414–415.

[196] Wolterstorff, *TRR*, 56–57; *H&R*, 414–415.

[197] Wolterstorff, *TRR*, 57; *CBGR?*, 174; *H&R*, 414.

[198] It may be noted here that Christians *ought to be* in an epistemically superior position to non-Christians, for we have, by the work of Christ mediated to us by the Holy Spirit, regained access to the created order. (O'Donovan, 76–97). This, however, needs to be seen as a complex and variable phenomenon, for our noetic faculties, along with the rest of our beings, are caught up in the struggle between flesh and S/spirit which characterises Christian experience. However, it is a hopeful struggle, for we understand that God, by his Spirit, is effecting his universal reconciliation of all things in our very beings, a reconciliation which includes the redemption of our sinfully distorted intellects.

endowed by God, and in part the product of other reliable mechanisms ordained by God, even though they have been influenced by sin.[199] That we ought to trust them and so govern them that we get in touch with reality as well as we can is a consequence of the responsibilities we have to the God who has made us, the world, and the dispositions by means of which we come to know it.[200] Indeed, the very particularities of our cognitive constitutions which were so problematic for the project of generic learning are best seen as ways of accessing reality.[201] For this reason the Christian is able to reject cognitive relativism, antinomianism and anarchy, as Wolterstorff himself does. Thus Wolterstorff is able to provide an epistemology which avoids the Scylla of relativism and scepticism and the Charybdis of "vulgar absolutism", an epistemology which provides a needed and fruitful context in which to develop a meta-theory of *Wissenschaft*.[202]

---

[199] Wolterstorff, *TRR*, 57; *CBGR?*, 174; *H&R*, 414. Of course, to argue this way is to already trust the dispositions whose veracity is under question, in particular that of reasoning. But in reality we have no choice but to do so: all know or believe is the result of our trusting them. *TRR*, 57–58; *CBGR?*, 174–175; *H&R*, 414–415. This trust in "unjustified" faculties is only problematic on guilty-until-proven-innocent grounds, which have already been seen to be unfounded. cf. Reid, *Essays*, VI,5; *Inquiry*, V,7; VI,20; VI,24; and above (Chapter 1, B.).

[200] See the discussion of epistemic norms, and their relationship to God above (this chapter, A.3.).

[201] Wolterstorff, "Privileged Access", 89, 91–92.

[202] For the necessity of this, see Shapere, "Modern Science", 414–416; Siegel, 163–164.

CHAPTER 4

Wolterstorff's Meta-Theory

As we have seen, crucial to Wolterstorff's meta-theory is his rejection of traditional views of science and the models of rationality associated with them. Indeed, his rationality, which his meta-theory seeks to articulate in the realm of *Wissenschaft*, is predicated upon the failure of the Enlightenment ideal of rationality.[1] Fundamental to these Enlightenment models of rationality and science is the ideal of a rational consensus of scholars arising out of a commitment to shared methods and bases of rationality and scientific investigation.[2] With the collapse of classical foundationalism, and the associated Enlightenment ideal of objective, value-neutral knowledge, has come a recognition of the essential plurality of rationality and *Wissenschaft*.

A. Wolterstorff and Neo-Calvinist Meta-Theories

This critique and rejection of the Enlightenment ideal of rational consensus arises from Wolterstorff's own roots in Neo-Calvinist philosophy, although his model differs in certain crucial respects from earlier Neo-Calvinist views. He states:

> I myself was reared intellectually within this movement. It was the context in which my own intellectual life began. Its denial of the neutrality and autonomy of scholarship was something I embraced early on, and which I continue to embrace. Nonetheless, I have come to feel acutely that the first- and second-generation founders of the movement did not

---

[1] This is seen, for instance, in his early essay "Faith and Philosophy", where he outlines this failure in the discipline of Philosophy, and moves towards his later views on rationality from a Christian perspective. See esp pp. 3–9, 20–21, 29–33, where he argues for the non-neutrality of philosophy vis-a-vis faith commitments.

[2] Wolterstorff, "On Christian Learning" [from here on *OCL*], 56–58; *IFS*, 16–17; "Faith and Philosophy", 3–8.

succeed in pinpointing the connection between religion and the practice and results of scholarship. It was for this reason that I developed my own notion of "control beliefs" in my book *Reason within the Bounds of Religion*.[3]

Thus, while he shares the Neo-Calvinist rejection of classical foundationalism and the consensus and objective views of rationality and *Wissenschaft* allied to it, he does not embrace its program of *Wissenschaft*.[4] Before outlining his meta-theory, then, it is important to explore his understanding of Neo-Calvinist models of science, and his reasons for rejecting them for, having seen what models of *Wissenschaft* he rejects and why he rejects them, we will be able to see more clearly the nature and uniqueness of his alternative.

A central claim of the Neo-Calvinist movement was that competent scholarship is not religiously neutral.[5] This is no accident, nor is it to be attributed to a failure in the rationality of those engaged in *Wissenschaft*.[6] It is an ineluctable feature of the human enterprise of *Wissenschaft*, for all scholarship is influenced by the religious beliefs of the scholars who are engaged in it, and necessarily so.[7] Only religious conversion, not the search for rational consensus, can change that.[8] The only possible unity of *Wissenschaft* is an eschatological one:

> Until all God's children are religiously united in his Kingdom of Peace, there is no possibility of unified science. Pluralism in the academy, running along the fault-lines of religious divergence, cannot be eliminated.[9]

---

3   Wolterstorff, *OCL*, 68–69.

4   This is so in relation to its models of theorising and its heuristics. For Wolterstorff as a product, member and critic of the Neo-Calvinist movement, see R. J. Mouw, "Dutch Calvinist Philosophical Influences in North America", *Calvin Theological Journal* 24/1 (April 1989) 104–108.

5   Wolterstorff, *OCL*, 56. It is interesting to note that Wolterstorff views the provocative nature of this claim as being restricted to non-theological scholarship. However, the quest for confessionally neutral theological scholarship was at the heart of much critical biblical scholarship. Thus it too came under the aegis of the supposed neutrality of scholarship. For these claims and their critical evaluation, see above (Chapter 1, A.).

6   Wolterstorff, *OCL*, 56–58.

7   For the significance of these claims in Neo-Calvinist philosophy, see Mouw, 104–110; H. Hart, "A Theme from the Philosophy of Herman Dooyeweerd", *Faith and Philosophy* 5/3 (Jul 1988) 270–271, 275–276, 277–278.

8   Wolterstorff, *OCL*, 58.

9   Ibid., 56.

The specific formulations of meta-theories of science which accounted for this phenomenon were varied. Wolterstorff, however, refers specifically to the work of two notable exponents of Neo-Calvinist meta-theories, namely Abraham Kuyper and Herman Dooyeweerd.[10] While he also briefly refers to the work of others in the movement, for the purpose of this discussion I shall limit myself to Kuyper and Dooyeweerd as the most significant representatives of first and second generation Neo-Calvinist meta-theories respectively. I will outline and critique Kuyper's and Dooyeweerd's theories of science, before presenting the salient points of Wolterstorff's departure from their views of science, leading to an outline of his overall meta-theory.

A.1. KUYPER'S TWO SCIENCES

The foundation of Kuyper's analysis of science is not an empirical examination of the nature of scientific theorising but a theological appraisal of the nature of the human subjects of scientific reflection.[11] There is no unity of human subjectivity, for there are two kinds of people, divided along inescapably religious lines, those whom he calls the "normalists" and the "abnormalists".[12] There are those who have been regenerated, begotten anew, enlightened, and those who have not.[13] Those who have been regenerated have experienced a fundamental change in their very being, including their noetic faculties, and are thus separated from those who have not experienced this transformation.[14] This separation cannot be overcome by human resources, unlike other differences that arise out of the inter-subjective disunity of human community, for its cause lies *outside* the human subject in the will and action of the God who redeems.[15] Thus:

---

10 Wolterstorff, *OCL*, 58–66, 66–68.
11 Wolterstorff, *OCL*, 58–59. This, as Wolterstorff claims, can be seen clearly in Kuyper, *Principles*, II,iii,48, where he talks of the denial of his notion of "two kinds of science" as entailing a denial of the doctrine of regeneration. cf. A. Kuyper, *Lectures on Calvinism* (Grand Rapids: Eerdmans, 1931) 131–132, 133–136, 137; cf. G. A. Remelts, "The Christian Reformed Church and Science, 1900–1930: An Evangelical Alternative to the Fundamentalist and Modernist Responses to Science", *Fides et Historia* 21/1 (Jan 1989) 69–71.
12 Kuyper, *Principles*, II,iii,48; *Lectures*, 136–138; cf. Wolterstorff, *OCL*, 59. "Normalist" is a term he uses in reference to the non-Christian rejection of the existence and effects of sin in the objective world and subjective human consciousness, while "abnormalist" refers to the avowal of these, and related notions, in Christian views. See Kuyper, *Lectures*, 132–133.
13 Kuyper, *Principles*, II,iii,48; Wolterstorff, *OCL*, 59.
14 Ibid.
15 Ibid.

We speak none too emphatically, therefore, when we speak of two kinds of people. Both are human, but one is inwardly different from the other, and consequently feels a different content arising from his consciousness; thus they face the cosmos from different points of view, and are impelled by different impulses. And the fact that there are two kinds of *people* occasions of necessity the fact of two kinds of human *life* and *consciousness* of life, and of two kinds of *science*; for which reason the idea of the *unity of science*, taken in its absolute sense, implies the denial of the fact of palingenesis, and therefore from principle leads to the rejection of the Christian religion.[16]

However, even as there is commonality in the two kinds of people, inasmuch as they are all human, so there is commonality in the two kinds of science.[17] This is necessarily so, in Kuyper's view, for science is the product of human subjectivity, and acquires its nature from the nature of the ones who generate it.[18] This accounts for the common features as well as the distinctives of the two kinds of science. The distinctives, as he has said, arise from the fact that there are two kinds of people, regenerate and unregenerate. The commonalities arise from the fact that they are both people, and regeneration, despite its radical comprehensiveness, effects no change in some human faculties, notably the senses and "the formal processes of thought" by which we apprehend entailments.[19] These, he believed, while affected by sin, are capable of correction "through the discourse of the community of scholars".[20] This common ground means that there can be discussion of why one group of scholars diverges from the common starting point, as well as its limiting unnecessary polemics between the two groups.[21] There is, therefore, a common basis for the two kinds of science in empirical facts and reason, but as soon as they go beyond these very basic levels, the two kinds of science diverge.[22]

---

16   Kuyper, *Principles*, II,iii,48, italics in original.

17   Kuyper, *Principles*, II,iii,49; Wolterstorff, *OCL*, 60; Marsden, 251.

18   Kuyper, *Principles*, II,i,39; Wolterstorff, *OCL*, 60; Marsden, 251. Remelts, 69, 71, argues that this founding of his meta-theory of science upon a given understanding of the human subject is a function of Kuyper's roots in German Idealist philosophy. For a similar idea in Dooyeweerd's thought, see H. Dooyeweerd, *A New Critique of Theoretical Reason* (3 vol; Philadelphia: Presbyterian and Reformed, 1953; vol 1) 20, 99; L. Kalsbeek *Contours of a Christian philosophy: An introduction to Herman Dooyeweerd's thought* (ed. B. and J. Zylstra; Toronto: Wedge, 1975) 47–51.

19   Kuyper, *Principles*, II,iii,49; Wolterstorff, *OCL*, 60.

20   Wolterstorff, *OCL*, 60; cf. Kuyper, *Principles*, II,ii,48.

21   Kuyper, *Principles*, II,iii,49.

22   Kuyper, *Principles*, II,iii,49; Wolterstorff, *OCL*, 60–61; cf. Remelts, 68.

This divergence, according to Kuyper, is as radical as the psychological divergence which gives rise to it. The workings of observation and reason fall far short of what is required in the development of any given *Wissenschaft*, and thus two kinds of science are inevitable, for once we leave the realm of observation and reason we enter the realm of divergence.[23] This is found even in the natural sciences, for though they have a more significant empirical component than do the social sciences, nonetheless the religious antithesis is operative, for these *Wissenschaften* too require the exercise of investigative skills and conviction in order to develop theories.[24] The result is two kinds of science, totally distinct from, sundered from, and hostile to each other, corresponding to the two kinds of scientific agents.[25] They are like grafted and ungrafted branches on a fruit tree: once they part, there is no possibility of their joining, nor of their producing common fruit.[26] From thereon their growth and products, though sharing common roots and trunk, are totally separate, distinct and unique.[27] Once this stage is reached, in which the two kinds of science diverge, "there is no hope of the rational adjudication of disagreements".[28] Rather, the two scientific camps are arrayed against each other like warring armies.[29] The conflict, then, is not between *faith* and *science*, for all scholarly investigation requires faith in something, if just the dependability of our senses and reasoning, but between two incompatible scientific enterprises each articulating a different faith stance.[30]

The similarities between Kuyper and Kuhnian views of science are striking. The two types of science have different starting points, have different sets of presuppositions derived from different sources and run in different directions.[31] They see things and do things differently, as a result of their different presuppositions and constitutions.[32] With the exception of their common basis in observation and reason,[33] polemics between the two

---

[23] Kuyper, *Principles*, II,iii,49; Wolterstorff, *OCL*, 61.
[24] Ibid.
[25] Kuyper, *Lectures*, 136–138; *Principles*, II,iii,49; cf. Marsden, 251.
[26] Kuyper, *Principles*, II,iii,49.
[27] Kuyper, *Principles*, II,iii,49; cf. Marsden, 251.
[28] Wolterstorff, *OCL*, 61; cf. Kuyper, *Principles*, II,ii,49, 50; *Lectures*, 133–136.
[29] Wolterstorff, *OCL*, 61; cf. Kuyper, *Principles*, II,ii,49, 50; *Lectures*, 133–136.
[30] Kuyper, *Lectures*, 131–133; *Principles*, II,ii,46; cf. Marsden, 248.
[31] Kuyper, *Principles*, II,iii,49; cf. Wolterstorff, *OCL*, 63–64; Marsden, 251; Remelts, 69.
[32] Kuyper, *Principles*, II,iii,49; cf. Wolterstorff, *OCL*, 63–64.
[33] This common basis is denied by Kuhn and Feyerabend by virtue of the theory-dependence of observation statements. See above (Chapter 2, A.3.).

groups of scientists is pointless.[34] Indeed, Kuyper asserts that the proponents of one kind of science will deny the title of true science to those who operate within the rival system.[35] There is no possibility of a rational consensus arising out of discourse between proponents of rival systems. Indeed, given that each regards its own *Wissenschaft* as being true, and therefore necessarily all others are seen as being false, it will claim that there is only *one* science – theirs.[36] Thus there will and must be a "stand-off in persuasion and rationality".[37]

This, however, is a *rational* stand-off, for both sets of scientists are conducting their science in a manner consistent with the rules of their own science.[38] Neither Christians nor non-Christians are obliged to surrender their beliefs in the face of disagreement across the boundaries of the two kinds of science: they are equally justified in holding the beliefs they do.[39] Kuyper states:

> He, who subjectively looks upon his inner being and objectively upon the world around him as normal, *cannot* but speak as he does, *cannot* reach a different result, and would be *insincere* in his position as a scientific man, if he were to represent things in a different light. And therefore from a moral point of view, not thinking for the moment of such a man's responsibility in the judgement of God, nothing can be said against his personal stand-point...[40]

As Wolterstorff puts it: "What Kuyper sees when surveying science is a pluralism of contrary, but nevertheless rationally held, positions."[41]

There are a number of points on which Kuyper's account of science can be called into question, such as the clear distinction he makes between

---

34   Kuyper, *Principles*, II,iii,49; Wolterstorff, *OCL*, 61–62.
35   Kuyper, *Principles*, II,iii,49, 50. cf. the detailed discussion of the incommensurability thesis in Chapter 2 above.
36   Kuyper, *Principles*, II,iii,49; Wolterstorff, *OCL*, 62.
37   Wolterstorff, *OCL*, 62.
38   Ibid.
39   Wolterstorff, *OCL*, 62. He notes that there is obviously a different notion of rationality to the classical foundationalist one operative here. Indeed Kuyper's views, inasmuch as they reflect elements adopted by Wolterstorff in his meta-theory, are entirely consistent with the model of rationality developed in Chapter 3 above. For the inescapable – and justifiably so – plurality of science and its solution only in the final judgement of God in the eschaton, see Kuyper, *Lectures*, 136, 137–138, 141; *Principles*, II,iii,51. cf. Remelts, 70, who stresses the legitimacy of *Christian science* in Kuyper's view.
40   Kuyper, *Lectures*, 136.
41   Wolterstorff, *OCL*, 62.

the observational and theoretical,[42] and the idea that the communal pursuit of science removes the distortions of observation and reason resulting from our subjectivity.[43] The central issue, however, is the nature and function of the religious antithesis which Kuyper sees as central to the idea of "two sciences".[44] It is this core component of Kuyper's theory that Wolterstorff claims is unsatisfactory.[45] While Kuyper repeatedly stresses the *fact* that the religious antithesis gives rise to a scholarly antithesis, he does not analyse this supposed fact of scholarship, but merely presents a plethora of metaphors for it.[46] There is no discussion of *how* the religious antithesis influences scholarship, nor is there any support evinced for the claim that this influence *must* give rise to a scholarly antithesis.[47] Despite this, while there were attempts made to rescue the antithesis of science from apparent empirical contradictions by arguing that neither Christians nor non-Christians are consistent in theorising in line with their religious convictions, the fundamental thesis that two kinds of people of necessity produce two kinds of science remained uncontested by Kuyper and his followers.[48]

The reason for this adherence to the doctrine of "two people – two sciences" is, Wolterstorff claims, a function of the "religious totalism" of

---

42   This is noted in passing by Wolterstorff, *OCL*, 63. For the theory-dependence of observation statements, see above (Chapter 1, B.2.).

43   This is noted in passing by Wolterstorff, *OCL*, 63. For a discussion of the (limited, but real) effects that different "paradigms" can have upon the very notion of what is reasonable and the nature and relevance of the "facts", see above (Chapter 2, B.2.). Kuyper does note in *Principles*, II,iii,49, that differences persist within the "two kinds of science" of Christian and non-Christian, thus accounting for the plurality of theories held to by Christian and non-Christian scholars, and the disputes that arise within these two bodies of scholarship, but he does not recognise the role that beliefs can have in determining "facts" and "rationality" in theorising.

44   Wolterstorff, *OCL*, 63. cf. Remelts, 71–74, where he notes that Dooyeweerd follows Kuyper's more radical line regarding the nature of the anthesis. He also notes another tradition arising out of the thought of Herman Bavinck which was more irenic in nature.

45   Wolterstorff, *OCL*, 63. In passing it is interesting to note Wolterstorff's phrasing of this criticism. It is, he says "at the very core, not somewhere out in the periphery of details" that Kuyper's theory is unsatisfactory. Here, I think, Wolterstorff is implicitly adopting a Lakatosian model of the structure of theories or research programs in his analysis of Kuyper.

46   Wolterstorff, *OCL*, 63–64. Note the passages he cites there from Kuyper, *Principles*, II,ii,49, 50, 51, in support of this contention, as well as *Lectures*, 136–138.

47   Wolterstorff, *OCL*, 64.

48   Wolterstorff, *OCL*, 64–65. For support of this contention from Kuyper, see *Lectures*, 133, 134, 138; *Principles*, II,iii,49. In the latter passages he also cites the popularity of "detail-study", with its more assured results and lesser influence of the antithesis, as occasioning an apparent lack of bifurcation in science. For similar arguments in Dooyeweerd's thought, see Dooyeweerd, *New Critique (I)*, 523–524; Kalsbeek, 142–150.

the Neo-Calvinist movement.[49] This entails the notion that "one's whole life must be lived in obedience to God-in-Christ, that faith must penetrate all."[50] As Christians we are called to obey all the commands of God, to serve nothing but God. The Neo-Calvinists interpret this to mean that "all life is to consist of obeying the commands of God... all life is to consist of service to God."[51] Underlying this is a tendency to deny any commonality between Christian and non-Christian, and thus to deny that there is anything in the non-Christian's life or thought that is rooted in a common human nature rather than idolatry.[52] Indeed, Kuyper has been criticised by some later Neo-Calvinists on just this issue: he is, they say, guilty of dualism in dividing human faculties into indigenous capacities and those which arise from regeneration.[53] Based on this view of human life, the claim is made that all of life is religion, it consists either in obedience or disobedience to the commands of God, and thus there must be two kinds of science, lest we be guilty of dualism and the denial of the fundamentally religious nature of all of human life.[54] While this goes beyond Kuyper, it serves to explain why his central thesis of "two kinds of people, two kinds of science" was accepted almost uncritically by later Neo-Calvinists.[55]

A.2. DOOYEWEERD AND THE REDUCTIONISM OF IDOLATRY

There were two main strategies adopted by second generation Neo-Calvinists to demonstrate the link between religion and scientific enquiry, in line with the notion of "two kinds of science": world-view, and the reductionism of idolatry, both of which are prefigured in Kuyper, and consist of an articulation of inchoate suggestions in his writings.[56] These

---

[49] Wolterstorff, *OCL*, 65.

[50] Wolterstorff, *OCL*, 65. This contention is supported by Mouw, 96, 97–98.

[51] Wolterstorff, *OCL*, 65.

[52] Wolterstorff, *OCL*, 65–66; cf. Mouw, 97, 103, re the significance of sin in Neo-Calvinist epistemology and the lack of common ground even in the notion of common grace.

[53] Wolterstorff, *OCL*, 66.

[54] Wolterstorff, *OCL*, 66; cf. Dooyeweerd, *New Critique (I)*, 99, 542–543; Kalsbeek, 46, 173; Remelts, 71. For this idea prefigured in Kuyper, see *Lectures*, 133, 134, 135.

[55] Wolterstorff, *OCL*, 66. An interesting sociological, as opposed to philosophical, explanation for the tenacity of the antithesis in Neo-Calvinist thought is proffered by Mouw, 115–117. This, of course, does not invalidate the philosophical roots of the antithesis: they are compatible explanations.

[56] See Kuyper, *Lectures*, 133, 134, for the idea of world- and life-view, and of the unity of this being tantamount to a different faith-stance (hence idolatry) on the part of the non-Christian scholar. The idea of these being basically Kuyperian notions is supported by Mouw, 106.

are not exclusive options, as can be seen by Dooyeweerd's adoption of both strategies.[57] The first strategy argues that all human beings have a world-view, or "mind",[58] which shapes all their practices and beliefs, including in the realm of scholarship.[59] Dooyeweerd's notion of *ground-motive* is, Wolterstorff argues, best understood within the overall world-view approach.[60] According to Wolterstorff:

> A particular ground-motive is the fundamental dimension of how those who share the world-view see reality, and a basic determinant of their action – it is both motif and motive.[61]

According to Dooyeweerd all philosophies have such a ground motive, expressed in its *wetsidee*,[62] which, regardless of the philosopher's recognition of its existence, shapes and governs the philosophical system.[63] This *wetsidee* is derived from that system's adoption of a transcendent *Archimedean point of departure*, and its correlative centre and organising principle which shape and express the associated world-view.[64] It is the *wetsidee* of a philosophy, and its related ground motive, which are the characteristic and determinative features of the world-view embodied and articulated in a given philosophical system.[65]

---

57   H. Dooyeweerd, *A New Critique of Theoretical Reason*, vol 1 [from here on *New Critique (I)*], 93–99, on *ground motive*; cf. Wolterstorff, *OCL*, 66–68; Kalsbeek, 69–70.

58   The latter is the formulation of W. H. Jellema, Wolterstorff's former teacher. See Wolterstorff, *OCL*, 66, 67 n. 4; "Teaching for Justice", *Making Higher Education Christian*, ed. J. Carpenter and L. Shipps (Grand Rapids: Eerdmans, 1987) 205–206.

59   Wolterstorff, *OCL*, 66.

60   Wolterstorff, *OCL*, 67; cf. Mouw, 106–107; Remelts, 74.

61   Wolterstorff, *OCL*, 67; cf. J. Douma, *Another Look at Dooyeweerd* (Winnipeg: Premier, 1976) 44.

62   Dooyeweerd, *New Critique (I)*, 93, suggests that *cosmonomic Idea* is the best English translation of the Dutch term, which literally means "law-idea", for "law" in English has a juridical flavour which would distort what he means by *wetsidee*; cf. Kalsbeek, 69.

63   Dooyeweerd, *New Critique (I)*, 93–99; Kalsbeek, 69.

64   Dooyeweerd, *New Critique (I)*, 7–11, 20–21, 57, 82–93, 501–506; Kalsbeek, 56–57, 62–63; R. D. Knudsen, "The Idea of Christian Scientific Endeavour in the thought of Herman Dooyeweerd", *Philosophia Reformanda: Reflections on the Philosophy of Herman Dooyeweerd* (R. Knudsen; 1971) 3, 4, 6; R. D. Knudsen, "Dooyeweerd's Philosophical Method", *Philosophia Reformanda: Reflections on the Philosophy of Herman Dooyeweerd* (R. Knudsen; 1971) 14–15.

65   Dooyeweerd, *New Critique (I)*, discusses the notion of world-view and its relation to philosophical systems, and in 169–495, identifies a number of different ground motives in Western thought and expounds their roots and impact upon various world-views. See also Knudsen, "Philosophical Method" 14, 16, for the connection between *wetsidee* and world-view. For a similar perspective on the recent history of biblical interpretation, adopting

The idea behind the world-view, or *Weltanschauung* theory is that, out of the total set of beliefs and affects that a person has, we can extract those beliefs which make up her world-view.[66] These are the beliefs which provide the impetus for a given form of life and which shape the form of that life.[67] Now there is no real problem with the idea of continua of beliefs of various complexity, firmness, and centrality.[68] For the notion of world-view to be a useful tool in the analysis of thought patterns and theorising, however, the idea of world-view needs to be carefully articulated. Just which of a person's beliefs and values constitute her world-view? Are world-views shared by all members of a given religious, scientific or social community, and if so, how are those world-views communicated, how are people inducted into a world-view, and how does a person's belonging to more than one community affect her personal world-view?[69] How does a change in one belief influence the world-view, and when is such change sufficient to be considered a change in the world-view itself? How, specifically, does a world-view influence theorising, and how can this be demonstrated? These have proven to be extraordinarily difficult questions, leading to the suspicion that world-view (or *Weltanschauung*) analysis is of little value in elucidating the patterns of scientific theorising, and may well be a false line.[70] Wolterstorff states:

> My own judgement is that this line of thought, at least as developed so far, constitutes little advance on Kuyper... the person who adopts this approach assumes the obligation of explaining and refining the concept of a *worldview*, and that has proved to be no easy task... I myself doubt, however, that any benefit is to be gained from refining the vague notion

---

Dooyeweerd's notions of two sciences, and the influence of philosophical stances on hermeneutical strategies adopted in different interpretive schools, see Gruenler, *Meaning and Understanding*.

66 Wolterstorff, *OCL*, 67.
67 Wolterstorff, *OCL*, 67. cf. Dooyeweerd's idea of the function of *wetsidee* and ground motives in philosophy: Dooyeweerd, *New Critique (I)*, v, vi, 93–99; Douma *Another Look*, 44; Kalsbeek, 46, 53–54, 69–70.
68 Wolterstorff, *OCL*, 67.
69 That these ideas are central in world-view theories of scholarship can be seen by reference to the work of Jellema, for which see: Wolterstorff, "Teaching for Justice", 205–206, where he sees Jellema as arguing that everyone adopts the mind of a *civitas*, a particular world-view accepted by adherents to a specific faith community. For this idea of the communal nature of world-view in relation to the philosophy of *wetsidee*, see Knudsen, "Philosophical Method", 16.
70 See, e.g., Shapere, "The Paradigm Concept", 53; Suppe, "Introduction", 217–221.

of worldview so that we can pick out that cluster of beliefs that constitutes his worldview, or so that we can answer all these questions about the similarities and differences between worldviews.[71]

If the Kuyperian notion of "two kinds of people, two kinds of science" is to be used as the basis for a model of science, therefore, another formulation is required.

Such a formulation was presented in the compatible idea of faith and idolatry as the organising principles, or *wetsidee*, of the two kinds of science.[72] The central claim is that people have an irresistible impulse to organise their lives and views of reality around something – be it God, a philosophical system, or anything else in the created order – which then becomes their absolute.[73] If God is taken as absolute, then this impulse is *faith*; if anything else is substituted, then this impulse is *idolatry*.[74] Only from the standpoint of faith is reductionism avoidable, it is claimed, for otherwise some dimension of the created order becomes the clue to the understanding of the whole, with the result that the whole is reduced to that part, or a function of it.[75] Indeed, Dooyeweerd claimed that true knowledge of God was necessary for true knowledge of the cosmos, true

---

[71] Wolterstorff, *OCL*, 66–67.

[72] Wolterstorff, *OCL*, 67. That these notions are compatible is seen in the close association in Jellema's thought between the adoption of the mind of a given *civitas*, and the answers people give to the question of the identity of God, an issue which lies at the heart of the structure of beliefs of a given world-view or mind. See Wolterstorff, "Teaching for Justice", 205–206.

[73] Dooyeweerd, *New Critique (I)*, v, vi, 20–21, 46–48, 57, 103–104, 129–138, 149–150, 508–527; H. Dooyeweerd, *In the Twilight of Western Thought: Studies in the Pretended Autonomy of Philosophical Thought* (Nutley: Craig, 1975) 20–21; cf. Hart, "Philosophy of Dooyeweerd", 274–276; Kalsbeek, 46, 49–51, 54, 56–60, 109–113; Knudsen, "Christian Scientific Endeavour", 4, 6; "Philosophical Method", 14–15; Wolterstorff, *OCL*, 67.

[74] Wolterstorff, *OCL*, 67. Strictly speaking, they are both applications of the faith principle. It is just that in idolatry faith is directed to the creation rather than the Creator. See Dooyeweerd, *New Critique (I)*, 61–68; Kalsbeek, 132–136; H. Hart, "The Articulation of Belief: A Link Between Rationality and Commitment", *Rationality in the Calvinian Tradition*, ed. H. Hart, *et al* (Boston: University Press of America, 1983) n. 9, pp. 217, 225, 230. This idea of the "faith principle" as a specific function derived from the heart is stringently criticised by Douma, *Another Look*, 22–24, 41–45.

[75] Dooyeweerd, *New Critique (I)*, 35–51, 46–48, 61–68, 99–100, 103–104, 331–337, 501–506, 542–543; *In the Twilight of Western Thought*, 35–51; Kalsbeek, 69–71, 109–113, 132–136; Knudsen, "Christian Scientific Endeavour", 4; "Philosophical Method", 13–14, 17–18; Wolterstorff, *OCL*, 68. This is so regardless of whether the idol is an unsophisticated deification of a natural force as in animism, or a sophisticated cultural form of idolatry in which the ground of faith is reason, science, or whatever.

Wissenschaft.[76] This claim is related to his acceptance of the Kuyperian notion that the body of scholarship produced by a given scholar is a function of his subjectivity, and thus reflects the nature of his subjectivity.[77] He argues that the transcendent condition for knowledge is the selfhood, the heart, the religious root of the activity of knowing, and thus all human experience, including knowing, is determined by its orientation towards or away from God.[78] True knowledge of the cosmos is thus bound to true self knowledge, and given that true self-knowledge is impossible outside of the knowledge of God, true knowledge of God is required for true knowledge of the cosmos.[79]

The basis of the antithesis between Christian and non-Christian scholarship is clear. The Christian's life and thought is rooted in and controlled by the sovereign agency of God in the Holy Spirit, whereas the non-Christian's is pervaded by his alienation from God.[80] The antithesis, then, is rooted in the "heart", understood as the origin of the issues of life, that which governs the direction of faith.[81] All of life is the product of the "heart", the source of the inner life, and therefore the orientation of the heart pervades all of life.[82]

> Dooyeweerd's philosophy stands or falls with the conviction that the spiritual antithesis has marked philosophical thinking itself during the course of history, and therefore the Christian philosopher must discern between Christian and non-Christian ground motives which gave birth to various traditions of thought.[83]

---

[76] H. Dooyeweerd, *A New Critique of Theoretical Reason* (3 vol; Philadelphia: Presbyterian and Reformed, 1955; vol 2) 562; cf. Kalsbeek, 175; Knudsen, "Christian Scientific Endeavour", 5. For a similar claim in relation to biblical interpretation, arising, I believe, from the adoption of a meta-theory analogous to Dooyeweerd's, see Gruenler, *Meaning and Understanding*, esp xi–xviii, 60–61, 64–71, 168–175.

[77] See above, this chapter, n. 18. For a recent presentation of this view along the lines of Dooyeweerd, see Hart, "The Articulation of Belief", 220.

[78] Dooyeweerd, *A New Critique of Theoretical Reason*, vol 2 [from here on *New Critique (II)*], 542–565; *New Critique (I)*, 5–6; Kalsbeek, 173.

[79] Dooyeweerd, *New Critique (II)*, 560–563; Kalsbeek, 175. Dooyeweerd specifically includes recognition of our own sinfulness in true self-knowledge, an idea which clearly entails some apprehension of the gospel.

[80] Dooyeweerd, *New Critique (I)*, 99, 523–524; Kalsbeek, 45–46.

[81] Dooyeweerd, *New Critique (I)*, 61–68; Kalsbeek, 132; Knudsen, "Philosophical Method", 14–15.

[82] Dooyeweerd, *New Critique (I)*, 99; Kalsbeek, 46.

[83] Kalsbeek, 46.

These ground motives are essentially religious in nature: they are rooted in faith or idolatry.[84] It is this understanding of the antithesis which gives rise to Dooyeweerd's claim that there is no possibility of a synthesis between Christian and non-Christian philosophy.[85]

This model has the advantage of specifying what features of a scientific theory we are to look for in order to discover the operation of non-Christian, idolatrous science – namely reductionism.[86] However, it has certain crucial flaws. It illegitimately limits the impact of religious beliefs upon science to the phenomenon of reductionism, when many other factors are at work in connecting a non-Christian scholar's theorising with her underlying commitments.[87] It also makes the universal claim that "*whenever* scholars fail to take God as their absolute, their scholarship will display the tell-tale structure of being illicitly reductionist".[88] This, however, seems unreasonable, for there are many cases in which the operation and results of science do not show evidence of reductionism.[89] And despite their commitment to this idea of the relation between religion and science: "Neither Dooyeweerd, who especially embraced and elaborated this approach, nor anyone else has ever succeeded in showing otherwise."[90]

A.3. WOLTERSTORFF'S REJECTION OF NEO-CALVINIST META-THEORIES

These reflections led Wolterstorff to doubt the central tenets of the Neo-Calvinist meta-theory. The first of these is the whole idea of there being "two kinds of science". The Neo-Calvinists claimed that *faithful* Christian scholarship must always be *different* to non-Christian scholarship, once the bases of sense and reason were left behind.[91]

> But surely this is flagrantly false to the experience of all of us. All of us who are Christian scholars find ourselves agreeing with our non-

---

84   Dooyeweerd, *New Critique* (I) v, 61–68; Kalsbeek, 54, 132–136.
85   Dooyeweerd, *New Critique* (I) v, vi, 114–124; Kalsbeek, 53–55. This is also found in his claim that the knowledge of God is required for true knowledge of the cosmos.
86   Wolterstorff, *OCL*, 69; cf. Dooyeweerd, *New Critique (I)*, 46–48, 103–104; *In the Twilight of Western Culture*, 20–21; Kalsbeek, 109–111; Knudsen, "Christian Scientific Endeavour", 4; "Philosophical Method", 13–14, 17–18.
87   Wolterstorff, *OCL*, 69.
88   Wolterstorff, *OCL*, 69; cf. Kalsbeek, 111–113.
89   Wolterstorff, *OCL*, 69.
90   Ibid.
91   Wolterstorff, *OCL*, 69; cf. Dooyeweerd, *New Critique (I)* 114–124.

Christian colleagues on vastly more than the deliverances of the senses and "reason". And where we do disagree on matters other than such deliverances, it is our experience that there often exist rational methods of adjudication. It is not true that all each party can do is declare, Here I stand.[92]

The reason for this is that it is not the case, as assumed in the Neo-Calvinist tradition, that all of the unregenerated, but redeemable, faculties of a non-Christian scholar will produce results unacceptable to the regenerated Christian scholar.[93] This can be seen by examining the actual cases of disagreement amongst scholars in a given *Wissenschaft*. Once we set aside the deliverances of the senses and reason, we can discover that consensus and dissension do not follow "the fault lines of the break between Christian and non-Christian".[94]

This means that, not only is the Neo-Calvinist diagnosis of the cause of dissension flawed, but so is the underlying anthropology.[95] It is not the case that all fallen but unredeemed faculties are misleading: Christian epistemology, in science and in general, needs to be cognisant of the effects of the created as well as the fallen nature of non-Christian scholars.[96] Many changes in beliefs, many human actions do not arise from a decision to serve God or something else, they arise out of dispositions and habits.[97] Of course, many of our habits and dispositions are distorted by sin, and where we discover this is the case, we are obliged to so govern our dispositions as to overcome this distortion to the best of our ability.[98] However, this does not mean that the disposition is eliminated, rather it is

---

[92] Wolterstorff, *OCL*, 69. This bears striking resemblance to many of the criticisms levelled against Kuhn's notion of the incommensurability of paradigms. This is not surprising, for in reality the Neo-Calvinist notion is a limited precursor of Kuhnian views, as I have mentioned above (this chapter, A.1.). For a detailed critique of the "Incommensurability Thesis", see above (Chapter 2, B.2.).

[93] Wolterstorff, *OCL*, 69. This, according to Mouw, 108, means that Wolterstorff would be seen by many Neo-Calvinists as down-playing the noetic effects of sin. That this is not the case can be seen by examining his discussion of this matter. See above (Chapter 3, A.4.) though note my critical expansions of his thought, and below (this chapter, C.2.).

[94] Wolterstorff, *OCL*, 69.

[95] Ibid., 71–72.

[96] See the comments in Mouw, 108, and above (Chapter 3, A.1., A.4., B.3.) This view is endorsed by Klapwijk ("Rationality", 100–110) specifically in terms of the operation of common grace.

[97] Wolterstorff, *OCL*, 72. This is clearly related to his overall epistemology, for which see Chapter 3 above.

[98] Wolterstorff, *OCL*, 71–72; and see above (Chapter 3, A.4.).

altered.⁹⁹ Many others of our dispositions are not, and need not, be modified. They function quite well as they are with appropriate governing for both Christian and non-Christian.¹⁰⁰ This overall epistemological perspective adequately explains the lack of clear "fault lines" in science. It is a function, not of the inconsistency or infidelity of Christian or non-Christian scholars, but of their sharing of common belief-dispositions. Such a view lets "the differences fall where they may", rather than forcing them to follow lines of Christian versus non-Christian scholarship.¹⁰¹ It allows us to see that not all non-Christians are naturalists or humanists, that there are "many 'kinds' of science, not just two".¹⁰² It also allows us to recognise the real similarities and commonalities between Christian and non-Christian scholarship, and thus to "balance suspicion with gratitude".¹⁰³

A further area of difficulty in Neo-Calvinist meta-theories is that they consider that it is only legitimate for faith to influence science, and not *vice versa*.¹⁰⁴ Thus:

> A crucial failing in Kuyper and many of his followers is that they overlook the fact – or resist acknowledging the fact – that developments in scholarship sometimes lead persons to alter their religious convictions, and that sometimes at least this is fully justified, even obligatory.¹⁰⁵

This, Wolterstorff believes, is due to the Neo-Calvinist idea that science is a product of human subjects.¹⁰⁶ Thus, if there are two kinds of subjects

---

99 Wolterstorff, *OCL*, 72.

100 Ibid.

101 Ibid., 70.

102 Ibid. He cites here the possibility of faithful Jewish and Muslim scholarship which, while not Christian, are clearly not humanist or naturalist, and may not in fact be *idolatrous*.

103 Wolterstorff, *OCL*, 70. It is interesting to note Kuyper's endorsement of the value of much non-Christian scholarship for Christians, as a result of the workings of common grace, *Lectures*, 121–126, and the tension between this and his notion of "two kinds of science". For this tension in Kuyper's meta-theory of science, see Klapwijk, "Rationality", 98–99, 101–110, where he presents criticisms of Kuyper similar to those of Wolterstorff.

104 See Hart, "The Articulation of Belief", 235–237, for a recent presentation of this view. Remelts, 66, who accepts this general approach, notes that at times *minor* changes in theology were permissible. But this was rare, and did not ultimately challenge the *conceptual* primacy, even inviolability, of central theological tenets, cf. Remelts, 67. As Wolterstorff argues, *RWBR*, 94–96, this openness to minor change may have been a forced violation of the principle of the pretheoretical nature of faith. See below (this chapter, B.2.).

105 Wolterstorff, *OCL*, 72.

106 Ibid., 72–73, and see above (this chapter, A.1., A.2.) for this in the thought of Kuyper and Dooyeweerd.

engaging in science, there must be two kinds of science produced by them.[107] The emphasis was on the way the self influences culture and science, despite their recognition of a created order which we are to discover, and to which we must be conformed, almost ignoring the impact that culture, science and society have on the self.[108] But:

> Science is not solely an expression of the self, however. It is likewise the outcome of the impact of the world on us, coupled with the impact of the social practice of science. Self, world, social practice: it is from the interplay of these three that science emerges.[109]

It is for these reasons that Wolterstorff chose to abandon the Neo-Calvinist approach to science in order to develop his own.[110] The key idea for Wolterstorff is that Christian scholars are called to be *faithful*, rather than *different* in their scholarship.[111] This faithfulness will on balance produce *distinctive* scholarship, though it need not.[112] At times there will be little real difference between faithful Christian and non-Christian scholarship.[113] This, however, presents no problem to his view for, while distinctiveness will be a general feature of faithful Christian science, "difference must be a consequence, not an aim... Difference is not a condition of fidelity – though, to say it once more, it will often be a consequence."[114] It is this notion of *faithful Christian scholarship* that Wolterstorff expounds in his meta-theory of *Wissenschaft*.

---

[107] Wolterstorff, *OCL*, 73.

[108] Ibid.

[109] Wolterstorff, *OCL*, 73. I will look at Wolterstorff's idea of the social practice of science in Chapter 5.

[110] Wolterstorff, *OCL*, 68–69. Of course, this does not mean he abandons the idea of the control function of religious beliefs that was at the heart of the Neo-Calvinist model.

[111] Wolterstorff, *OCL*, 69, 70, in clear contrast to the Neo-Calvinist belief that faithful Christian *Wissenschaft must be different* to non-Christian *Wissenschaft*.

[112] Wolterstorff, *OCL*, 70; "Faith and Philosophy", 31. For the clear distinction between this and the Kuyperian line, see Mouw, 108.

[113] Wolterstorff, *OCL*, 70.

[114] Wolterstorff, *OCL*, 70; cf. *OCL*, 69; "Scholarship and Conviction", 48. For an insightful application of this to political philosophy, see Wolterstorff, "From Liberal to Plural", 201–215; and his engagement with the liberal alternative of Robert Audi in, R. Audi and N. Wolterstorff, *Religion in the Public Square*. For its implications for theological scholarship, see N. Wolterstorff, "Is it Possible and Desirable for Theologians to Recover from Kant?", *Modern Theology* 14/1 (Jan 1998) 1–18.

B. Wolterstorff's Meta-Theory

As we come to examine Wolterstorff's meta-theory, it is vital to recognise that it is by no means restricted to the physical sciences – it is not a theory of the philosophy of science – nor is it restricted to *Wissenschaft* – it is not just a theory of *academic* rationality.[115] It is a model which has bearing on all human theorising, for all such actions, be they "scientific" or not, share essential features in common. He presents no definition of what constitutes a theory other than that it makes general assertions about the properties of, or relationships among, the entities in its scope.[116] What he does claim is that the practice of theorising is not limited to the physical sciences, or even *Wissenschaft*, for theorising is a common practice in every-day life.[117] It is not even the case that *Wissenschaft* is characterised by a particular *kind* of theory, for there is a constant movement of theories out of *Wissenschaft* into everyday life, and *vice versa*.[118] Nor can *Wissenschaft* be seen as performing unique actions with respect to theories, for in everyday life people devise and weigh theories, even as they do in *Wissenschaft*.[119] The practice of *Wissenschaft* is not a unique discipline, sundered in kind from all other forms of human life. Rather:

> Science and ordinary life can be viewed as on a continuum with respect to the presence of theories and with respect to the actions performed on those theories. What is eminently characteristic of science is the use of theories to suggest and guide research programs. But on reflection even this can be best seen as making science different only in degree from ordinary life.[120]

---

[115] Wolterstorff, *RWBR*, 64–65.
[116] Wolterstorff, *RWBR*, 63–64; *C&T*, 118–119.
[117] Wolterstorff, *RWBR*, 64.
[118] Ibid.
[119] Ibid., 64–65.
[120] Wolterstorff, *RWBR*, 65. Indeed, Wolterstorff clearly rejects the notions that there exist clear demarcations between science and other human activities, between the natural sciences and other *Wissenschaften*, for which see, "Privileged Access", 82–85; "Scholarship and Conviction", 36–41. In making such claims, Wolterstorff defies a significant tradition in the philosophy of science which sought to demonstrate both that science was unique, and in what ways it differed from non-scientific enterprises. See, for example, Popper, "Normal Science", 57–58, where he specifically states that theology is a non-scientific, and psychology and sociology are pre-scientific disciplines; I. Lakatos, "Introduction: Science and Pseudoscience", *Philosophical Papers, vol 1: The methodology of scientific research programmes*, ed. J. Worrall and G. Currie (Cambridge: Cambridge University Press, 1978) 1–7; *MSRP*, 173–177, for true science as characterised by progressive research programs; Kuhn, *SSR*, 10–22, for true science as characterised by a shared paradigm, and *SSR*, 23–34, for different sciences as sharing different paradigms. Similar views of the uniqueness of

B.1. BELIEFS AND THEORIES

Wolterstorff proceeds to present his model of how people go about weighing theories, despite the fact that he believes that scholars spend substantially less time weighing theories than they do in articulating them.[121] This he does because it illuminates principles that are applicable to other actions that are performed with respect to theories. They must be applied with care, however, recognising that they are different actions, and that beliefs may therefore function differently.[122] It is important to note that from here on he avoids the term "theorising", which he has used freely up to this point, on the grounds that it is too vague, and tends to conflate a number of distinct actions that can be performed with respect to a theory.[123] In the course of this analysis Wolterstorff deals with three distinct types of beliefs that operate in the process of theory-weighing: *data beliefs*, *data-background beliefs* and *control beliefs*. These will be examined in turn.

Data beliefs are beliefs one has about the entities within the scope of the theory which are taken to be data concerning those entities.[124] They are those beliefs with which a theory must be consistent if it is to be an acceptable theory.[125] It is important to stress that these are *beliefs* one has

---

science are found in Dooyeweerd, *In the Twilight of Western Thought*, 12–19; *New Critique (I)*, 38–44, 82–86; in relation to pre-theoretical thought; *New Critique (II)*, for the clear distinctions he makes between different types of science characterised by distinct methods, integrative centres, and so on; H. Dooyeweerd, *A New Critique of Theoretical Reason* (3 vol; Philadelphia: Presbyterian and Reformed, 1957; vol 3) for the application of this method to the social sciences and the structure of society. cf. Kalsbeek, 160–171; Knudsen, "Christian Scientific Endeavour", 1–2; "Philosophical Method", 10, for the uniqueness of theoretical thought, and Kalsbeek, 181–295; Knudsen, "Philosophical Method", 10, 13, 14, for the discussion of distinct spheres of existence and science. For a criticism of his approach, see Douma, *Another Look*, 58–65; Hart, "Philosophy of Dooyeweerd", 276.

121   Wolterstorff, *RWBR*, 65. The term "articulating theories" is taken from Kuhn and involves, amongst other things, making the theories more precise, engaging in research programs suggested by the theories, increasing the scope and precision of the data the theories cover, and so on. Wolterstorff cites Kuhn and Lakatos as supporting this claim. This notion is discussed in Chapter 5 below.

122   Note Wolterstorff, *RWBR*, 101–108.

123   Wolterstorff, *RWBR*, 65 n. 28. He does resume its use in Part 2, of *RWBR* and in *J&P*, 162–176, probably in part because it was written later, but mostly, I believe, because he is not concerned there with the actions that scholars perform on theories, but with a general heuristic strategy.

124   Wolterstorff, *RWBR*, 65; *C&T*, 119. From this point "Commitment and Theory" and Part One of *Reason Within the Bounds of Religion* are substantially the same, with the exception of some longer footnotes in *RWBR*, and so I shall cite only the latter work from here on.

125   Wolterstorff, *RWBR*, 65.

about the entities in the scope of the theory, not "brute facts".[126] One needs to make a decision to adopt these beliefs as data beliefs, but this decision is not based on foundations which thereby produce indubitable "facts", it is a true decision, an act of commitment.[127]

> If I am to weigh a theory's claim there is no option to my taking as data that which I find myself believing to be true. Confronted as we are with the fact that we lack a shared foundation each of us has no choice but 'to one's own self be true'.[128]

It must be recognised, however, that data beliefs are not the only beliefs by which a theory is measured, for otherwise no theory choice could be made in a great number of cases.[129] But they are crucial to the task of theory weighing:

> Now it happens repeatedly that more than one competing theory will be consistent with all that I take as data. My decision between them must be made on other grounds. Yet it remains true: there can be no weighing of theory with respect to what is claimed without taking as data some of one's beliefs about entities in the theory's scope.[130]

One can not examine a theory only in the light of what one takes to be the data, for one always brings along a "cloak of beliefs" which is impossible to strip off.[131] Some of these beliefs are known, others of them are unknown, all of them influence our weighing of theories.[132] Wolterstorff identifies just two types of these beliefs, though he does not thereby exclude others, one of which he labels *data-background beliefs*.[133] Data-

---

126 Wolterstorff, *RWBR*, 66. This is discussed further above (Chapter 1, B.2.).

127 Wolterstorff, *RWBR*, 66. It is worth noting that Wolterstorff has modified his ideas to restrict the role of volition and decisions in belief, as seen in his *CBGR?*; see Chapter 2 above for further discussion of this. In the light of this data beliefs may be more appropriately construed as the products of the triggering of belief-dispositions, rather than as the product of specific decisions. This would be consistent with what he goes on to say in *RWBR*, 66, about taking as data "that which I find myself believing to be true", this data then being the product of the corresponding disposition.

128 Wolterstorff, *RWBR*, 66.

129 Ibid.

130 Wolterstorff, *RWBR*, 66. In 65 n. 30, he notes that aesthetic qualities, by which I take him to mean such things as "beauty", "elegance", and "simplicity" are often important in weighing theories.

131 Wolterstorff, *RWBR*, 66, *OCL*, 75; "Scholarship and Conviction", 46.

132 Wolterstorff, *RWBR*, 67; *J&P*, 165.

133 Wolterstorff, *RWBR*, 67.

background beliefs are those beliefs which we must have in order to accept others of our beliefs as data.[134] "That which the scientist takes as data he does so because of his acceptance of an enormously complicated web of theory."[135] This web of theory includes theories about the reliability of one's senses, the functions and deliverances of instruments, and so on.[136] At the time in which a given theory is being weighed these theories are taken to be unproblematic, even though at some other time they may *be* the theory being weighed.[137]

For the purpose of Wolterstorff's analysis of theory weighing, the second component of the "cloak of beliefs" is more important, the beliefs he labels *control beliefs*.[138] These are those amongst our set of beliefs that determine what is an acceptable sort of theory on the matter under consideration.[139] These *control beliefs* deal with such things as the kind of logical or aesthetic structure and scope an acceptable theory must have, the range of entities which one may believe in, and so on.[140] In short, they deal with the acceptability of certain cognitive goals and standards and the methods of achieving them.[141] Control beliefs have two main functions: they lead us to *reject* some theories because they do not comport well with our control beliefs; and they lead us to *devise* theories which comport as well as possible with our control beliefs.[142] He cites, along with the (in)famous case of the Congregation of the Index's rejection of Copernican cosmology, several instances of scientific bodies and researchers accepting or rejecting theories on the basis of control beliefs in order to support his contention that this is usual in theory weighing.[143]

---

[134] Ibid.

[135] Ibid.

[136] Ibid. On this idea, see above (Chapter 1, B.2.).

[137] Wolterstorff, *RWBR*, 67, 69–70.

[138] Ibid., 67.

[139] Wolterstorff, *RWBR*, 67, *OCL*, 76; "Theology and Science", 98–99; "Scholarship and Conviction", 48.

[140] Wolterstorff, *RWBR*, 67–68. He notes in 69 n. 32 that the relationship that a given theory needs to have with the relevant data beliefs in order to be acceptable may be more stringent than simple logical consistency.

[141] Wolterstorff, *OCL*, 75, 76.

[142] Wolterstorff, *RWBR*, 68; *J&P*, 166. In *RWBR*, 68 n. 31, Wolterstorff notes that he can not define the notion of "comporting as well as possible with", though it is possible to determine when a theory does or does not do this.

[143] Wolterstorff, *RWBR*, 15–17 (the Copernican theory); 17–18 (initial rejection of Newton's Celestial Mechanics); 18–19, 68 (Ernst Mach's attempt to redefine physics); 68–69 (B. F. Skinner's behaviouristic psychology).

The consigning of such a significant role to control beliefs in theory weighing and devising constitutes a significant departure from traditional meta-theories such as are found in the history of the philosophy of science. For Wolterstorff does not accept the clear distinction that is normally made between the logic of discovery and of confirmation.[144] His reasons for rejecting this distinction are that he doubts that it is possible to frame a satisfactory concept of confirmation, and that the testing of a theory is inextricably caught up with its articulation.[145] Thus he argues that, contra Gutting, one should weigh a theory with respect to its acceptability, not its promise of proving acceptable in the course of testing.[146] It is this that led him to develop his notion of the role of control beliefs in theory weighing.[147] Thus Wolterstorff believes that control beliefs do play a legitimate role in the devising of theories, as well as in their being weighed.[148]

It is also of great importance to note that the distinction between data, data-background and control beliefs is not one of ontology or essence, but of function.

> What functions as a data-background belief, or as a control belief, in a given person's weighing of a given theory on one occasion may on another occasion be the theory under consideration... What also happens sometimes is that a belief which on a given occasion functions as a data belief against which a theory is weighed is on another occasion itself weighed by taking the theory as unproblematic.[149]

This means that one must be careful to note not only what beliefs are influencing one in devising or weighing a theory, but also how they are functioning.

---

[144] Wolterstorff, *RWBR*, 69 n. 32, cites G. Gutting, "A Defence of the Logic of Discovery" *Philosophical Forum* vol IV, no 3, as one who proposes such a distinction. It has been very forcefully presented also by Popper; see e.g., *Logic*, 31–33, 109–111; *Conjectures and Refutations*, 21–22.

[145] Wolterstorff, *RWBR*, 69 n. 32; *Educating for Responsible Action* (Grand Rapids: Eerdmans, 1980) 115, on the development of a comprehensive Christian psychological theory. Similar points were made in the discussion of Kuhn, see above (Chapter 2, B.1.).

[146] Wolterstorff, *RWBR*, 69 n. 32.

[147] Ibid.

[148] Ibid., 68.

[149] Ibid., 69–70.

B.2. Authentic Christian Commitment and the Function of Control Beliefs

Wolterstorff's contention is that "the religious beliefs of a Christian scholar ought to function as *control beliefs* in his devising and weighing of theories."[150] All scholars have certain beliefs which function as a control on their theorising: what makes a certain body of scholarship *Christian* in character is that this control function is performed, in part at least, by Christian beliefs.[151] He states further:

> And not only is this true as a matter of fact, but it is entirely right and proper that Christians should practice theorising thus: it is, in fact, their obligation to do so.[152]

And:
> *Christian* scholars are not only fully justified but even obligated to govern their own theorising so as to assure that what they accept will be compatible with authentic Christian conviction.[153]

While this role as control is not the only way a Christian scholar's religious beliefs ought to function, it is central.[154] This assertion, he acknowledges, is an unpopular one even amongst Christian scholars.[155] This, he believes, is in part due to psychological and sociological factors.[156] It is also due, however, to the widespread acceptance by Christian scholars of the notion that to let faith intrude upon the domain of scholarship is inappropriate, even in defiance of the canons of rationality.[157] Central to their acceptance of this notion is the consensus model of

---

150 Wolterstorff, *RWBR*, 70; "The Integration of Faith and Science" [from here on *IFS*], 16.

151 Wolterstorff, *J&P*, 166; *OCL*, 76; "Scholarship and Conviction", 46.

152 Wolterstorff, *J&P*, 166. cf. *OCL*, 76, 77, where he stresses that this depends upon those convictions being epistemically justified for that person. This justification, of course, is not made on foundationalist grounds, but with respect to the criterion of rationality he elsewhere develops, for which see Chapter 3 above.

153 Wolterstorff, *J&P*, 170.

154 Wolterstorff, *RWBR*, 70.

155 Wolterstorff, *IFS*, 16.

156 Ibid. He specifically notes the lack of a comprehensive Christian belief system amongst western Christians, resulting in large areas of life being seen as outside Christian commitment, and the longing for professional acceptance and the associated sense of intimidation Christian scholars feel when their theorising does not conform to the accepted canons of scholarly rationality.

157 Wolterstorff, *IFS*, 16; cf. "Scholarship and Conviction", 47. For an articulation and defence of this view, see below (Chapter 5, A.1.).

rationality which excludes religious beliefs from rational discourse since they give rise to plurality rather than consensus in beliefs.[158] Wolterstorff's assertion of the role of authentic commitment as a control on theorising becomes much more plausible in the light of the collapse of the Enlightenment ideal of rational consensus pursuant to the collapse of foundationalism.[159]

To be specific, Wolterstorff asserts that the *authentic commitment* of a Christian scholar ought to have this control function.[160] In order to clarify this notion of *authentic commitment*, Wolterstorff proceeds to draw a contrast between the content of a Christian's *actual commitment* and that of her *authentic commitment*. Central to one's being a Christian is commitment: without some kind of commitment one cannot in fact be a Christian.[161] Wolterstorff argues that the notion of *commitment* is more crucial to Christianity than that of *faith* for two reasons.[162] First, he sees God's speaking as far more importance than God's revealing, even his revealing of himself, and since the notion of faith is traditionally linked with that of revelation, it is a misleading notion to use.[163] Secondly, faith, while it is a central Christian *virtue*, is not the *sine qua non* of the Christian's response to God's speaking.[164] This is a role much more suited to the idea of *commitment*.[165] At the core of this commitment are the decisions to be a Christ-follower, to join the Church, understood as a community with a tradition that centres on following Christ, and to accept the sacred literature of the Old and New Testaments as authoritative in some way for faith and action.[166] This in turn means that "anyone who is a

---

158 Wolterstorff, *IFS*, 17.

159 Ibid., 18, and see the extensive discussion in Chapter 1 above.

160 Wolterstorff, *RWBR*, 71.

161 Ibid.

162 Ibid., 72 n. 34.

163 Ibid. Further support for this contention is found in "The Assurance of Faith", 397–401, where Wolterstorff argues that especially in Hebrews, wherein is found the clearest discussion of faith, faith is related, not to accepting revealed propositions, but to trust in God's promises. Thus commitment is a better notion than the traditional idea of faith, for essential to commitment is trust, which is also central to the writer of Hebrew's discussion of faith, and it avoids the ambiguity in contemporary usage between faith as assent to revealed propositions and faith as trusting commitment. For similar arguments in relation to the nature of faith, see C. S. Evans *Philosophy of Religion* (Leicester: IVP, 1982) 178–179; B. Mitchell, "Faith and Reason: A False Antithesis?", *How to Play Theological Ping-Pong: And Other Essays on Faith and Reason*, ed. W. J. Abraham and R. W. Prevost (London: Hodder and Stoughton, 1990) 132–150.

164 Wolterstorff, *RWBR*, 72 n. 34.

165 Ibid.

166 Ibid., 71.

Christ-follower will in consequence say and do certain things", for such commitment must be realised in belief and action.[167] The way in which this commitment is in fact expressed in the life of a particular Christian is her *actual* Christian commitment.[168]

There is more than mere commitment, however, to being a Christian, for the very commitment to following Christ entails a conviction about the way this commitment *ought* to be realised.[169] There is, of course, wide divergence in the ways that this commitment is envisaged by different Christians from different traditions, but common to all is some notion of how Christian commitment ought to be expressed in action and belief.[170] This "complex of action and belief that its realization *ought* in fact to assume, for any given person, is what I shall call his *authentic* Christian commitment."[171]

Wolterstorff briefly outlines his idea of authentic commitment,[172] and asserts that while authentic commitment incorporates subscription to dogmas, it is not to be identified with the believing of propositions.[173] For authentic commitment is a complex of actions *and* beliefs, and thus is not to be reduced to either action alone or belief alone.[174] The belief content of authentic Christian commitment is non-dualistic, for it includes propositions about "this world and its inhabitants" as well as propositions about "the supernatural".[175] It is moreover relative to persons and times: "For authentic Christian commitment is how one's Christ-following *ought* to be actualised. And that varies not only from person to person but from time to time within a person's life."[176] It may be claimed that certain propositions will be common to all forms of authentic Christian commitment: while this is true, they will be "few and simple".[177] "So authentic Christian commitment as a whole, but also the belief content thereof, is relative to persons

---

167 Ibid., 72.
168 Ibid.
169 Ibid.
170 Ibid.
171 Ibid.
172 Ibid., 72–73.
173 Ibid., 73.
174 Ibid., 72, 74.
175 Ibid., 74.
176 Ibid. This, it must be stressed, is clearly related to his overall situation- and person-specific model of rationality. See above (Chapter 3, B.2.).
177 Wolterstorff, *RWBR*, 75. In n. 38 he notes that the belief authentic commitment is different to those propositions that one needs to be a Christian at all. The former are maximally obligatory, the latter are minimally obligatory.

and times."[178] However Wolterstorff's own understanding of authentic Christian commitment is thoroughly orthodox as well as being committed to the cause of justice-in-*shalom*: he includes belief in "those things taught in the creeds",[179] as well as the unity and authority of the message of the Bible,[180] as being central to the belief-content of authentic Christian commitment.[181]

Having identified the nature of *authentic Christian commitment*, Wolterstorff proceeds to outline its function in the weighing of theories. He asserts:

> The Christian scholar ought to allow the belief-content of his authentic Christian commitment to function as control within his devising and weighing of theories.[182]

It is important to note that it is only the Christian scholar's *authentic* commitment, not her *actual* commitment that is to so function, for when they differ, by the very nature of authentic commitment, she is obliged to conform the latter to the former.[183] Of course, this controlling role of authentic commitment assumes that she wishes to have consistency and integrity in the total structure of her beliefs and commitments.[184] In this case, since the fundamental commitment to follow Christ ought to be "decisively ultimate" in a Christian's life, all other aspects of life, including the intellectual, must be conformed to it.[185]

The function of authentic commitment as control is both positive and negative.[186] It functions positively in that it prompts one to devise theories

---

[178] Ibid., 75. This relativity, and its legitimate role in scholarship, is reinforced by Wolterstorff's comment in the preface to the first edition of *Reason Within the Bounds of Religion* that the structure of his meta-theory applies equally well to those committed to other religions, such as Buddhism (*RWBR*, 11–12).

[179] Ibid., 74. By this I presume he means the so-called Ecumenical Creeds – the Apostolic, Nicean and Chalcedonian Creeds – and the propositions affirmed therein. Thus Wolterstorff is committed to orthodox Trinitarian faith.

[180] N. Wolterstorff, "The Bible and Economics: The Hermeneutical Issues", *Transformation* 4/3&4 (June–Dec 1987) 13–14.

[181] Further details of the propositional content of Wolterstorff's Christian commitment will be dealt with where relevant to the analysis of specific exegetical theories below.

[182] Wolterstorff, *RWBR*, 76.

[183] Ibid., 76 n. 39.

[184] Ibid., 76.

[185] Ibid.

[186] Ibid.

which are consistent with, or better still, comport well with the belief-content of authentic commitment.[187] It functions negatively in that it prompts one to reject theories that are inconsistent with, or do not comport well with that content.[188] These functions need to be understood together as a special case of the governance of belief-dispositions, which he calls *acceptance governance*.[189]

> We can govern our belief-dispositions in such a way that when in situations in which a certain disposition would normally have been activated, we can resist such activation and avoid automatic acceptance of the proposition in question."[190]

Similarly we can foster the action of a given disposition so as to ensure we will be more likely to accept a given proposition, belief in which would be triggered by the operation of that disposition.[191] Thus our acceptance governance obligations determine what steps we ought to take when confronted with a proposition or theory.[192] This, in part, is what Wolterstorff understands by the control function of certain beliefs: they prompt us to resist or foster the operation of certain belief forming mechanisms in certain circumstances.

Wolterstorff outlines how that ought to operate in psychology as a paradigm case.[193] The belief-content of authentic Christian commitment incorporates the idea that humans are uniquely responsible to God for their actions, which further entails that humans are free agents, at least with respect to the responsibilities God "graces" us with.[194] It also includes the claim that human beings are sinful creatures, and that this sinfulness affects us at all levels of our being, and that there are therefore clear limits on our ability to improve ourselves.[195] These beliefs ought to function as control for a Christian scholar leading her to reject behaviourist, Freudian

---

[187] Ibid.

[188] Ibid.

[189] Wolterstorff, *J&P*, 168. For the nature of belief-dispositions and their governance, see *J&P* 167–168, for a brief discussion, and Chapter 3 above (A.3., A.5., B.1.) for an extensive exposition.

[190] Wolterstorff, *J&P*, 168–169; cf. *CBGR?*, 153–154, 155.

[191] Wolterstorff, *CBGR?*, 153, 155.

[192] Wolterstorff, *J&P*, 169.

[193] Wolterstorff, *RWBR*, 77; *IFS*, 12–19, though he does not use that terminology.

[194] Wolterstorff, *RWBR*, 77; *IFS*, 12–13.

[195] Wolterstorff, *IFS*, 13.

and self-actualisation psychologies, and further, to develop psychologies that comport well with the notions of human freedom and sinfulness.[196]

> Only when the belief-content of the Christian scholar's authentic Christian commitment enters into his or her devising and weighing of psychological [and other] theories can it be said that he or she is fully serious both as scholar and as Christian.[197]

This function of the belief content of authentic commitment as control must not be misunderstood. The belief-content of a Christian scholar's authentic Christian commitment in general does not contain her theories, for it does not touch upon every area of scholarship.[198] It is simply not the case that either the authentic or the actual commitment of a Christian scholar contains theories of scholarship, or even the propositions required for those theories.[199] Nor does it always suggest a theory to her, although sometimes it does that, and so a Christian scholar needs to use "the same capacities of imagination that scholars in general use".[200] At times, of course, this imagination may fail the scholar, for the belief-content of any person's authentic Christian commitment is "a wonderfully rich and complex structure".[201] This means that the scholar, and her predecessors, may have missed an important point of connection between those beliefs and the area in question.[202]

---

[196] Wolterstorff, *RWBR*, 77; *IFS*, 13, 15–16; cf. *Educating for Responsible Action*, for a general theory of moral education, and p. 115 for its need to arise out of an overall Christian psychological model; and "Teaching for Justice", 201–216, for the specific application of such a theory of moral education in the context of Christian collegiate education.

[197] Wolterstorff, *RWBR*, 77, addition mine. cf. *IFS*, 16, where he asserts that it is for precisely these reasons that other models of the relationship between faith and theorising are inadequate.

[198] Wolterstorff, *RWBR*, 77–78.

[199] Ibid.

[200] Ibid., 78. This is probably the case even when a theory is suggested by the belief-content of her authentic commitment, for in that case she still needs to specifically articulate the suggested theory, an action that her commitment can not perform for her. Wolterstorff also makes the same observations about the Bible itself.

[201] Ibid., 107.

[202] Ibid. He cites two reasons in particular which lie behind this today: firstly, most of our ways of thinking are moulded by western scientific world-views more than biblical patterns of thought; secondly, most Christians outside the disciplines of philosophy and theology are ignorant of the issues pertaining to the development of a Christian world-view. Thus Christian philosophy and theology are central disciplines, for they are those disciplines in which the Christian scholar reflects upon the belief-content of her authentic Christian commitment.

Furthermore, authentic commitment does not necessarily determine which specific theory is to be adopted, for more than one may comport well with it. Thus Christian scholars can (and do) differ in their acceptance of theories.[203] It does not generally provide all, or sometimes any, of the data beliefs by which a scholar may weigh a theory, for many theories lie outside its scope.[204] At times the belief-content of a Christian scholar's authentic commitment may provide *some* of the data-beliefs which she uses in devising and weighing theories.[205] Even so, they will usually be insufficient for the development of an adequate theory, and so they will need to be augmented by the normal process of observing and reflecting on reality.[206] It is not even the case that it provides all the control beliefs of a Christian scholar, for no one is *just a Christian*: everyone has a range of beliefs lying outside her authentic commitment which influence theory choice.[207] All these are limitations on the role of the belief-content of authentic Christian commitment that need to be born in mind by Christian scholars when they devise and weigh theories.

However the belief content of authentic Christian commitment should have an impact upon theory devising and weighing which transcends the normal conformism of Christian scholarship to the canons of contemporary *Wissenschaft*.[208] The three strategies Wolterstorff identifies: *harmonising*, in which a scholar modifies the belief-content of her authentic commitment in line with current theories of *Wissenschaft*; *contextualisation*, in which she tries to establish a more general theory into which both theories of *Wissenschaft* and Christian commitment can cohere; and *applying*, in which she proposes "Christian" applications to life problems for theories of *Wissenschaft*; all see the various *Wissenschaften* as being acceptable as they are.[209] This is inadequate, for Christian commitment

---

203 Wolterstorff, *RWBR*, 78–79; cf. Kuyper, *Principles*, II,iii,49.

204 Wolterstorff, *RWBR*, 79.

205 Wolterstorff, *RWBR*, 80; *OCL*, 76. This is more likely in philosophy and theology than in other disciplines.

206 Wolterstorff, *RWBR*, 80.

207 Wolterstorff, *RWBR*, 82–83; *OCL*, 76.

208 Wolterstorff, *RWBR*, 81.

209 Wolterstorff, *RWBR*, 81–82. In *IFS*, 13–14, he presents a slightly different typology: harmonising, compatibilism, and delimitation. The latter two strategies are probably subsets of contextualisation. He pays most attention to delimitation, largely because it offers the most promise. However, it is also inadequate, unless the Christian scholar develops a specifically *Christian* theory of her *Wissenschaft*, which shows both how a given theory is limited, and how she proposes to cover the territory previously claimed by that theory. This, he sees, either is an example of his model at work, or would be best done from within his meta-theory. See *IFS*, 14–15.

should function *internally* to the scholar's practice of scholarship, if necessary challenging and rejecting the assumptions and techniques of a given *Wissenschaft*.[210] For it is often the case that, when a Christian scholar encounters incompatibility between the theories of *Wissenschaft* and her Christian commitment, it is due to the operation of the control beliefs of a rival belief-system.[211] Thus even the data-beliefs of a given *Wissenschaft*, and certainly its theories, can be called into question, for they have been devised with the control beliefs of those who devised the theories.[212] And in relation to these control beliefs: "There is no reason to believe that mine are theirs, or that a science in accord with theirs will be in accord with mine."[213]

The result of this approach is a thoroughly pluralistic body of *Wissenschaft* which, far from being a sign of the *dis*-ordering of *Wissenschaft*,[214] is a sign of its proper ordering.[215] From Wolterstorff's perspective the plurality of scholarship is not to be excused or lamented, but rather embraced as an indication that scholars are articulating their view of life, in relation to reality and in the context of the community of scholarship, in an entirely appropriate manner.[216] Scholarship does, and ought to, reflect the core commitments of scholars, and since they do not share a consensus with respect to their core commitments, neither will they produce consensus in their *Wissenschaft*.[217] Christians then, rather than being cowed by an illusion of consensus into attempting to conform their scholarship to it, should boldly and rigorously articulate their Christian convictions in the context of their *Wissenschaft*.[218] This does not mean,

---

210 Wolterstorff, *RWBR*, 81–82; *IFS*, 16; *OCL*, 77. He notes that some, on the grounds of the non-realist construal of science and or religion, claim there is no possibility of real tension: it is only apparent. He rejects this, while not arguing the case, because the gospel speaks about the world and about God, as do scholars. For his realist stance re theoretical entities, and its relation to theology and exegesis, see below (Chapter 5, B.1.).

211 Wolterstorff, *J&P*, 169–170; "Theology and Science", 103. For examples of this at work in theology, see Wolterstorff, "The Travail of Theology", 35–46; "Is it Possible and Desirable for Theologians to Recover from Kant" [from here on "Can Theologians Recover from Kant?"], 1–18. For examples in philosophy of religion, see Wolterstorff, "Between the Pincers", 13–20.

212 Wolterstorff, *RWBR*, 82; "Theology and Science", 103–104.

213 Wolterstorff, *RWBR*, 82.

214 This is clearly contrary to the Enlightenment ideal of consensus rationality which Wolterstorff outlines and critiques in *IFS*, 17–18.

215 Wolterstorff, *IFS*, 18–19; cf. my discussion of pluralism above in Chapter 3, B.2.

216 Wolterstorff, *IFS*, 18–19.

217 Wolterstorff, *IFS*, 19; "Theology and Science", 104.

218 Wolterstorff, *IFS*, 19; *J&P*, 166, 170.

however, that a Christian and a non-Christian scholar can never agree on a theory's acceptability, for the same theory may fit both their sets of control beliefs.[219] However, it may be that there is less common ground than appears to be the case, for most theories are connected with theories on other levels which may conflict with the control beliefs of one of the scholars.[220] In all of this Wolterstorff stresses again that neither the data beliefs nor the control beliefs by which a theory is weighed are derived from a foundation of certitude.[221] Thus our theories are always possibly false, our knowledge is always defeasible.

This latter point is further developed by Wolterstorff in relation to the way that a Christian scholar's devising and weighing of theories can and does influence the belief-content of her authentic Christian commitment.[222] This possibility arises when she recognises that there is a discrepancy, be it a logical contradiction, or less rigorously, a lack of comportment, within the web of her beliefs.[223] The responsible course of action is for the scholar to revise the total content of her belief-system in such a way as to remove the contradiction.[224] For the physical scientist such a contradiction often arises between what she takes as the deliverances of true science, and what she takes as the belief-content of her authentic Christian commitment.[225] For the case of the physical scientist, and this holds true in general for other scholars, the options are two: she can either revise her scientific views, even to the extent of rejecting fundamental assumptions and methods of her *Wissenschaft*, or she can modify the belief-content of her authentic Christian commitment, and thus of her actual commitment.[226]

---

219 Wolterstorff, *RWBR*, 83–84; *OCL*, 70; "Scholarship and Conviction", 47. This is in clear distinction to the Neo-Calvinist line, outlined and critiqued above (this chapter, B.) as Wolterstorff notes in *OCL*, 69–70.

220 Wolterstorff, *RWBR*, 84.

221 Ibid.

222 Wolterstorff, *RWBR*, 92–97; *OCL*, 77; "Scholarship and Conviction", 49–50.

223 Wolterstorff, *RWBR*, 92; "Scholarship and Conviction", 49.

224 Ibid. For why this is the *responsible* course of action, see p. 76.

225 Wolterstorff, *RWBR*, 92. It is important to recognise that at this stage Wolterstorff is addressing contradiction between what is *taken* to be the belief content of that commitment, not what actually *is* that content; see p. 94. The picture is a little more complicated than this, for the deliverances of science include "what we tak or are disposed to take as data, [and] what we take or are disposed to take as theory", and so the perceived conflicts may be three way, namely, between data, theory and control beliefs. For this see Wolterstorff, "Theology and Science", 99.

226 Wolterstorff, *RWBR*, 92–93; "Scholarship and Conviction", 49. Again, as Wolterstorff notes in "Theology and Science", 99, the picture is a little more complicated: given the three-way nature of the possible conflicts, "we try to eliminate the conflict and achieve equilibrium by making a revision in one of the three-preferring that complex of data, theory

Often it is difficult to decide *which* of these is the correct option, and more, *how* the appropriate option is to be implemented once it is chosen.[227] These decisions need to be made situationally, relative to a specific scholar with a specific body of beliefs in a specific context.[228] Nonetheless, it is important to determine how in principle this may be done, recognising that at some point it will almost certainly need to be done. The former option has been addressed earlier: Wolterstorff now proceeds to examine the latter.[229]

It is apparent that it is frequently the case that developments in *Wissenschaft* have led to changes in what is perceived to be the belief-content of authentic, and thus actual, Christian commitment.[230] This revision may be more or less extreme – ranging from the abandonment of belief, through to major or minor revisions of belief-content – as well as being plausibly made at a number of different points.[231] Such revisions are easily recovered from post-Renaissance intellectual history.[232] Wolterstorff believes that not only is it the case that scholars *have* modified the belief-content of their authentic, and thus actual, Christian commitment, it is also in some instances what they *should have done*,[233] "for he [the Christian scholar] may have been mistaken as to what constitutes the belief-content of his authentic commitment".[234] This, to cite an example, is what he believes happened in the case of post-Renaissance developments in cosmology.[235] Not only have the majority of Christians, almost without exception for those Christians who are physical scientists, modified their view of what constitutes the belief-content of authentic Christian commitment so that geocentricity is no longer included in it, but this is what they should have done, for such a change constitutes an improvement in the shared notion of this belief-content.[236] Thus developments in

---

and control belief which seems to us to have the most likelihood as a whole of being true."

227 Wolterstorff, *RWBR*, 93; "Theology and Science", 103.

228 This is related to his model of rationality as a specific case of the situated character of all rational belief. Indeed, it is a specific example of his criterion of rational belief at work.

229 Wolterstorff, *RWBR*, 94.

230 Ibid., 93.

231 Ibid.

232 Ibid., 93 n. 46, cites R. Popkin "Scepticism, Theology and the Scientific Revolution in the Seventeenth Century" *Philosophy of Science*, ed. I. Lakatos and A. Musgrave (Amsterdam, 1968) as presenting supporting examples of such revisions.

233 Wolterstorff, *RWBR*, 93–94.

234 Ibid., 94.

235 Wolterstorff, *RWBR*, 94; *OCL*, 78.

236 Wolterstorff, *RWBR*, 94. This of course assumes that heliocentric cosmologies are better cosmologies – an assumption that Wolterstorff acknowledges he makes.

Wissenschaft, in this case specifically in the physical sciences, have legitimately resulted in alteration in the belief-content of a Christian scholar's authentic commitment.[237]

Such a view of the relationship between faith and science contradicts those views of faith and commitment, exemplified in the Neo-Calvinist tradition, that hold to the impossibility, or at least the inappropriateness or inadvisability, of allowing one's weighing and devising of theories to influence one's commitment.[238] Wolterstorff sees that such views, which typically assert that faith is *pre-theoretical* in that it influences the processes of devising and weighing theories but is not in turn influenced by those processes, as mistaken, hopeless and misguided.[239] They are mistaken in as much as history demonstrates that people have in fact allowed their theories to influence their faith.[240] They are hopeless, in as much as it is not possible to so structure communities, faith, or *Wissenschaft* in such a way as to prevent such changes from occurring.[241] They are misguided in as much as some of the changes prompted by theories of *Wissenschaften* have been justified, for Christians can be mistaken in their beliefs about what constitutes authentic commitment, and *Wissenschaft* can make those mistakes apparent.[242] Thus:

---

[237] Wolterstorff, *RWBR*, 94; cf. "Theology and Science", 101–103, where he discusses alterations in authentic Christian commitment in terms of the role in religious communities of canonical texts, canonical benefits (especially true beliefs arising from interpretation of those texts), practices of interpretation, practices of appropriating or applying those interpretations and their application to canonical benefits. Generally speaking alterations in the canon will be unacceptable, whereas alterations in benefits or practices of interpretation will be acceptable ways of re-establishing reflective equilibrium. And examples of just such changes in these aspects of authentic Christian commitment are evident in the history of Christian theology and Christian engagement in natural sciences.

[238] Wolterstorff, *RWBR*, 94; *OCL*, 77. For a recent presentation of this view, see Hart, "The Articulation of Belief", 209–243.

[239] Wolterstorff, *RWBR*, 95; *OCL*, 77. It is interesting to note that Hart, "The Articulation of Belief", 228 n. 43; 233 n. 58, accuses Wolterstorff of being overly rationalistic, and allowing reason to dictate to faith. This is an altogether extraordinary claim and justifies the criticism of W. Hasker, "Review of *Rationality in the Calvinian Tradition*", *Christian Scholar's Review* 14/3 (1985) 260, that Hart demonstrates the typical Neo-Calvinist inability to really engage in dialogue with people of other persuasions, and instead to unnecessarily confront them. He wonders, in fact, whether the Neo-Calvinists as typified by Hart (and I would add in contrast to Wolterstorff) are opposed to the idea of *philosophy* as such. For an endorsement of Wolterstorff's practice of allowing reason and faith to inform each other, see A. F. Holmes, "Commitment and Rationality", *Rationality in the Calvinian Tradition*, ed. H. Hart, *et al* (Boston: University Press of America, 1983) 191–208.

[240] Wolterstorff, *RWBR*, 95.

[241] Ibid.

[242] Ibid.

Though authentic commitment ought to function as control within our theory-devising and theory-weighing, such activities will forever bear within them the potential for inducing, and for *justifiably* inducing, revisions in our views as to what constitutes authentic commitment, and thus, revisions in our actual commitment.[243]

Wolterstorff believes that this holds true for authentic commitment itself – what one ought to believe and do as a Christian – as well as for what one perceives that commitment to be.[244] He cites in support of that contention recent (then) studies demonstrating the danger of excess mercury levels in fish populations.[245] This he believes, and I think rightly, has resulted in a change in what we ought to do as Christians, for if we fail to stop the discharge of mercury into bodies of water we will be "defecting from our authentic commitment".[246]

This general approach, and especially the function of control beliefs, gives rise to a thoroughly defeasible view of both scholarship and Christian commitment: "The scholar never fully knows in advance where his line of thought will lead him... We are all profoundly *historical* creatures."[247] It is entirely possible that as a result of the undertaking of scholarship the Christian scholar will be forced to revise her belief system.[248] Indeed, in a sense, scholarship if it is at all honest must have that possibility constantly in mind, even at times as a potential *goal* for the scholarly enterprise. Such a revision may be in the direction of changing accepted theories of *Wissenschaft*, even the methods or assumptions of a given discipline.[249] Alternatively, the scholar may need to modify her actual, or even her authentic, Christian commitment, discarding some of her beliefs as no longer appropriately functioning as control.[250] This process may well lead to a further restructuring of the web of her beliefs, specifically the belief-content of her authentic Christian commitment along Lakatosian lines.[251] This results in more essential beliefs being placed nearer the core of the belief-system, and less essential ones being placed

---

243 Ibid., 95–96.
244 Ibid., 96. This, he says, is for some people "the ultimately alarming possibility".
245 Ibid.
246 Ibid.
247 Ibid., 96, 97.
248 Ibid., 96.
249 That is the burden of the argument in Wolterstorff, *RWBR*, 76–84.
250 Wolterstorff, *RWBR*, 96; *OCL*, 78.
251 Wolterstorff, *RWBR*, 96 n. 47, although the designation of this as a *Lakatosian model* is mine.

nearer the periphery.²⁵² This does not call into question the objectivity of the Word of God, nor of Christian commitment and practice. It is not the objective and absolute truth claims of the Word of God that are here being rejected, but the objective and absolute truth claims of religious theories and existence.²⁵³ And the gospel itself calls these into question inasmuch as it calls us to recognise the fallenness, and thus fallibility, of all areas of life, including religious commitment and theology.²⁵⁴ It is particular *formulations and practices* of Christian commitment that are here asserted to be fallible, not Christian commitment or its revelational core themselves.

While it is clear from what Wolterstorff has said that he does not consider a complementarist model of faith and science to be an adequate one, it must be noted that he does not accept a preconditionalist approach either.²⁵⁵

> The preconditionalist is correct that there ought to be some internal relation between one's commitment and one's devising and weighing of theories, but that relation is not quite the simple one of true faith as a condition of true learning.²⁵⁶

That this is true is seen in the fact that the same theory may satisfy the control beliefs of a Christian and a non-Christian scholar.²⁵⁷ Thus it is not the case that being a Christian, and allowing the belief-content of authentic

---

252 Wolterstorff, *RWBR*, 96 n. 47; cf. "Scholarship and Conviction", 50, where he speaks different beliefs being more crucial than other, being more or less *deeply ingressed* in the belief-system. This delineation of "core" and peripheral beliefs bears striking resemblance to Lakatos' *Methodology of Scientific Research Programmes* and his designation of "hard core" and "protective belt" in the theoretical (and meta-theoretical) structure of scientific research programs. The protective belt of the Christian's belief system can be seen as having a distinctively "apologetic" function, a function which is the purview of all Christians, not just theologians and apologists (see 91 n. 45). This resemblance, even to the extent of dependence, or perhaps better, genetic relationship, is made clearer by his comments that "scientists expend more time and energy pursuing research programs suggested by theories than in devising and weighing theories", Wolterstorff, *RWBR*, 105, cf. 65. Indeed, Wolterstorff sees it as a major flaw in most Christian scholarship that the Christian scholar's commitment does not suggest any research programs, Wolterstorff, *RWBR*, 105–106. These Lakatosian intimations will be explored further below (Chapter 6, B., C.).

253 Wolterstorff, *OCL*, 78; "Scholarship and Conviction", 50.

254 Ibid.

255 Wolterstorff, *RWBR*, 98. Such a preconditionalist approach is clearly endorsed by Hart, "The Articulation of Belief", 209–248.

256 Wolterstorff, *RWBR*, 98.

257 Ibid. This is discussed in relation to Neo-Calvinist views of the interaction of faith and theorising, in *OCL*, 59–73, and above (this chapter, A.3.).

Christian commitment to function as control in theorising, is a criterion for developing a set of comprehensive, coherent, consistent and true theories in *Wissenschaft*.[258] This is reinforced by two further points.

First, it is not the case that one who exhibits authentic commitment, if such a person were to exist, would be guaranteed the attaining of such a satisfactory set of beliefs.[259] For it is entirely possible that more than one theory in a given area may comport well with her control beliefs, and in choosing between them she may choose the wrong one, if in fact there is an unambiguously correct one to choose.[260] So too, given that the theories of *Wissenschaft* are not contained within the belief-content of her authentic commitment she would need to use imagination in the devising of her theories, just as any other scholar would, and this imagination may be defective or lacking in her.[261] It is also possible that some propositions that are properly part of her authentic commitment were strictly false, even though they are not only useful, but also necessary beliefs for her at that point in time.[262] All of these factors mean that it is possible for a Christian scholar in using her noetic faculties in a correct manner to arrive at a body of beliefs which she *ought to accept* but which are not strictly speaking true.[263]

Second, it is entirely possible that a non-Christian scholar may serve the purposes of the growth of knowledge, *by virtue of their non-Christian stance*.[264] "In their opposition to what they knew as Christianity, they have sometimes explored lines of thought that proved fruitful and important."[265] Examples of this are found in the development of evolutionary theory and of behaviourism.[266] Both of these theories were devised specifically in opposition to Christian beliefs, and in the light of history, they could only have been developed by non-Christians.[267] Yet they have furthered our understanding of humanity and the world in ways that would not have been possible to those who had an authentic Christian commitment *at the*

---

258 Wolterstorff, *RWBR*, 98. This is clearly in contrast to Dooyeweerd, *New Critique* (II) 542–562; cf. Kalsbeek, 173–175.
259 Wolterstorff, *RWBR*, 99.
260 Ibid.
261 Ibid.
262 Ibid.
263 Ibid. This is related to his general epistemology, where he notes that a belief's being rational is no guarantee of its truth, for which see above (Chapter 3, B.2.).
264 Wolterstorff, *RWBR*, 99.
265 Ibid.
266 Ibid., 99, 100.
267 Ibid., 99–100.

time, for "the requisite motivations were lacking" for a Christian to develop those theories.[268] Thus, being a Christian is not a criterion for the attainment of truth.[269]

Indeed, the question of how we attain truth, if ever, is not a simple one. For while it is the goal of theoretical enterprises to attain "a consistent, coherent (ie., not *ad hoc*), and comprehensive body of true theories",[270] this goal is not easily attained. Indeed, the *heuristic* question of what theories we ought to accept in order to advance the cause of truth needs to be clearly distinguished from the normative question of what theories we are warranted in accepting, and how they are to be warranted.[271] This must be done if we are to avoid relativism, scepticism and epistemological anarchy, positions Wolterstorff is eager to avoid.[272] For often the theories that a scholar was warranted in accepting impede the growth of the body of true theories, as was the case, for example, for the phlogiston theory of combustion in Chemistry.[273]

> It is only by looking back (if then) that we can tell what hindered and what advanced the goal for theorizing. It is never a question that we can with any confidence answer at the time.[274]

Nor does this retrospective vision of heuristic benefit enable us to develop a *general heuristic*, "a strategy that will always tell what is the most efficient way of arriving at the goal of theorizing."[275] For not only is it unable to provide tools for analysis of future heuristic prospects, by its very nature, but as Wolterstorff says:

---

[268] Ibid., 100. This is so even though, as noted above, they are to be rejected: unacceptable theories may nonetheless add true propositions to the body of true, or at least justified, beliefs.

[269] Wolterstorff, *RWBR*, 100. This is in clear contrast to Dooyeweerd's notion that true self-knowledge, and thus the knowledge of God in Jesus Christ, is required for true knowledge of the world. See above (this chapter, A.2.).

[270] Wolterstorff, *RWBR*, 103.

[271] Ibid. It is important to remember, here, that in the following discussion Wolterstorff uses *warrant* as synonymous with *rationality*; that is, it is an internalist, normative notion, in stark contrast to Plantinga's externalist, non-normative notion. It is, indeed, roughly equivalent to *entitlement*.

[272] Ibid., 102, 103; cf. 56–57.

[273] Ibid., 103. One could add many other theories to this, such as medical theories using the notion of the four *humours*, or pre-germ theory theories of disease, and so on.

[274] Wolterstorff, *RWBR*, 103. This is one point on which he disagrees profoundly with Lakatos (see below, Chapter 5, B.2.).

[275] Wolterstorff, *RWBR*, 103.

What seems in fact to have contributed to the growth of theory is the most astounding succession of human foibles, follies and frailties. Perhaps it is true, as Lakatos has suggested, that what leads most efficiently to the advance of theorizing is *a proliferation of tenaciously held theories*, no matter what the motive for the proliferation or the tenacity. But at best this is a very rough generalization. *How* tenacious? And *how* proliferative?[276]

Thus even this, as loose as it is, provides no basis for a *general heuristic*.[277]
Nor is there a general warrant for theory acceptance and rejection, despite the separation of the notions of warrant and heuristic.[278] This is not to say, however, that there is no such thing as warranted theory acceptance or rejection.[279] Wolterstorff assumes that there are such actions, even though he does not demonstrate that this is the case.[280] What he does do is present a non-foundationalist formulation of warranted theory acceptance or rejection, in which warrant is made relative *to a body of beliefs, not a body of certitudes*.[281] This formulation is, roughly:

Given such-and-such a body of beliefs, is the scholar warranted in accepting or warranted in not accepting theory T?[282]

Thus there are cases of warranted theory choice, there may even perhaps be general norms for theory choice, even though we cannot formulate and specify "*general norms* for theory acceptance and nonacceptance".[283] This commitment to the possibility of warranted theory choice, and the concomitant rejection of agnosticism and antinomianism, Wolterstorff recognises to be a function of his control beliefs.[284] Indeed, our notion of warrant, or rejection of such a notion at all, is always a result of the operation of control beliefs.[285] In this area of knowledge, as in all others,

---

276   Wolterstorff, *RWBR*, 103–104; cf. *IFS*, 18.
277   The issue of heuristic principles for Christian scholarship is of sufficient importance that a separate, detailed analysis of Wolterstorff's heuristic is warranted. For a brief discussion, see below (Chapter 5, B.2.).
278   Wolterstorff, *RWBR*, 104.
279   Ibid., 102, 104.
280   Ibid., 102. This, he says, is well beyond the scope of his essay.
281   Ibid.
282   Ibid. This is very closely related to the criterion for rationality he developed later in *CBGR?*, which has been discussed in detail above (see Chapter 3). I will explore how this criterion relates to his meta-theory below (Chapter 5, A.2.).
283   Wolterstorff, *RWBR*, 104.
284   Ibid.
285   Ibid.

there is no foundation of certitudes to which we can refer, and so we must recognise that there will be different perspectives on this issue, arising from different scholars' differing control beliefs.[286]

C. Wolterstorff's Heuristics of *Shalom*

Earlier I noted that Wolterstorff rejects the idea of a *general heuristic*.[287] This rejection, I think, needs to be understood not as a rejection of the existence of justifiable guidelines for research, but of the idea that there can be a heuristic calculus (or algorithm) that enables a scholar to determine which lines of research are going to best further the cause of "truth" in every circumstance. He does not deny that there ought to be general principles or strategies which guide a Christian scholar's choice of research programs,[288] instead he asserts that the traditionally accepted criterion of "furthering the cause of truth" is impossible of fulfilment.[289] The question of how a Christian scholar ought to make heuristic decisions is the focus of Part Two of *Reason Within the Bounds of Religion*.[290] There he discusses the issue of what matters a scholar ought to investigate, in particular focusing on the debate between pure theory and praxis-oriented theory.[291]

C.1. HEURISTICS AND *SHALOM*

The framework for his discussion is the notion that a Christian scholar's theorising, like all other human endeavours, ought to contribute to God's ultimate goal for human existence, namely *shalom*.[292] This ultimate goal is contrasted with traditional notions of the *telos* of humanity as being the

---

286 Ibid.
287 See my discussion of Wolterstorff, *RWBR*, 103–104, in the previous section.
288 See Wolterstorff, *RWBR*, 105–108.
289 This, as I understand it, is the force of Wolterstorff's argument in *RWBR*, 103–104.
290 Part Two of the 1984 edition of *RWBR*, 111–146, is a reprint of N. Wolterstorff, "Theory and praxis", *Christian Scholar's Review* 9/4 (1980) 317–334. He does not there *identify* his discussion as one concerning heuristics, but the very fact that he is dealing with choice principles for the Christian scholar's adoption of a given line of research, or even area of scholarship, indicates that this is what he is doing.
291 Wolterstorff, *RWBR*, 111. I cannot explore this issue in too much detail, intriguing as it is, as heuristics for biblical scholarship lies beyond the scope of my thesis. For my purposes, what is primary is the way in which this approach enables Wolterstorff to separate *direction governance* from *acceptance governance* so as to avoid Feyerabendian epistemological anarchy. For this, see below (Chapter 5, B.2.).
292 Wolterstorff, *RWBR*, 113–114.

beatific vision of God, as found for instance in the Westminster Confession and Aquinas, as well as with contemporary notions of liberation as the goal of human life.[293] Neither of these provides an adequate view of the *telos* of life as presented in the Bible, though both contain elements of truth.[294] *Shalom* is both a more inclusive, and a more Biblically warranted notion of the goal of human life than either of these alternatives.[295]

> The goal of human existence is that man should dwell at peace in all his relationships: with God, with himself, with his fellows, with nature, a peace which is not only absence of hostility, though it certainly is that, but a peace which at its highest is *enjoyment*. To dwell in shalom is to enjoy living before God, to enjoy living in nature, to enjoy living with one's fellows, to enjoy life with oneself. A condition of shalom is justice, and a component of justice is liberation from oppression. Never can there be shalom without justice. Yet shalom is more than justice. Justice can be grim. In shalom there is delight.[296]

Wolterstorff relates his heuristic to this idea of *shalom* being the ultimate *telos* of human life under God.

> I suggest that if the activities of the scholar are to be justified, that justification must be found ultimately in the contribution of scholarship to the

---

[293] Wolterstorff, *RWBR*, 111–113. This receives more detailed treatment in relation to Reformed and Liberationist perspectives in *J&P*, Ch. 3, 42–68.

[294] Wolterstorff, *RWBR*, 113. See also *J&P*, 69, where he notes that we need a vision of world-formative Christianity which incorporates Reformed theology's emphasis on creation and freedom-by-mastery and Liberation theology's emphasis on salvation and freedom-of-self-determination.

[295] Wolterstorff, *RWBR*, 113–115; *J&P*, 69–72. The passages cited by Wolterstorff in support of this contention include Is. 32:16–18, 11:1–8; Lk. 1:79, 2:24, 29; Eph. 2:17. His thesis that *shalom* is the biblical ideal and goal for human life, indeed all of creation, and his idea of the nature of *shalom* are supported by: B. C. Birch, *Let Justice Roll Down: The Old Testament, Ethics and Christian Life* (Westminster: Louisville, 1991) 83–84; W. Brueggemann, *Living Toward a Vision: Biblical Reflections on Shalom* (United Church Press: New York, 1976); S. C. Mott, "The Partiality of Biblical Justice: A Response to Beisner", *Transformation* 10/1 (Jan/April 1993) 23–29; C. R. Padilla, "The Fruit of Justice will be Peace", *Transformation* 2/1 (Jan/Mar 1985) 2–4; J. P. Wogaman, "Toward a Christian Definition of Justice", *Transformation* 7/2 (April/June 1990) 18–23; P. B. Yoder, *Shalom: The Bible's Word for Salvation, Justice and Peace* (Faith and Life Press: Newton, 1987). Mott and Wogaman specifically focus on a communitarian notion of justice rather than on the idea of *shalom* itself, however their views of justice comport well with and support Wolterstorff's presentation of *shalom*.

[296] Wolterstorff, *RWBR*, 114; cf. *J&P*, 69–70.

cause of justice-in-shalom. The vocation of the scholar, like the vocation of everyone else, is to serve that end.[297]

He asserts that: "A seesaw battle is taking place in history between the forces that advance and the forces that retard shalom."[298] It is the Christian scholar's calling, he believes, to engage in theorising so as to "participate in that battle", to serve to advance the cause of justice-in-shalom, and to combat those forces which retard it.[299] This calling is not, however, simply a duty, it is also a privilege and a delight. In their work as scholars Christians integrate their Christian faith and their scholarly practice, thereby serving the Christian community: they also respond in thankfulness to God's invitation to scholarship, and participate in the delight of shalom. The delight of shalom is an integral part of the practice of Christian scholarship.[300] It is this idea of scholarship serving the *telos* of shalom that provides the heart of Wolterstorff's heuristic.[301]

This, it must be noted, is again a specific articulation of his general epistemology in the context of scholarly rationality.[302] Heuristics, he asserts, deals with the *direction governance* of our belief-dispositions.[303] It is entirely possible for us, *without in any way affecting or impairing the function of our reasoning disposition*, that is without in any way compromising the rational status of our theorising, to turn our attention as scholars to one thing instead of another.[304] In relation to that ability to govern the *direction* of operation of our belief-dispositions we have obligations, just as in the case of our acceptance governance.[305] And as is the case with our

---

[297] Wolterstorff, *RWBR*, 116.

[298] Wolterstorff, *J&P*, 163.

[299] Wolterstorff, *J&P*, 163. This is not an affirmation he makes easily, for it is contrary to the traditional heuristic of Neo-Calvinist views of scholarship, the theological tradition which nurtured Wolterstorff and within which he sees himself as working, *J&P*, 163.

[300] N. Wolterstorff, "Should the Work of Our Hands Have Standing in the Christian College?", *Keeping Faith: Embracing Tensions in Christian Higher Education*, ed. R. A. Wells (Grand Rapids: Eerdmans, 1996) 133–151, esp pp. 139–141.

[301] Again, it must be noted that this is my assessment of the force of Wolterstorff's argument in relation to his meta-theory, rather than a specific identification made by Wolterstorff himself.

[302] Again, he relates his heuristic to his broader discussion of belief-dispositions as he does his understanding of control beliefs in Wolterstorff, *J&P*, 167–169.

[303] Wolterstorff, *J&P*, 169.

[304] Ibid. This, as Wolterstorff, *J&P*, 170–171, notes, provides a rationale for the negation of the charges of irrationality that are brought against praxis-oriented theorising. In relation to the non-irrational and non-relativist nature of Wolterstorff's meta-theory, see below (Chapter 5, B.).

[305] Wolterstorff, *J&P*, 169.

noetic obligations in general, so with these direction governance obligations, our governance obligations relate to our obligations in general.[306]

This, then, given that he sees the quest for justice-in-shalom as the ultimate obligation of humans, and the source for our other more specific obligations, provides a cogent, even ineluctable reason for his taking the advancement of the struggle for shalom to be the primary direction-governance obligation for scholars. Given the relation of scholarly obligations to more general obligations this engagement of scholarship with issues of social responsibility is not just a matter of the results of pure scholarship being responsibly applied, nor should scholarship be just a contextually relevant pursuit which relates pure theory to a given context.[307] Rather, in providing the governing interest of Christian scholarship, the *telos* of shalom requires the integration of social commitment and scholarly theorising in such a way that that theorising "places itself in the service of the cause of struggling for justice".[308] Thus scholarship guided by the heuristic of *shalom* is at the very least closely allied with those who call for praxis-oriented theory.[309] This means that the identification of, and commitment to, certain social goals, the recognition that *Wissenschaft* can foster those goals, and the pursuit of those directions of scholarship which will further those goals are integral to the task of responsible Christian scholarship.[310] In calling for a heuristic of shalom Wolterstorff is calling for Christian scholars to be engaged in this kind of responsible Christian scholarship.

C.2. *SHALOM* AND PURE VERSUS PRAXIS-ORIENTED THEORY

In identifying the cause of *shalom* as the ultimate justification for the scholarly enterprise in general, and for a scholar's choice of research programs in particular, the issue of pure versus praxis oriented theories arises.[311] From the perspective of a heuristic of *shalom* it is obvious that at least some praxis-oriented theories are justifiable, for otherwise the burdens of the poor cannot be lifted, and the needs of society cannot be met.[312] The question then becomes whether some pure theory can be seen

---

306 Ibid. cf. the detailed discussion of this point in relation to Wolterstorff's general epistemology above (Chapter 3, A.2., B.2.).
307 Wolterstorff, *J&P*, 163–164.
308 Ibid., 164.
309 Ibid., 162–163, 170.
310 Ibid., 170.
311 Wolterstorff, *RWBR*, 117.
312 Ibid., 117, 125–126.

as furthering the cause of *shalom*.[313] In order to answer this question so as to provide real guidelines for the Christian scholar, the issues need to be clarified. Thus Wolterstorff's clarifying question: "But what *is* pure theory? And what, correspondingly, is praxis-oriented theory?"[314]

Wolterstorff identifies three traditions in the justification of scholarship. The first is the *Pythagorean justification* in which theorising is justified "by reference to the self-improvement that inherently results from gaining theoretical knowledge".[315] This is a teleological theory of epistemic virtue, in as much as the justification of theorising lies in an end which is extrinsic to the scholarly task itself, namely the conformity of the theoriser's mental processes with the orderliness of the cosmos.[316] Such a view has its proponents today, who see scholarship as freeing its practitioners from prejudice and intolerance and fostering "scientific" thought processes.[317] The second is the *Baconian justification*, in which theorising is justified by "the power it places in our hands by the cognitive states attained".[318] This power is seen as the power to mould one's circumstances in line with one's own ends, traditionally seen as technological control of the physical environment.[319] This view is the most commonly espoused justification of theorising today, and has been applied even to "technologies of society", in which the goal is the control of humans themselves and their communities.[320] This justification can best be described as a teleological theory of epistemic utility, for the cognitive states attained in the scholarly pursuit are not valued for themselves, but for their application

---

[313] Wolterstorff, *RWBR*, 117. It is clear that Wolterstorff sees that praxis-oriented theory has a prima facie legitimacy that pure theory does not have. R. McInerny, "Thoughts on Wolterstorff's 'Theory and Praxis'", *Christian Scholar's Review* 9/4 (1980) 335–336, criticises him for this basic stance, at the same time *mis*-construing it as a call to embrace *only* praxis-oriented theory. While recognising that other obligations may override the practice of scholarship, McInerny seems to believe that once engaged in scholarship, only pure theory is appropriate. This line of argument is effectively countered by Wolterstorff's general argument, as outlined below.

[314] Wolterstorff, *RWBR*, 117.

[315] Ibid., 118. In n. 2 he notes that there may be problems in ascribing this justification to the Pythagoreans *per se*, but the identification of the general stance is nonetheless valid.

[316] Ibid., 118, though the categorisation of these as teleological theories of epistemic virtue is my own.

[317] Ibid., 119.

[318] Ibid., 123. Note: for my purposes I have reversed the order of his second and third categories.

[319] Ibid., 124–125.

[320] Ibid., 125. He makes the interesting observation in n. 5, that the Pythagorean tradition is being absorbed by the Baconian in contemporary psychological and sociological theories.

to practical problems in various technologies.[321] The third is the *Aquinian justification*, which is "the justification of theoretical inquiry by reference to the inherent worth of the cognitive states achieved".[322] The relative value of certain cognitive states may be determined by the *object* of knowledge, such as was the case for Augustine and Aquinas,[323] or by reference to their *formal characteristics*, as was the case for Kant.[324] This, in contrast to the teleological theories mentioned above,[325] is an explicitly deontological epistemic theory, in as much as it is the intrinsic value of the cognitive states attained, rather than the ends to which they are applied, that justifies the theoretical enterprise.[326]

Having identified these different traditions, Wolterstorff applies them specifically to the debate over the justification of pure versus praxis-oriented theory. It is obvious that the Aquinian justification legitimises pure theoretical pursuits, for it allows one to choose a line of research simply because it promises to yield knowledge that is inherently valuable.[327] This is labelled by Wolterstorff as *objective* pure theory.[328] This version of the pure theory choice principle may be stated thus:

> Choose those directions of inquiry which hold the greatest promise of yielding knowledge of greatest inherent worth for the greatest number of people.[329]

It is equally clear that the Baconian justification legitimises praxis-oriented theories, for lines of inquiry are to be chosen because of their promise of

---

321 Ibid., 124, though the categorisation of these as teleological theories of epistemic utility is my own.

322 Ibid., 119.

323 Ibid., 120, where he notes that knowledge of God was seen by them as the highest knowledge.

324 Ibid., 120–121, for whom completeness of explanation and systematic unity were what determined the relative value of different forms of knowledge.

325 Wolterstorff, rather loosely in my opinion, identifies them as *utilitarian* theories. See *RWBR*, 124, 125. As I have mentioned earlier, they are both *teleological* theories; but only the second is *utilitarian per se*.

326 Ibid., 119, though again the classification of these as deontological epistemic theories is my own.

327 Ibid., 128–129.

328 Ibid., 131.

329 Ibid., 129. In n. 6 Wolterstorff recognises that there are variations on this choice-principle, and the possibility of choices within it.

yielding knowledge that is useful for ends other than cognitive states.[330] This praxis-oriented choice-principle may be stated thus:

> Choose those directions of inquiry which hold the greatest promise of yielding knowledge useful in altering our human circumstances in the most desirable ways.[331]

Pure theory can also be justified, however, by reference to pragmatic epistemic theories. For while the Baconian justification proposes that theorising ought to be done with pragmatic ends in mind, it can also justify pure theory by reason of the pragmatic disadvantages of all theorising being praxis-oriented, and the pragmatic benefits of allowing some scholars to pursue lines of inquiry just because they are interesting to them.[332] This is labelled by Wolterstorff as *subjective* pure theory.[333] This version of the pure theory choice principle can be formulated thus:

> The best way to serve the technological interests of mankind is to allow a sizeable body of researchers to pursue whatever matters they find of greatest intellectual interest to themselves.[334]

From here, Wolterstorff proceeds to discuss the issue of pure versus praxis-oriented theory in the heuristics of Christian scholars.[335] It is obvious, as stated above, that praxis-oriented theorising is justified in terms of the heuristics of *shalom*, for it is useful, even necessary in "lifting the burdens of deprivation and oppression and advancing the cause of shalom".[336] This is the case even when pure theory is thought of in subjective terms as a means to pragmatic ends, for although often non-praxis-oriented theory has proven to be of practical benefit, at times the theoretical knowledge we require for the attainment of some human goal is unavailable.[337] Thus people need to engage in specifically pragmatic theorising in order for that goal to be achieved.[338] Pure theory does not

---

330 Ibid., 130.
331 Ibid.
332 Ibid.
333 Ibid., 131. In n. 9 he suggests that the subjective/objective pure-theory distinction is not as stark as might appear from this discussion, but is valid nonetheless.
334 Ibid., 131.
335 Ibid.
336 Ibid., 125–126.
337 Ibid., 132–133.
338 Ibid., 132.

always serve the needs of praxis, as has been noted particularly by thinkers from the Third World.[339] Thus in order to serve the needs of human community in line with the goal of furthering *shalom*, specifically praxis-oriented theorising is required, and thus is justified in terms of the heuristics of *shalom*.

However, pure theory is also justifiable, for the having and acquiring of knowledge can lay claim to having intrinsic worth.[340] They are components in human fulfilment, and hence an aspect of *shalom*.[341] Wolterstorff states:

> To me it seems evident that understanding, comprehension, knowledge, constitutes a fulfilment of our created nature. To me it seems evident that human fulfilment is less than God meant it to be insofar as there is ignorance in place of understanding, bewilderment in place of comprehension... a theoretical comprehension of ourselves and of the reality in the midst of which we live – of its unifying structure and explanatory principles – is a component in the shalom God meant for us. Where knowledge is absent, life is withered.[342]

This endorsement of pure theory further distinguishes Wolterstorff's position from those of liberationists: "Not every legitimate *logos* is the *logos* of a *praxis*."[343] However in justifying the legitimacy of pure theory, Wolterstorff does not endorse strictly subjective pure theory, but only objective pure theory.[344] For the *responsible scholar* can never bear in mind only her own interests but must also consider the interests of human beings in general.[345] Thus pure theory is to be justified on objective grounds, with respect to its intrinsic *value* as knowledge, not on subjective grounds, with respect to its intrinsic *interest* as knowledge.[346]

Thus the intrinsic value of knowledge and its extrinsic consequences both have claims on the Christian scholar.[347] Consequently, in determining which matter she should pursue, the Christian scholar needs to decide

---

[339] Ibid., 132–133.
[340] Wolterstorff, *RWBR*, 132, 134; *J&P*, 171.
[341] Wolterstorff, *RWBR*, 126.
[342] Wolterstorff, *RWBR*, 126–127. Similarly, *J&P*, 171.
[343] Wolterstorff, *J&P*, 171, italics in original.
[344] Wolterstorff, *RWBR*, 135.
[345] Ibid. I suspect Wolterstorff is here operating on the principle expounded so frequently by Paul, for instance in Phil. 2:4.
[346] Ibid.
[347] Ibid.

which of these considerations has priority in a particular instance.[348] The question is not the simple one of just choosing to engage in pure *or* praxis-oriented theorising, but the much more complex one of determining which line of research will best further the cause of *justice-in-shalom*.[349] Of course, at times this will not be difficult, as the results of the choice principles of pure and praxis-oriented theory may coincide in a particular case.[350] However, this will not always be so: at times a difficult decision must be made in favour of either pure theorising or praxis-oriented theorising, for often their claims conflict.[351] This decision can never result in a once-for-all answer, for the needs of humanity for knowledge vary with time and place, and the capacities of one scholar will vary from those of another.[352] Such heuristic decisions are always situation and person specific.[353]

Wolterstorff contrasts his with the alternative visions of Christian scholarship developed in the Thomist and Reformed traditions, which tended, for different reasons, to favour pure over praxis-oriented theory. In the Thomist and Augustinian tradition, the knowledge of God was seen as the highest of all possible goods, the noblest *telos* of all.[354] This resulted in an individualistic and elitist view of life and scholarship, a view which is necessarily out of line with Wolterstorff's heuristic of *shalom*.[355] The Reformed tradition, on the other hand, was thoroughly non-elitist, for it saw the scholarly enterprise as just one human task among many tasks, all of equal value.[356] However, it was also an inadequate vision of scholarship,

---

348 Ibid., 133.
349 Ibid., 133–134.
350 Ibid., 131 and 132, nn. 9 and 10.
351 Ibid.
352 Ibid., 134.
353 Ibid.
354 Ibid., 136–139.
355 Wolterstorff, *RWBR*, 139–140. G. Gutting, "Review of *Reason Within the Bounds of Religion* (2nd ed)", *Faith and Philosophy* 4/2 (April 1987) 227, claims that Wolterstorff misrepresents Aquinas's position on this matter, confusing the ultimate telos of human life in the beatific vision, and the telos of human scholarship, and other human enterprises, as ministering to human needs. While an analysis of Aquinas's position is beyond the scope of my thesis, it seems apparent, however, that conceptually and historically an emphasis on the contemplative knowledge of God results in a devaluing of practical human needs in life and in scholarship.
356 Wolterstorff, *RWBR*, 140–141. See Wolterstorff, "The Work of Our hands", 133–151, for a discussion of the implications of this for the Christian academy, including the role of the academy as a locus for Christian scholars to reflect with their non-academic counterparts on everyday life, business, the arts, and so on. He states: "The Christian college and university should be a place where the Christian community does its thinking about the

for it failed to consider the needs of humanity in the pursuit of scholarship, thus all too often irresponsibly favouring pure over praxis-oriented theory.[357] This was inevitable given its view that the direction-governance obligations of scholars were totally determined by the goal of developing a body of pure nomological theory.[358] Even more, the fallenness of creation, and the need for scholarship to serve the ends of salvation and renewal were surprisingly absent in traditional Protestant views of the cultural mandate.[359] Indeed, this inadequate grounding of scholarship in the cultural mandate alone inevitably results in the development of pure theory over-against praxis-oriented theory.[360] This, in turn, resulted in their ignoring the goals of lifting the burdens of oppression and deprivation, which need to be a particular focus of the heuristics of *shalom*.[361]

However, this avowal of the legitimacy of praxis-oriented theory does not entail a rejection of pure theory, as is the case in the critiques of pure theory found in liberation thinkers, who claim that any theory that is not oriented to praxis is illegitimate, and a denial of the reality of the socially conditioned nature of all scholarship.[362] This rejection of liberationist commitment to strictly praxis-oriented theory does not mean that their critiques of western scholarship are also rejected.[363] These critiques in part arise out of, and are reinforced by, the searching analyses of Marx and

---

major social formations of contemporary society – its normative and strategic thinking." ("The Work of our Hands, 135).

357   Ibid., 141, 142.

358   Wolterstorff, *J&P*, 163, 165–166.

359   Wolterstorff, *RWBR*, 142. This, in my view, is especially surprising in the light of the Protestant, particularly Reformed Protestant, tradition's endorsement of various formulations of the doctrine of human depravity.

360   Wolterstorff, *J&P*, 172. Indeed, the relationship between the Neo-Calvinist's grounding of scholarship in the cultural mandate with no reference to the needs of a fallen world is directly related, I believe, to their inadequate vision of the *telos* of humanity. For with no incorporation of the broader relational concerns of *shalom* into their vision of the goals of human existence it is not surprising that the needs of those broader relationships are ignored in the pursuit of scholarship as a result of the focus on fulfilling their obligations to God in the cultural mandate.

361   Wolterstorff, *RWBR*, 142–143. Wolterstorff levels similar criticisms against contemporary Christian collegiate education in "Teaching for Justice", 201–216. These are in large part derivative of the ideas developed here.

362   Wolterstorff, *RWBR*, 134; *J&P*, 171; cf. the calls for solely praxis-oriented theory in theology in J. Miguez-Bonino, "Theology as Critical Reflection and Liberating Praxis", *The Vocation of the Theologian*, ed. T. W. Jennings (Philadelphia: Fortress, 1985) 37–48; J. Kroger, "Prophetic-Critical and Strategic Tasks of Theology: Habermas and Liberation Theology", *TS* 46/1 (Mar 1985) 3–20.

363   See, for instance, Wolterstorff, *RWBR*, 144–146; *J&P*, 171–172, 173–176.

Freud, who demonstrated that all too often the *reasons* people, including scholars, give for their actions, in this case their engagement in pure theory, are no more than *rationalisations* of their efforts to maintain their own positions of power and privilege.[364] These critiques, while not invariably correct, are frequently accurate, for often the scholar who says he is engaged in pure theory is actually working to maintain his position of power and prestige.[365] So too, generally Western scholarship has ignored the needs of those who live in the Third World in its theorising, be it pure or praxis-oriented, thus neglecting truly global *justice-in-shalom*.[366]

These ideas were to some degree pre-empted in the Neo-Calvinist movement, in particular in Kuyper's discussion entitled "Science and the Fact of Sin".[367] Sin, Kuyper believed, distorted our belief-dispositions, and to an extent, our acceptance governance of those dispositions in a systematic, law-like manner.[368] These effects are seen in "the ways in which our social goals, antipathies and background distort the workings of our belief-dispositions (and of our acceptance governance of them)".[369] While the precise operation of these laws, and the empirical evidence for them, have not been developed, the existence of these effects is clear.[370] Indeed, Wolterstorff believes that Marx's notion of *ideology* is a specific, and well articulated example of such a socially determined distortion of our noetic faculties resulting from sin.[371] It is regrettable, Wolterstorff says, that due to his emphasis on the role of religion and idolatry on theoretical enterprises Kuyper did not analyse these socially determined factors in more detail.[372] What is important to recognise in this regard,

---

364 Wolterstorff, *RWBR*, 144–145; *J&P*, 174–175. These assertions are supported by Riggs, 136–170; D. N. Livingstone, "Science and Society: Reflections on the Radical Critique of Science", *Faith and Thought* vol 113, no 1 (April 1987) 17–32; "Farewell to Arms: Reflections on the Encounter Between Science and Faith", *Christian Faith and Practice in the Modern World: Theology from an Evangelical Point of View*, ed. M. A. Noll and D. F. Wells (Grand Rapids: Eerdmans, 1988) 253–255; who recognise these factors as playing a role in scientific practice, but do not see them as telling the whole story, thereby holding to the rationality of science.

365 Wolterstorff, *RWBR*, 145.

366 Ibid., 134.

367 Kuyper, *Principles*, II,i,41; Wolterstorff, *J&P*, 173.

368 Wolterstorff, *J&P*, 173. For a more detailed discussion, see above (Chapter 3, A.4.).

369 Kuyper, *Principles*, II,i,41; Wolterstorff, *J&P*, 173. Wolterstorff gives some examples of these in *J&P*, 173–174.

370 Wolterstorff, *J&P*, 174.

371 Ibid., 174–175, although, of course, Marx did not hold to its being the result of rebellion against God.

372 Ibid., 175.

however, a point that Kuyper failed to appreciate, is that socially conditioned deformations of our noetic apparatus influence our religious beliefs and practices.[373] Thus we need to practice the "hermeneutics of suspicion" so as to uncover the workings of "socially produced malformations" as well as of "religiously determined malformations" of our belief-dispositions and our governance thereof.[374] The reason for this is that such malformations produce false beliefs, and thus we have the responsibility, knowing that they may be operative, to so govern our dispositions that we overcome their effects to the best of our ability, and thus fulfil our overall noetic obligation of getting more amply in touch with reality.[375]

Thus we must recognise that:

> even when scholars are not engaged in praxis-oriented theory, social reality will consistently shape their judgements about what is important enough to investigate, thus influencing direction. By refusing to allow considerations of what is useful for some goal of social reform into their assessment of importance, they do not automatically free such assessments from all considerations save those native to the world of scholarship.[376]

This problem needs to be addressed if our scholarship is to be both rational and faithful to the cause of justice-in-shalom. Wolterstorff states:

> it seems to me imperative that in our practice of scholarship we do our best to break out of the bondage of our situation as relatively well-to-do members of the First World in order to be able to hear the cries of the deprived and oppressed of humanity.[377]

The solution to this problem is not to be found in the abandonment of pure theory, for that would be to deny a major component of shalom.[378] Rather it is found in a self-conscious heuristic of shalom, in which the

---

[373] Ibid.

[374] Ibid.

[375] Ibid., 176; and see above, (Chapter 3, A.2.) for the reality component obligation of our believings, and (Chapter 3, A.4.) on the effects of sin on our belief-dispositions and our obligation to overcome those effects to the best of our ability.

[376] Wolterstorff, *J&P*, 171.

[377] Ibid., 173.

[378] Wolterstorff, *RWBR*, 126–127. This idea, that knowledge is an important component of *shalom*, while controversial, does provide Wolterstorff with good reasons for rejecting the idea that all theory is "implicitly praxis-oriented", contra Gutting, "Review", 227. It may not specifically deal with the charge that pure theory is impossible, but its possibility is clearly entailed in its being included as a component of the *shalom* we are meant to pursue on earth.

scholar, out of compassion for the needs of her brothers and sisters in the Third World, listens actively to the voice of God in his Word, and the voice of the poor in the world.[379]

> The person who turns one of his ears to the prophetic unmasking word of the gospel and the other to the cries of those who suffer deprivation and oppression is not likely to suffer from the illusion that he is engaged in pure theory when in fact he is working to shore up his own position of privilege.[380]

Thus, an important strategy in the discovering of the workings of these malformations of our noetic faculties is that we listen to those who come from a different social *milieu* to our own, people who can thus challenge our assumptions and practices in the light of their different social goals and commitments.[381] The most powerful strategy, of course, is "listening attentively to the prophetic word of the Bible, that great unmasker of self-deceit."[382] These two strategies need not be seen to be in conflict:

> Perhaps we shall discover, though, that these paths join: by listening to the cries of the oppressed and deprived we are enabled genuinely to hear the word of the prophets – and of him who did not count equality with God a thing to be grasped at, but took the form of a servant, walking the path of humble obedience even to the point of accepting execution as a despised criminal: the Prince of Shalom.[383]

Thus, by its openness to God, his Word, and the needs and perspectives of the marginalised in our world society, Wolterstorff's heuristic of shalom avoids the problems of traditional Christian models of theorising, while answering the criticisms of Western scholarship proffered by people in the Third World.

---

[379] Wolterstorff, *RWBR*, 145–146; *J&P*, 176; cf. "Privileged Access", 91–93, where argues that both experiences of suffering and Christian commitment provide us with privileged access to the truth, to aspects of reality.

[380] Wolterstorff, *RWBR*, 146.

[381] Wolterstorff, *J&P*, 176.

[382] Ibid.

[383] Ibid.

PART THREE

A Critical Analysis of Wolterstorff's Meta-Theory

Introduction to Part Three

Having outlined Wolterstorff's meta-theory in the previous chapter, I will now critically analyse it, first identifying its main features, then dealing with relevant criticisms of his position and its allies, before discussing its meta-epistemological structure. This is necessary primarily in order to articulate his meta-theory by making it more rigorous, and demonstrating more adequately that it is justified.[1] This process will show that Wolterstorff's is a reasonable meta-theory to adopt in the analysis of *Wissenschaft*, including theological scholarship. It will also, by means of critical testing, result in the theory itself becoming more rigorous and comprehensive, and thus more capable of explaining a range of scholarly practices. These results will be valuable in the application of Wolterstorff's meta-theory to theological theorising.

---

1   That this is needed is seen in the suggestions made by G. Gutting "Review of *Reason Within the Bounds of Religion*", 225–228. There he specifically states that Wolterstorff needs to justify his meta-theory, for the rejection of foundationalism does not provide sufficient justification for adopting his version of situated rationality.

CHAPTER 5

An Articulation and Defence of Wolterstorff's Meta-Theory

A. Wolterstorff's Meta-Theory and his Situated Rationality

A.1. EMPIRICAL AND SITUATED

Wolterstorff's theory of rationality is empirical, in that it attempts to do justice to the nature of human believings.[1] The corresponding empirical nature of Wolterstorff's meta-theory is clearly seen in *Reason Within the Bounds of Religion*, in which on many occasions he refers to the history of science and details of scientific practice to support his contentions.[2] Support for the use of the history of science in the development of the philosophy of science has already been adduced with respect to Kuhn's theory of science.[3] It can also be found in the work of Lakatos who specifically attempted to develop a meta-theory which did justice to the nature of scientific practice, as is evident in his explicit claims and liberal use of examples from the history of science.[4]

However, for Lakatos the epistemologically significant history of science is not that which a historian of science would see, but a philosopher's *rational reconstruction of the history of science*.[5] This reconstruc-

---

[1] See above (Chapter 3, B.1.).
[2] See Wolterstorff, *RWBR*, 15–20, 43–45, 68–69, 94. It is important to realise that for Wolterstorff it is not just the products of theorising in *Wissenschaft* that are epistemologically significant, but also the practice of *Wissenschaft* itself. This has bearing on the role of control beliefs in the devising and weighing of theories, for which see below (this chapter, A.1.).
[3] See above (Chapter 2, B.1.).
[4] Lakatos, *MSRP*, 91–93, 98–100, 114–116, 138–154, 159–173; cf. N. Murphy, *Theology*, 51–87; M. Pera, "Methodological Sophisticationism: A Degenerating Project", *Imre Lakatos and Theories of Scientific Change*, ed. K. Gavroglu, *et al* (Dordrecht: Kluwer, 1989) 169, 171, 183–184.
[5] Lakatos, *MSRP*, 138 n. 2; 140 n. 4.

tion entails the use of footnotes to identify where the actual history of science differed from its rational reconstruction, in order to remove the personal and non-rational elements from the development of science.[6] It is at just this point, however, that Lakatos's theory is open to question. For if his methodology of scientific research programs, which was supposed to be true to the history of science, requires the effective falsification of that history for its support, then it is open to the same criticisms as the theories it attempted to replace.[7] In this regard Wolterstorff's meta-theory is more empirically adequate since, due to its flexibility and its ability to incorporate personal and social factors into a model of rationality, it is able to deal with a wider range of unreconstructed historical material.[8]

This commitment to empiricism in his epistemology does not, however, lead Wolterstorff to endorse the program of naturalised epistemology and its attendant rejection of trans-historical norms for believing.[9] Rather, it is an attempt to ensure that his epistemology is consistent with the real constraints that bear upon human believings on the grounds that "ought implies can".[10] Naturalised epistemology claims that science is the canon of rationality, that truth-claims are ultimately to be

---

[6] Lakatos, *MSRP*, 138 n. 2; 140 n. 4; cf. Kuhn, "Reflections", 256–259; Pera, 183. Pera, 172–184, argues that this is a reflection of Lakatos's "Cartesian Dilemma", in which a theory is either rational *or* subject to personal and social forces in its development. See further below (this chapter, B.2.).

[7] Kuhn, "Reflections", 256–259; Pera 183–184. J. A. Kourany, "Towards an Empirically Adequate Theory of Science", *Philosophy of Science* 48 (1982) 526–548, esp 537–546, argues that Lakatos's rational reconstruction of science is in fact empirically adequate. Her arguments, however, seem to be no real advance over Lakatos's position, and do not answer the crucial criticisms of Kuhn and Pera, but cf. Murphy, *Theology*, 69–73, who also supports Lakatos's line.

[8] Indeed, many of the features of the history of science that are so problematic for Lakatos are used by Wolterstorff to illustrate his meta-theory. See Wolterstorff, *RWBR*, 17–20, 68–69, 99–100. N. C. Murphy, "Acceptability Criteria for Work in Theology and Science", *Zygon* 22/3 (Sept 1987) 284–287; *Theology*, esp 51–87, asserts that Lakatos's meta-theory of science is the best-to-date. For the reasons adduced here, and others mentioned elsewhere, I disagree with this assessment in favour of Wolterstorff's meta-theory. For a more detailed discussion of Lakatos' theory and its empirical and conceptual problems, see below (Chapter 6, B.).

[9] N. Wolterstorff, "On Avoiding Historicism", *Philosophia Reformata* 45/2 (1980) 178–185; *pace* E. J. Echeverria, "Towards a Critique of the Subject", *Philosophia Reformata* 44/1 (1979) 86–105. Echeverria's major concerns focus on the person- and situation-specific nature of Wolterstorff's meta-theory, rather than specifically on Wolterstorff's use of the history of science. However, in large part the former is a product of the latter, and so his comments are relevant to Wolterstorff's empirical focus.

[10] For a similar notion, see Duran, 121. This position does not, of course, lead to Wolterstorff's accepting her particular version of an empirically adequate meta-theory.

settled at the "tribunal of science", and there are, therefore, no transcendent reference points or norms by which science is to be assessed.[11] The only norms which exist are internal to science, and consist of those "virtues" which have been found to best serve the goals of science.[12] This is clearly in contrast to Wolterstorff who believes that transcendent obligations pertain to the governing of belief-dispositions which, while their form may change in the light of a specific belief system or believing community, are nonetheless constant norms which are to govern our believings.[13] While pragmatism and the practice of science may be useful guides to the truth content of a theory, ultimately the goal of rationality is to get in touch with reality, rather than to develop theories that work, or comport well with currently accepted scientific standards.

However, both Wolterstorff's use of the history of science in the development of his meta-theory, and the nature of the obligations which he sees as governing theorising, clearly indicate that his meta-theory is as situation- and person-specific as is his theory of rationality. This situation- and person-specificity is a central feature of his meta-theory as a whole. His functional distinction between data, data background and control beliefs is clearly situated, in that the very function a belief performs depends in part on the context of a particular case of believing.[14] This results in a situation- and person-specific account of theory acceptance, for theory acceptance or rejection is always made relative to a particular body

---

11   W. V. O. Quine, "Comments on Lauener", *Perspectives on Quine*, ed. R. B. Barrett and R. F. Gibson (Oxford: Basil Blackwell, 1990) 229; *Pursuit of Truth* (Cambridge: Cambridge University Press, 1990) 19–21.

12   Quine, *Pursuit*, 19–21, where he identifies these as, preeminently empiricism, and secondarily the five virtues he noted with Ullian in *The Web of Belief*, 42–53, namely conservatism, generality, simplicity, refutability and modesty. These are, however, specifically *historicist* virtues, giving rise to a strictly historicist criterion of scientific rationality, as can be seen in his discussion of simplicity in W. V. Quine, "On Simple Theories of a Complex World", *The Ways of Paradox and Other Essays* (New York: Random House, 1966) 242–245, and in general in relation to rationality, in *Pursuit*, 19–21; cf. L. Laudan, *Progress and its Problems: Towards a Theory of Scientific Growth* (Berkley: University of California Press, 1977) 127–131, who adopts purely pragmatist norms for believing; Rorty, "Pragmatism, Relativism and Irrationalism", 165, 166, 173–174; Rosenbaum, 98–99. Kourany, 526–548, also argues, on Lakatosian lines, for a specifically historicist theory of science.

13   Wolterstorff, "On Avoiding Historicism", 182–185; *EB&G*, 455. For a discussion of this idea of universal norms with situation specific forms in relation to ethical virtues, see McIntyre, *After Virtue*, 186–222; C. S. Layman, *The Shape of the Good: Christian Reflections on the Foundations of Ethics* (Notre Dame: University of Notre Dame Press, 1991) 128–135. Their arguments can be applied, *mutatis mutandis*, to noetic norms and virtues.

14   See above (Chapter 4, B.1.).

of beliefs.[15] Given the importance of control beliefs in Wolterstorff's meta-theory, it is of particular significance that these control beliefs are themselves always situation- and person-specific and defeasible.[16] This aspect of his meta-theory warrants exploration, particularly in the light of some criticisms that have been levelled against it.

Wolterstorff's meta-theory is both descriptive and prescriptive.[17] Central to his prescription for Christian scholarship is the claim that the belief-content of a Christian scholar's authentic Christian commitment ought to function as a control in her devising and weighing of theories.[18] This notion clearly reinforces the situation- and person-specific character of his meta-theory, for the authentic commitment which is to guide a scholar's theorising is situation- and person-specific.[19] It needs to be stressed that, in contrast to a person's *actual* commitment which is a "certain selection from the totality of his *doings and believings*", a person's *authentic* Christian commitment is a "certain selection from the totality of his *obligations*".[20] It is, therefore, a normative notion, which shares the situation- and person-specificity of Wolterstorff's idea of the nature and function of noetic norms in general. It follows from this that, since the authentic commitment which is to guide a scholar's devising and weighing of theories is legitimately subject to alteration, any criterion of warranted theory choice will be situated and defeasible.[21] It will be situated, for the norms which govern theory choice are subject to situational modification, and it will be defeasible, for these norms are not themselves incorrigible but are subject to justified modification. There is, therefore, no algorithm of warranted theory choice, and *Wissenschaft* itself will be a pluralistic and corrigible enterprise.[22]

Such a situated model of rationality and the scientific enterprise is supported by a number of people who are committed to the objective

---

15 See above (Chapter 4, B.2.)

16 See above (Chapter 4, B.1.).

17 This aspect of Wolterstorff's thought was clearly missed by Echeverria, 95–96. For a discussion of this, see Wolterstorff, "On Avoiding Historicism", 179–180.

18 See above (Chapter 4, B.2.).

19 See above (Chapter 4, B.2.).

20 Wolterstorff, "On Avoiding Historicism", 178.

21 This is reinforced by Wolterstorff's recognition that even the same set of control beliefs may allow different appraisals of a given theory by different scholars by virtue of the complexity of belief systems and the varying skills of scholars. See above (Chapter 4, B.2.).

22 This is central to Wolterstorff's meta-theory, as argued at length in Chapter 4 above. For further articulation of Wolterstorff's criterion of theory choice, see below (this chapter, A.2.).

nature of science and rationality. Siegel, Helm, Newton-Smith and Thorson, for instance, argue from perspectives different both to Wolterstorff and each other for a revisable, fallible model of science in which certitude is ruled out, but objectivity is not.[23] There is no unique, privileged epistemic framework, nor are there rules which pertain to all times and persons and contexts.[24] There is an inescapably personal component to all human knowing, including scientific knowing.[25] However, objectivity, even a particular kind of absolutism, are possible so long as researchers recognise the claims of rival theories and ensure that all theories, their own included, are fairly and non-question-beggingly assessed.[26] An essential component of this rational critical – and self-critical – assessment of truth-claims of rival theories is the recognition and critical analysis of the presuppositions of the theories being assessed.[27] Claims to truth, objective truth, are possible and rationally supportable if, in the context of rational debate, these claims are seen to be the best available option so far developed.[28] A similar situated, defeasible perspective has been advanced for the rational assessment of rival theological and interpretive theories.[29]

This notion of situated scientific rationality needs to be examined in the light of Wolterstorff's later suggestion that the control function of beliefs needs to be understood in the context of the *social practice* of scholarship. While he recognises that scientific equipment and results are significant in the philosophical analysis of science, these results and equipment "emerge from, or gain their significance from, scientific practice".[30] Just what a social practice is, and how it functions, has not

---

[23] Siegel, 160–167; P. Helm, "Understanding Scholarly Presuppositions: A Crucial Tool for Research?", *Tyndale Bulletin* 44/1 (1993) 143–154. Newton-Smith, *The Rationality of Science*; W. R. Thorson, "Scientific Objectivity and the Listening Attitude", *Objective Knowledge*, ed. P. Helm (Leicester: IVP, 1987) 59–83. Other examples could be cited but these suffice for my purposes.

[24] Siegel, 162, 165.

[25] Thorson, "Scientific Objectivity and the Listening Attitude", 61–62. He draws particularly on the work of Michael Polanyi in his discussion of these issues. For a brief exposition of the main tenets of Polanyi's position, see Polanyi, *Science, Faith and Society*.

[26] Siegel, 167.

[27] Helm, "Scholarly Presuppositions", 152–154.

[28] Newton-Smith, 208–236, 266–273; Siegel, 162.

[29] See Barbour, 66–92; Bosch, *Transforming Mission*, 186–187; G. R. Osborne, *The Hermeneutical Spiral: A Comprehensive Introduction to Biblical Interpretation* (Downers Grove: IVP, 1991) esp 397–415; Polkinghorne, *One World*, 26–42; *Reason and Reality*, 4–33, 49–59; D. R. Stiver, "Much Ado About Athens and Jerusalem: The Implications of Postmodernism for Faith", *RevExp* 91 (1994) 83–102.

[30] Wolterstorff, *OCL*, 73.

been subject to rigorous analysis, so Wolterstorff turns to MacIntyre for a brief elucidation of these matters.[31] A social practice is a complex, learned activity with traditions and histories.[32] Novices are inducted into these practices through explicit teaching and apprenticeship-type modelling.[33] The goal of such induction is "to assimilate goals for one's engagement in the practice, and standards of excellence for one's performance of it".[34] These goals and standards, however, "are not for the most part analytic of the practice", they do not merely *reflect* the universally accepted patterns of a given practice.[35] Amongst practitioners of a discipline there are often competing standards and goals, and at certain times there will be major changes in the predominant goals and standards operant in a given practice.[36] Over time, and even at a particular time within a practice, goals and standards are malleable, open to change and development.[37]

> An implication of this openness is that it is a mistake to ask for *the* goals and *the* standards and *the* methods of a social practice such as art or science, as though art and science were some sort of static, Platonic essences descending into history in the fullness of time.[38]

Rather, there will be different goals and standards and methods for different communities within a given practice, and for the same community at different times.[39] And these goals, standards and methods will be

---

[31] Wolterstorff, *OCL*, 73, where he refers to A. MacIntyre, *After Virtue: A Study in Moral Theory* (2nd ed; Notre Dame: University of Notre Dame Press, 1984) as the source for this analysis. Since Wolterstorff wrote this article, however, more work has been done on the nature and function of social practices. Indeed, some of the salient points are present in the work of Michael Polanyi. A detailed study of the sociology of knowledge lies outside my scope here, so I will only deal with this issue briefly, and to the extent that it is relevant to my overall argument. For an interesting discussion of some of the dimensions of social practices in science, see M. Polanyi, *Science, Faith and Society*, Ch. II and III, pp. 42–84; and for some intriguing parallels between science and theology, see A. Thomson, *Tradition and Authority in Science and Theology*.

[32] Wolterstorff, *OCL*, 74; "Scholarship and Conviction", 42–43; MacIntyre, *After Virtue*, 187, 189–190, 220–224, 274.

[33] Wolterstorff, *OCL*, 74; "Scholarship and Conviction", 43; MacIntyre, *After Virtue*, 190.

[34] Wolterstorff, *OCL*, 74; "Scholarship and Conviction", 43–44; MacIntyre, *After Virtue*, 190.

[35] Wolterstorff, *OCL*, 74.

[36] Ibid.

[37] Wolterstorff, *OCL*, 74; "Scholarship and Conviction", 44; MacIntyre, *After Virtue*, 189, 274.

[38] Wolterstorff, *OCL*, 74.

[39] Wolterstorff, "Scholarship and Conviction", 44–45.

justifiable for those communities at those times, so long as the appropriate conditions for rationality are met. This provides further support for Wolterstorff's notion of a pluralism of rational sciences. Whether it is compatible with his disavowal of relativism and historicism remains to be seen.[40]

Quite clearly such a social practice account of science is susceptible to historicist interpretation and development. This is evident in the way that MacIntyre articulates his theory of morality in *After Virtue*, where he adopts a specifically historicist account of the virtues.[41] This account, *mutatis mutandis*, applies equally to scientific practice, and rationality in general. MacIntyre states:

> For all reasoning takes place within the context of some traditional mode of thought, transcending through criticism and invention the limitations of what had hitherto been reasoned in that tradition; this is as true of modern physics as of medieval logic.[42]

According to MacIntyre there is no historically transcendent point from which the arguments of tradition can be appraised, nor are there historically transcendent norms by which they are judged.[43]

From Wolterstorff's perspective, such historicist conclusions are unacceptable, for there are transcendent norms by which different traditions may be assessed.[44] It seems, in fact, that in *Whose Justice? Which Rationality?* MacIntyre backs away from strict historicism and adopts a situated notion of rationality which bears striking resemblance to that of Wolterstorff.[45] Indeed, the seeds of a non-historicist interpretation

---

[40] This will be discussed below (this chapter, B.). See also MacIntyre, *After Virtue*, 265–277.

[41] MacIntyre, *After Virtue*, 190, 222, 267–271, 276–277, makes it clear that he is a historicist, and that his position is not to be identified with relativism.

[42] Ibid., 222.

[43] Ibid., 267–271.

[44] This is clearly seen in Wolterstorff, *OCL*, 74–78, where he affirms both the importance of the social practice account of *Wissenschaft*, and also the reality of non-historicist norms for believing in Christian scholarship.

[45] A. MacIntyre, *Whose Justice? Which Rationality?* (London: Duckworth, 1987) 6–8, 356–357, 363–364. There he maintains his idea that rationality is crucially connected to the historical context of the argument, and in the problem-solving value, relative to its predecessors within a tradition and rivals in other traditions, of a given notion of rationality. However he also clearly argues for a correspondence theory of truth, and asserts that while rational justification and warranted assertibility are historically conditioned notions that only have meaning within the history of a given tradition, the notion of truth is timeless and not historically conditioned. This seeming change in perspective is susceptible to a number of

and development of a social practice account of *Wissenschaft* and rationality are seen in MacIntyre's idea of a broader vision of a *telos* of human life into which practices, and the virtues they engender, fit and to which they must conform and which they must further.[46] For MacIntyre these goals, and the overall *telos* to which they contribute, are part of the continuing conversation of tradition: they are as such historically determined and non-transcendent, as are the virtues and practices they nourish.[47] For Wolterstorff, on the other hand, the overall goal of human life is not historically determined. It is, rather, history-transcendent, and is found in the vision of *shalom* which is the Bible's view of the goal of all existence, including human existence. There may be different visions of what constitutes the flourishing of different communities,[48] but the Christian vision of *shalom* is constant and objective, despite the fact that its implications and implementation for different communities at different times may vary. For Wolterstorff the different rules and norms and virtues of a (noetic) community are justifiable inasmuch as they further the *flourishing*, the *shalom*, of a given community. While noetic obligations are clearly a function of situation-specific practices, then, they are not *historicist* in nature, for they are governed by the over-arching *telos* of *shalom*.[49]

This situation- and person-specificity of Wolterstorff's meta-theory has been subject to two main criticisms: that it results in a type of historicism; that it illegitimately imports Christian commitment into scientific theorising thereby defying the "naturalised" quality of the natural sciences. Both criticisms in effect relate to the use, and manner of use, of

---

possible interpretations: he has modified his notion of rationality in such a way as to be consistent with Wolterstorff's ideas; he was either ambiguous or misleading in his avowal of historicism in *After Virtue*; I have misconstrued his position in either (or both) *After Virtue* or *Whose Justice? Which Rationality?*; he is simply inconsistent. It seems to me, in the light of *After Virtue*, 267–271, and comments he makes in the preface to *Whose Justice? Which Rationality?* that the first is the most cogent (and charitable) option. This, from my perspective, is reinforced by his correspondence theory of truth and non-historicist account of the nature of truth which, as I argue below (this chapter, B.1.) do not comport well with the historicist thesis.

[46] MacIntyre, *After Virtue*, 201–203.

[47] MacIntyre, *After Virtue*, 222. In *Whose Justice? Which Rationality?*, 401–403, he acknowledges the historically conditioned nature of different accounts of justice and practical rationality in a manner reminiscent of Wolterstorff's notion of the plurality of *Wissenschaft*. Indeed, his general argument seems quite consistent with Wolterstorff's position.

[48] Wolterstorff, *EB&G*, 455.

[49] The different rules, norms and values which inform and are informed by the life of a community can be seen as the historical incarnation of the trans-historical rule of *shalom*.

authentic Christian commitment as a norm in Christian (scientific) scholarship. The first of these criticisms is levelled against Wolterstorff by Echeverria in a paper in which he misleadingly identifies Wolterstorff's meta-theory as a variety of historicism.[50] His chief reason for doing so is that Wolterstorff argues that authentic Christian commitment is person and situation specific. If that commitment is to function as normative control over Christian scholarship, then it is supposed that there is in fact no history-transcendent norm which governs our believings.[51]

One argument against this interpretation of Wolterstorff has already been outlined in relation to *shalom* as the ultimate norm which grounds all historically shifting norms for believing (including the belief-content of authentic Christian commitment). In light of Wolterstorff's understanding of *shalom*, of the central role that relationship with God through faith in Jesus Christ and of the function that the Bible as authoritative source of belief has in that notion, it is clear that the belief content of authentic Christian commitment is not totally historically conditioned. Wolterstorff's specific argument against Echeverria's construal of his position is connected to this. He asserts that the biblical *kerygma*, which he believes includes the work of Christ and the biblical meaning of Creation, is "fixed no matter what transpires in history".[52] The biblical *kerygma*, on which all faith depends, is not subject to historical change, but the specific way in which Christian faith is actualised in belief and life certainly is.[53] Thus,

---

50 See Echeverria, 100–105; cf. Wolterstorff, "On avoiding historicism", 180–181, 183–185. For reasons why Wolterstorff is not historicist, see below (this chapter, B.).

51 Echeverria, 101–103. This, he believes, leads Wolterstorff to embrace what Echeverria calls his "qualified immanent historicism". For support of the idea that authentic Christian commitment is not subject to change, see Hart, "The Articulation of Belief", 216, 226–237. M. H. Rienstra, "History, Objectivity and the Christian Scholar", *History and Historical Understanding*, ed. C. T. McIntire and R. A. Wells (Grand Rapids: Eerdmans, 1984) 78–80, has problems with Wolterstorff's idea that authentic commitment is "relative to persons and to times", see Wolterstorff, *RWBR*, 74. However, his problem is more with the word than with the idea, largely due to his concern that it may lead to the "horrors" of relativism. This is a legitimate fear, but as I have shown to some extent, and will show in more detail below (this chapter, B.), Wolterstorff's is not a relativist meta-theory. For an endorsement of the reciprocal relationship of commitment and rationality, see Holmes, "Commitment and Rationality", 191–208.

52 Wolterstorff, "On avoiding historicism", 184.

53 Ibid. Indeed, these ideas were already present in *RWBR*, 71–75. Perhaps Echeverria was unable to see these claims, or their implications, because of his concern that Wolterstorff had given too much ground to the situation- and person-specificity of belief, in particular seeing that Wolterstorff claimed that the propositions which every believer in every context has to accept are "few and simple", Wolterstorff, *RWBR*, 75. Perhaps Echeverria ultimately cannot allow for an objective and absolute ground in revelation co-existing with fallible and situation-specific doctrinal and ethical formulations of the

while Wolterstorff clearly recognises that the specific belief content of authentic Christian commitment is person- and situation-specific, it can function as a history-transcendent norm for theorising for Christian scholars because it does have at least some fixed content, which in turn is constrained by the nature of *shalom*.

Whether, in fact, it should function as a norm at all is the burden of the second criticism raised by de Vries.[54] This criticism requires more substantial treatment, in large part because it cuts to the heart of the notion that rationality is guaranteed by value-free neutrality of method and assumptions.[55] De Vries presents three main arguments against Wolterstorff's perspective on the integration of faith and science. First, he argues, the contradictions that scholars may identify between their Christian commitment and their scholarly practice may be more apparent than real.[56] Wolterstorff, of course, agrees with this perspective: his concern is with cases of real rather than apparent contradiction.[57] Secondly, he states that Christian commitment ought to function, not at the level of specific theories, but at the level of the assumptions and methods which lie at the foundation of any discipline.[58] In the case of a specific theory's contradicting our genuine control beliefs he argues that we can question or alter the assumptions of the discipline, restrict the theory's scope, or revise our control beliefs.[59] Again, Wolterstorff always recognised the role of control beliefs in the challenging of disciplinary assumptions and methods.[60] However what de Vries fails to recognise is that a given theory may well embody the questionable assumptions and methods in such a way that the rejection of those foundations entails the rejection of the theory.[61] In this

---

content of that revelation.

[54] P. de Vries, "Naturalism in the Natural Sciences: A Christian Perspective", *Christian Scholar's Review* 15/4 (1986) 388–396; "Multifaceted Perspective: A Rejoinder to Nicholas Wolterstorff", *Christian Scholar's Review* 16/1 (1986) 59–65.

[55] de Vries often seems to caricature the idea of integration rather than arguing against it, as in his repeated statements that there is no need to introduce the God hypothesis into natural sciences, and thus there is no need for the kind of integration Wolterstorff commends. See de Vries, "Naturalism in the Natural Sciences", 388, 389; See also his claim that Wolterstorff must reject determinism in chemistry as well as in psychology, "Multifaceted Perspective", 63.

[56] de Vries, "Naturalism in the Natural Sciences", 391.

[57] N. Wolterstorff, "Reply to Paul de Vries", *Christian Scholar's Review* 16/1 (1986) 57.

[58] de Vries, "Naturalism in the Natural Sciences", 393. I have reversed the order of the second and third of de Vries' arguments against Wolterstorff.

[59] Ibid.

[60] Wolterstorff, "Reply to Paul de Vries", 55, 58.

[61] Ibid., 57–58.

case even a narrow focus on disciplinary foundations will have consequences for the acceptance or rejection of a particular theory. It is not possible to restrict the control function of Christian commitment just to disciplinary foundations without thereby also influencing theory choice.

The third argument that de Vries proffers is that Wolterstorff has not advanced any convincing cases of a Christian scholar's beliefs leading to the rejection of a specific theory.[62] He argues that Wolterstorff's examples of Freudian and behaviourist psychology are not examples of the rejection of a scientific theory because it is incompatible with Christian belief but of the rejection of illegitimate and reductionist extra-scientific philosophical extrapolations of those limited theories.[63] In this matter Wolterstorff and de Vries continue to disagree: for Wolterstorff sees de Vries' strategy as an example of the conformist strategy he rejects, and the result of a failure to consider the *practice* as well as the *results* of science.[64] From the perspective of the *practice* of science the "philosophical" pronouncements of Skinner are not extra-scientific extrapolations of his scientific theories, but control beliefs which determine the very nature of his theory.[65]

The idea that Christian commitment cannot function internally to scholarship is supported by de Vries with three further claims. The first is that Wolterstorff presents more examples of *Wissenschaft* altering Christian belief than *vice versa*. This, he claims, means that Christian commitment is not really functioning as a control.[66] This criticism ignores a crucial component of Wolterstorff's meta-theory: the defeasibility and situation-specificity of authentic Christian commitment.[67] Given this notion of authentic Christian commitment functioning as a control,

---

62 de Vries, "Naturalism in the Natural Sciences", 392–393; "Multifaceted Perspective", 61–65.

63 de Vries, "Naturalism in the Natural Sciences", 392; "Multifaceted Perspective", 63–64. However, it is important to note that in effect de Vries is allowing his Christian beliefs to influence his assessment of a particular theory's claims in stating that it has transgressed the limits of its discipline. While this is a compatibilist as opposed to a transformationalist strategy (for these terms, see below, 267–270) it nonetheless shows that de Vries is tacitly allowing his Christian commitment to function internally to his scholarship. Thus he is unwittingly, I believe, adopting the strategy he criticises Wolterstorff for adopting.

64 Wolterstorff, "Reply to Paul de Vries", 57–58. de Vries briefly articulates a conformist or complementarist strategy and presents arguments in its favour in "Naturalism in the Natural Sciences", 394–396. Again, Wolterstorff sees this as an inadequate attempt to do just what he suggests scholars in general should do, Wolterstorff, "Reply to Paul de Vries", 58.

65 Wolterstorff, "Reply to Paul de Vries", 57–58.

66 de Vries, "Naturalism in the Natural Sciences", 391–392.

67 For this, see above (Chapter 4, B.2.).

de Vries' criticism fails.[68] His second claim is that in order to be consistent Wolterstorff would need to reject current practice in chemistry and physiology, for they both operate on deterministic assumptions.[69] This, however, is to misunderstand the nature of the control function of authentic Christian commitment in Wolterstorff's meta-theory. He freely acknowledges that Christian and non-Christian scholars may share many assumptions and methods, and that there may be little or no difference between Christian and non-Christian scholarship. Given that his is not a Neo-Calvinist meta-theory and his demand is that Christian scholarship be *faithful* rather than *different*, this is again no real criticism of his theory.[70] It is not important that there be a demonstrable *difference* between the scholarship a Christian practices and that of her non-Christian colleague. Rather, if they share assumptions and methods, then this must result from reasoned reflection on the part of the Christian in the light of her authentic

---

[68] This, of course, is a controversial view of authentic Christian commitment. This criticism of de Vries's is similar to Echeverria's. For the idea that science can contribute to theories in theology, see N. Murphy, "Postmodern Apologetics: Or Why Theologians *Must* Pay Attention to Science", *Religion and Science: History, Method, Dialogue*, ed. W. M. Richardson and W. J. Wildman (New York: Routledge, 1996) 105–120; "Acceptability Criteria", 287–288.

[69] de Vries, "Multifaceted Perspective", 63–64. This is similar to a criticism noted by Nelson, "Strategies", 328 n. 6, of Wolterstorff's meta-theory. Two comments are relevant here. First, Wolterstorff rejects *psychological* determinism because it conflicts with human freedom; he says nothing about laws of chemical or physiological processes conflicting with Christian control beliefs. Thus, unless chemical and physiological theories were developed along lines inconsistent with human freedom, this problem does not arise. Of course, if they are developed so as to be inconsistent with *divine* freedom and *divine* agency, as they have been, then a Christian is entitled or even obliged to reject those formulations, conflicting, as they do, with Christian control beliefs. Which brings me to the second point. It is interesting to note that J. Polkinghorne, *Science and Creation* (London: SPCK, 1988) *Reason and Reality* (London: SPCK, 1991) 34–48; "Science and Providence: How God Works in the World" (Sydney: Morling College Annual Lecture, 1993) presents a line that comports well with Wolterstorff's meta-theory in relation to physics, a discipline which has been seen to be the paradigm of deterministic science. He argues that the new physics with its view of a non-mechanistic, non-deterministic universe which is open to real becoming is more consistent with Christian belief than the old mechanistic theories. While I do not claim that he has adopted Wolterstorff's meta-theory, I do believe his argument supports Wolterstorff's notion over-against de Vries'. For examples of the integration of theological propositions in a coherent and fruitful research program, see Murphy, "Acceptability Criteria", 289–294. The provision of examples, including those from the domain of physics and anthropology, in the work of Polkinghorne and others undermines this criticism of Wolterstorff's meta-theory.

[70] See above (Chapter 4, A.3.).

commitment rather than the uncritical acceptance of current scholarly practice.[71]

The third claim is that the complexity and subsidiary nature of the belief-content of Christian faith make Wolterstorff's position difficult or impossible to implement.[72] Christian commitment is first to the Word of God, and at best only secondarily to a set of control beliefs derived from that commitment. To focus, then, on the latter and not on the general *perspectival* approach offered by the former is to mistake the nature of Christian faith and scholarship.[73] These derivative beliefs are in turn sufficiently complicated to make any comparison between those beliefs and the theories of scholarship "either highly interpretive or literally impossible.[74] In fact, however, these claims are directly paralleled by claims made by Wolterstorff. He sees the primary component of Christian belief and life to be commitment: the belief-content of this commitment is both derivative of that commitment and person specific.[75] So too, authentic Christian commitment, and the practice of scholarship are so complex, and human abilities are so limited, that mistakes and lacunae in thought are inevitable.[76] This presents no problem to Wolterstorff's theory, despite de Vries' contentions, just because Wolterstorff rejects the notion of an algorithm of rationality and embraces the reality of pluralism in scholarship.[77] Thus, in my view, de Vries' counter-arguments are either specifically defeated by Wolterstorff, or apply only to a misconstrual of his position.

To some extent the judgements I have made are impossible to definitively adjudicate, for the cogency of the arguments which support

---

71 Thus, subject to suitable reflection, the Christian scholar can adopt the pattern of complementarist scholarship outlined below from within a broadly transformationalist strategy.

72 de Vries, "Multifaceted Perspective", 61–62. A similar claim is made by Helm, who believes that in light of the qualifications Wolterstorff places upon the role of authentic Christian commitment in devising and weighing theories, "it would appear that the role of Christian commitment being internal to and controlling the devising, accepting or rejecting of theories has, by these qualifications, all but vanished" (P. Helm, *Faith and Understanding* (Grand Rapids: Eerdmans, 1997) 50). He does note, however, that such a judgement cannot be made *a priori*, but must await the production of such theories. Irrespective of such empirical demonstration of Wolterstorff's account, I believe that my discussion of Wolterstorff's meta-theory shows that Helm's claim is mistaken.

73 Ibid., 61.

74 Ibid., 61–62.

75 See above (Chapter 4, B.2.).

76 See above (Chapter 4, B.2.).

77 See above (Chapter 4, B.2.).

them depends upon the conceptual framework in which they are situated. This in turn leads me to note what I see as a root cause of the differences between Wolterstorff, de Vries and Echeverria: they adopt different and incompatible strategies for integrating faith and scholarship. Three main integrative strategies have been identified by Wolfe and articulated by Nelson and Hasker and are helpful, I believe, in understanding and resolving these disputes.[78] The first of these is the *compatibilist* strategy, which roughly equates with Wolterstorff's category of *conformist* views of faith and *Wissenschaft*.[79] In this strategy the assumptions and methods of a given discipline are accepted as they are, and the Christian scholar's task is to demonstrate the compatibility of her discipline with her Christian commitment.[80] This is clearly the line adopted by de Vries, and is inadequate, I believe, for the reasons Wolterstorff notes in *Reason Within the Bounds of Religion* and elsewhere.[81] The second strategy is the *reconstructionalist* one, which roughly equates with the Neo-Calvinist vision of Christian scholarship.[82] In this strategy the assumptions and methods of a given discipline are seen as incompatible with Christian commitment, and so a separate, faithful body of learning must be constructed along Christian lines in accord with Christian presuppositions.[83] While Echeverria does not specifically argue for this strategy, it seems to be the one which best fits with his concern that the basic tenets of

---

[78] See D. L. Wolfe, "The Line of Demarcation between Integration and Pseudointegration", *The Reality of Christian Learning: Strategies for Faith-Discipline Integration*, H. Heie and D. L. Wolfe (Grand Rapids: Eerdmans, 1987) 3–11; R. R. Nelson, "Faith-Discipline Integration: Compatibilist, Reconstructionalist and Transformationalist Strategies", *The Reality of Christian Learning: Strategies for Faith-Discipline Integration*, H. Heie and D. L. Wolfe (Grand Rapids: Eerdmans, 1987) 317–339; W. Hasker, "Faith-Learning Integration: An Overview", *Christian Scholar's Review* 21/3 (Mar 1992) 234–248.

[79] Wolfe, "Demarcation", 7–11; Nelson, "Integration", 320–324; Hasker, 239; cf. Wolterstorff, *RWBR*, 81–82.

[80] Wolfe, "Demarcation", 7; Nelson, "Strategies", 320; Hasker, "Integration", 239.

[81] This is evident in many of de Vries's assertions and most of his arguments. See de Vries, "Naturalism in the Natural Sciences", 388–396; "Multifaceted Perspective", 59–65. These problems are noted above (Chapter 4, B.2.). Note also the problems Nelson identifies with this strategy, and his preference for the transformationalist strategy (Nelson, "Integration", 320–324, 327–339). For a general defence of a version of the compatibilist strategy, see Wolfe, "Demarcation", 7–11.

[82] Wolfe, "Demarcation", 7–8; Nelson, "Strategies", 324–327; Hasker, "Integration", 239–240. R. Sweetman, "Christian Scholarship: Two Reformed Perspectives", *Perspectives* 16/6 (June/July 2001) 14–19, calls this the "integralist" strategy of Reformed presuppositionalism, especially those who follow Dooyeweerd's line. cf. Wolterstorff's discussion of neo-Calvinism, above (Chapter 4, A.).

[83] Wolfe, "Demarcation", 7–8; Nelson, "Strategies", 324–325; Hasker, "Integration", 239–240.

the faith not be subjected to criticism and alteration in the light of advances in *Wissenschaft*.[84] This line is also inadequate, largely for reasons already adduced.[85]

The third line, and the one which Wolterstorff clearly endorses, is the *transformationalist* strategy.[86] This strategy recognises that some of the assumptions and methods of the discipline may be acceptable, but that others are not: what is required is a reformation of the discipline along Christian lines.[87] I believe that this strategy not only conforms to Wolterstorff's meta-theory, but is also the most adequate one.[88] Once the integrative strategies which nourish the specific criticisms of Wolterstorff's position are identified and called into question, the arguments themselves are largely defeated. Further, Wolterstorff's views, while needing further articulation, best explain the nature of *Wissenschaft*, and provide a fruitful strategy for the integration of Christian commitment and scholarly endeavour.[89]

---

[84] This is an example, as noted above, of the immunity of the fundamentals of faith to rational criticism and fits with the Neo-Calvinist idea of faith as a precondition for true scholarship.

[85] See above, (Chapter 4, A.); cf. Wolfe, "Demarcation", 7–8, who argues that the reconstructionalist strategy is not an example of true, but of pseudo-integration. This is too harsh a judgement, as Hasker, "Integration", 240–241, notes. However, his strictures, and the more detailed arguments of Nelson, "Strategies", 326–327, support Wolterstorff's contention that it is an inadequate strategy for the integration of commitment and theorising.

[86] Wolfe, "Demarcation", 7; Nelson, "Strategies", 327–339; Hasker, "Integration", 239; cf. Sweetman, 14–19, who calls this the "integrationalist" strategy. That this is Wolterstorff's approach is clear from the line of his argument in general, and is endorsed by Nelson, "Strategies", 328 n. 6.

[87] Wolfe, "Demarcation", 7; Nelson, "Strategies", 327–339; Hasker, "Integration", 239.

[88] For further defence of the main lines of this strategy, see Nelson, "Strategies", 327–339.

[89] Wolterstorff's meta-theory is specifically supported by Rienstra, 75–82, in relation to historical scholarship, and is generally supported by Nelson's ideas of integration, Nelson, "Strategies", 327–339, and many discussions of the integral relationship between commitment and theorising, see Helm, "Christian Philosophy of Science", 3–4; Holmes, "Commitment and Rationality", 192, 197, 198–200; B. Mitchell, "Reason and Commitment in the Academic Vocation", *How to Play Theological Ping-Pong: And Other Essays on Faith and Reason*, ed. W. J. Abraham and R. Prevost (London: Hodder and Stoughton, 1990) 98–112; "Neutrality and Commitment", *Theological Ping-Pong*, 113–131; "Two Approaches to the Philosophy of Religion", *For God and Clarity: New Essays in Honour of Austen Farrer*, J. C. Eaton and A. Loades (ed) (Allison Park: Pickwick, 1983) 177–183. In the latter essay he argues that Wolterstorff is a fideist. This is a mistaken claim, and in fact Wolterstorff's position is close to the general lines endorsed by Mitchell, for Wolterstorff clearly accepts the possibility and necessity of the critical assessment of Christian commitment.

A.2. Entitled Theory-Choice and his Criterion of Rationality

The way in which authentic commitment ought to function as a control needs to be specified if it is to be useful in the development of a criterion of warranted theory devising and weighing. This in turn requires the articulation of the links that exist between his notion of situated rationality and his meta-theory. Once these links are established his general criterion of rationality can be articulated as a criterion, or set of related criteria, of theory devising and weighing.

Wolterstorff's rationality is one in which beliefs are innocent-until-proven-guilty; indeed that is central to his theory.[90] It may seem at first glance that this is inconsistent with the general strategy of theory-testing, and with the practice of scholarship as a whole. For the testing of theories and the process of demonstrating that a given theory is more adequate than its rivals is at the heart of scholarship, and it seems that this will not allow an innocent-until-proven-guilty stance. This, however, is a misconception, both of the nature of scholarship and of the nature of the innocent-until-proven-guilty stance. An innocent-until-proven-guilty approach to theorising comports better with accepted scholarly practice, and provides a workable strategy for this practice. It is not the case that in normal scholarly practice belief in a theory is suspended during the course of its testing. In all types of *Wissenschaft* theories are tested by the process of dialogue and debate in various scholarly fora. The normal practice is not for the proponent of a theory to proffer it tentatively and withhold belief in her theory until it passes the critical appraisal of the community.[91] Rather they are held tenaciously and presented as the best available explanation of the data in their scope. When challenged, the normal response is not to give up the theory as falsified,[92] but to defend the theory, if necessary modifying related hypotheses in order to articulate the theory. Thus the practice of *Wissenschaft* is not generally conducted along guilty-until-proven-innocent lines.

---

90   See Chapter 3 above.

91   Even Popper's falsificationist criterion of an acceptable theory does not require tentativeness in the holding of a theory under test. Certainly Lakatos's modification of falsificationism does not: indeed for Lakatos it is the proliferation of tenaciously held theories which best characterises the practice of true and successful science. While there are flaws in Lakatos's view and it does not provide an adequate criterion of theory choice, these views support my claim. See also Mitchell, "Reason and Commitment", 98–112; "Neutrality and Commitment", 113–131.

92   See the criticisms of falsificationism for a justification of this claim, above (Chapter 1, B.2.).

Furthermore, an innocent-until-proven-guilty stance provides a workable strategy for the devising and weighing of theories. It is not the case that the critical appraisal of theories requires the suspension of belief in those theories. A theory is not taken to be guilty-until-proven-innocent in the course of testing, but rather when subjected to testing it becomes a suspect belief or set of beliefs.[93] That theory does not need to prove its rational acceptability before it is an acceptable theory, even as a suspect does not need to prove her innocence. It is still presumed innocent, but all avenues of "guilt", all beliefs or mechanisms which can be seen as reasonable sources of doubt about its rational acceptability, need to be explored in order to settle beyond reasonable doubt that it is an innocent belief. Only if it fails this judicious weighing of the evidence does it lose its status as an entitled belief. Thus a theory being weighed is still innocent-until-proven-guilty, but it needs to undergo a more rigorous testing process than a belief in everyday life in order to be taken as rational.

It is important to remember, of course, that this is only true of those beliefs which are the product of *innocent* belief-dispositions. Those which are the product of *non-innocent* belief-dispositions are not innocent-until-proven-guilty.[94] This is important in relation to scholarship for theories may be the product of such non-innocent belief-dispositions as a desire for power or prestige.[95] When this is the case, such theories become more than suspect, they lose their "innocence": they are beliefs, or sets of beliefs, which to all intents and purposes need to demonstrate their innocence. This reinforces the point made earlier that the devising of theories is not separable from their weighing. While it is true that the sources of belief are often difficult or impossible to identify, and that a belief may be rational or irrational regardless of the mechanisms that produced it, it is not possible

---

[93] Here I am deliberately using forensic language, for the notions of a belief's presumed guilt or innocence evoke comparisons with a person's legal status before a court.

[94] See above (Chapter 3, A.4.).

[95] See above (Chapter 4, C.2.). This deprives the theories of their innocence only if those dispositions give rise to the theories or crucial beliefs therein, and not if they govern the direction of research. The latter is *morally* rather than rationally unjustified. For instance, a medical researcher who enters into studies of children's cancer may be motivated by a desire for prestige and funding from large drug companies. This is a morally unjustifiable defect in the *direction-governance* of her noetic faculties. She is thus defective in her heuristics. However, if she accepts a theory of carcinogenesis because it is the best explanation of her data within the context of her belief-system, then this theory choice is entirely rationally justified. If, however, she accepts a particular theory because it best serves her interests and those of the company, particularly in relation to academic prestige and drug royalties, then her choice of that theory is both morally and epistemologically culpable.

to strictly distinguish between the logic of discovery and the logic of confirmation and testing. Theories are tested in the process of their being articulated, and articulated in the process of their being tested.[96] If that process of articulation is one which is characterised at its heart by such non-innocent belief-dispositions as a desire for power or privilege, then the theory is not one we are entitled to believe without good reasons to do so.

These two ideas lead to the question of the role of belief forming mechanisms, or belief-dispositions, and their related obligations in theorising. Wolterstorff sees belief-forming mechanisms as having epistemic priority over specific beliefs. These mechanisms give rise to beliefs in certain conditions, and are the locus of what volitional control we have over our beliefs.[97] He relates the notion of the control function of certain beliefs to the acceptance-governance of belief-dispositions.[98] These control beliefs perform their control function via the modification of the belief-dispositions which relate to a particular belief or theory thereby determining whether they operate so as to produce belief in the proffered propositions. In the case of a theory which is unacceptable in the light of control beliefs, these currently held beliefs function as inhibitors of the belief-dispositions producing belief in that theory. They will do so by directing the reasoning process, observation, and so on, to take note of counter-evidences and give them more weight in the process of weighing the theory than the evidences that support belief in it. In the case of an acceptable theory, the reverse happens: abettors of the belief-dispositions operate so as to reinforce the evidence for the theory and undermine counter-evidences.

These processes, while meaning that believing a proposition, or nexus of propositions such as a theory, is not under *direct* voluntary control, do not mean that there is no role for volition in coming to believe or giving up belief in theories. This volitional control is, however, *indirect*, via the governance of belief-dispositions, as are the obligations associated with them. These obligations, however, are person- and situation-specific, and are related to other obligations that pertain in the scholar's life. It is not just the obligations which are thus specific, so too is the weight of a particular obligation: it may be overridden by more important obligations. Equally, it is neither possible nor desirable to subject all beliefs to the same degree of testing. This relates to the relative weight of the obligations which pertain to the scholar's holding those beliefs. The greater her obligations with

---

[96] See above (Chapter 2, B.1.; Chapter 4, B.1.).

[97] See Chapter 3 above.

[98] See above (Chapter 4, B.2.).

respect to that belief, i.e. the more it is important that she get in touch with that aspect of reality, the greater care she should exercise in its testing. In this regard, important considerations are how important and controversial the belief is.[99]

These considerations relate to the practice of scholarship: if a belief is not generally accepted by the scholarly community, then this constitutes a reason for its being carefully tested. This is not so because a belief's being the subject of dispute counts against it *per se*: for that to be the case a social-evidentialist, consensus view of rationality must obtain, a view Wolterstorff clearly rejects, and for good reasons.[100] Rather, it is so because its being controversial is an indicator of the existence of possible counter-arguments that need to be examined by a scholar if she is to be justified in accepting this belief.[101] Furthermore, if it is a belief that is central to the life of the scholar, or to the practice of her scholarship, then it matters greatly whether it is true or false. In both these circumstances the justifying process may be needed in order for that belief to be justified. So too, these considerations help clarify the general expectation that scholars be more careful in their believings than other people. It is generally the case that the critical testing of beliefs to determine their adequacy is more central to the practice of *Wissenschaft* than to most practices in daily life, and that beliefs are often a matter of considerable controversy in particular scholarly communities.

In the practice of scholarship it is also necessary that theories be subject to more rigorous testing than beliefs in ordinary practices due to the very nature of scholarship and the demands it makes upon truth. Scholarship is at its heart the quest for truth; it is the conscious and committed concentration of a person's energies on intellectual life.[102] The

---

99 McKim, 46–47.
100 See Wolterstorff, "Once Again, Evidentialism", 58–73. For a version of social-evidentialism in relation to science and Christian belief, see P. Clayton and S. Knapp, "Rationality and Christian Self-Conceptions", *Religion and Science: History, Method, Dialogue*, ed. W. M. Richardson and W. J. Wildman (New York: Routledge, 1996) 131–142. Wolterstorff argues that such a view fails once we renounce all forms of generic, consensus rationality, for which see "Entitled Christian Belief", *Religion and Science: History, Method, Dialogue*, ed. W. M. Richardson and W. J. Wildman (New York: Routledge, 1996) 148–149. Interestingly, Clayton and Knapp fail to respond to this criticism in their reply to Wolterstorff, for which see, P. Clayton and S. Knapp, "Is Holistic Justification Enough?", *Religion and Science: History, Method, Dialogue*, ed. W. M. Richardson and W. J. Wildman (New York: Routledge, 1996) 161–167.
101 This question also has bearing on the issue of the corroborated content of a theory and its related research tradition, and the need for them to convert counter-evidences into evidences over time in order to be justified, for which see below (Chapter 6, C.).
102 It must be noted that this means that scholarship is different to normal intellectual life,

aim of intellectual life is the pursuit of truth and the avoidance of error,[103] and since scholarly practice is a distillation of intellectual life such practice has an especial obligation to get in touch with reality. To enter into the practice of scholarship is to accept the obligation to get in touch with reality as a principal concern, at least within the practice of scholarship. It may well be that other obligations may take precedence over this quest at some times, in which case the practice of scholarship itself may need to be temporarily suspended.[104] However, as a scholar, the quest for truth is a particularly important obligation, one that warrants the exercise of greater care in the testing of beliefs than is necessary in normal life. The scholar, then, has a particular obligation to ensure that in terms of her practice of scholarship her beliefs comport as well as possible with reality.[105] While, as discussed above, these beliefs are still innocent, there is an extra burden of proof upon her weighing of them just because she has entered into the practice of a particular *Wissenschaft*.[106]

---

but is different only in degree, not in kind. It is the particular focus of a life on one component of life in general, even as the helping professions or government are particular focuses on other aspects of life with related concentration of obligations in certain spheres (ie avoiding harm and practicing beneficence for medicine, controlling social disorder and injustice and maximising social cohesion and justice for politics). This concentration of life, and its associated distillation of one particular kind of obligation, means that the adoption of these practices as a focus of life entails the acceptance of the related obligations as a major focus of responsibility. Similar points are made by Wolfe, *Epistemology*, 45–50, where he talks about criteria of rationality as the result of the adoption of a particular intellectual project.

103   See above (Chapter 3, A.2.).

104   For instance in the case that a member of my immediate family is seriously ill, I will surrender the practice of scholarship, to a greater or lesser extent, in order to meet my family obligations. Of more importance in this discussion is the recognition that belief in God generally takes precedence over all other obligations in Christian thought (cf. Mt. 22:34–40). As has been shown by Wolterstorff, and discussed above (Chapter 3, B.2.) this does not necessarily mean that the believer is left no recourse but to count herself as irrational, subject to an intellectual trial, although this is a possibility. For she is quite entitled to develop a new notion of rationality which is compatible with her faith, and even to transform her whole discipline so as to comport well with belief in God.

105   A scholar has these particular obligations only in relation to her particular discipline, and other disciplines that she does, or ought to believe, have relevance to her practice of that particular *Wissenschaft*. In all other areas of belief her obligations are roughly the same as another person, with the exception, perhaps, that her intellectual skills should be more finely honed than other people's, thus increasing her ability to get in touch with reality. Since intellectual obligations require her to do as well as can reasonably be expected of her, and more can be expected of her due to her greater intellectual skills, her obligations are thereby greater (cf. Lk. 12:48).

106   Picking up again the forensic metaphor, this correlates to a lawyer's obligation to her clients to do the best that can be expected of her to ascertain their legal standing, given, of

It is important to note before proceeding something which is implicit in Wolterstorff's meta-theory but which is not explicitly dealt with in relation to his criterion of rational theory devising and weighing. The theories of Lakatos, Kuhn and Laudan, for all their flaws, demonstrate the importance of situating the analysis of a theory in the context of a "world-view", belief-system, research program or research tradition.[107] This situating works in a number of directions. An essential component of the justification of a particular theory is determining how it fosters the development of its scholarly tradition. A theory which is in other ways acceptable, but which results in either no empirical or theoretical progress, or in retrogressive steps in that tradition, is unacceptable.[108] Progressiveness, while not the only factor in the rational justification of theories, is an important criterion in their assessment.[109]

Another direction in which a theory needs to be judged in the light of its traditional context, is the role the theory itself plays in adding to or subtracting from the net justification of the tradition. Certain theories, by solving recalcitrant problems in a research tradition, may not only be themselves justified thereby, but revive a flagging or moribund tradition.[110] Other theories, while being developed within a particular tradition, and coming to be seen as highly acceptable, may in fact come to be seen as incompatible with the tradition that gave them birth. Their status may be so great, however, that rather than the theory's being rejected because it is seen to no longer comport with its tradition, the tradition itself gives way, and either changes or is superseded.[111]

A final direction for the working of a theory's context in its intellectual tradition is that part of the weighing of a theory is the weighing of the

---

course the initial presumption of their innocence.

[107] This is discussed in relation to Kuhn (Chapter 2, above) and specifically in connection with the belief-system context of rational theorising, and the meta-epistemic structure of Wolterstorff's meta-theory, below (Chapter 6). See also, Wolfe, *Epistemology*, 55–69.

[108] This point is made strongly by Laudan, 6, 117, 124, in relation to scientific research traditions. See also MacIntyre, *Whose Justice? Which Rationality?*, 1–10, 350, for a similar point in relation to intellectual traditions.

[109] See Riggs, 171–180, for a discussion of the merits of Laudan's focus on progressiveness and the problems of his restriction of rationality to progress.

[110] Lakatos and Laudan in particular discuss the way in which progressive problem shifts may revive flagging research programs or traditions. See below (Chapter 6, B.).

[111] This type of process is discussed in relation to my epistemological metaphor below (Chapter 6, C.). Such a critique of a tradition or belief-system by beliefs and theories, either internal or external to it, also provides good reasons for the rejection of relativism from Wolterstorff's perspective. Instead of being locked within a "world-view" we are able to critically analyse belief-systems even from a point of view internal to the belief system.

belief-systems which nourish it. A theory which is acceptable in the context of a rationally unjustified and unjustifiable tradition loses justification thereby. Indeed, if it is justified only in the context of an unjustifiable tradition, then the theory itself is unjustified.[112] Thus no theory can be weighed without weighing it in the light of its tradition. This is, in fact, a crucial component of the "web of belief" that Wolterstorff recognises plays such a vital part in the devising and weighing of theories.

From this it is clear that personal and social factors play a crucial role in Wolterstorff's notion of scholarly rationality. A scholar's background and traditions – intellectual, social, personal and religious – play an important role in the developing of her control beliefs. The stock of beliefs against which theories are weighed, and the rules and very notion of rationality she employs in their assessment, are the product of her traditions and background.[113] So long as these beliefs, rules, notions and values are rationally justified along the lines developed by Wolterstorff, then they can play a legitimate role in the *rational* assessment of theories. However, these personal and social factors may also play roles which are non-rational or even irrational. These non-rational factors may play a legitimate or an illegitimate role in scholarship, but their functioning is not a part of the rational appraisal of theories. It is rather an aspect of the use of the heuristics of *shalom* in determining whether a line of research is justifiable or unjustifiable. Since these concerns do not relate to the goal of getting in touch with reality, but rather reflect social, personal and political concerns, they are not rational matters, and so should play no part in the

---

[112] This idea adequately explains the fate of many theories, such as strict bipartite or tripartite anthropologies. These theories comported well with a generally dualistic intellectual tradition. They entailed the idea that purely mental processes, such as stress or despair, should only influence mental states and not physical processes, with the exception of neurotic paralyses and so on. These theories, nourished by a particular anthropological tradition, denied the effective reality of psychosomatic illness and the role of mental influences on disease states. Once that tradition was undermined, including the undermining it experienced from the medical evidence against strict compartmentalisation of mind and body, the theories it supported became less tenable. Thus medical theories that deny the influence of mental events on disease processes are generally unacceptable. This is due, not only to the undermining of those specific theories, but to the undermining of the intellectual tradition that supported them. This demonstrates the reciprocal relationship between theories and belief-systems or research traditions. Particular theories lose or gain ground in relation to the belief-systems in which they are situated. The erosion of a particular theory is both a product of and a contributor to the erosion of its associated belief-system. This point is well presented in relation to ethical reasoning in particular by MacIntyre, *Whose Justice? Which Rationality?*, 350–370.

[113] See MacIntyre, *Whose Justice? Which Rationality?*, for a discussion of "practical rationality" in ethics, and its relevance to general concepts of rationality.

appraisal of particular theories. If they do, then entirely appropriate heuristic concerns deprive a scholar of rationality in her weighing of theories.[114]

I mentioned earlier the important, but not unique role, that progressiveness plays in the rational devising and weighing of theories. This idea is drawn in particular from Lakatos and Laudan. There are other ideas from the philosophy of science that need to be incorporated into a criterion of theory-choice. Such factors may be seen as rational criteria, or more appropriately in my opinion, as values that function in the devising and weighing of theories. These are those "criteria", which are traditionally recognised as features of acceptable theories in science: accuracy, consistency, scope, simplicity and fruitfulness.[115] Kuhn identifies them as values that control the appraising work of scientists but which are not sufficient for the construction of a criterion or algorithm of rationality. While I agree with his claim that there is no algorithm of rationality, I do not believe that this means, as he claims, that there is only the psychology of research.[116] These values can, I believe, be incorporated into a situation-specific criterion of rational or entitled theory devising and weighing.[117] They function as control beliefs in relation to the qualities which characterise a good theory.[118] The precise nature of these values, how they are construed and applied, and the relative weight given to them, differs in various disciplines, and in different research traditions within a discipline. Thus, for example, simplicity and fruitfulness are differently construed and applied in theology and the natural sciences, but they are, for all their

---

[114] It is worth noting that thus, while Wolterstorff's heuristics of *shalom* rescues scholarship from some of the charges of irrationality made by sociologists of knowledge, some of their criticisms are sound. At times social and political agenda do influence a scholar's choice of a theory, in which case that choice is irrational. Where a scholar's decision to pursue a particular *line* of research is based on the same concerns, but her choice of specific theories within that line of research is governed by the motive of getting in touch with reality, then regardless of the moral justification of her line of research, her theorising is rational. For more on the moral justification of research, heuristics, and rationality, see below (this chapter, B.2.).

[115] Newton-Smith, 223–236; Wolfe, *Epistemology*, 50–55, while accepting these general values, adopts the criteria of consistency, coherence, comprehensiveness and congruence (cf. Quine's criteria noted above, 4 n. 13). They are, I believe, a different categorisation of the same predominant values that guide theoretical practice in *Wissenschaft*.

[116] See above (Chapter 2, B.1., B.2.).

[117] See Newton-Smith, 223–236; Wolfe, *Epistemology*, 50–69.

[118] Wolfe generalises them as criteria for the assessment of rival belief-systems as well as rival theories. There is some value in that and it comports well with my epistemological metaphor, see below (Chapter 6, C.).

person- and situation-specificity, shared values by which theories in science and theology are weighed.[119]

Having discussed these connections between Wolterstorff's theory of rationality and his meta-theory, and the virtues of good theories identified in the philosophy of science, I can proceed to relate his criterion of rationality to his understanding of the devising and weighing of theories so as to articulate the former as a criterion of theory devising and weighing. The criterion he specifically proffers in his meta-theory is this:

> *Given such-and-such a body of beliefs*, is the scholar warranted in accepting or warranted in not accepting theory T?[120]

This can be made more specific in relation to his criterion of rational justification, thus:

> A scholar *S* is rational in her eluctable and innocently produced belief in theory *T* if and only if *S* does believe *T* and either:
> (i) *S* neither has nor ought to have adequate reason to cease from believing *T*, and is not rationally obliged to believe that she *does* have adequate reason to cease; or
> (ii) *S* does have adequate reason to cease from believing *T* but does not realise that she does, and is rationally justified in that.[121]

Such reasons *for or against* belief in a theory are those I have discussed above.

These reasons, however, also need to be applied to the weighing of a new belief, a theory which is offered to a scholar for her acceptance. For many theories are new beliefs or sets of beliefs that are devised by a scholar or her colleagues and are not yet held by that scholar. Thus a criterion which is limited to justified ceasing to believe them is irrelevant to their acceptance. In relation to this Wolterstorff's criterion of warranted theory choice provides clearer guidance than does his criterion of rationality. In that criterion he states that such choices are always made relative to a given body of beliefs *already accepted by the scholar*. Now, given that those beliefs are innocent-until-proven-guilty, the new beliefs of the proposed theory must be assessed with respect to them. In particular they must be judged in relation to those justified beliefs, or beliefs to

---

[119] cf. Polkinghorne, *One World*, 36–42.

[120] Wolterstorff, *RWBR*, 102.

[121] Here I am rewording Wolterstorff's criterion of rationality as a criterion of theory-choice, Wolterstorff, *CBGR?*, 168.

which a scholar is entitled, that function as control in relation to the theory's set of belief.[122] This may be formulated as an expansion of the above criterion thus:

> A scholar S is rational in her eluctable and innocently produced belief in theory T if and only if S does believe T and either:
> (i) S neither has nor ought to have adequate reason to cease from believing T, and is not rationally obliged to believe that she *does* have adequate reason to cease; or
> (ii) S does have adequate reason to cease from believing T but does not realise that she does, and is rationally justified in that.

And:

> A scholar S is rational in her eluctable and innocently produced acceptance of theory T if and only if S does accept T and either:
> (i) S neither has nor ought to have adequate reason to believe that T conflicts with her rationally justified control beliefs, and is not rationally obliged to believe that she *does* have adequate reason to so believe; or
> (ii) S does have adequate reason to believe that T conflicts with her rationally justified control beliefs but does not realise that she does, and is rationally justified in that.

This criterion can also be framed negatively as a criterion of rational theory rejection, thus:

> A scholar S is rational in her eluctable and innocently produced disbelief in theory T if and only if S does not believe T and either:
> (i) S neither has nor ought to have adequate reason to believe T, and is not rationally obliged to believe that she *does* have adequate reason to believe T; or
> (ii) S does have adequate reason to believe T but does not realise that she does, and is rationally justified in that.

And:

> A scholar S is rational in her eluctable and innocently produced rejection of theory T if and only if S does reject T and either:
> (i) S neither has nor ought to have adequate reason to believe that T comports well with her rationally justified control beliefs, and is not rationally obliged to believe that she *does* have adequate reason to so believe; or

---

[122] This process of assessment may result in the acceptance or rejection of the theory, or the modification of the scholar's control beliefs. This process is discussed in detail below (Chapter 6, C.).

(ii) *S* does have adequate reason to believe that *T* comports with her rationally justified control beliefs but does not realise that she does, and is rationally justified in that.

Turning now to Wolterstorff's later notion of entitlement,[123] the criterion can be framed in terms of entitled theory choice, thus:

A scholar *S* is entitled to her eluctable and innocently produced belief in theory *T* if and only if *S* does believe *T* and there is no doxastic practice, *D* pertaining to *T* such that *S* ought to have implemented *D* and she did not, or she ought to have implemented *D* better than she did.

And:

A scholar *S* is entitled to her eluctable and innocently produced acceptance of theory *T* if and only if *S* does accept *T* and there is no doxastic practice *D* pertaining to *T* such that *S* ought to have implemented *D* and she did not, or she ought to have implemented *D* better than she did; and that, had she done so, she would have been entitled to believe that *T* conflicts with the set of her entitled control beliefs.

This criterion can also be framed negatively as a criterion of entitled theory rejection, thus:

A scholar *S* is entitled to her eluctable and innocently produced disbelief in theory *T* if and only if *S* does not believe *T* and there is no doxastic practice, *D* pertaining to *T* such that *S* ought to have implemented *D* and she did not, or she ought to have implemented *D* better than she did.

And:

A scholar *S* is rational in her eluctable and innocently produced rejection of theory *T* if and only if *S* does reject *T* and there is no doxastic practice *D* pertaining to *T* such that *S* ought to have implemented *D* and she did not, or she ought to have implemented *D* better than she did; and that, had she done so she would have been entitled to believe that *T* comports well with the set of her entitled control beliefs.

This criterion, be it a criterion of rational justification or of entitlement, whether in its positive or negative form, does not allow for the devising of an algorithm of rational theory-choice, a criterion or list of

---

[123] Remembering that a scholar's being *entitled* to a particular belief or set of beliefs is equivalent to her not having failed in any of her noetic obligations, these obligations being understood as those which arise out of and are related to her particular scholarly practice.

criteria which can be applied in a rule-like manner in all contexts. It is, rather, a defeasible, situation- and person-specific criterion, that depends upon the beliefs and standards a scholar actually holds, or those that she could be reasonably expected to hold. Thus, for instance, if a specific scholar believed that for a particular theory, or perhaps even for all theories, simplicity was not a desirable trait, and she had good reasons so to believe, then she would be entitled to accept a complex over a simple theory, all other things being equal.[124]

B. Wolterstorff's Meta-Theory is Rational and Non-Relativist

From this outline of Wolterstorff's meta-theory it may seem that, in a manner similar to Kuhn, he has effectively embraced the relativism he began by rejecting.[125] Such a construal, while having *prima facie* force, is erroneous: for not only does Wolterstorff reject such a position, he has good reason to do so within the context of his belief-system.[126] The first is related to his ontology. Wolterstorff's great advantage over Kuhn is that he specifically believes that the entities predicated by theories do in fact exist, and that epistemological and ontological realism is a valid stance. The second is related to the disjunction he posits between the process of theory-warrant, and the question of heuristics. This is his alternative to the traditional dichotomy between the context of theory devising and theory weighing which he rejected. This distinction allows him to incorporate such issues as learning for *shalom* into his meta-theory, without embracing

---

[124] Of course, similar comments could be made for the other features I have discussed earlier. So too, similar points can be made about the notion of simplicity that a particular scholar accepts, and how she sees it is to function in theorising. All of these factors mean that there is no algorithm of rationality. It does not mean, however, that there is no *criterion* of rational theory-choice, and that such choices are, therefore, non-rational.

[125] So H. Meynell, "Faith, Foundationalism and Nicholas Wolterstorff", *Rational Faith*, ed. L. Zagzebski (Notre Dame: University of Notre Dame Press, 1993) 79–109. His identification of Wolterstorff as (implicitly) relativist depends upon a crucial misconstrual of his meta-theory from Meynell's broad foundationalist perspective. He sees Wolterstorff's control beliefs as being analogous in nature and function to Plantinga's properly basic beliefs, and thus immune from rational critique. So too, he believes that reasons play no role in Wolterstorff's theory of rationality, at least in relation to control beliefs. As has been seen above in regard to his theory of rationality, and will be further demonstrated below specifically in regard to control beliefs, this is a misconstrual of Wolterstorff's meta-theory.

[126] Of course, such a defence assumes Wolterstorff's epistemology. But that is simply being consistent with that epistemology itself: for no theory, or argument can be proposed or defended outside a system of beliefs, and all weighing of such arguments *according to his meta-theory* can take place only in such a context. For Wolterstorff to defend himself in any other manner, or for me to do so, would be self-referentially inconsistent, and would probably be taken as a good reason for rejecting his meta-theory.

the epistemological anarchy of a philosopher such as Feyerabend. In general this distinction allows us to incorporate the positive features of Kuhn and Feyerabend and their colleagues without accepting the relativism which their position on the whole implies or asserts. These chief reasons for Wolterstorff's meta-theory's being non-relativist will be examined in turn.[127]

B.1. REALISM AND RELATIVISM

An anti-realist approach to the existence of theoretical entities has been a close ally and supporter of naturalised epistemology, historicism, and epistemic pragmatism and relativism, as can be seen variously in the work of Quine,[128] Kuhn,[129] Feyerabend,[130] Rorty,[131] Goodman,[132] and even

---

[127] I noted, above (Chapter 3, A.3., this chapter, A.2.) that Wolterstorff believes there are obligations which are to govern our believings. This constitutes another reason for him to reject relativism and historicism, for these obligations are history-transcendent and thereby provide non-relativist and non-historicist controls on theorising. See Wolterstorff, "On Avoiding Historicism", 182–185. A further aspect of his theory that allows him to avoid relativism is the way in which theories, beliefs and experiences are not only interpreted and assessed in the context of a belief-system or intellectual tradition, but they also critically assess the traditions in which they are situated. Thus, while there may be no value-independent assessment of rival belief-systems, they are open to critical analysis leading to modification and even rejection. For this, see above, Chapter 2. For a general exposition of this position, see Wolfe, *Epistemology*, 43–69. See also, F. Ferré, *Basic Philosophy of Religion* (London: Allen and Unwin, 1967) 371–406; E. J. Carnell, *An Introduction to Christian Apologetics: A Philosophical Defense of the Trinitarian-Theistic Faith* (5th ed; Grand Rapids: Eerdmans, 1956) 103–121, for a belief-systems approach to the defence of theism as a whole. It is to be noted that neither of them adopt a correspondence view of truth. G. Gutting, *Religious Belief and Religious Skepticism* (Notre Dame: University of Notre Dame Press, 1982) 109–142, argues that theism as a belief-system cannot in fact be justified by reference to the joint criteria of scope, accuracy, fruitfulness or simplicity, as Ferré and Carnell propose. This suggests that it is not so much the better meeting of such criteria by which a belief-system such as theism is justified, but rather by the surviving of the process of critical testing over time. This is in fact what Wolfe suggests, and is cogently argued by MacIntyre, *Whose Justice? Which Rationality?*, 350–388; and Runzo, "World-views and Theism", 37–51. The latter's argument is flawed in that he adopts a specific world-view perspective with all its problems. However, both Runzo and MacIntyre present good arguments for the possibility, and even the necessity of the critical analysis of competing belief-systems or intellectual traditions in the process of dialogue with their rivals. Indeed, MacIntyre asserts that the very truth claims that traditions make implicitly or explicitly presuppose the willingness of their proponents to subject them to critical testing in dialogue with their rivals. It is such testing which shows that those traditions correspond to reality better than their rivals, and thus are more or less true. Truth is correspondence to reality: critical testing in the market-place of ideas is the means to the end of determining which traditions correspond best to reality, and thus have the most justified claims to truth.

[128] W. V. Quine, "Posits and Reality", *The Ways of Paradox and Other Essays* (New

Laudan.[133] One of the crucial ways in which Wolterstorff is able to avoid relativism, despite his defeasible person- and situation-specific epistemology is by embracing a (critical) realist stance on the existence of theoretical entities. This position, while unfashionable in many philosophical circles,[134] is not only defensible, but given certain beliefs which are central to Christian commitment, is a view which Christian scholars can, and perhaps should support.[135]

York: Random House, 1966) 233–241; "Two Dogmas", 42, 44, 46; "Simple Theories", 242–245; *Pursuit*, 19–21. It has been argued that Quine is in fact not an anti-realist, or that, if he is, his anti-realism is compatible with realism in the context of his overall naturalised epistemology. See Gibson, *Enlightened Empiricism*, 16–17, 52. There he argues that Quine views scientific theories and the entities posited therein in anti-realist terms when analysed from a perspective *external* to the scientific enterprise, but in realist terms when analysed from a perspective *internal* to the practice of science. Given, however, that Quine sees the external perspective as essentially flawed, for science is the most successful of all human epistemic exercises, Quine's view is, he believes, at heart a realist one. This is supported by comments Quine makes in *Pursuit*, 3–6, in relation to observation sentences, and in "Comments on Lauener", 229, and *Pursuit*, 93–102, in relation to the truth-status of statements. This assessment is endorsed by C. Hookway, *Quine: Language, Experience and Reality* (Cambridge: Polity, 1988) 50–57, 200–202, 207–209, 219–220, who argues, however, that Quine's epistemic naturalism, which illegitimately restricts epistemology to empirical science, undermines the claims he makes regarding the truth-status of science, thereby undermining the whole notion of realism. From the perspective of someone who does not accept this restriction, and who therefore looks at scientific theories from an external as well as an internal perspective, Quine's theory is inescapably anti-realist.

129   See above (Chapter 2, A.3., B.1.).

130   See above (Chapter 2, A.3.).

131   See above (Chapter 2, A.).

132   See above (Chapter 2, A.1.).

133   Laudan, 121–133.

134   N. Wolterstorff, "Are Concept-Users World-makers?" *Philosophical Perspectives* 1 (1987) 251.

135   There are, however, those who argue that anti-realism is a Christian option, e.g. M. S. McLeod, "Making God Dance: Postmodern Theorizing and the Christian College", *Christian Scholar's Review* 21/3 (Mar 1992) 275–292, who calls his view "Christian Multi-World Realism", which is a version of what Wolterstorff calls creative anti-realism; N. C. Murphy, "From Critical Realism to a Methodological Approach: Response to Robbins, Van Huyssteen, and Hefner", *Zygon* 23/3 (Sept 1988) 287–290; *Theology*, esp 197–198; S. McFague, *Metaphorical Theology* (London: SCM, 1982); *Models of God* (Philadelphia: Fortress, 1987) esp xi–xii, 29–57. For the claim that Christian anti-realism comports better with Christian beliefs than does realism, on the grounds that the former rightly denies "the God's-eye view", see M. Westphal, "Taking Plantinga Seriously: Advice to Christian Philosophers", *Faith and Philosophy* 16/2 (Apr 1999) 173–181. Marshall, on the other hand, rejects realism without embracing anti-realism, and does so in order to develop a non-relativist theory of truth from a Christian perspective, for which see Marshall, *Trinity and Truth*, esp 217–282. Nancey Murphy has adopted a similar position in her more recent

It must be noted that Wolterstorff's realism is not restricted to theoretical entities or human beliefs but rather extends to a general metaphysical and ontological realism, which in turn provide crucial support for his realist epistemology.[136] The way in which Wolterstorff's realist ontology supports his realist metaphysics and epistemology can be readily seen. He asserts:

---

work, for which see N. Murphy, *Anglo-American Postmodernity: Philosophical Perspectives on Science, Religion, and Ethics* (Boulder, Colorado: Westview, 1997) esp 49–62. However, while I do not claim that a Christian cannot adopt an anti- or non-realist stance without conflict with crucial Christian beliefs, I do believe that such a stance has important drawbacks from a Christian perspective, and does not comport as well with authentic Christian commitment as does a realist position, especially given that epistemological realists tend to *reject* the possibility of attaining a "God's-eye view". For a defence of these claims and the associated non-neutral objectivity in theorising, see e.g. Polkinghorne, *Science and Creation*, 18, 71, 75–82, 95; *Reason and Reality*, 4–19, 20–33 (in the latter chapter he specifically argues against McFague's metaphorical theology); Barbour, 31–65; D. M. MacKay "Objectivity as a Christian Value", *Objective Knowledge*, ed. P. Helm (Leicester: IVP, 1987) 15–27; P. Helm, "Why be Objective?", *Objective Knowledge*, 29–40; Thorson, "Scientific Objectivity and the Listening Attitude", 59–83; M. Ross, "Who is Telling the Myth?", *Objective Knowledge*, 129–143; Van Huyssteen, "Postmodernist", 385–386, and his criticisms of Murphy's perspective. While not all of their arguments are necessarily compelling, and I do not accept all of their views, their general arguments support my contentions. I should note two things in passing. First, most of the Christian opponents of realism specifically reject relativism: hence *their* non- or anti-realism cannot be used in support of relativist conclusions. Second, Wolterstorff's arguments in favour of his version of (critical) realism engage with and counter non- and anti-realist criticisms of epistemological and ontological realism, for which see below.

[136] Early signs of his ontological realism are found in his rejection of Quine's thesis that meanings of terms do not determine the identity of properties and attributes. N. Wolterstorff, "Are Properties Meanings?" *Journal of Philosophy* 57/ 8 (April 1960) 277–281. This line is taken further by Wolterstorff in his *On Universals: An Essay in Ontology* (Chicago: University of Chicago Press, 1970) 4, 6, 157–158, 194–218, where he not only reaffirms his rejection of Quine's view, but argues that ontology and linguistic analysis are distinct philosophical disciplines. Subsequently, after arguing that ontological nominalism and realism are complete, internally consistent but incommensurable positions, each of which has its problems and advantages, N. Wolterstorff, "Qualities", *PhRev*, 69 (1964) 183–200, Wolterstorff firmly adopted a realist ontology, N. Wolterstorff, *On Universals*, xi–xii, 1–6, 105–218; "Response to Dennis Casper", *Philosophical Studies* 30 (1976) 121–124. This development was specifically in response to criticisms levelled against his arguments by Dennis Casper, "On Wolterstorff's Nominalistic Theory of Qualities", *Philosophical Studies* 30 (1976) 115–119. It is also relevant to other criticisms of his position found in D. Brownstein, "Wolterstorff on Qualities", *Philosophical Studies* 23 (1972) 98–104; M. J. Loux "Recent Work in Ontology", *American Philosophical Quarterly* 9/2 (April 1972) 126. Wolterstorff's realist position has been criticised by E. B. Allaire, "Wolterstorff and Bradley on Ontology", *Journal of Philosophy* 70/19 (Nov 1973) 727–733. However Allaire, in my view, fails to do justice to the nuances of Wolterstorff's view of the nature of the existence of predicables, for which see *On Universals*, 158–170.

> Ontology, as I understand it and shall try to practice it, is a description of the most general structure of what there is… For I hold that we can know not only our conceptual scheme but that to which our conceptual scheme applies. Indeed, one of the main uses of our conceptual scheme is to gain knowledge of that to which the scheme applies.[137]

It is also clear that his is not a naive realism, for interpretation and experience and so on play a crucial role in our view of reality. It also recognises that people other than professional philosophers have a real awareness of reality:

> It is my conviction that all of us, apart from ontology, are aware of the structure of reality – always, of course, dimly, always somewhat askew, always overlooking things, never getting the whole picture.[138]

This also reveals the connections between his ontology and his epistemology, indeed his general understanding of the nature of academia. Indeed, these connections are quite pervasive, for his is a situated, defeasible concept of ontology, one in which rational consensus is no more assured of attainment than in other disciplines:

> But let us not be snared by the delusion that the ontologist's description of the structure of reality can be unbiased, unprejudiced. It will invariably be shaped and formed by many factors – cultural, linguistic, religious, and more. The ontologist explores how things seem to him to be. In the course of doing so he finds others claiming that things are different from the way they seem to him to be. He should, then, if he does not conclude that he was mistaken, search for considerations in favour of his own view that his disputants will find decisive. Sometimes he will find such, sometimes he will not. Sometimes, that is, he will find that when productive argument has ceased, disagreement remains. What he needs then is just the courage of his convictions.[139]

It is plain that Wolterstorff is conducting his ontological theorising along the lines he develops in his meta-theory. His ontological theorising is consistent with his meta-theory.[140]

---

137 Wolterstorff, *On Universals*, xii.
138 Wolterstorff, *On Universals*, xiii.
139 Wolterstorff, *On Universals*, xiii.
140 This is also seen in his adoption of an "innocent until proven guilty" stance in relation to the existence of predicable entities, Wolterstorff, *On Universals*, 5, 105–172. Indeed, this rather extensive argument is conducted along the line that there are no good reasons *not* to hold to the existence of predicable entities, and that the existence of such entities provides us

Just as it is consistent with his meta-theory in the way it is presented, so his ontology is consistent with his metaphysical realism, and thus supports his realist epistemology.[141] Essential to Wolterstorff's metaphysical realism is the assertion that reality has a structure which is largely independent of human beings, which we are nonetheless able to grasp in our believings.[142] This grasping of reality involves two components: the objective order which exists independent of us; our concepts of that order which act as bridges between us and the structure of reality.[143] The structure of that world consists in at least the following things: individual entities, common substances or natures, natural kinds and common essences.[144] Our concepts are clearly theory-laden, dependent upon socially determined linguistic conventions and fallible, yet they are still able to function as effective links between us and our conceptual schemes and reality.[145] Our apprehension of reality is via perception, which while concept-laden, is still a veridical link between us and the world which enables us to know it: "for concepts are graspings of properties, and

---

with a better way of explaining the world than do the alternatives. He repeatedly asserts that he does not, and can not, provide compelling arguments *for* this belief, but that it nonetheless seems to him to be obviously true. See for instance, *On Universals*, 123–125, 126, 149.

141 Both of these points are well illustrated in N. Wolterstorff, "Realism vs Anti-Realism: How to Feel at Home in the World", *Proceedings of the American Catholic Philosophical Association* 54 (1985) 182–205, and "Concept-Users", 233–267, which will form the core of the following discussion of metaphysical realism and its connections with Wolterstorff's realist epistemology. The realist/anti-realist debate is a complex and wide-ranging one, and lies outside the scope of this thesis. I will deal with the debate only when it has direct bearing on Wolterstorff's realist epistemology. Wolterstorff's two articles on this matter, cited here, present detailed critiques of the two central theses of anti-realism, being the "truth thesis" and the "world-constitution thesis". For a more extensive discussion of these issues, see Wolterstorff, *Presence to Practice*, Part One, "Undoing Reality's Recession", especially the chapter entitled "Awareness Under Concepts".

142 Wolterstorff, "Concept-Users", 235; "Realism vs Anti-Realism", 202–203. It is important to note that we do partly determine the structure of reality, for not only are humans part of the reality we grasp, but we also interact with reality in ways that alter it. But these are the *only* ways in which we determine the nature of reality: we do not do so by means of our concepts or theories.

143 Wolterstorff, "Concept-Users", 235; "Realism vs Anti-Realism", 202–203.

144 Wolterstorff, "Concept-Users", 263–264. For the anti-realist argument against essences and Wolterstorff's defence of realism, see pp. 248–252.

145 Wolterstorff, "Concept-Users", 235; "Realism vs Anti-Realism", 187–188; *Locke*, 99. For a discussion of anti-realist attacks on the felicity of concepts as ascertaining real properties, see "Concept-Users", 241–248, 251–252, 258–261; "Realism vs Anti-Realism", 188–190, 201–202; and *Locke*, 97–100, in relation to perception. Note that this is associated with a rejection of the representationalist view of perception. See Wolterstorff, "Concept-Users", 243; cf. Alston, "Christian Experience and Christian Belief", 103–134; Evans, 81–84.

objects have properties".[146] Simply because reality can be divided up in different ways either in the context of different frameworks, or by using different concepts, does not mean that those divisions are "invented" and have no bearing on the independent structure of reality. Indeed, there must be a mind-independent structure of reality for these conceptual divisions to have any point of reference. They do not divide up reality in different ways, but simply recognise the different ways and kinds of ordering that are already present in reality.[147]

This perspective impacts our understanding of biblical interpretation, for the recognition of the pluralistic nature of the practice and results of exegesis can be used to support claims to radical pluralism or relativism in biblical scholarship.[148] Wolterstorff's critical realism would suggest, however, that there is a determinative meaning for a given (biblical) text, which, no matter how multi-faceted or even ambiguous, has been encoded in the text by its author. The goal of exegesis, then, as one example of the search for truth, is to recover that meaning.[149] The existence of a plurality of interpretive methods and interpretations of texts can be seen as a reflection of the partial and context-dependent nature of our knowledge, rather than as an illustration of the invention of meaning.[150] Meaning is not

---

146 Wolterstorff, "Concept-Users", 251–252; "Realism vs Anti-Realism", 201–203; cf. Evans, 81–88.

147 Wolterstorff, "Concept-Users", 258–263; "Can Theologians Recover From Kant?", 17–18, where he speaks of such awareness as an activation of our noetic faculties so as to grasp reality. cf. Banner 37–39; Vision, 75–76.

148 For the pluralist perspective, see M. G. Brett, "Motives & Intentions in Genesis 1", *JTS* 42/1 (1991) 1–16; "Four or Five Things to do With Texts: A Taxonomy of Interpretative Interests", *The Bible in Three Dimensions*, ed. D. J. A. Clines, *et al* (Sheffield: JSOT, 1990) 357–377; "The Future of Reader Criticisms?", *The Open Text: New Directions for Biblical Studies?*, ed. F. Watson (London: SCM, 1993) 13–31; D. J. A. Clines, "Reading Esther From Left to Right: Contemporary Strategies for Reading a Biblical Text", *The Bible in Three Dimensions*, ed. D. J. A. Clines, *et al* (Sheffield: JSOT, 1990) 31–52; F. Watson, "Introduction: The Open Text", *The Open Text: New Directions for Biblical Studies?*, ed. F. Watson (London: SCM, 1993) 1–5; For the relativist perspective, see Fowl, "Ethics of Interpretation", 379–398; Gunn, "Reading Right", 53–64; cf. above (Chapter 2, B.1.) on the influence of anti-realism on relativism.

149 Davies, "Reader-Response Criticism", 578–580; Goldingay, "How far do readers make sense?", 5–10; B. Meyer, 3–12; Osborne, *Hermeneutical Spiral*, esp 5–8, 397–415; A. C. Thiselton, "On Models and Methods: A Conversation with Robert Morgan", *The Bible in Three Dimensions*, ed. D. J. A. Clines, *et al* (Sheffield: JSOT, 1990) 345–347, 353–356; *New Horizons in Hermeneutics: The Theory and Practice of Transforming Biblical Reading* (Grand Rapids: Zondervan, 1992) esp 55–75, 499–508. For Wolterstorff's own views on this, see below (Conclusion: Retrospect and Prospect).

150 Goldingay, "How far do readers make sense?", 6–9; Osborne, 401–411; Thiselton, *New Horizons*, esp 499–508, 546–550, 582–592, 597–619.

created by readers, it is discerned by them, more or less accurately, more or less faithfully, more or less truthfully.[151] In light of Wolterstorff's ontological and epistemological realism, pluralism in biblical interpretation, as in other scholarly practices, does not justify relativism.[152]

Clearly associated with this view is a correspondence theory of truth: "given the reference of our words, (some, at least of) our sentences are true by virtue of how the world is".[153] Such a view does not necessitate holding to the idea that there must be one true theory which provides a complete and cohesive picture of all that there is.[154] There are many ways of looking at reality, many of which correspond to certain aspects of or ways of ordering reality, but regardless of the diversity of theories there is one reality to which they all relate, and by virtue of which they are (more-or-less) true or false.[155] Such a way of looking at the world, he argues, best fits our understanding of normal mature human perception and belief,[156] and best enables normal humans to "feel at home in the world".[157]

Certain of our ways of looking at the world, he argues, "may have a fundamental *rightness* about them which others lack: a rightness which inheres, not in reality as such, but in the fit between our own contingent nature and reality".[158] Correspondence to reality is what constitutes

---

[151] Goldingay, "How far do readers make sense?", 7–8; Osborne, 368–415; Thiselton, "On Models and Methods", 353–356; *New Horizons*, 63–68.

[152] cf. Poythress, 75–89, 103–120, 135–143, who, despite his acceptance of Kuhn's general theory of science, rejects his relativist implications, largely because of a critical-realist epistemology.

[153] Wolterstorff, "Concept-Users", 241; "Realism vs Anti-Realism", 185. This is what Newton-Smith, 37–38, 43, calls the "ontological ingredient" of (critical) realism. Wolterstorff notes in "Concept-Users", 241, that anti-realism can adopt a correspondence theory of truth, though this is not normally the case, as he notes in "Realism vs Anti-Realism", 185.

[154] Wolterstorff, "Concept-Users", 262.

[155] Ibid., 262–263.

[156] Ibid., 263. Indeed, he argues that anyone who adopts a position in which nothing is counted as a material object or a person would be naturally seen as immature of malformed. Here he is clearly using the idea that beliefs are innocent until proven guilty: we implicitly adopt a correspondence view of truth and believe our noetic endeavours strive to attain some grasp of reality. Unless we have good reasons to the contrary, this common-sense view is justified. There are not such reasons, and so a correspondence theory of truth, while not *proven*, is *justified*.

[157] Wolterstorff, "Realism vs Anti-Realism", 203.

[158] Wolterstorff, "Concept-Users", 263; cf. "Privileged Access", 91–93, where he argues that the particularities of our programming can, and in many cases do, provide us with privileged cognitive access to reality – including both experiences of suffering and Christian commitment.

truth,[159] but it is not a criterion of truth, nor is it a useful notion in the justification of beliefs: it in no way guarantees the attainment of the goal of truth.[160] Rather the correspondence theory of truth claims that "truth-bearers" (statements, beliefs and so on) are made true by things in the world, and that their truth consists in their discerning or discriminating those things, which are themselves mind-independent.[161] Whether we know them or not, or even whether we are able to know them, is irrelevant to their truthfulness.[162] Truth is a profoundly *non-epistemic* notion.[163]

This clearly has bearing on Wolterstorff's non-relativist epistemology. His belief that, in spite of the conceptualised and socially determined nature of all observation, we have access to reality, enables him to avoid the idea of incommensurable "worlds" which is so prominent amongst relativists. So too his belief that there is a real structure to reality which is independent of our conceptual schemes means that there is something "out there" to which theories can conform. When this is coupled with his commitment to our ability to grasp crucial elements of this reality, such as properties, kinds and so on, by means of our concepts, it is clear that not only is Wolterstorff not a relativist, his position can only be construed as relativist by means of misconstrual. For Wolterstorff there is a sense in which reality forces itself upon our beliefs, when we govern our belief forming mechanisms appropriately, in such a way as to constrain our beliefs. Such a view ensures that Wolterstorff's epistemology, for all of its person- and situation-specificity, is an objectivist one.

---

[159] Note that this is *not* the same as a definition of the use of the term "truth" or of the assertion that something "is true", although this is a common charge made against those who adhere to a correspondence view of truth. See Wolterstorff, "Realism vs Anti-Realism", 194; Vision, 75.

[160] Vision, 81. cf. Wolterstorff's notion of situated defeasible rationality.

[161] Wolterstorff, "Concept-Users", 241; 263–264; "Realism vs Anti-Realism", 193–194. Banner, 34–39; Newton-Smith, 19–43; Vision, 75, adopt a viewpoint similar to Wolterstorff's, with its inclusion of ontological and epistemological ingredients in the critical realist stance.

[162] Vision, 79. Wolterstorff, "Realism vs Anti-Realism", 191, says that he varies in his belief in the idea that for something to be true it must be in principle capable of being known to be true. I do not accept this idea at all. It is also worth noting that while there is no guarantee that the truth is knowable in a correspondence theory of truth, if it is rejected, and an epistemic notion of truth adopted, there is no possibility of ever attaining it. See Wolterstorff, "Realism vs Anti-Realism", 195–200. Indeed, he claims on p. 197 of the latter article that "it is often much easier to tell how much it snowed than whether some belief is rationally acceptable."

[163] Wolterstorff, "Realism vs Anti-Realism", 186; cf. Vision, 75–76.

B.2. Heuristics of *Shalom*, Historicism and Relativism

Lakatos specifically attempted to fuse the questions of theory-choice and heuristics in his methodology of scientific research programs, effectively replacing the former with the latter. Lakatos shifted the primary concern of science and its philosophical analysis away from theory choice to heuristics.[164] Indeed for Lakatos, the progressiveness of a research program was a primary factor in the rational appraisal of scientific decisions to accept it, and the theories associated with it.[165] The major problem with this concept is that the progressiveness of a research program can only ever be determined *retrospectively*, for no matter how regressive a research program becomes, there is always the possibility of a "progressive shift" by means of the development of an auxiliary hypothesis which deals with recalcitrant anomalies.[166] Thus, while there are grounds for the appraisal of research programs, there are no grounds for advice concerning which program a scientist should adopt, for decisions about the rational acceptability (i.e. progressiveness) of a research program can only be made retrospectively, thereby robbing scientists of grounds for making prospective rational choices between research programs.[167]

Such a view may be developed in one of two directions, both of which are consistent with Lakatos's theory and are found in his writings at different points.[168] The first is more compatible with Lakatos's goal of establishing a rational methodology of science. While there are no explicit rules of rationality which can deal with all situations and eliminate all personal and social factors, science is nonetheless a rational enterprise.[169]

---

[164] Lakatos, *MSRP*, 132; "Introduction", 4–5; cf. Chalmers, 73–76.

[165] Lakatos, *MSRP*, 158, 173; "Introduction", 4–5. Indeed his claim that the idea of instant rationality is moribund is a direct consequence of this notion.

[166] Lakatos, *MSRP*, 173; cf. Chalmers, 82–83.

[167] I. Lakatos, "The problem of appraising scientific theories: three approaches", *Philosophical Papers: vol 2; Mathematics, Science and Epistemology*, ed. J. Worrall and G. Currie (Cambridge: Cambridge University Press, 1978) 110; *MSRP*, 173–176; "Introduction", 7; cf. N. Avgelis, "Lakatos on the evaluation of scientific theories", *Imre Lakatos and Theories of Scientific Change*, ed. K. Gavroglu, *et al* (Dordrecht: Kluwer, 1989) 157–167; Chalmers, 82–83; Laudan, 77–78; Pera, 181–182; Riggs, 93–94. Avgelis and Pera both suggest that there is an element of internal inconsistency in Lakatos's refusal to provide criteria for advice as well as appraisal of research programs and theories.

[168] Certain passages in Lakatos's works can be read either way. See I. Lakatos, "History of Science and its Rational Reconstructions", *Philosophical Papers, vol 1: The methodology of scientific research programmes*, ed. J. Worrall and G. Currie (Cambridge: Cambridge University Press, 1978) 102–138; "Appraising", 110; cf. Chalmers, 83–84; Pera, 181–184; Riggs, 93–94.

[169] Chalmers, 83; Riggs, 93.

The second is consistent with Feyerabend's radical relativism, which sees that there is in fact no rational methodology of science.[170] It seems, however, that in the light of Lakatos's refusal to suggest criteria for choosing one theory or even research program over another, his theory comports better with the second, irrationalist position.[171] Following Pera, this can best be seen as a consequence of Lakatos's acceptance of the "Cartesian dilemma", in which a belief or noetic enterprise must be free from all personal and social influences, and subject to explicit rules, or it can not be considered rational.[172]

It follows from this that Feyerabend and others who reject objective rationality are victims of the Cartesian syndrome. Once the possibility of defeasible, situation- and person-specific rationality is allowed, then a belief or noetic enterprise may well be rational in the absence of an algorithm of rationality and in the presence of personal and social influences. The separation of heuristics and theory choice seems to me to be a strategy which can only assist the program of developing a non-Cartesian rationality. Wolterstorff's heuristics of shalom provides an insightful and fruitful means of making that distinction, and allows for the development of just such a defeasible and situated model of rationality and rational theory choice.

The primary way in which Wolterstorff's perspective does this is by allowing us to distinguish between the rational goal of theorising as getting more adequately in touch with reality, and heuristic concerns about what line of research to pursue. For Wolterstorff such criteria of pursuit may focus on the question of which line of research will best foster the growth of knowledge, as is the case in the justification of pure-theory.[173] Equally,

---

170   Feyerabend, "Consolations", 215–216; Chalmers, 83; Pera, 181–184; Riggs, 93.
171   So Pera, 183–184.
172   Pera, 169–187.
173   Such justification is related to but distinct from rationality *per se*. The choice of a "progressive" theory is *ceteris paribus*, a rational choice. The decision to pursue a progressive or potentially progressive research tradition is not strictly a matter of rationality. Its justification is more broadly "moral", in relation to the furthering of the quest for understanding as an aspect of *shalom*. This means that our inability to determine ahead of time which research tradition is going to be most fruitful does not threaten scholarly rationality, for such decisions are a matter of heuristics and not the rationality of theory-choice. It is, however, related to rationality, for the comportment of a theory to a progressive or non-progressive tradition is an aspect of its justification, even as the progressiveness of a tradition is a component in its rational assessment. Thus, a scholar's initial decision to pursue a certain line of research because it has potential to further our knowledge of the world is justified "morally" in relation to the heuristics of *shalom*. However, if after a certain period that promise is unfulfilled, her commitment to that tradition may become irrational, if it becomes clear that the tradition is not as adequate (including progressiveness as a criterion of adequacy) as one of its rivals.

pursuit criteria may focus on social factors, such as the alleviation of suffering, as is the case in the justification of praxis-oriented theory. These social concerns may be illegitimate, in that a line of research may be prompted and sustained by a desire for personal prestige, security, the benefit of a powerful elite, and so on. However these unjustifiable reasons for pursuing a line of research are not irrational. Their failure is not epistemic, depriving them of rational status, but moral, depriving them of justification overall. Similarly, a line of research may be prompted by a concern for the liberation of a particular minority group or oppressed class, and thus be justified.[174] This again, however, is not a matter of rational justification, for it is not motivated by the quest for truth. Rather, it is a matter of moral justification.

Thus these social and personal factors may play an important and legitimate role in the direction of research, be that appraised positively or negatively, without touching on the rational justification of the theories developed in that research. That is to be established on independent grounds in line with the criterion of rational or entitled theorising outlined above. These social factors cannot play a part in rational justification, no matter how much they may be justified by their fostering of *shalom*, for they do not relate to the goal of rationality, which is getting in touch with reality. Thus if a scholar accepts a particular theory over another within her field of research because, while it is less intellectually justified than the other, it is more *morally* acceptable, then her choice of that theory is irrational.[175] This perspective allows Wolterstorff's meta-theory to incorporate the reality of justifiable non-rational concerns within an overall picture of rational scholarly practice without allowing those factors to encroach upon the rationality of theory choice. This provides further justification for Wolterstorff's rejection of relativism.

---

[174] This justification may be lost over time if it appears that an initially promising line of research no longer offers promise of alleviating human suffering. It may be possible, however, that a scholar may be justified in pursuing that line of research, or a related one, if it provides reasonable promise of furthering the growth of knowledge. It then becomes a justified line of pure-theory. Of course, it would be important for a Christian scholar to ensure that this pure-theory justification was not a cover for maintaining a position of security and prestige. This would rob it of legitimacy in terms of the heuristics of *shalom*.

[175] It may well be that her choice of that theory is nonetheless justified overall. This, however, must not detract from the irrationality of her choice. It may well be an intellectual trial, as Wolterstorff rightly suggests, but it still results in her being irrational in her belief. Of course, there is nothing to stop her from attempting to construct a theory of rationality that allows her to accept that theory on rational grounds. This, however, is a different matter, and ultimately relates to the reconstruction of a noetic framework in order to ensure it survives a threat. This kind of response is discussed below in my epistemological metaphor (Chapter 6, C.).

CHAPTER 6

The Structure of Wolterstorff's Meta-Theory

The epistemological structure of Wolterstorff's meta-theory is of some moment in its critical analysis, for the structure of any epistemological theory has an influence on its workings, as can be seen from the discussion above of classical foundationalism. Whether a meta-theory is broadly foundationalist, coherentist, or whatever, determines the nature of the connections between propositions and the theories which are derived from or connected with them which serve to justify those theories, and whether those theories in turn can justify in part the propositions which justify them. Thus it is important to try to identify the structure of Wolterstorff's meta-theory before proceeding to apply it and analyse its functioning in relation to theological theorising.

A. Wolterstorff's Meta-Theory is Non-Foundationalist

That Wolterstorff's meta-theory is not a classical foundationalist theory goes without saying. However it has been claimed that Wolterstorff adopts a broad foundationalist epistemology similar to that of Plantinga.[1] This identification seems to be made for the following reasons: Plantinga and Wolterstorff co-edited *Faith and Rationality* and identify their views as belonging to the school of "Reformed Epistemology", and since Plantinga is avowedly a broad foundationalist Wolterstorff must be one too;[2]

---

1   G. Mavrodes, "Jerusalem and Athens Revisited", *Faith and Rationality: Reason and Belief in God*, ed. A. Plantinga and N. Wolterstorff (Notre Dame: University of Notre Dame Press, 1983) 202; T. A. Russman "'Reformed' Epistemology", *Thomistic Papers IV*, ed. L. A. Kennedy (Houston: University of St Thomas, 1988) 187, 188, 197; H. B. Veatch, "Preliminary Statement of Apology, Analysis, and Critique", *Thomistic Papers IV*, ed. L. A. Kennedy (Houston: University of St Thomas, 1988) 37, 50, 51; K. Clark, 140.
2   Russman, 185–189; Veatch, 7, where he introduces the shorthand expression "P. W. and Co." for the contributors to the volume *Faith and Rationality*. That it is illegitimate to assume that such a broad affiliation entails the adoption of the same views can be seen by

Plantinga and Wolterstorff both assert that belief in God may be rational without its being established on the basis of reasons or evidences, and since Plantinga establishes his case on the notion of "properly basic belief" so must Wolterstorff;[3] or simply some loose association between the men and their ideas.[4]

I think, however, that Wolterstorff is best construed as adopting a specifically non-foundationalist epistemology, whether foundationalism be construed in the classical or broad sense.[5] Indeed, he specifically repudiates foundationalism in relation to his criterion of rationality:

> The criterion offered is clearly not a foundationalist criterion. Fundamental to the foundationalist's vision of the structure of rational belief is the distinction between immediate beliefs and mediate beliefs. As the reader will have surmised, I judge this to be a tenable distinction. And for many purposes it is an important distinction to have in mind... But for a criterion of rational belief the distinction proves otiose. The criterion I have offered is a unified criterion, applying in the same way to mediate and immediate beliefs alike.
>
> Is it then a coherence criterion? Yes, perhaps it is so. In the central place it gives to the phenomenon of *no adequate reason to surrender one's belief* it is an example of what John Pollock has called "negative coherence theories". However in its incorporation of a normative component it goes beyond traditional coherence theories. Perhaps the time has come for us to discard the supposition that the foundationalist/coherentist dichotomy is an illuminating principle of classification.[6]

As this passage indicates, Wolterstorff clearly rejects the foundationalist structure of believings, even though he accepts the usefulness of the

---

Mavrodes' criticisms of both Plantinga and Wolterstorff in his essay "Jerusalem and Athens Revisited", 192–218, in that same volume.

[3] Russman, 197; Veatch, 37, 50–51. This also seems to be the assumption made by K. Clark, 140, where he specifically asserts that Wolterstorff's notion of control beliefs, and his acceptance of Christian belief as control, is identical to the proper basicality of such beliefs.

[4] This seems to be the underlying rationale for the claim of Mavrodes, 202. That there is an association of ideas between Wolterstorff and Plantinga is true, as can be seen by Wolterstorff's endorsement of Plantinga's critique of classical foundationalism, Wolterstorff, *CBGR?*, 142. This, however, does not mean that he accepts Plantinga's alternative epistemology, as can be seen in his preference for entitlement over Plantinga's notion of warrant see above (Chapter 3, A.5.).

[5] This impression has been confirmed in private correspondence with Wolterstorff, in a letter dated June 1, 1993.

[6] Wolterstorff, *CBGR?*, 172; cf. "Once Again, Evidentialism", 56, for the validity of the distinction between mediate and immediate beliefs.

immediate/mediate distinction in beliefs. This rejection of all versions of foundationalism and the associated affinities with coherentist notions of rationality is seen in Wolterstorff's idea that the connections which exist between a particular belief and an individual's network of beliefs are what justify that belief for that person. This is particularly the case given that this criterion of justification applies equally to immediate beliefs, which are taken to be the foundation in foundationalist theories and thus necessarily independent of justification by other beliefs, and mediate beliefs. However, the fact that he maintains that the distinction between immediate and mediate beliefs has some validity and usefulness, as well as the clear normative component of his model of rationality, indicates that his theory of rationality is not a coherentist one.[7] Thus his epistemology, as reflected in his criterion of rationality at least, is specifically and avowedly neither foundationalist nor coherentist, but contains ideas from both. As I will demonstrate, the central ideas of Wolterstorff's meta-theory, in particular the nature and function of control beliefs, serve to reinforce the non-foundationalist nature of his notion of rationality and further explicate it.

In this regard the notion of control beliefs is central, for it is that notion which enables him to hold to the rationality of belief in God without that belief being established on evidences or arguments, and without adhering to Plantinga's broad foundationalism. This is particularly important to establish, for otherwise his understanding of the relationship between evidence and belief in God will be subject to the same criticisms as Plantinga's notion of properly basic belief.[8] I shall, therefore, briefly outline Plantinga's notion of *properly basic beliefs* and the conceptual problems associated with it, before showing how Wolterstorff's notion of control beliefs differs from it and is conceptually superior to it.

Plantinga's notion of proper basicality clearly requires a foundationalist meta-epistemology, though of course not a *classical* foundationalist

---

[7] This suggestion is reinforced by his rejection of key elements of Murphy's Quinean coherentist theory of science and theology. For this theory, see Murphy, "Postmodern Apologetics", 105–120; for Wolterstorff's rejection of its coherentist character, see Wolterstorff, "Entitled Christian Belief", 148–150. Interestingly, Murphy fails to respond to this criticism in her reply to Wolterstorff, for which see, N. Murphy, "On the Nature of Theology", *Religion and Science: History, Method, Dialogue*, ed. W. M. Richardson and W. J. Wildman (New York: Routledge, 1996) 151–159.

[8] In relation to this he claims that while there is no need to establish belief in God on the basis of reasons or evidences, it is not illegitimate, and at times it may be obligatory, for a believer to do so. See Wolterstorff, *CBGR?*, 171–172, 173; *EB&G*, 455; "Is Reason Enough?", 22, 23, 24. For the relevant criticisms of Plantinga, see below.

one.⁹ A properly basic belief is one which is justifiably held or, alternatively, that is *warranted*, in a given instance, without its being held on the basis of evidence, inference from other beliefs, or evidence.¹⁰ It is a species of immediate belief.¹¹ A properly basic belief functions in such an epistemology as the grounds of justification of other beliefs which are linked to it by arguments, evidences and so on, without itself needing to be justified by such evidences or arguments.¹² Where Plantinga's foundationalism differs from the classical model is in his inclusion of memory beliefs, beliefs about external reality, acceptance of testimony, belief in other persons, and belief in God in the set of properly basic beliefs.¹³ It is the claim that belief in God is a properly basic belief for Christian theists that has been at the heart of Plantinga's project,¹⁴ and the source of greatest controversy. It also most clearly demonstrates the problems inherent in his notion.

The crucial problems with Plantinga's theory, for my purposes, are the rationality of non-inferred beliefs, the role of arguments in relation to basic beliefs, and whether Plantinga's criterion for proper basicality implies or necessitates a relativist notion of rationality. Plantinga's notion that belief in God can be rational even though it is not based on evidence has been criticised as fundamentally irrational.¹⁵ This criticism is based, however, on a rival model of rationality, namely medieval foundationalism, one which Plantinga argues is inadequate.¹⁶ To criticise Plantinga for not adhering to a criterion of rationality he rejects as untenable is illegitimate:

---

9 Plantinga, *R&BG*, 72–73; cf. Cooke, 279; J. Zeis, "A critique of Plantinga's theological foundationalism", *International Journal for Philosophy of Religion* 28 (1990) 173–179. For an outline and justification of such a "minimalist foundationalist" epistemology, see Alston, *Epistemic Justification*, 39–56. For a general critique of it, see Zeis, 173–189.

10 Plantinga, *R&BG*, 50–51. It must be noted that for Plantinga a belief may be properly basic in one instance but not in another. I will attempt to show this idea comports better with Wolterstorff's epistemology than with Plantinga's. For the distinction between the proper basicality of belief in God with reference to *justification* and *warrant*, see Plantinga, *Warranted Christian Belief*, 175–178 and 178–179 respectively.

11 For a defence of this notion of immediate belief, see Alston, *Epistemic Justification*, 57–78.

12 Plantinga, *R&BG*, 47–55; Clark, 140–141.

13 Plantinga, *R&BG*, 72–74, 81–82; Clark, 141; Cooke, 279.

14 That Plantinga sees belief in God as properly basic is beyond contention. See Plantinga, *R&BG*, 63–91.

15 Veatch, 38–50.

16 This is clearly seen throughout Veatch's article, but most particularly in 38–50. For Plantinga's rejection of Thomistic foundationalism, see *R&BG*, 39–63. There are problems with his identification of Aquinas as a classical foundationalist and an evidentialist, for which see Wolterstorff, "Migration", 78–81; Cooke, 278.

for it assumes the very point in question, namely that Plantinga's rejection of that theory, and his development of an alternative theory are unjustified. What is needed instead is evidence that Plantinga's model of rationality is internally incoherent, or does not adequately deal with the nature of human believings or alternative models of rationality.

This type of criticism is levelled against Plantinga's theory with respect to the relation of properly basic beliefs to arguments. Plantinga claims that belief in God, while it *ought* to be taken as properly basic, may nonetheless be established on the basis of arguments,[17] that it is not groundless or immune to arguments,[18] and that a belief may be properly basic in some instances but non-basic in others.[19] While there are questions as to whether theistic belief can be properly basic for western intellectuals,[20] my major concern is with the role that arguments play in relation to properly basic beliefs. It seems to me that the idea of a properly basic belief being grounded in particular conditions which then confer justification on that belief is cogent. This notion has been criticised on the grounds that these conditions are merely the *causes* of a belief and not grounds for its justification,[21] or that what Plantinga calls *grounding* is in reality a

---

17   Plantinga, *R&BG*, 73.
18   Ibid., 78–90.
19   Ibid., 50–51.
20   See S. C. Goetz, "Belief in God is not Properly Basic", *RelS* 19/4 (Dec 1983) 475–484; J. W. Robbins, "Is Belief in God Properly Basic?" *International Journal of the Philosophy of Religion* 14/4 (1983) 246–247; Quinn, 479–484. These arguments, in particular those of Quinn, are countered by Plantinga ("The Foundations of Theism: A Reply", *Faith and Philosophy* 3/3 (July 1986) 306–312). R. Grigg argues that there are crucial disanalogies between belief in God and beliefs which can justifiably be taken to be basic ("Theism and Proper Basicality: A Response to Plantinga" *International Journal for Philosophy of Religion* 14 (1983) 125–126; and "The Crucial Disanalogies between Properly Basic Belief and Belief in God", *RelS* 26/3 (Sept 1990) 389–401). These disanalogies have been effectively countered (Evans, 88–95; Alston, "Christian Experience", 103–134; M. S. McLeod, "Can Belief in God be Confirmed?" *RelS* 24 (1988) 311–323). Gutting argues that the presence of disagreement on belief in God amongst one's epistemic peers vitiates Plantinga's proposal (*Religious Belief*, 79–92). This is effectively countered by Wolterstorff ("Once Again, Evidentialism", 53–74). More modest concerns about the proper basicality of belief in God for such people are raised by McKim, 45–53. M. Hester makes the interesting claim that belief in some specific personal God, which is what is typical in theistic belief as opposed to belief in an abstract notion of God's existence, is generally properly basic only for those who already believe in the reality of that God ("Foundationalism and Peter's Confession", *RelS* 26/3 (Sept 1990) 403–413). This claim seems plausible, and comports well with the notion of rationality I develop in this thesis. For an extensive discussion of these points, see Plantinga, *Warranted Christian Belief*, especially his discussion of the "Freud-and-Marx Complaint".
21   Veatch, 40–50.

weaker, and inadequate notion of evidence.[22] However once a Reidian epistemology is adopted, an epistemology which clearly lies behind Plantinga's theory,[23] this criticism loses its force, for all beliefs are the product of belief-forming mechanisms, and it is the epistemic status of those mechanisms which, in part, confers justification on the beliefs they produce.[24]

What is more problematic is the assertion that a belief may be the result of reasoning or evidences at some stage in its career, but be properly basic at another, since the reasons which initially gave rise to the belief no longer function in its maintenance.[25] Related to this is the idea that a basic belief may be subject to critical analysis without losing its basic status. Plantinga's discussion of this is not inconsistent with his general thesis, for it is true that such a belief may function basically in one situation but not in another, and that it may be subject to criticism and still be basic.[26] However, it does comport better with a dynamic, non-foundationalist epistemology, such as that proposed by Wolterstorff.[27]

---

22 Zeis, 177–179.

23 See above for the relationship of Plantinga's theory of rationality to Reid's (Chapter 3, A.5.).

24 See Chapter 3 above for a detailed discussion of such a Reidian epistemology. Cooke, 284–285, supports the notion from what he calls a criteriologist perspective.

25 Plantinga, *R&BG*, 50–51, 73; cf. Alston, *Epistemic Justification*, 63–64.

26 For the latter, see Plantinga, *R&BG*, 82–87. Quinn, 478–484, argues that if arguments against belief in God are countered, then these counter-arguments become the basis of belief in God, and thus belief in God loses its status as a basic belief. This is effectively countered by Plantinga, ("Foundations", 306–312). Alston suggests that, in fact, belief in God may be properly basic, even if it is now believed on the basis of reasons or evidence ("Plantinga's Epistemology", 291–293). What matters in proper basicality, he asserts, is that belief in God does not *need* reasons to justify it, not that it is not in fact supported by reasons. This assertion is in line with what he calls "minimal foundationalism", for which see (Alston, *Epistemic Justification*, 39–56); cf. J. Gowan's helpful discussion ("Foundationalism and the Justification of Religious Belief", *RelS* 19/3 (Sept 1983) 391–393). While I agree with this general notion, it seems to fit uneasily with a foundationalist epistemology. The idea does, however, comport very well with Wolterstorff's notion of control beliefs, which gives added weight to his theory.

27 See McKim, 45 n. 12, where he specifically endorses Wolterstorff's model of rationality over-against Plantinga's, and his general argument 45–53, which comports very well with the nature and function of control beliefs in Wolterstorff's theory of rationality. See also Gowan, 391–406, who shows that if foundationalism can support theistic belief, Plantinga has not demonstrated that it does so. This suggests that an alternative model may well do a better job, as I believe Wolterstorff's does. Zeis, 177–179, 181–186, attempts to show that Plantinga's theory is untenable. In this I think he is unsuccessful, largely for the reasons he adduces against Plantinga's critique of coherentism: namely that it illegitimately employs a rival criterion of rationality in the assessment of Plantinga's theory (see Zeis, 179–186). What Zeis does do, in my view, is show that many of Plantinga's insights

The role performed by properly basic beliefs in Plantinga's theory is performed in Wolterstorff's by control beliefs.[28] These beliefs may be derived from a number of sources, including reasoning, and may function differently at different times without affecting their function of control in the appropriate circumstances.[29] Indeed, unlike basic beliefs which cannot in fact be basic at a particular time if they are truly believed on the basis of reasons or evidences, control beliefs may be developed and sustained by reasons or evidences without changing their control function at all.[30] Nor is there a conceptual problem in a control belief being subject to critical assessment, for if necessary it can change from being a control belief to being a proposition under question without threatening its function as control, unless it fails the test. The advantage that this notion has over Plantinga's is that there is no infelicity in the notion that a control belief may change its nature or function, while there is in the idea that a belief which supports higher level propositions could at some other time not be

---

comport better with a non-foundationalist, dynamic model of rationality. For his version of such a model, see Zeis, 184–187.

[28] This is correctly noted by K. Clark, 140, even though he falsely asserts that Wolterstorff is a foundationalist.

[29] Zeis, 182–183, argues, successfully in my view, that what are called basic beliefs really depend upon other beliefs for their formulation, significance, and so on. Thus, as soon as they are formulated *as beliefs*, or incorporated into an overall conceptual scheme, they lose their basicality, for interpretation, theories of reality and so on, affect their form, content and function as beliefs. This seems to me to be a straightforward implication of the notion of the theory-dependence of data.

[30] This idea is supported by Gowan, 403–406. In relation to belief in God in particular, it is interesting to note that Wolterstorff has reservations about the legitimacy of arguments which support belief in God, so called "positive apologetics", but not about countering arguments against belief in God, so-called "negative apologetics" ("Is Reason Enough?", 20–24). Mavrodes, 197–204, argues that both positive and negative apologetics may at times be appropriate strategies, and suggests that a dynamic alternative to the static foundationalist model of rationality be developed to overcome some of the typical problems in apologetics. This, however, is just what Wolterstorff has done. What he has failed to do, I believe, is recognise the significance of his model of rationality for the apologetic enterprise. His dynamic theory, in particular the nature and function of control beliefs, allows for the legitimacy of belief in God being established and maintained *as a control belief* by evidence and arguments, without jeopardising the strength, constancy and function of that belief which is so important to Reformed philosophy and theology. His failure to recognise this important implication of his theory is due, I believe, to remnants of foundationalism in his thought patterns, and the vehemence of the Reformed epistemologists' antipathy to traditional versions of natural theology and evidentialist apologetics. However positive apologetics can easily be reinterpreted and developed along lines consistent with Reformed epistemology, in particular Wolterstorff's own theory. This can only be noted here, as such a development lies beyond the scope of this thesis.

in the foundations of the belief-system at all.[31] It seems better to me to specifically adopt Wolterstorff's dynamic model instead of Plantinga's apparently more static foundationalist model with its attendant problems of changing functions and "positions" of beliefs in an apparently static noetic structure.[32]

Significant criticisms have also been levelled against Plantinga's criterion of proper basicality. He claims that despite the fact that there is no *a priori* criterion for proper basicality this does not mean that the way is opened for any and every belief to be seen as properly basic.[33] Rather, in the light of a broadly inductive approach to the establishment of a criterion of rationality,[34] suitable cases of properly basic beliefs are to be collected and from them a general criterion is to be inferred.[35] However, given that different people, and more importantly, different believing communities and intellectual traditions, will have differing notions of what beliefs are or are not properly basic, there will be no consensus amongst such individuals or communities as to this criterion of proper basicality.[36] Indeed, given that Christian theists in the Reformed tradition will accept the proper basicality of belief in God while others, especially atheists will not, there will be no general agreement on the proper basicality of belief in God.[37]

---

31   Zeis, 185–186, calls this "local foundationalism", and argues that it is compatible with a non-foundationalist, dynamic model of rationality in which there is no ultimate justification of a noetic structure. However, I believe that a noetic structure can be justified in toto, but only defeasibly, and generally only piecemeal; i.e., by examining certain crucial elements of the belief-system in relation to a rival system. Thus it is not justified in relation to an arbitrary, transcendent criterion of justification, but only provisionally, and in relation to alternative belief-systems which have bearing on related matters. This notion is briefly developed below (this chapter, C.).

32   As suggested by Mavrodes, 202–204, although he does not note the dynamic nature of Wolterstorff's meta-theory. I should note here that this is a problem for the *model* or *metaphor* that Plantinga uses, namely (broad) foundationalism, rather than for the theory *per se*. Indeed, given that he allows for such dynamism, it seems to me that the theory is ill served by his use of a static, foundationalist metaphor.

33   Plantinga, *R&BG*, 74–77. Hatcher, 91, argues that without such an *a priori* criterion we are reduced to Rortian relativism. However, given the cogency of the epistemology underlying the rejection of such a criterion, and the possibility of a non-relativist solution to the problem of the criterion, Hatcher's claim is unjustified.

34   Plantinga specifically adopts Chisholm's approach as found in *The Problem of the Criterion*.

35   Plantinga, *R&BG*, 76–77; cf. Cooke, 279.

36   Plantinga, *R&BG*, 77. As McKim, 31, notes, it is not clear whether the inductive procedure is to be used with respect to individuals or faith communities. This detail could be resolved, and has little bearing on my discussion here.

37   Plantinga, *R&BG*, 77.

Thus, it is only from within a specific faith context that belief in God will be justifiably taken to be basic.

This idea raises the issue of implicit relativism in Plantinga's notion of rationality,[38] an implication Plantinga rejects.[39] That his is not a relativist notion is clearly seen in his recognition that when two people disagree in relation to a criterion of proper basicality then at least one of them is wrong and the other may be right, even if there is no way to establish which is wrong or possibly right by further discussion.[40] Thus those who claim that his is a relativist notion are mistaken.[41] However, this charge, and the nature of Plantinga's defence, raises a further issue in relation to his epistemology: while it is not, strictly speaking, a relativist theory, it seems to imply or necessitate the acceptance of the incommensurability thesis in relation to criteria of proper basicality, and thus of models of rationality.

Plantinga's initial response to the subjectivist and relativist critique is to assert that "The Christian community is responsible to *its* set of examples",[42] and that since there is no Great Pumpkin there can be no natural tendency to believe in the Great Pumpkin such as exists for belief in God.[43] Such a position is not only particularist,[44] it makes Christian and non-Christian belief systems effectively incommensurable.[45] There is no way to assess the rival claims of belief systems or the notions of rationality associated with them. All we can do is agree to differ with our opponents.[46] Thus, while his is not a specifically relativist position, there are aspects of his earlier work that point to a framework relativist position in relation to criteria of proper basicality and thus notions of rationality.[47] His

---

[38] Hatcher, 90–91; Robbins, 246.

[39] Plantinga, *R&BG*, 74, 78.

[40] Plantinga, *R&BG*, 78; cf. Alston, "Plantinga's Epistemology", 300; A. M. Matteo "Can Belief in God be Basic?" *Horizons* 15/2 (1988) 269–270; P. C. Appleby, "Reformed epistemology, rationality and belief in God", *International Journal for Philosophy of Religion* 24/3 (Nov 1988) 137–139.

[41] cf. A. M. Matteo, "Can Belief in God be Basic?" *Horizons* vol 15, no 2 (1988) 270.

[42] Plantinga, *R&BG*, 77.

[43] Ibid., 78. A more adequate counter-argument against the "Great Pumpkin Objection" is proffered by Appleby, 137–139, which avoids some of the relativist implications of Plantinga's defence in *R&BG*.

[44] As Plantinga asserts in *R&BG*, 78.

[45] Matteo, 270–272. However, he wrongly accuses Plantinga of being *nonfoundationalist*.

[46] The similarities between Plantinga and Neo-Calvinist epistemology, and even Kuhn's meta-theory are clear in this regard.

later discussion, however, largely avoids these difficulties, focussing as it does on warrant and proper basicality.[48] Given, however, that Plantinga's later theory deals with *warrant* and not *rationality* or *entitlement*, it is not directly relevant to normative dimension of belief-governance.

Wolterstorff's model of rational justification or entitlement has advantages over Plantinga's earlier theory of rationality for, while recognising that different faith communities have differing control beliefs, he proposes a general epistemology which allows for such belief systems to be critically assessed and opened to modification.[49] This allows him to recognise the person and community specific nature of rationality without embracing or implying incommensurability. Thus, not only is Wolterstorff's model of rationality substantially different both to Plantinga's theory of rationality and of warrant, it is a more adequate theory rationality, for it explains all that Plantinga's does, it does so without the crucial problems associated with the notion of properly basic belief, and it explains more facts than Plantinga's model.

Russman has claimed that such an avowedly post-foundationalist epistemology is incompatible with Christian faith,[50] and so is an unacceptable theory of rationality for Wolterstorff to adopt as a Reformed Christian.[51] Indeed, despite the fact that Wolterstorff rejects the antinomian and agnostic views of Rorty and Feyerabend,[52] Russman claims that:

---

47 Similar points are made by Alston, "Plantinga's Epistemology", 301; Matteo, 269–270; Runzo, 37–39; McKim, 33–43. The latter specifically states that Wolterstorff's model of rationality is more adequate than Plantinga's in this respect (45 n. 12). Runzo, 31–51, provides an alternative conceptualisation in terms of world-views which, while not without flaws, with suitable modification can be reconciled with Wolterstorff's account of rationality.

48 See Plantinga, *Warranted Christian Belief*, 342–353.

49 This follows a similar line to that of Runzo, 31–51, but is a more adequate view in toto. For a brief discussion of this in relation to Wolterstorff's theory, see Wolfe, *Epistemology*, 50–55.

50 Russman, 186–189.

51 In a similar vein, H. Netland claims that the very notion of rationality "seems to demand a foundationalist epistemology of some kind" ("Review of *Faith and Rationality: Reason and Belief in God*", *Journal of the Evangelical Theological Society* 29/1 (Mar 1986) 93). It is interesting that he also implies that Wolterstorff is a foundationalist, perhaps because he is unwilling to charge him with being fundamentally irrational. Meynell, 79–87, is not so circumspect. He claims not only that rationality entails at least a broad foundationalism, but also that Wolterstorff's is a fundamentally irrational and antinomian meta-theory. This largely depends upon his mistaken assumption that all reasons for (or against) a belief must function as foundations in a static epistemological structure. These criticisms are thus vitiated in light of the non-foundationalist construals of evidence and reasons presented in this thesis.

52 Wolterstorff, "Introduction", 4, as acknowledged by Russman, 187.

Wolterstorff's enthusiasm for the contemporary, postfoundationalist dialogue in epistemology is precisely the point which might seem at first to put his Christianity in doubt.[53]

Indeed, he forcefully asserts:

> Let's state the matter categorically – Christianity is epistemologically a foundationalist enterprise. It claims that revelation has taken place, that, whatever developments in Christian understanding may emerge, the validity of those developments is always to be checked against the foundation in revelation... And so, if some of our Reformed brothers and sisters were at this late hour to embrace antifoundationalism, they would be abandoning some of the most central and most commonly held tenets concerning Christian revelation. The grounds on which they would call themselves "Christian" would not be the grounds on which *Christians* have called themselves Christian through the centuries to the present.[54]

There are a number of important claims made in this quote,[55] but I shall limit myself to the question of the Bible as a foundation for Christian thought.[56] The assertion that the Bible provides Christians with a foundation of certitudes for theorising fails for three main reasons.[57] First, this claim assumes that biblical revelation is primarily or solely propositional in character, or that it can be reduced to propositions without distorting its character,[58] a view that is at best questionable and incom-

---

[53] Russman, 186. Indeed, it seems that it is only Russman's fallacious identification of Wolterstorff's theory as a broadly foundationalist theory like Plantinga's that saves him from this charge in his view (Russman, 187.)

[54] Russman, 187.

[55] For example, the historical question of the tacit or implicit epistemologies of classical Christian thinkers, and the importance of foundationalist epistemologies to the self-understanding of Christians. Plantinga, *R&BG*, 63–73, argues that the Reformers rejected *classical* (including medieval) foundationalist epistemology at least.

[56] Assertions about the foundational character of Christian revelation are made by Schaeffer and Henry (F. A. Schaeffer, *He is There and He is not Silent* (London: Hodder and Stoughton, 1972) 83–114; C. F. H. Henry, *God, Revelation and Authority*, vol 1 (6 vol; Waco: Word, 1976) 213–244). Henry specifically states it provides grounds for the reasonable certainty of Christian truth claims.

[57] These are outlined in Wolterstorff, *RWBR*, 58–62; and applied in detail to the theological theories of Carl Henry by R. R. Topping ("The Anti-Foundationalist Challenge to Evangelical Apologetics", *EvQ* 63/1 (1991) 47–52).

[58] See for instance, D. B. Knox, "Propositional Revelation the only Revelation", *Reformed Theological Review* 19/1 (Feb 1960) 1–9; Schaeffer, *He is There*, 118–120; C. F. H. Henry, *God, Revelation and Authority*, vol 3 (6 vol; Waco: Word, 1979) 455–487, esp

plete.[59] Second, it assumes that a God who cannot err reveals propositions and that the Bible contains only these propositions,[60] claims that are difficult if not impossible to prove in the light of textual criticism and possible doubts about the original record being an indubitable record of just those propositions.[61] Third it assumes that, even if the Bible may be seen as a source of indubitable propositions, we are able to interpret it accurately so that the conclusions we come to are indubitable,[62] a claim that seems implausible in the light of widespread, persistent and significant exegetical and theological debate.[63] There is, therefore, no plausible way in which the Bible may be seen as a source of foundational propositions, and so the claim that Christian reliance upon Scripture mandates a foundationalist epistemology is unwarranted.[64] Thus, there is no good reason to claim that Wolterstorff's rejection of foundationalism is inconsistent with his Christian profession, and so this rejection is permissible.

477–478 and 409–418, where he responds to Wolterstorff's notions of God speaking, for which see below (Conclusion: Retrospect and Prospect).

[59] Wolterstorff, *RWBR*, 58–59; Topping, 47–48, 51–52; Evans, 99–107.

[60] cf. Knox, 5, 8–9; Schaeffer, *He is There*, 120–121; Henry, *God, Revelation and Authority*, vol 1, 215–224.

[61] Wolterstorff, *RWBR*, 60–61; Topping, 48–49. It is important to note that these doubts do not need to be accepted in order to undermine the Bible as a foundation for theorising, only that they cast legitimate questions upon its status. Topping, 49–51, notes that for Henry certain logical criteria are used to justify the epistemic status of the biblical text. These become, in effect, the real (but inadequate) foundation of the Bible's truth claims, as can be seen in Henry's own work (see Henry, *God, Revelation and Authority*, vol 1, 232–238), and in that of Hackett who attempted to provide a more adequate foundationalist justification of theology (see S. C. Hackett, *The Reconstruction of the Christian Revelation Claim* (Grand Rapids: Baker, 1984) 13–83; Topping, 52–59, for a critique). It is important to stress here that I am not calling into question the value of logical tests in theological theorising. Rather I am noting that they function as foundations for Henry and Hackett, but that they cannot support the weight of the noetic structure they purportedly support. Thus they are valuable, but they are not adequate foundations. Nor am I, or Wolterstorff, calling into question the legitimate control function that the Bible exercises over a Christian scholar. The point is that this control function cannot be adequately conceived of in (classical) foundationalist terms.

[62] C. F. H. Henry, *God, Revelation and Authority*, vol 4 (6 vol; Waco: Word, 1979) 350–351. Here he acknowledges the "fallibility of the exegete", but claims that this does not threaten the objectivity and absolute status of theological conclusions when they are controlled by the propositional revelation of Scripture.

[63] Wolterstorff, *RWBR*, 61.

[64] Wolterstorff, *RWBR*, 61–62. This, as he clearly states, does not rob Christian faith of its justification, or even its potential status as knowledge.

B. Wolterstorff and Other Non-Foundationalist Meta-Theories

There are many similarities between Wolterstorff's meta-theory and those of Quine and Lakatos. While these are important, and provide considerable support for Wolterstorff's theory, there are crucial differences between Wolterstorff, Quine and Lakatos, and in general Wolterstorff's model is able to overcome the problems inherent in the theories of Quine and Lakatos. There is a large body of literature on both these theories, and their general appraisal lies beyond my scope here.[65] Thus I will limit my discussion of their theories to those aspects which have direct bearing on Wolterstorff's meta-theory.

Quine has developed a specifically coherentist model of rationality and scientific theorising. In his view no theory or observation exists in isolation, but rather they are all connected in a network of beliefs which provides the necessary context for their evaluation.[66] He states: "The unit of empirical significance is the whole of science."[67] In the event of a conflict between experience and our belief system, some change needs to be made in the system.[68] There is much latitude in what the actual change may be, for it is not dictated by the anomaly itself, but is the result of conscious choices to change our belief.[69] At the periphery of the network of beliefs lie our experiences of reality and the beliefs we form in relation to those experiences.[70] These beliefs are more amenable than others to

---

65   For such appraisals, see, for example, C. Hookway, *Quine: Language, Experience and Reality*; R. F. Gibson, *Enlightened Empiricism: An Examination of W. V. Quine's Theory of Knowledge* (Tampa: University of South Florida Press, 1988); K. Gavroglu, Y. Goudaroulis, and P. Nicolacopoulos, (ed); *Imre Lakatos and Theories of Scientific Change* (Dordrecht: Kluwer, 1989); N. Murphy, *Theology*, esp 51–87, 174–211, who specifically adopts Lakatos' methodology of scientific research programs as her descriptive and prescriptive meta-theory of theology.

66   Quine, "Two Dogmas", 42; Quine and Ullian, 6–8. Indeed, the very title of the latter work is a specific allusion to a coherentist model of rationality.

67   Quine, "Two Dogmas", 42.

68   Quine, "Two Dogmas", 42; Quine, *Pursuit*, 13–16; Quine and Ullian, 13.

69   Quine, "Two Dogmas", 42–43; *Pursuit*, 13–16; Quine and Ullian, 10–11. This notion of conscious choices to change belief influenced Wolterstorff's ideas in *Reason Within the Bounds of Religion*. He has since shifted away from this perspective due to his view that our beliefs are in general not subject to direct volitional control.

70   Quine, "Two Dogmas", 42; Quine and Ullian, 12–13. Strictly speaking, Quine asserts that we do not believe in external entities, but in statements we make about those entities. Thus, in relation to the periphery of a belief system he refers to *observation statements or sentences* and not beliefs, see Quine, "Two Dogmas", 43; *Pursuit*, 3–5; Quine and Ullian, 4–5. For a critique of this representationalist view of perception and experience, see Evans, 81–84; Alston, "Christian Experience and Christian Belief", 108–110. In the light of these

change in the light of conflicts between our belief system and our experience of reality.[71] The reason these peripheral beliefs are changed rather than those more distant from the empirical edge of the belief system is that changes to them require less adjustment to the overall system than do changes to more central beliefs.[72] Such a notion of rationality has obvious bearing on the nature of theorising in science.[73]

There are some clear similarities between this model of rationality and Wolterstorff's meta-theory. Both recognise that theories are weighed in the context of a network of beliefs rather than in isolation, and that inconsistencies between the belief system and experience dictate only that some change in the network of beliefs takes place, but not the specific change.[74] This provides added support for Wolterstorff's meta-theory. There are, however, important areas in which Wolterstorff and Quine differ which have bearing on the epistemological structure of their theories. One difference is that Quine's is clearly a voluntarist model of rationality. He believes that beliefs are subject to voluntary control, and that we can and ought to choose which beliefs we alter in the event of an empirical anomaly.[75] Wolterstorff on the other hand does not believe that beliefs are subject to voluntary control, rather they are generally the product of belief-dispositions which ineluctably produce beliefs in the appropriate circumstances.[76] This then means that changes to the belief system are not and cannot be the result of decisions to believe or disbelieve, but are instead the product of much more complex mechanisms which relate to the function of control beliefs.

Another significant difference between Quine's and Wolterstorff's models is that the former is a relatively static coherentist model, as is the metaphor he uses to articulate it. While beliefs and their connections within a person's belief system must be modified in the light of recalcitrant evidence, certain beliefs lie at the core of the noetic structure and, due to the relative inertia of human believings, are relatively immune from change.[77] Such core beliefs thus play a predominantly passive role in the

---

critiques, I will refer to beliefs about reality, and experiences of reality rather than using Quine's terminology.

[71] Quine, "Two Dogmas", 43; Quine and Ullian, 12–13.
[72] Quine, "Two Dogmas", 44; *Pursuit*, 13–16.
[73] For an outline of this, see Quine and Ullian, 42–90.
[74] cf. Wolterstorff, *RWBR*, 42–47, 63–70.
[75] Quine and Ullian, 10–11. It is worth noting in passing that Quine ignores conceptual anomalies and deals only with empirical problems which, as Laudan, *Progress*, 45–69, demonstrates, is at best a partial explanation of science and scientific change.
[76] Wolterstorff, *CBGR?*, 162; *EB&G*, 452.
[77] See Quine, "Two Dogmas", 44; *Pursuit*, 13–16.

development of a belief system, in that they control the shape of a person's structure of beliefs largely because they are resistant to change.

Wolterstorff's model is both more dynamic than this and also involves a much more active role for certain core beliefs, those he calls control beliefs. It is more dynamic in as much as control beliefs are subject to critical assessment, even though they are relatively resistant to change.[78] Indeed, the very nature of control beliefs, and the meta-theory they are part of, entails that such beliefs can and do change their function in different circumstances. They are not statically embedded at the core of the noetic structure, distanced from the empirical periphery. Rather, they are core beliefs in some conditions and data-beliefs in others, depending on the matter under review.[79] So too control beliefs have a more positive role in Wolterstorff's meta-theory than do core beliefs in Quine's, for control beliefs are not just resistant to change, they dictate the kinds of changes that may be made in the belief system as a whole. Thus, in the right conditions, control beliefs can affect a person's total noetic structure, from the core out, rather than being isolated at the centre, and so they play a crucial and positive role in the belief system.

Lakatos's model of scientific rationality was devised as a critical development of Popper's falsificationism, incorporating certain of Kuhn's notions of the nature of scientific discovery.[80] The crucial development for Lakatos was the shift from the appraisal of individual theories to series of theories, or Research Programs.[81] This entailed a major shift in the focus of both the philosophy of science and the pursuit of science, from theory choice to heuristics. There were two primary elements in Lakatos's conception of a scientific research program: the "hard core" or "negative

---

[78] It must be noted that core beliefs are subject to critical assessment in Quine's view, for which see Quine and Ullian, 6–10. However his model does not include a mechanism for the revision of core beliefs in the event of insurmountable problems as does Wolterstorff's, for which see above (Chapter 4, B.2.). Thus, this is a problem for the *model* or *metaphor* that Quine uses, namely coherence in the web of belief, rather than for the theory *per se*. Indeed, given that he allows for such dynamism, it seems to me that the theory is ill served by his use of a static, coherentist metaphor.

[79] This notion, and its impact upon Wolterstorff's meta-theory will be examined in more detail below (this chapter, C.).

[80] Lakatos, *MSRP*, 180–184; Chalmers, 76, 85; Feyerabend, "Consolations", 211; Murphy, *Theology*, 58–59; Newton-Smith, 77; Laudan, 4 n. 6, claims that Lakatos's ideas do not comport well with the Popperian program. This comment exposes certain crucial problems with Lakatos's model of scientific rationality which are explored by Pera, 169–187.

[81] Lakatos, *MSRP*, 132; "Introduction", 4–5; Chalmers, 73–76.

heuristic", and the "protective belt" or "positive heuristic".[82] The hard core of a research program was envisaged as a set of unchanging presuppositions and methodological rules adopted by the decision of the adherents to the program which cannot be modified or rejected without abandoning that research program.[83] It is thus a negative heuristic, identifying areas and methods of research which are closed to adherents of the program.[84] This is a rational conventionalism, according to Lakatos, in that the growth of corroborated empirical content provides empirical and logical reasons for the acceptance or rejection of a research program, and thus there are good reasons for or against the conventions which make up a research program's hard core.[85] It is this hard core of commitments and beliefs which gives the research program its continuity and partially constitutes it as a conceptual scheme.[86]

The second major constituent of a research program is the set of auxiliary hypotheses which surround the hard core protecting it from refutation in the event of anomalies.[87] The protective belt becomes the target of refutation rather than the hard core, and the auxiliary hypotheses which constitute it are modified in order to deal with new or recalcitrant evidence, thereby ensuring that there is no change to the hard core of the research program.[88] The goal of any research program is to extend and modify the protective belt so as to more adequately articulate the theories which constitute it.[89] The result is an increase in corroborated empirical content, which he also calls the discovery of novel facts, by which a research program's progressiveness may be determined.[90] Any hypothesis is acceptable so long as it is not *ad hoc*; i.e. so long as it opens the way for fresh tests or new discoveries, or the reinterpretation of old contrary evidence, thereby converting it from an anomaly to a confirmation of the research program.[91]

---

[82] Lakatos, *MSRP*, 133–134; "Introduction", 4; cf. Chalmers, 76–77; Riggs, 73–74, 76–77.
[83] Lakatos, *MSRP*, 133–134; "Introduction", 4; cf. Chalmers, 76–77; Riggs, 73–74.
[84] Lakatos, *MSRP*, 132–133.
[85] Ibid., 134.
[86] Ibid., 132 and n. 1.
[87] Lakatos, *MSRP*, 133; "Introduction", 4; cf. Chalmers, 77; Riggs, 76–77.
[88] Lakatos, *MSRP*, 77; cf. Chalmers, 77; Riggs, 76–77.
[89] Lakatos, *MSRP*, 116–132, 138–154, and the examples explored there; cf. Chalmers, 76, 80–81.
[90] Lakatos, 116–119, 122–123; "Introduction", 4–7; cf. Chalmers, 79; Riggs, 77.
[91] Lakatos, *MSRP*, 137; cf. Chalmers, 80. There is, however, a tension in this aspect of Lakatos's thought, for he criticises Marxism and Freudian psychology for hypotheses which retrospectively explain anomalies (Lakatos, *MSRP*, 175–176). It seems there is a fine line

This growth in corroborated empirical content is the hallmark of progressiveness which, along with coherence, are the criteria by which a research program must be appraised.[92] This appraisal can, however, only ever be retrospective, and new research programs are, and should be, immune from criticism for a (unspecified) period to enable them to become sufficiently articulated.[93] This immunity from empirical refutation not only allows for the maturation of new research programs, it also explains the relative autonomy of theoretical science from refutation by empirical science.[94] Thus research programs are relatively autonomous entities which define and guide a particular area of scientific investigation.

There are many similarities between Lakatos's and Wolterstorff's models of science, such as the recognition of the role of some noetic obligations in the governance of belief,[95] the adoption of a fallible but rational model of science,[96] the situated nature of this rationality,[97] and the use of empirical data from the history of science in the development of his philosophy of science.[98] Here I will restrict myself to those aspects of Lakatos's theory which have bearing on the epistemological structure of Wolterstorff's meta-theory.

Wolterstorff's central notion of control beliefs bears certain crucial similarities to Lakatos's notion of the hard core of a research program. For Wolterstorff a person's control beliefs, which for a Christian are partially constituted by the belief-content of her authentic Christian commitment, ought to function as a negative control excluding certain beliefs and

---

between a progressive hypothesis which converts a "refutation" into a "verification", and an *ad hoc* hypothesis which merely rationalises the program's failure in a given area, the line being, it seems, that the conversion must involve an extension of the explanatory power of the program. See Banner, 130–140, for problems of the internal and external justification of Lakatos' methodology in light of the nature and definition of *ad hoc* hypotheses, and Murphy, *Theology*, 66–68, for an articulation and defence of it.

92   Lakatos, *MSRP*, 116–132, 142–143; cf. Chalmers, 79, 81.
93   Lakatos, *MSRP*, 137, 158, 173; cf. Chalmers, 79, 82; Riggs, 77.
94   Lakatos, *MSRP*, 137. This latter idea is criticised by Laudan, 78, and Riggs, 80, as being inconsistent with the history of science, for anomalies do play a significant role in the development of research programs and theoretical science.
95   Lakatos, "Introduction", 1, 4, 6, and on norms in believing and non-relativism in Wolterstorff's meta-theory see above (Chapter 3, A.3.; Chapter 5, A.2. and n. 126).
96   Lakatos, *MSRP*, 179, 188.
97   Lakatos, *MSRP*, n. 2, pp. 164, 154–173.
98   Lakatos, *MSRP*, 138–151, 159–173, although, as he notes, he uses a *rational reconstruction* of the history of science in his meta-theory of science, Lakatos, *MSRP*, 138 n. 2; 140 n. 4. For similarities and differences between this, and Wolterstorff's meta-theory, see above (Chapter 5, A.1.).

theories because they do not comport well with it, in much the same way as the hard core functions in Lakatos's research programs.[99] So too, Wolterstorff and Lakatos share the belief that an empirical anomaly does not give rise to the refutation of a given theory, for it merely shows that there is some problem in the total system of beliefs and theories, and thus that some adjustment must be made in that system.[100] Thus there are important structural similarities between Wolterstorff's and Lakatos's epistemologies, in that there is a core of commitments at the heart of any noetic structure which is surrounded by a network of defeasible theories and beliefs. This provides general support for central ideas in Wolterstorff's meta-theory.

There are, however, crucial differences between Wolterstorff and Lakatos, many of which correlate to crucial problems in Lakatos's methodology of scientific research programs. Despite his attempt to minimise the conventional component of scientific investigation, decisions still play a central role in Lakatos's theory, be they in relation to the way that certain beliefs are taken to be data in the course of anomalies being processed by a research program,[101] or the manner in which the hard core is adopted.[102] This not only conflicts with Wolterstorff's claim that at least some important beliefs are not subject to volitional control, particularly in relation to our taking certain beliefs to be data or control,[103] it is also too subjective,[104] and comports poorly with Lakatos's general idea of rationality.[105] Perhaps most importantly, however, Lakatos's description of the nature of these decisions, and how they are to be made with respect to the hard core of a research tradition, is vague, overly generalised, and open

---

[99] Wolterstorff, *RWBR*, 76, cf. Lakatos, *MSRP*, 132–133. It is, of course, significantly different in that Wolterstorff's control beliefs also function positively, in that the (Christian) scholar ought to devise theories which comport to her control beliefs to the best of her ability, Wolterstorff, *RWBR*, 76, and that it is not a rigid and unchanging core, Wolterstorff, *RWBR*, 69–70, 74–75.

[100] Lakatos, *MSRP*, 119–120, 129–130; Wolterstorff, *RWBR*, 42–45, 63–70. There are striking similarities particularly in the notions of the role of rival theories and networks of theories in scholarly activity in these passages.

[101] Lakatos, *MSRP*, 106–107, 129–130; cf. Pera, 179–180.

[102] Lakatos, *MSRP*, 133–134; "Introduction", 4; cf. Chalmers, 77; Riggs, 73–74; Pera, 179–180.

[103] See, for instance, Wolterstorff, *RWBR*, 66, where he states that our data beliefs are "that which I find myself believing to be true". However, it is to be stressed that he does maintain a role for decisions and volition, particularly in relation to noetic obligations, Wolterstorff, *RWBR*, 70.

[104] Chalmers, 60, 77.

[105] Pera, 179–180.

to at least two contrary interpretations.[106] Given the importance of the hard core to the establishment and progression of a research program, this is a crucial flaw in his meta-theory.[107]

If there are problems with Lakatos's discussion of how a research program's hard core is established, there are equally significant problems with his discussion of its constancy and rigidity throughout the life of the program. The central problem is simple: the history of science provides examples of "research programs" in which the hard core has been changed, or even refuted, within the life of the research program, thus contradicting Lakatos's claim that the hard core is irrefutable by methodological convention.[108] Laudan develops this observation in his notion of evolving research *traditions* in science, an idea which is a critical modification of Lakatos's methodology of scientific research programs.[109]

Laudan sees a research tradition as comprising a number of different theories which exemplify and partially constitute it, and as having a set of methodological and metaphysical assumptions at its core.[110] Like Lakatos's research programs, Laudan's research traditions guide the development of theories within it by limiting the nature, scope and methodologies of acceptable theories, defining possible and impossible entities, and providing hints on acceptable future research.[111] These research traditions are crucially different to research programs, however, in that they evolve over time so that over the history of a given tradition it will have many different forms, some of which may be mutually incompatible.[112] This evolution includes changes not only in the tradition's constituent theories, but also in the assumptions, ontology and methodology which lie at the core of the tradition.[113] The continuity of the tradition

---

[106] Kuhn, "Reflections", 239–240; Riggs, 75.

[107] Riggs, 75.

[108] Banner, 111; Newton-Smith, 82–84; Riggs, 78–79; Laudan, 78–79. Clayton, 315–335, argues that the clarity and rigidity of research programs in the natural sciences become progressively more opaque and softer as we move through the social sciences to hermeneutics and theology. While this may be true, it is also the case that this opacity and softness is present in the natural sciences, and so this does not vitiate the truth-claims of these disciplines as he suggests. This suggests, as argued below, that for the analysis of *Wissenschaft* in general the notion of a research tradition is better than that of a Lakatosian research program.

[109] Laudan, 70–120; cf. Riggs, 95.

[110] Laudan, 78–79; cf. Riggs, 110.

[111] Laudan, 81, 93, 96–97; cf. Riggs, 110, 112.

[112] Laudan, 78–79, 81; cf. Riggs, 110–111.

[113] Laudan, 96–97; cf. Riggs, 112–113.

consists, then, not in the constancy of its make-up, but in the relative slowness of its evolution and the fact that at no time in its history may the essence of the "soft core" be rejected by adherents to the research tradition.[114]

This is close to Wolterstorff's notion of control beliefs, and provides added support for it, particularly in relation to the soft core's control function with respect to the ontology, methodology and assumptions which are allowed in acceptable theories. However it suffers from important historical and conceptual problems which Wolterstorff's meta-theory is able to overcome. Its major conceptual problem is that key articulated assumptions cannot all be subject to change over time within a single tradition and have that tradition maintain its integrity.[115] So too, Laudan's theory suffers from historical evidence of at least one common assumption or premise being found in the soft core throughout the life of a research tradition.[116] For Wolterstorff's theory these problems do not exist, for many of a scholar's control beliefs are implicit, and thus may change dramatically over time without her abandoning her central commitment.[117] Furthermore, for Christian scholars at least, there are certain beliefs which cannot be removed from the belief content of authentic Christian commitment, and which thus provide the constancy required over time for the integrity of research traditions.[118] Thus Wolterstorff's central notion of control beliefs provides both the flexibility and the stability required for the continuance of a research tradition. This demonstrates the value of Wolterstorff's meta-theory and its attendant epistemological structure. Indeed, I believe that Wolterstorff's meta-theory constitutes a Lakatosian or Laudanian refutation of their meta-theories, as it incorporates the empirical and conceptual problem solving ability of both, while avoiding their empirical and conceptual anomalies.[119]

---

[114] Laudan, 98–99; cf. Riggs, 113. It is interesting to note, with Riggs, 114, that Laudan does not specify how a scientist may decide which elements of the soft core are subject to change at a given time.

[115] Riggs, 114.

[116] Ibid.

[117] Note Wolterstorff, *RWBR*, 66–67.

[118] Ibid., 71–75, though that he believes that these beliefs are "few and simple", in relation to the belief-content of authentic Christian commitment (Ibid., 67).

[119] For these as criteria for choosing a theory or research tradition over its rivals, see Lakatos, *MSRP*, 116–119, 122–123, 142–143; Laudan, 11–69.

C. A Dynamic Model of Wolterstorff's Meta-Theory

A number of times in the course of the preceding discussion I have suggested the need for a dynamic meta-epistemology in order to do justice to the nature of both human noetic enterprises and Wolterstorff's meta-theory. The chief reason for this is that both foundationalist and coherentist models of rationality suffer from an overly rigid noetic structure. Traditional foundationalist theories use the image of a building to describe the structure of warranted belief, while coherentist theories use the image of a web or network. As I have shown, neither these images nor their attendant meta-epistemological models are adequate descriptions of either Wolterstorff's meta-theory or the nature of scientific or other human belief systems, and so an alternative needs to be developed. Here, following a suggestion made by Mavrodes,[120] I will present a dynamic model for a noetic structure which, I believe, does justice to Wolterstorff's meta-theory and the nature of human noetic enterprises. Unfortunately I will not be able to articulate it as rigorously as I would like, as that would be well beyond the scope of this work. Rather I will present the broad outline of such an epistemic schema, recognising the programmatic and generalised nature of the model, looking to future work to further articulate it.

The dynamic nature of Wolterstorff's meta-theory is seen clearly in the manner in which beliefs can change their function depending upon the context and the matter under review. At one point we take certain beliefs to be true, i.e. data, while on another occasion the same belief may well be treated as a theory which is subject to review. Similarly, at one point theories about instruments and initial conditions within a system may be taken as background beliefs, while at a later date, perhaps due to some recalcitrant anomaly, the instrumental theory will itself be subjected to critical appraisal. Thus beliefs may shift from being viewed as unequivocally true, to being the subject of critical testing. Of course, it may well be that subsequent to its testing, such a belief is again accepted as true, and functions once more as an unquestioned belief. The same dynamism is seen in the nature and origin of control beliefs. The origin of a control belief is of little importance in its current function and justification. It may well have been established, and at times be maintained or retained, on the basis of evidences and other beliefs, but so long as at the appropriate time it functions as a valid control on theorising its control function is legitimate.

---

[120] Mavrodes, 202–204.

These ideas are far from new, being present in the theories of Plantinga, Quine and Lakatos. What is new is the way in which Wolterstorff's meta-theory is able to make use of this dynamism in the construction of a noetic model, incorporating dynamism and change in belief function into the epistemological structure of his meta-theory. Instead of having to justify control beliefs as being properly basic in the problematic manner of Plantinga, Wolterstorff can let these beliefs function as control, or data, or data-background regardless of their relation to other beliefs. Similarly, beliefs which are at the centre of a Quinean network of beliefs can have only minimal and indirect contact with the empirical periphery, thus causing problems for their critical appraisal. In a Wolterstorffian meta-theory, using the (inadequate) image of a network of beliefs, such beliefs can be brought to the periphery for critical appraisal, the network of beliefs being adjusted in the process, and then returned to the core if they pass the test. In the same way, the dynamism of Wolterstorff's model allows for both continuity and the possibility of change in the set of core beliefs of a research program or tradition, as per Lakatos and Laudan respectively, without the belief system as a whole being abandoned.[121]

The image or metaphor which I believe best encompasses the dynamism of Wolterstorff's meta-theory is an organic or biological one in which belief systems are envisaged as individual organisms which are also members of a species of belief.[122] The belief system itself can be seen as an individual organism which seeks to survive and grow in its environment. This environment contains inimical as well as amicable elements, to

---

[121] There is a certain infelicity in referring or alluding to Lakatos's meta-theory in terms of belief systems, since he specifically subordinated the question of an individual's belief system and the theories she accepts to the question of research programs. However, as I will argue below, once the idea of a *species* of belief systems is utilised, the crucial connections between the two questions, and the relevance of some of Lakatos's answers to my questions, can be seen.

[122] This metaphor arose out of my medical background. Having studied, and briefly practised, as a medical doctor before turning to theology, I have some understanding of the workings of biological systems. They have, I believe, the necessary dynamism and functional integrity to metaphorically represent Wolterstorff's epistemology. I have deliberately tried to keep the language non-technical in order to make it accessible to the non-medical reader. As I develop the model at various times the metaphor or that to which it refers will be discussed in the text or footnotes. This "swapping" from one to the other in the text is done for ease of exposition. I should note here that Wolterstorff has outlined an epistemological metaphor drawn from the operation of computers. While this is a dynamic metaphor which allows for the integration of new beliefs and practices in the noetic system, it has a different focus to mine, dealing, as it does with our doxastic apparatus, or hardware, and our being programmed with belief. For a brief presentation of this metaphor, see Wolterstorff, "Privileged Access", 86–89. It will be more fully articulated in Wolterstorff, *Presence to Practice*, in the chapter entitled "Programmed with Belief".

which the organism must respond. Amicable elements, in this case supporting evidences, confirming beliefs and theories, confirmatory experiences, and so on, are processed by the belief system and incorporated into it. This processing may be portrayed as the digesting of nourishment in which food is ingested, digested, deconstituted and reconstituted in the growth and maintenance of body systems. By such processes belief systems "live", in that they continue to be held by the person who adheres to them, and "grow", in that they are articulated so as to explain reality more adequately. The inimical elements, in this case rival belief systems, conceptual problems arising from the marketplace of ideas, empirical problems arising from experience or rival belief systems, and so on, must be overcome if the organism is to live and grow.

These environmental stresses, depending on their nature and significance, may be envisaged as taking a variety of forms. There are obvious threats, such as rival belief systems which, by virtue of their alternative explanations of reality, compete with the person's current belief system. Depending on how significant a threat it is, and how much it impinges on the person's environment, a rival may be seen as a predator or a competitor, in which case it must be defeated or avoided. To put it concretely rather than metaphorically, if a rival belief system, say atheism, claims to explain the same data and experiences as, say, theistic belief, then the theist must counter it, and so defeat its threat. If it is an incompatible belief system, but one which does not claim to explain the same data and experiences, say certain versions of a scientific theory, then it may be avoided if it does not encroach upon the believer's domain.[123]

Other threats are more insidious, akin to poisonous plants or animals in an organism's environment. There may be no obvious threat to the organism's survival, but if they are ingested, then they will eventually destroy the organism unless internally countered. Such internal defence mechanisms include the enzyme systems of the liver which neutralise organic poisons, and the immune system which recognises foreign proteins and rejects them. Whatever form the threats take, they must be countered if the organism is to survive. For a belief system such defence mechanisms include defeaters of anomalous beliefs,[124] reinterpretation of anomalous experiences,[125] the denial of the claimed implications of an argument or

---

[123] It must be noted that for some theists certain scientific theories do comprise a more serious threat, in which case they must be defeated, or digested and incorporated into the theist's belief system in a substantially modified form.

[124] Such as Plantinga's free will defence against the problem of evil.

[125] Such as theist's explanations of personal disasters as being somehow the "will of God"

belief,[126] or even alterations to accepted patterns of reasoning so as to deny the supposed implications of an anomalous belief.[127] It may be that as a result of this processing certain components of a threatening theory may be incorporated into the belief system, as happens biologically in the metabolism of alcohol, in which after detoxification by liver enzymes it is utilised as an energy source.[128] It is also possible that they may need to be rejected outright, as happens biologically in response to infective agents, in which they are combated by various immune mechanisms.[129] To extend the immunological image, response to a threatening agent may be facilitated by apologetic "inoculation" of a person against it by means of preemptive counter-arguments to the threatening belief, enabling the person to reject that belief without the "illness" of a crisis of faith and recovery from it.[130] This does not mean, however, that the belief system is irrationally indoctrinated against change, for the effectiveness of the "inoculation" is only as great as the soundness of the defeater presented, and it may be by-passed by the development of a new form of the counter-argument,[131] or the presence of another, unforseen counter-argument.[132]

Control beliefs play a dual role in this model, being both the vital organs of the belief system and its defence mechanisms, in much the same way as vital organs play a dual role in the life of an organism. For instance, in the event of an immunological stress to an organism, such organ systems as the bone marrow, lymphatic system, spleen and liver, are

---

which will work for their benefit. (Of course that is only one possible move that a theist can take in such an instance).

126   For instance the claim that the existence of evil in the world is evidence, not of God's non-existence, but of the existence and effects of human sin.

127   For instance the claim that there is no logical incompatibility between divine sovereignty and human free will, in this case relating it to theodicy.

128   As seen, for instance in some evangelical responses to evolutionary theories.

129   As seen, for instance, in Wolterstorff's response to Freudian psychology. It is worth noting, however, that even in the latter case, certain elements of Freudian psychology may be incorporated into a Christian scholar's belief system, so long as they are adequately "detoxified".

130   This idea is developed from suggestions Wolterstorff makes in relation to educating children in *Educating for Responsible Action*, 60–61.

131   As can be seen by analogy in the evolution of the influenza virus and the lack of cross-immunity between different forms of the virus.

132   As can be seen by analogy in the ineffectiveness of 'flu vaccines against small pox and *vice versa*. However, it must be noted that there is some degree of "cross-immunity" in both these cases: those who have been inoculated against some defeater of their belief system are more able to counter other threats to it, Wolterstorff, *Educating for Responsible Action*, 61. This may be likened to the general immunological robustness which develops as a result of exposure to disease.

simultaneously the organs which respond to the threat and organs which are protected by the immune system. Similarly, the gut is both the processor of nutrients and an organ system which is nourished by the digestive system, while the heart and lungs work to enable the body to function, both in normal life and in crises, and in turn are maintained and protected by their own function. In the event of their failure, it is often the responding organ system which suffers the most. Again, to put it non-metaphorically, control beliefs both determine what experiences and beliefs are to be counted as threats to the system and how the system will respond, and also are the beliefs which are most threatened by an anomalous experience or belief.[133]

How, then, does the model allow for the kind of critical appraisal of control beliefs which is required for scholarly integrity?[134] Again, parallels to organ systems within the life of an individual organism seem to offer fruitful metaphorical clues. In the case of, say, the immune system, its normal function is to identify baneful and non-baneful substances, particularly proteins, and trigger or permit the appropriate response, be it rejection or metabolic integration.[135] This parallels one of the normal functions of control beliefs in the accepting or rejecting of certain beliefs as being incompatible with them. However, as Wolterstorff recognises, control beliefs function as control only in certain circumstances,[136] and at

---

[133] This can be seen again in relation to theistic belief. Belief in God (or more precisely, a particular form of belief in a particular God) is threatened by certain claims of science, for instance the astrophysical theories of Stephen Hawking, but also determines that those theories are a threat to it and how that threat may be effectively countered.

[134] This requirement is normative, in that such objectivity, in which control beliefs or systematic presuppositions are exposed to ongoing analysis, is obligatory for a Christian scholar in her quest for the truth. It is also descriptive, in that critical analysis of presuppositions is often demanded by the threat that rival beliefs present to an individual scholar's control beliefs. For the former point, see Helm, "Scholarly Presuppositions", 143–154; for the latter, see Wolterstorff, *RWBR*, 92–97.

[135] Similar functions are performed by other organ systems, such as the hepato-biliary system with toxins and metabolites, the renal system with waste products and vitamin and hormone production, the cardio-vascular and pulmonary system with changes in environmental conditions such as temperature and partial pressure of gases and differing needs of various organ systems, and so on.

[136] Again, the parallel with organ systems is apparent: each system, while it may have multiple functions, is limited in its tasks. For instance, the immune system plays no role in oxygen transfer, even though, of course, it requires oxygen for its own function. Some systems, for instance the cardio-vascular system, are involved in nearly all body functions, including metabolism, immune responses, gaseous transfer and so on. As I will argue, this has certain crucial analogies to the pervasive role of certain crucial control beliefs within particular belief systems.

times are themselves subject to critical appraisal as provisional beliefs which need to be assessed to determine whether they are to be retained or not. However, depending on the significance of a particular control belief within the system, particularly the nature and extent of its influence upon other beliefs, including other control beliefs, it may be more or less directly involved in its own defence. This may be likened to the way that a particular organ system may be subject to a disease process or be the target of a particular stress, which needs to be overcome if the organ system is to survive and function effectively. In the process it may play a role in its own survival (or demise), such as occurs in diseases of the immune system. In the same way a control belief may be called into question by a particular belief or experience, or complex of beliefs and or experiences, in which case this challenge must be defeated, possibly involving the control belief in accepting or rejecting auxiliary hypotheses, if it is to survive and resume its control function.

These belief-and-experience-complexes, call them "challenges" for convenience, may come in a number of ways, roughly paralleling the different types of disease processes to which an organism needs to respond: acute inflammatory or infectious diseases; delayed immune responses or chronic diseases; and auto-immune or neoplastic diseases.[137] The first corresponds to an external belief which challenges a particular control belief, such as is the case with certain arguments against theistic belief. The second corresponds to a set of previously accepted beliefs which now are seen to be incompatible with a particular control belief. The last corresponds to changes within the belief system, within a particular control belief, or in the relation of the two, which give rise to a perceived incompatibility between the two, and the possibility of an altered control belief rejecting crucial aspects of the belief system.

The response of a belief system to such challenges also parallels an organism's response to different disease processes. An acute challenge and its resolution results in the threat being defeated, generally because it comports less well with the belief system than does the currently held control belief. If, however, the challenge is successful, then the control belief will be rejected, possibly, though not necessarily, being replaced by the challenging belief. Depending on the significance of the control belief in question, such a result may be of varying degrees of importance to the life of the belief system. If it is a control belief which has relatively little systematic ramification, then its loss may not affect the overall network of

---

[137] There are also congenital abnormalities and syndromes with which an organism may need to cope. These may be likened to inherent problems within a particular belief system. These may be ignored for the sake of this discussion.

beliefs much at all.[138] If, on the other hand, it has a wide impact on the belief system as a whole, the rejection of the control belief may result in significant morbidity for the system, or even its "death" following a crisis of faith.[139] Long term challenges and those that arise due to unforeseen relations among beliefs, may or may not be resolved. If they are resolved, then the belief system after a prolonged period of decreased efficiency at handling new beliefs,[140] will return to health. The control belief will have survived intact, and be able to function as effectively as before, with the added benefit of immunity to that type of challenge.[141] If the challenge is not adequately dealt with, then the belief system as a whole may "die", or suffer prolonged disability or illness, making it unable to deal with a range of challenges relating to the area covered by the control belief.[142] These metaphors enable us, I believe, to helpfully conceptualise the nature and consequences of challenges to control beliefs within a belief system.

It is worth noting that in this model there is no necessity for conscious decisions to be made with respect to accepting or rejecting beliefs, or even with respect to the need or manner of response to a particular challenge. Indeed, an emphasis on consciously deciding to accept or reject certain beliefs would comport poorly with the nature of the metaphor. This is in line with Wolterstorff's belief that belief is generally not subject to conscious control.[143] Decisions may be required in some cases of exposing a belief to critical reappraisal and in determining which beliefs need to be reappraised and how that ought to be done. However in general belief systems have a certain autonomy which parallels that of organic systems. Control over them is often a product of changing their environment and choosing to look at some things rather than others, and so on, rather than

---

[138] This may be likened to tonsillitis or appendicitis, which have little effect on the life of a person once the acute illness has resolved and the offending organ has been removed.

[139] This can be likened to disease in a limb or major organ system. Loss of a limb means the organism can still survive, but at greatly reduced efficiency. Loss of a major organ or organ system, such as may follow acute hepatitis or myocarditis, will inevitably lead to the death of the organism. These effects are seen analogously in belief systems. The infelicity of death as a metaphor for belief system failure is discussed below.

[140] There may well be associated feelings of "wrestling in faith", which may be likened to the symptoms of chronic illness.

[141] And, following Wolterstorff, *Educating for Responsible Action*, 61, a generally improved chance of fighting off other types of illness.

[142] The latter state corresponds to the debilitating effects of unresolved chronic illnesses.

[143] For this, see Wolterstorff, *EB&G*, 452, "Beliefs are not the outcome of decisions but of dispositions."

conscious decisions to change beliefs. Thus this model relates well to the non-voluntarist nature of Wolterstorff's epistemology.

However it is important to acknowledge that the dynamic and organic model of human belief systems here presented is even more dynamic than the images I have used so far may suggest. In looking at an organism's response to its environment, and the multiple roles of organ systems and immunological responses to certain stresses, it must be acknowledged that a single individual organism is not as malleable as an individual human's belief system. An organism, within its lifetime, is not able to so change that it is transformed into another species of organism. If it is unable to meet a particular challenge of its environment it will die: a leopard cannot change its spots. Human belief systems are much more malleable, for in the process of responding to certain stimuli or stresses the belief system may well be transformed into another species of belief system. For instance in the case of a theistic belief system, a particular challenge, such as one form of the argument from evil, may prove to be insurmountable for an individual's theistic belief. In such an instance the theistic belief system may be seen as having "died"; but that is a misleading image, for no person operates without a network of beliefs. In fact what has happened is that one belief system has been replaced by another, incompatible one. In terms of that person, her original theistic belief system has, as a result of insurmountable environmental forces, evolved into a new, rival species of belief.

It is this kind of radical evolution within a person's beliefs which comprises the phenomenon of conversion, be it religious or scholarly. Conversion is the response of a person, or more specifically the response that a person and her belief system makes, to an insuperable problem in her intellectual environment.[144] In the case of either religious,[145] or academic conversion,[146] a particular complex of experience and theory and

---

144 Note that talk of a response does not necessitate conscious choices on the part of the believer.

145 This conversion may be conversion to a theistic belief (say Christian belief), conversion from one type of theistic belief to another (say from Islam to Christianity, or from "liberal" to "evangelical" Christian belief or *vice versa*), or conversion out of theistic belief (say from Christian belief to atheism). All such moves involve analogous changes in the total network of a person's beliefs such that a new belief system can be said to have come into being, or to put it more strictly in my terms, a new species of belief system has evolved from the original network of beliefs.

146 Such academic conversion is similar to Kuhn's notion of paradigm shift, such as the shift from Newtonian Celestial Mechanics to Einsteinian Relativity Theory. It is, however, not an a-rational shift, as there are good reasons for such changes of belief system, although it is, as Kuhn suggests, irreducible to an algorithm of choice. However, once a non-Cartesian form of rationality is accepted, the existence of good reasons in the absence of

the beliefs which attend it,[147] are beyond the belief system's ability to cope and give rise to a crisis of faith. If the crisis is unresolved, and another species of belief is seen to more adequately deal with this challenge,[148] then the person's belief system evolves, perhaps all of a sudden, into one which conforms to the more adequate species. Of course, it may be that the crisis is resolved, in which case the resources of that individual belief system, or perhaps those of its species of belief, have been adequate to meet the challenge, and the belief system survives, with suitable modification.

This less radical evolution within a person's belief system is what lies behind the phenomenon of evolving research traditions. Within this dynamic, biological model of rationality, both Lakatos's and Laudan's insights into the nature of scientific change can be incorporated. Lakatos's notion of an unchanging hard core, while too rigid and extensive, recognises that certain beliefs are necessarily held by all proponents of a certain species of belief within the life of that species. The individuals within the species may evolve, at times quite dramatically, but certain characteristics must be common to all individuals which belong to the species.[149] Any individual which changes crucial characteristics is likely to be rejected by the others within that species.[150] In terms of belief systems

---

rules or an algorithm of change constitutes sufficient grounds for the rationality of such a shift.

[147] This assumes that experience or belief on their own are never sufficient causes of conversion. This can be substantiated, I believe, for instance by reference to the way that the problem of evil functions in conversion out of theistic belief. But such a demonstration lies outside the scope of this thesis.

[148] Other environmental stresses may also be involved, depending on the importance of this particular challenge. This idea parallels (with suitable modification) Kuhn's regarding the number, nature and importance of anomalies in the precipitation of a scientific revolution.

[149] A biological illustration may help clarify this idea. An examination of horses, from the time of Genghis Khan to the present will show dramatic changes in the characteristics of the horse both over time and within the species. Compare for instance Przbylsky's Horse with a thoroughbred, or a thoroughbred with a Shetland Pony. While these individuals differ greatly from each other, they are clearly of the one species, and will breed true to the species, even though there may be greater similarities between an individual of the species and an individual of another species (say donkey).

[150] Perhaps certain kinds of scholarship function as herd or hive organisms in which quite clear physical criteria are required for acceptance into the herd or hive. Failure to evince those qualities results in expulsion from the herd or hive. This phenomenon may be a helpful metaphor for the sociological processes Kuhn and others have identified within scientific communities. Other types of scholarship are more "open", or less communal in nature, thus allowing for greater heterogeneity within the species of belief. Fundamentalist

and species thereof, unless certain core beliefs are adhered to, an individual scholar has abandoned the research program and her belief system belongs to another species of belief. Laudan, on the other hand, while failing to acknowledge the necessity of some continuity within an research tradition, recognises that change and evolution are necessary in the history of all living species. Thus a perspective which sees belief systems as dynamic organisms which are also individuals of a species enables us to incorporate the valid insights of Kuhn, Quine, Lakatos and Laudan within a single model.[151] Such a model fits Wolterstorff's meta-theory and the reality of human believings, and offers, I believe, a more adequate metaphor for human noetic structures than its foundationalist or coherentist rivals.

---

and some critical theologies may be seen as examples of the former type of species of belief, some evangelical and critical theologies may be seen as examples of the latter.

[151] It also has interesting parallels with the account of MacIntyre in *Whose Justice? Which Rationality?*, 348–369.

Conclusion to Part Three

It can be seen from this analysis of Wolterstorff's meta-theory that I consider it to be superior to those of its rivals I here assessed. There are, I believe, good reasons for this assertion. It offers a more adequate explanation of the descriptive features of scholarly practice than its rivals, including the epistemological structure of beliefs, theories and intellectual traditions. It presents a more cogent outline of the normative criteria which should govern the rational practice of *Wissenschaft*. It is able to deal with the history of science, as well as current practice, and provides a suitable model for a non-relativist situation- and person-specific model of scholarly rationality. Thus general studies in the history and philosophy of science and in epistemology support my contention that Wolterstorff's meta-theory is a rationally acceptable, and perhaps the most rationally justified, meta-theory currently available. It remains to be seen whether this is borne out in its application to the analysis of the practice of scholarship, including theology in general and biblical scholarship in particular.

Conclusion

Retrospect and Prospect

In this work I have outlined, articulated and defended Wolterstorff's meta-theory, in so doing claiming that it provides Christian scholars with a cogent alternative to foundationalist and relativist views. For these claims to stand, however, his meta-theory needs to be applied to actual scholarly practice, testing whether it provides an adequate descriptive and prescriptive account of the practice of scholarship. A thorough empirical testing of Wolterstorff's meta-theory would require its application to the full range of scholarly practice, a task which is beyond the scope of any one study. Even its application and testing in relation to theological theorising as a whole is a prohibitive task, due to the range of method and content of the different disciplines within theology. The scope of this study does not permit such an analysis, even of exegetical theorising. However, having begun this study with an interest in the pluralism of OT scholarship, it would be remiss of me not to comment on the application of Wolterstorff's meta-theory to theological scholarship, at least in passing. This, of course, means that many important areas of research, including within the epistemology of hermeneutics, will have to be left to one side.[1]

---

1 For instance, the issue of evolving research traditions or species of belief in critical methodology in OT exegesis would be a profitable line of research. It seems to me that, from the perspective of this meta-theory, critical scholarship as a whole is a tradition or species which has evolved significantly in response to empirical and theoretical challenges. Thus classical source criticism has given rise to form criticism, which in turn has been influential in the development of rhetorical criticism, tradition criticism, and these later generations of belief systems have in turn been productive of other species of belief. However the historical investigation of the development of these research traditions, and the way in which the control beliefs of earlier traditions have been modified and adopted in later traditions, lies beyond the scope of this work.

In dealing with the application of Wolterstorff's meta-theory to exegetical theorising a number of matters need to be addressed. In order to do this I will outline and assess Wolterstorff's notion of hermeneutics, and the way in which he sees control beliefs operating within the practice of exegesis and biblical theology. I will then outline how his more general meta-theory can be applied to exegetical theorising, identifying the major steps in the epistemological analysis of this scholarly practice, and present general criteria and procedures for the analysis of the rational status of exegetical theories.

An interesting and important area of Wolterstorff's meta-theory is its application to theology and biblical hermeneutics. Dogmatic and biblical theology are "idiosyncratic" cases of the workings of his meta-theory, in which it is particularly important to remember that the distinction between data, data-background, and control beliefs is not ontological, but "a distinction as to how beliefs function relative to a given person's weighing of a given theory on a given occasion".[2] As was discussed earlier,[3] data beliefs are beliefs about the entities within the scope of a theory which are taken to be data for that theory and with which it must be consistent. Data-background beliefs are beliefs about the nature of the entities in question and the tools of research, which enable a scholar to accept a certain range of beliefs as data in her theorising. Control beliefs are beliefs about the nature of cognitive goals and standards, and acceptable means of attaining them, which lead a scholar to accept some theories and reject others. Particular (sets of) beliefs may perform different functions for a particular scholar's theoretical practice at different times or for different theories, depending upon the nature of the theory and its scope.

The dogmatic theologian is engaged in the task of devising theories about "God and his relation to us and the world (or, on the view of some, concerning how we ought to *think* about God and his relation to us and the world)".[4] These theories are then weighed by taking as at least a part of her data, beliefs which belong to the belief-content of her authentic commitment, which is that set of beliefs which comprises how her Christian commitment *ought to be* realised in the cognitive realm.[5] While both of these actions are taking place the belief-content of her authentic Christian commitment will *also be functioning as control*. Thus, for the dogmatic theologian, the self-same beliefs may function as data in her devising and

---

2   Wolterstorff, *RWBR*, 85.
3   See Chapters 4 and 5 above.
4   Wolterstorff, *RWBR*, 85.
5   See above (Chapter 4, B.2.).

weighing of theories, inasmuch as they may be included amongst those beliefs which she takes to be true and which need to be included in the theory's scope, and as control for those same theories, inasmuch as they may also be included amongst that set of beliefs which determines which theories are or are not acceptable.[6]

Wolterstorff's application of his meta-theory is somewhat different in relation to biblical theology and exegesis. The interpreter's primary task is to use principles of interpretation in order to determine the meaning of biblical texts.[7] This often entails the formulation of specific hermeneutic principles and their being proposed as normative principles of interpretation.[8] In these tasks, "the content of his Christian commitment will function mainly as control beliefs rather than as data beliefs".[9] It will "condition his acceptance and formation of theories" of the meaning of biblical writings, but will not itself be included amongst the beliefs about which he is theorising.[10] For his data will consist of, not what he takes to be God's relation to us and the world, but what he takes the *Bible to say* about those matters.[11]

Of course, in as much as these conclusions are about the content of the Scriptures, which Christians take as authoritative, they will influence the belief-content of authentic commitment.[12] Even more, the biblical theologian's methodological conclusions will also necessarily influence the belief-content of authentic commitment, for often a particular reading strategy is taken to be a part of that belief-content.[13] Thus a change in hermeneutical principles may be seen as a change in the content of authentic commitment, and resisted as a departure from authentic

---

6   Wolterstorff, *RWBR*, 86. Wolterstorff also has an extended discussion of the relationship, often complex and dialectic, between the dogmatic theologian's theoretical activity and the belief-content of authentic commitment (see pp. 86–88). While this is interesting and important, I shall not deal with it in detail, for my focus here is on biblical theology and exegesis, not dogmatic theology. It is worth noting, however, that Wolterstorff specifically applies his meta-theory to dogmatic theology, and notes some of the problems in doing so.

7   Wolterstorff, *RWBR*, 88. Strictly speaking, this task is to determine what the writer used the text to say. For this issues, see the discussion later in this chapter; Wolterstorff, *EB&G*, 431–432, 440–442.

8   Wolterstorff, *RWBR*, 88.
9   Ibid.
10 Ibid., 88–89.
11 Ibid., 89.
12 Wolterstorff, *RWBR*, 89; *EB&G*, 433.
13 Wolterstorff, *RWBR*, 90.

commitment.[14] However, the impact of hermeneutics upon Christian belief is inevitable, and is not necessarily a cause for alarm.[15] For there is no clear line between biblical theology or interpretation and the careful reading of Scripture by a committed follower of Christ.[16] All reading entails a reading strategy, all reading involves the use of interpretive principles, and the scholar is able to provide the general reader with better interpretations and principles of interpretation of the Scriptures.[17] Thus the scholar can, and should, influence general views of what comprises authentic Christian commitment.[18]

Thus, as in general theorising, when a conflict arises between the belief content of a biblical scholar's authentic Christian commitment and a particular theory of the meaning of a text or a hermeneutical research tradition, the conflict may be resolved by rejecting or modifying the theory or research tradition, rejecting or modifying a particular (set of) control beliefs, or rejecting or modifying the perceived connection between the apparently conflicting beliefs.[19] Which of these options is (the most) rational for a particular scholar in a particular case of conflict will depend upon the specific nature of the conflict and the significance of the beliefs in question.[20] Wolterstorff's notion of the control function of authentic Christian commitment is, then, significantly different to (contemporary caricatures of) dogmatic pre-critical exegesis. In such views of traditional dogmatic exegesis, traditional theological beliefs are seen as a set of *a priori* categories through which all texts are read, and with which biblical interpretation cannot conflict by *a priori* substantive and methodological decisions. There is, then, no systematic openness to the revising of pre-understanding in light of the text and new interpretations of it. The control function of the propositional content of authentic Christian commitment in Wolterstorff's meta-theory differs markedly from this perceived pattern, for control beliefs are not immune to critical appraisal in the process of devising and weighing theories. Indeed, integral to that process is the determination, be it voluntary or not, of which set of beliefs are to be rejected or modified in case of conflict between the propositional contents of an exegetical theory and authentic Christian commitment.

---

14 Wolterstorff, *RWBR*, 90; *EB&G*, 433.

15 Wolterstorff, *RWBR*, 90.

16 Ibid.

17 Ibid. For the notions of reading strategies and choices in their adoption, see the discussion later in this chapter.

18 Wolterstorff, *RWBR*, 90.

19 See Wolterstorff, *EB&G*, 433; "Theology and Science", 101–102.

20 For a discussion of this process, see above (Chapter 6, C.).

Specific issues in relation to the task of exegetical theorising that Wolterstorff raises in *Reason Within the Bounds of Religion* but does not discuss in detail, are those of hermeneutics and authority, *viz*: "how ought the Scriptures be interpreted?" and "how ought the Scriptures function for the work of the Christian scholar?"[21] These are important issues in relation to his meta-theory, for essential to Christian commitment is membership in a community which accepts the Scriptures as authoritative, which in turn means that they are to control the life and thought of those who are Christian.[22] Consequently, despite the fact that the belief content of authentic Christian commitment is person- and situation-specific, and that the propositions which are common to all authentic commitment will be few and simple, the acceptance of the authority of the Scriptures is seen by Wolterstorff as one such (complex of) belief.[23] But in order for the Scriptures to perform that control function we need to determine what we think they say, and how what they say, and what parts of what they say, are to function as authority.[24] The former question needs to be addressed because it has happened that beliefs which have been taken to be contained in Scripture, and which have been included in the belief-content of authentic commitment at a given time, have been discovered to be not in fact contained in Scripture.[25] The latter question needs to be addressed in order to determine which parts of the biblical message are to be authoritative for the formation of the belief-content of the Christian scholar's authentic commitment.[26] For there are some aspects of the Bible's message, such as the earth's being square and flat, that are not taken, and should not be taken, to be normative for belief by Christian scholars today.[27] Thus it is important to establish why some things are not taken to be normative, and how normative and non-normative statements of Scripture are to be distinguished.[28]

---

21 Wolterstorff, *RWBR*, 101. Wolterstorff tantalisingly raises these issues in a chapter entitled "Some Unanswered Questions", but does no more than that.

22 N. Wolterstorff, "On God Speaking", *The Reformed Journal* (Jul–Aug 1969) 7; "How God Speaks", *The Reformed Journal* (Sept 1969) 17–20; "Canon and Criterion", *The Reformed Journal* (Oct 1969) 10–15; *RWBR*, 101.

23 Wolterstorff, *RWBR*, 75, 71–72; "On God Speaking", 7; "How God Speaks", 17–20; "Canon and Criterion", 10–15.

24 Wolterstorff, *RWBR*, 101.

25 Ibid., 89–90.

26 Ibid., 102.

27 Ibid.

28 Ibid.

I will only be able to deal with these matters in passing, as they relate to the large and complex areas of general theories of hermeneutics and of biblical inspiration and authority, the pursuit of which would take me too far afield.[29] My concern here is to specify the nature and function of authentic Christian commitment in (exegetical) Christian scholarship. Wolterstorff contends that hermeneutics and authority are related but discrete issues. Interpretation is not a matter of simply discerning what a text says, for texts themselves do not say anything.[30] Rather it is a matter

---

[29] For extensive discussions of these issues, see N. Wolterstorff, *Divine Discourse*; "The Importance of Hermeneutics for a Christian Worldview", *Disciplining Hermeneutics: Interpretation in Christian Perspective*, ed. R. Lundin (Grand Rapids: Eerdmans, 1997) 25–47. There have been a number of criticisms of his notion of God's speaking by way of the human words of Scripture on the grounds of theological, biblical-critical or philosophical naivety. For instance, Westphal argues that the under-determination of interpretation by texts entails an indeterminant plurality of meaning incompatible with Wolterstorff's pre-Kantian idea of author-discourse interpretation (M. Westphal, "Post-Kantian Reflections on the Importance of Hermeneutics", *Disciplining Hermeneutics: Interpretation in Christian Perspective*, ed. R. Lundin (Grand Rapids: Eerdmans, 1997) 57–66; "Review Essay: Theology as Talking About a God Who Talks", *Modern Theology* 13/4 (Oct 1997) 525–536). M. Levine, on the other hand, argues that Wolterstorff's theory founders on the shoals of biblical criticism and the theology of revelation (M. Levine, "God Speak", *RelS* 34 (1998) 1–16; so also M. Wiles, "Review of *Divine Discourse*", *JTS* 47/2 (1996) 802–804. For Wolterstorff's rebuttal of Levine, and hence Wiles, see N. Wolterstorff, "Reply to Levine", *RelS* 34 (1998) 17–23.) For the contrary claim that, amongst other defects, Wolterstorff's view does not adequately anchor the authoritative meaning of Scripture, see I. H. Marshall, "'To Find Out What God is Saying': Reflections on the Authorizing of Scripture", *Disciplining Hermeneutics: Interpretation in Christian Perspective*, ed. R. Lundin (Grand Rapids: Eerdmans, 1997) 49–55; C. Gutenson, "An Examination of Nicholas Wolterstorff's *Divine Discourse* – Review Essay", *Christian Scholar's Review* 28/1 (Fall 1998) 140–154. However Wolterstorff anticipates most of these criticisms in both *Divine Discourse* and "The Importance of Hermeneutics". For a defence of his views, see G. Lindbeck, "Postcritical Canonical Interpretation: Three Modes of Retrieval", *Theological Exegesis: Essays in Honor of Brevard S. Childs*, ed. C. Seitz and K. Greene-McCreight (Grand Rapids: Eerdmans, 1999) 26–51; A. Thiselton, "Essay Review – Speech-Act Theory and the Claim that God Speaks: Nicholas Wolterstorff's *Divine Discourse*", *SJT* 50/1 (1997) 97–110. While I think his notion of Scripture being primarily a means of divine discourse is sound, I think it needs further articulation, especially in relation to the *manner* in which God appropriates and endorses the human speech of Scripture. For instance, it is only with difficulty that, say the Psalms or Wisdom literature, can be seen as God's speech, as Wolterstorff acknowledges (*Divine Discourse*, 208–218). If, however, God's appropriation of the Psalms were to include their being endorsed as means of addressing God, or reflecting about human life in the world, these difficulties would be obviated. Such a perspective can, I believe, be incorporated in a speech-act theory of Scripture as God's word, but to do so would, again, take me too far afield.

[30] Wolterstorff, *EB&G*, 431. For a critique of Frei's version of text-interpretation, see N. Wolterstorff, "Will Narrativity Work as Linchpin? Reflections on the Hermeneutic of Hans Frei", *Relativism and Religion*, ed. C. M. Lewis (New York: St Martin's Press, 1995) 71–107.

of "choice and habit" governed by criteria of interpretation or purposes which an interpretation is to serve, often codified (tacitly or explicitly) in sets of rules of interpretation.[31] While other purposes are possible, interpreters generally want "an interpretation which coincides with what the writer used the text to say. (Not with what he *intended* to use it to say; with what he *did* use it to say)."[32] Wolterstorff does not specify just how an interpreter adopts an interpretation of a text; rather he is concerned to show that there are options for interpreters which, while limited, are real.[33] And for those who take a text as canonical, who bind themselves to it as authoritative for their belief and practice, thereby accepting at least some of the content of interpretations of that text and ensuring that it exercises a control function on their beliefs on other matters, these options will be further limited.[34]

From this canonical perspective those interpretations which coincide with what the author used the text to say will be central to its control function.[35] Interpretation from this canonically driven perspective will not

---

31 Wolterstorff, *EB&G*, 431; cf. Thiselton, "On Models and Methods", 353–354.
32 Wolterstorff, *EB&G*, 431; cf. M. G. Brett, "Motives & Intentions", 1–16. He distinguishes between an author's *motives*, which are psychological states of affairs lying behind the text, and authorial *intentions*, which are embodied in the text and are unlocked by the study of semantics, genre, structure, context and so on. While I believe Brett focuses on the text too much at the expense of the context addressed by the author of the text, his distinction is a useful one, and closely parallels that made by Wolterstorff. It is worth noting, however, that, in line with his pluralistic perspective, Brett does not believe that what the author used the text to say is the only legitimate, or even the determinative, goal of exegesis. Thiselton recognises this plurality of interpretive interests, but nonetheless endorses a view analogous to Wolterstorff's ("On Models and Methods", 353–356).
33 Wolterstorff, *EB&G*, 432.
34 Ibid., 432, 442.
35 Wolterstorff, *EB&G*, 442. For an extensive discussion of this notion of "what the writer used the text to say" and its role the interpretation of Scripture in terms of speech-act theory and authorial discourse interpretation, see Wolterstorff, *Divine Discourse*, esp 37–57, 75–94, 183–260; "The Importance of Hermeneutics", 25–47. It is important to note here that Wolterstorff excludes neither other uses of Scripture, such as in liturgy, nor other interpretive approaches, such as "performance interpretation"; rather, he claims that author-discourse interpretation is crucial to Scripture's functioning as authoritative Scripture, and hence as a means of divine discourse. For this, see *Divine Discourse*, 183–186; "The Importance of Hermeneutics", 29–33. This is a controversial claim in the light of recent literary approaches to biblical interpretation, particularly those of a reader-response type. Radical reader-response criticism, and similar reading strategies are, however, subject to overwhelming criticism from the perspective of the epistemology I have developed. They are necessarily relativistic, as well as conflicting with the (modified) authorial intention perspective of Wolterstorff, and thus are to be rejected as research traditions. This is not to say, however, that a concern for the ways in which different readers respond to texts is

be an "autonomous, text-focussed" activity (let alone a relativistic, reader-focussed one), but will be concerned with the author's use of the text, its objective referents to history its historical and sociological context, and so on.[36] This in turn requires that reasons be given for adopting a particular (kind of) interpretation,[37] while recognising that those reasons, and the choices and habits of interpretation associated with them, are, and should be constrained by the canonical or control function of the Scriptures within authentic Christian commitment. Thus, for all the apparent circularity of the process, our understanding of what the Scriptures say does and ought to function as a control in our exegetical theorising.

This authoritative function has two related but distinct facets. The Bible functions for Christians as the criteriological and the canonical norm for faith and practice.[38] It is criteriological for our speaking, believing and

---

illegitimate, nor that readers from different perspectives may not see things in the text that others have previously not seen. However, it must be recognised that if at all legitimate, then these new insights must have been present in the text all along, even if they have only now been seen by these readers. For a discussion of these issues, see Goldingay, "How far do readers make sense?", 5–10; B. F. Meyer, 3–12; Thiselton, "Models and Methods", 345, 353–356; Osborne, *Hermeneutical Spiral*, esp 5–8, 366–415; and above (Chapter 5, B.1.). For the range of reader-oriented critical strategies, not all of which imply or assert this relativistic abandonment of determinative (text and author centred) meaning, see Brett, "The Future of Reader Criticisms?", 13–31.

36   Wolterstorff, *EB&G*, 440–441.

37   Ibid., 442.

38   Wolterstorff, "Canon and Criterion", 11. The general position endorsed by Wolterstorff and which is outlined in this paragraph has been criticised from both conservative and non-conservative view points. For conservative discussions of this issue, see Schaeffer, *He is There*, 83–114; Henry, *God, Revelation and Authority*, vol 3, 409–418; G. R. Lewis and B. A. Demarest, *Integrative Theology* (3 vol; Grand Rapids: Academie, 1987; vol 1) 131–171; W. A. Grudem, "Scripture's Self-Attestation and the Problem of Formulating a Doctrine of Scripture", *Scripture and Truth*, ed. D. A. Carson and J. D. Woodhouse (Grand Rapids: Zondervan, 1983) 19–59. For various non-conservative viewpoints, see K. Barth, *Church Dogmatics* (4 vol; Edinburgh: T&T Clark, 1936; vol I.1) 98–212; E. Brunner, *The Christian Doctrine of God: Dogmatics: vol 1* (3 vol; Philadelphia: Westminster, 1950) 14–34, 107–113; R. P. Carroll, *Wolf in the Sheepfold: The Bible as a Problem for Christianity* (London: SPCK, 1991); D. L. Edwards, "The Authority of the Scriptures", *Essentials: A liberal-evangelical dialogue*, D. L. Edwards and J. Stott (London: Hodder and Stoughton, 1988) 41–82; J. Macquarrie, *Principles of Christian Theology* (rev ed; London: SCM, 1977) 7–11, 378–382; W. Pannenberg, *Systematic Theology* (3 vol; Edinburgh: T&T Clark, 1991; vol 1) 230–257; P. Tillich, *Systematic Theology* (Welwyn, Herts: Nisbet, 1968) 118–177, esp 135–139, 140–142, 174–177. It must be stressed, however, that Wolterstorff's position, while controversial, is certainly defensible, and is accepted for good reasons by a number of scholars. For discussions which support his general line, see H. Boer, *Above the Bible? The Bible and its Critics* (Grand Rapids: Eerdmans, 1975); H. M. Conn, "Normativity, Relevance and Relativism", *Inerrancy and Hermeneutic: A Tradition, A Challenge, A Debate*, ed. H. M. Conn (Grand Rapids: Baker, 1988) 185–209; M. J.

acting inasmuch as the word that God has spoken to his people constrains our speaking and believing and acting.[39] It has a canonical function inasmuch as in it we find the record of, and instantiations of God's speaking, thereby functioning as the authoritative source for knowing the criteriological word spoken in the past.[40] However it is important to note that Wolterstorff does not consider that all that Scripture means is authoritative for our belief and practice. God's speaking to his people then and now comes via others who speak for him, who, as his authorised messengers, stamp the message with their own character and beliefs.[41] His messengers were not emptied of their cultural and personal beliefs in their being his messengers, and so the Bible records God's message to his people as well as the personal and cultural beliefs of the messengers.[42] However some of those beliefs of the ancient authors, such as those pertaining to cosmology and natural history, are wrong, and so cannot function as a criterion for our beliefs in cosmology or natural history.[43] This is not to say, however, that the Bible itself is not to function as criterion, or control, on our cosmological beliefs, or that where it conflicts with our contemporary beliefs on such matters its message is to rejected, for that would be a denial of its control function in the practice of *Wissenschaft*.[44] Rather, accepting the normative function of the text, we need to distinguish between the message and the media, examples, or

---

Erickson, *Christian Theology* (Grand Rapids: Baker, 1987) 120–127, 199–241; I. H. Marshall, "Using the Bible in Ethics", *Essays in Evangelical Social Ethics*, ed. D. F. Wright (Wilton: Moorehouse-Barlow, 1979) 39–55; L. Morris, *I Believe in Revelation* (London: Hodder and Stoughton, 1976) esp 136–147; J. Stott, "John Stott's Response to Chapter 2", *Essentials*, 82–106; C. J. H. Wright, *Living as the People of God* (Leicester: IVP, 1983) 19–64; "The Ethical Authority of the Old Testament: A Survey of Approaches. Part II", *Tyndale Bulletin* 43/2 (1992) 203–231, esp 225–231. Wolterstorff's position, then, can be seen as one that a Christian scholar is entitled to accept. Given the presence of good reasons in favour of his position, the lack of consensus on this issue does not undermine his view, but rather provides added support for his notion of a plurality of at least possibly rational scholarship.

39   Wolterstorff, "Canon and Criterion", 10–11. He discusses some philosophical problems with that contention on pp. 12–13, where he notes that the word spoken in Christ can and should give rise to reinterpretations and limitations of the significance of the word spoken by the prophets. See also Wolterstorff, "The Bible and Economics", 14.

40   Wolterstorff, "Canon and Criterion", 11.

41   Wolterstorff, "How God Speaks", 17; "Canon and Criterion", 12–13.

42   Wolterstorff, "Canon and Criterion", 12–13; "The Bible and Economics", 14.

43   Wolterstorff, "Canon and Criterion", 13–14. For this in contrast to evangelical inerrantists, *Divine Discourse*, 227–229; "The Importance of Hermeneutics", 45.

44   Ibid., 14.

incidental presuppositions of those who conveyed the message.⁴⁵ It is, therefore, the essential message of the Scriptures, as correctly understood as a unitive whole and in the light of Christ, that is to function as a part of the control which authentic Christian commitment exercises over our theorising, including our exegetical theorising.⁴⁶ When conflicts arise between what we understand to be the essential message of Scripture and our theorising, inasmuch as the theories are justified and our understanding of the Bible is not, it is frequently the case that either we have misunderstood the Bible, or have taken as essential a belief which is not.

In this process of hermeneutical theorising an important role is played by theological research traditions, or, as Wolterstorff terms them, types of "global exegesis".⁴⁷ As discussed earlier, these research traditions, or

---

45 Wolterstorff, "Canon and Criterion", 14; "Bible and Economics", 14. This is clearly consonant with the perspective of the Lausanne Covenant statement on Biblical authority in which it is affirmed that the Bible is authoritative and fully trustworthy (without error) in all it affirms. See J. Stott, *The Lausanne Covenant: An Exposition and Commentary* (London: Scripture Union, 1975) 6–7; and the statement of aims, beliefs and basic philosophy of Scripture Union issued by its International Council. It leaves open to question the truthfulness of beliefs held by the biblical authors which are embodied in the text, but which are not themselves affirmed as part of the message of the text. Of course, such a position does not prejudge the hermeneutical questions of what is and is not "essential" to the message and what is incidental. As is clearly evidenced in the debate concerning creation science and the interpretation of Genesis 1, and also recent discussions of literary approaches to OT interpretation, there is room for considerable disagreement amongst those who would endorse such an affirmation. The main strategies for making the move between the "first" and "second" hermeneutic (ie between understanding the human author's discourse and understanding God's discourse) are literal, tropic (or metaphorical) interpretation, and distinguishing between the main point and ancillary points being made by the author. Which of these strategies is to be used in a particular instance needs to be determined situationally. For this, see *Divine Discourse*, 202–218; "The Importance of Hermeneutics", 46.

46 For Wolterstorff's assertion that authentic Christian commitment, and its concomitant confession of the authority of Scripture, necessitates the quest for a unitive theme or message of the Bible as a whole in the midst of the diversity that exists within the canon, see "Bible and Economics", 13–14. He elsewhere speaks of this in terms of the influence that beliefs about God have on our interpretations of Scripture, namely that God speaks truly, and so consistently, and that God speaks lovingly. For this, see Wolterstorff, *Divine Discourse*, 202–208, 236–239; "The Importance of Hermeneutics", 46. The claim that the Bible can be read as a unitive whole has been challenged by critical scholarship, for which see the references listed in nn. 29 and 38 above. It is, however, defensible even in the light of critical research, as can be seen in D. Patrick and A. Scult, *Rhetoric and Biblical Interpretation* (Sheffield: Almond, 1990) 127–139.

47 Wolterstorff, "The Bible and Economics", 16. Due to the scope of his article he deals only with *theological* traditions. I think it is important, however, to recognise the significance of *methodological* traditions in the practice of exegesis. They play a similarly important role in abetting and inhibiting belief as do theological traditions. H. Schlossberg, "A Response to Nicholas Wolterstorff", *Transformation* 4/3&4 (Jun–Dec 1987) 20–25,

evolving species of belief, are characterised by a commitment by adherents to the tradition to certain beliefs, practices and methods which lie at the heart of the tradition. These traditions respond to their changing intellectual environments by modifying beliefs that are considered to be "peripheral" to the tradition whenever possible. Only if these minimal changes are ineffective will an adherent to the tradition modify or jettison core beliefs.[48]

All of us, he asserts, operate in our exegetical theorising within theological or interpretive traditions, which result in certain texts (or features of texts) being accented or de-emphasised.[49] These traditions thereby tend to blind us to certain themes of specific texts via their function as tacit or explicit controls on our exegetical theorising.[50] These traditions are often, at least in part, the product of "the self-interest of the powerful", which then read the Bible in such a way as to further their own vested interests.[51] However not all traditions, or at least not all components

---

denies the significance of such "global exegesis" in economic ethics, but operates with just such a tradition in his article.

[48] For a detailed discussion of the nature of research traditions, or species of belief, their control function in scholarly practice, and their modification in the light of challenges, see above (Chapter 6, B., C.).

[49] Wolterstorff, "Bible and Economics", 15–16.

[50] Wolterstorff does not specifically state that these traditions function as control, however inasmuch as he talks of them as factors which shape the "self interpreting the text", whose interaction with the text gives rise to an interpretation, I think they ought to be seen as a source of control beliefs.

[51] Wolterstorff, "Bible and Economics", 16. Here he refers specifically to *economic* interests, for that is the focus of his essay. However I think it is valid to see that such vested interests frequently operate in social, political and religious matters as well, as much recent feminist theology claims. Indeed, elsewhere Wolterstorff specifically deals with the operation of vested interests in the maintenance of patriarchalist interpretive traditions ("On keeping women out of office: the CRC committee on headship", *The Reformed Journal* 34/5 (May 1984) 8–14; "Hearing the Cry", *Women, Authority and the Bible*, ed. A. Mickelsen (Downers Grove: IVP, 1986) 286–294; "Between the Times", *The Reformed Journal* 40/12 (Dec 1990) 16–20). These may be seen as specific instances of rationalisation in scholarly practice which is discussed above (Chapter 4, C.2.). As such they are noetically defective, for the beliefs so produced are the product of non-innocent belief-dispositions. Not all traditions are so defective, and even defective traditions are flawed only in those matters that pertain to, or are affected by, the vested interests of a particular élite. A research tradition is not entirely invalidated by its unjustified blindness in one or more areas of belief. This idea is justified by and reflected in Wolterstorff's criticism of his own Reformed tradition from within that tradition of belief and praxis. While he accepts much that is central to the tradition, such as its commitment to the impact of Christian commitment on the totality of a believer's faith and practice, he rejects others, such as its tendency to demand that Christian scholarship be *different* as well as *faithful*, and its failure to respond

of all traditions, are ideologically driven. Many are the product of rational methods of exegesis, rational bodies of theological belief, heuristically fruitful patterns of research, and so on. They are, therefore, not only useful, but necessary and inescapable in the practice of exegetical scholarship. While they will inevitably blind their adherents to certain aspects of the Bible's message, to others they will give rise to greater sensitivity.[52] Inasmuch, however, as they do blind us to things that the writer used the text to say, these traditions are epistemologically flawed and need to be altered or even jettisoned.[53]

The problem is, how do we determine that they are so flawed, given that our understanding of the writer's meaning is limited by the "stranglehold" of these interpretive traditions?[54] One way in which the stranglehold of traditions can be broken, thereby opening us to previously hidden components of the author's message, is by our being placed in social or personal situations foreign to the tradition.[55] The resultant change in experience produces a new perspective which enables themes previously unseen to be brought to our attention.[56] Another way, one particularly

---

adequately to issues of justice and peace (Wolterstorff, *J&P*, viii–ix, 42–72, 162–176; *RWBR*, 111–146; *OCL*, 57–80; above, Chapter 4, A., C.2.).

52   Wolterstorff, "Bible and Economics", 15–16.

53   This, of course, assumes a realist epistemology and ontology, in which anything which is truly perceived about an entity, be it the Bible or any other entity in reality, is actually there, and always was. It is not the product of our noetic enterprises. Thus we do not *create* meaning, be it in the world or in texts, particularly when our interpretation is linked to, and constrained by, the canonical function of the biblical text as Wolterstorff contends. By our interpretive habits and choices we interact with the text in such a way as to understand what the writer used the text to say. There may be new nuances to that writer-generated, text-encoded, context-driven meaning, even whole new ways of reading the text to be discerned. But unless they coincide with the state of affairs projected by the writer and the stance the writer adopted towards that state of affairs, then they are unjustified interpretations. Similarly, if our interpretations and traditions thereof prevent us from discovering something that the author used the text to say, then they are defective. For the idea of speech actions as states of affairs and stances adopted to them, and their relation to interpretations of texts, see Wolterstorff, *EB&G*, 431–432, 440–443; for their role and nature in relation to the Bible, see "On God Speaking", 7–11; *Divine Discourse*; "The Importance of Hermeneutics", 25–47; for Wolterstorff's realistic ontology and epistemology, and specific issues relating to realism in biblical interpretation, see above (Chapter 5, B.1.).

54   This question assumes the rejection of cognitive, or framework relativism. If we are ineluctably bound by our traditions and are unable to break their stranglehold then, at least for biblical interpretation, framework relativism is correct. However, as I have shown above, framework relativism is untenable in relation to scholarship in general and hermeneutics in particular (Chapter 2). Thus the question is not *can* the stranglehold be broken? but *how* is it to be broken so as to allow us to see, and see around, the flaws in our own tradition?

55   Wolterstorff, "Bible and Economics", 16.

56   Wolterstorff, "Bible and Economics", 16. Wolterstorff uses the language of a theme

important in contemporary scholarship, is by exposure to different traditions, listening to the different interpretations adherents to those traditions propound, and by honestly listening to them, to expose the flaws within our own tradition.[57] Thus, as is the case with species of belief in general, in the process of dialogue and experience, anomalous beliefs and alternative traditions challenge our tradition, and are in turn challenged by them. By means of debate and discussion, the relative strengths and weaknesses of our traditions are brought to light, thereby presenting us with a challenge to their rationality.[58] In this way our exegetical traditions and theories can be tested, and can progress and evolve so as to become more methodologically and substantively adequate.

It is worth noting in relation to this process that Christian commitment is not a precondition for justified theorising in biblical or general theological scholarship.[59] Just as Wolterstorff argues that faith is not a precondition for knowledge in *Wissenschaft* in general, I see no compelling reason to claim that it is a precondition for theological scholarship. A Jewish, Moslem, Hindu, agnostic or even atheistic scholar can do such theorising, and in the process come to justified conclusions. Indeed, as was the case in the devising of evolutionary theory in the natural sciences, it may well be that only a non-Christian scholar is able to come to see certain truths that are present in the Scriptures, just because she does not have the set of control beliefs and interests that her Christian counterpart may have. There is nothing in Wolterstorff's meta-theory to preclude non-Christians from access to theological truth.[60]

"leaping to our attention". This, of course, is highly metaphorical language, but it does emphasise the ability that the Bible has in Christian experience to somehow act upon us in a way that transcends our own limited perceptions. It implies that someone, namely the God who speaks to us by means of the Bible, is able to show us something that we could previously not see in the message proclaimed by the writers of the texts. cf. "Hearing the Cry", 288; "Between the Times", 17–18; and his comments on the different perspectives of women and feminist scholars on biblical texts opening us to new ways of reading them.

[57] Wolterstorff, "Bible and Economics", 16; cf. Bosch, *Transforming Mission*, 186–187; Osborne, 371, 403–408, 411–415.

[58] For a general discussion of this, see above (Chapter 6, C.).

[59] *pace* Gruenler, xi–xvii, 60–61, 64–71, 168–175.

[60] Here I want to make an important, and from the perspective of Reformed Epistemology, crucial distinction: a non-Christian, scholar or not, may come to *know theological truths*, propositional truths about God, some of which may be inaccessible to Christians (at least at certain times in certain conditions for certain people); they cannot, without giving up their unbelieving stance, come to *know God*. The former is propositional knowledge which, while limited and of limited (non-salvific) value, can be known by all, under the right circumstances. The latter is personal, relational knowledge, which includes but is not limited

Of course according to Wolterstorff's meta-theory a Christian scholar must analyse a non-Christian scholar's exegetical theory for its comportment with her own control beliefs and not those of her non-Christian counterpart. These control beliefs will include the propositional content of her authentic Christian commitment, as well as many other beliefs and values, some at least of which will most likely be common to her colleague. It may be that in the course of testing, the weight of the theory overwhelms that of the conflicting control beliefs, or *vice versa*. So too, there is no certainty that the result will be *true*. All that can be asked of an exegetical scholar, as is the case for all scholars in all areas of scholarship, is that her conclusions be *rational*, not that they be *true*. Biblical scholarship is corrigible scholarship. Wolterstorff's meta-theory demands neither truth, nor uniqueness or exclusiveness of Christian scholarship, merely rational faithfulness to God.

How, then, would the epistemological appraisal of exegetical theories proceed? It would need to begin with an outline of a particular scholar's exegetical conclusions of the meaning and significance the text. For the purposes of further analysis these conclusions would be treated as exegetical theories of the meaning the text. The evidence or "data" and arguments used to justify them would then be identified. From this the substantive and methodological control beliefs that operate in a particular scholar's devising and weighing of theories of the meaning of the text, and the research traditions or species of belief to which she or he belongs, would be identified. This comprises the descriptive component of such an analysis. I would anticipate that, in general, biblical scholars operate within a theological and a methodological (or disciplinary) research tradition from which are derived a number of their respective control beliefs. These and other control beliefs function in their theorising so as to inhibit belief in some proposed interpretations of the text, and abet belief in others.[61] I expect that for those who specifically avow Christian commitment, the belief content of that commitment would play a crucial, but sometimes defective, role in the function of the set of control beliefs. Other beliefs, such as the nature of justified methods of interpretation and the rational status of particular interpretations in the scholarly community, would also function as control.

---

by the propositional, which is only available by God's gracious revealing of himself and his word, and received by faith. Thus a non-Christian may have a more complete and rationally justified body of theological theory than her Christian counterpart without knowing God.

61 See Wolterstorff, "Bible and Economics", 15–16, for a discussion of the role of "global exegeses" (which I believe correspond to my notion of research traditions) in interpretation of texts in relation to economics.

The next step is to assess the rational status or justification of their theories using the criterion of rationality developed above. There are two distinct but related perspectives in this analysis: internal and external. The internal analysis of the theories' justification focuses on their epistemological relationship to the research traditions which nourish them. This involves determining whether the theory comports well with its research traditions (methodological and substantive) and their associated control beliefs, and whether the theory results in the progress of these research traditions. It also requires that the theories be internally consistent and coherent as discrete entities. I expect that most theories, as the product of reputable scholarship, would be justified internally, i.e., from a perspective "internal" to a particular set of traditions, or species of belief. That is to say, a scholar who embraced such a tradition would be entitled to accept the theory.

The determination of the "external" justification of these theories is related to their status, and that of their research traditions, in relation to other well justified theories and traditions. If a theory's research traditions comport well with well-justified theories and traditions, then *ceteris paribus* they are justified, and this in turn contributes to the rationality of the theory, or a scholar's entitlement to it. If, on the other hand, they do not, then good reasons must be adduced in favour of the theory's traditions, or against its rival, for such a conflict may give rise to good reasons for the rejection of that theory and its traditions. They must, in Wolterstorffian terms, defeat the defeaters of belief in those traditions. The theory itself must pass similar tests in relation to well justified traditions and theories. If all of these tests are passed, which I expect to vary from one theory to another, then they are justified in terms of the general practice of scholarship. In terms of Wolterstorff's meta-theory a further question needs to be asked: how well do a given theory and its research traditions comport with the belief content of authentic Christian commitment? Where they do not, this will decrease or eliminate a Christian scholars' entitlement to accept these theories and their associated research traditions.[62]

Thus there are a number of levels in an epistemological assessment of exegetical theories. These levels correlate with levels of justification of or

---

[62] Given the person-specificity of Wolterstorff's meta-theory it would be legitimate to extend this appraisal to each scholar's moral and noetic justification in devising and accepting her or his theory and working within her or his research traditions. However, the focus of his meta-theory is whether a Christian scholar is justified in accepting or rejecting a given theory. Thus this final question, while interesting, will not be explored here.

entitlement to a given theory. If the theory passes the internal tests, then scholars within a particular tradition are entitled to accept it. There will, then, be at least a degree of justified pluralism within exegetical scholarship. However, given that a theory, its traditions, or both may be unjustified from a perspective external to the theory and its traditions, this may be a very limited justified pluralism. Some theories that are internally rational will be seen to be irrational from an external perspective. Equally, some theories which are otherwise well justified will be unjustified for a Christian scholar. Each of these contexts of justification is an important component of a "Wolterstorffian" epistemological analysis of exegetical theories.

Summary and Conclusions

In this book I have sought to demonstrate the need for the kind of person- and situation-specific rationality and meta-theory that Wolterstorff has developed, and to expound, critique, defend and articulate it. In Part One I indicated the need for Wolterstorff's defeasible, situated rationality and its associated meta-theory. This was done by means of a critical analysis of the two main alternatives to a situated, defeasible epistemology; namely absolutist classical foundationalist epistemologies and relativist theories which question the validity of objective rationality and the quest for truth. In Chapter 1 I outlined classical foundationalism and its attempt to attain value-neutral, incorrigible bodies of knowledge that would be accepted by all rational agents. I then outlined the arguments that have been levelled against this theory by Wolterstorff, and by recent contentions within the philosophy of science and epistemology. These arguments indicated that there is no incorrigible means of connecting theories with their foundations so as to transfer certitude from the foundations to the theories, and that there is no foundation of certitudes upon which theories can be based. In light of this, I concluded that the value-neutral, consensus, absolutist notions of rationality and *Wissenschaft* associated with classical foundationalism are philosophically and empirically untenable. Thus Wolterstorff is entitled to reject them.

Chapter 2 explored the relativist alternative to Wolterstorff's situated rationality. I outlined cognitive relativism and related views, focussing on Kuhn's radical theory of scientific revolutions, their main ally in recent philosophy of science. I identified and critiqued the main arguments that have been used to foster relativist theories, paying particular attention to Kuhn's notions of the history and sociology of science and the incommensurability of rival paradigms or disciplinary matrices. Given that these concepts have been shown to be problematic, and that relativist theories are self-referentially incoherent, I concluded that Kuhn's theory of science, and the relativist epistemologies it supports, are implausible. This, in turn, justifies Wolterstorff's rejection of relativism as a viable alternative to classical foundationalism. Given the implausibility of the alternatives, I concluded that the way is opened for the development of defeasible, situation- and person-specific theories of rationality and *Wissenschaft*.

In Part Two I outlined the nature of Wolterstorff's situated rationality and meta-theory. In Chapter 3 I presented his notion of defeasible, person- and situation-specific rationality in order to place his meta-theory in its broader context. Having presented his criterion of rationality, I demonstrated that central to his theory are the notions that our beliefs are the product of belief-dispositions or doxastic practices, and that they are, in general, innocent-until-proven-guilty. In light of this, his criterion of rational justification, or as he later develops it, entitlement, focuses on the removal of justification or entitlement from a particular person's acceptance of particular beliefs, and on the proper governance of doxastic practices so as to get in touch with reality. In outlining his theory of rationality I noted an important area in which it needs to be articulated, namely the noetic effects of sin, and the manner in which they rob beliefs of justification. I noted his passing reference to this phenomenon, and articulated his notion of rationality in light of his more detailed discussion of sinful doxastic practices in his meta-theory.

In order to illuminate crucial features of his meta-theory and draw out its connections to his general epistemology I identified three central features of Wolterstorff's theory of rationality. First, it is empirically oriented, inasmuch as he develops his theory in order to account for the actual nature of human believings: hence his focus on doxastic practices and their governance rather than choices in belief. Second, it is situated and non-absolutist, for a particular person's noetic obligations depend upon her particular context, and indeed are a function of her general obligations. So too, they only entail that she do as well as can be rightly expected of her to avoid error and attain truth, not that she actually do so. Third, it is, nonetheless, a rational epistemology, for he believes that we are constrained by the natures of reality and of God so as to make the quest for truth possible and necessary.

In Chapter 4, I outlined Wolterstorff's defeasible, person- and situation-specific meta-theory. I discussed its relationship to its Neo-Calvinist predecessors, noting the crucial problems in Kuyper's notion of "Two Sciences", and Dooyeweerd's concept of the reductionism of idolatry. These problems gave rise to and also justify Wolterstorff's rejection of their views. Nonetheless, his meta-theory was shown to share important elements of the Neo-Calvinist rejection of autonomous, religiously-neutral scholarship. The crucial difference between his and earlier Reformed theories of science was seen to be his claim that a Christian scholar is called to be *faithful* rather than *different* in her scholarly practice. This notion, and how it is fleshed out in his meta-theory, were shown to be dependent upon his understanding of the role of beliefs and commitments in the devising and weighing of theories. He distinguished between *data beliefs*, *data-background beliefs*, and *control beliefs*. I outlined his understanding of these different beliefs, noting that their differences are of function rather than kind. I also maintained that the nature and function of control beliefs lie at the heart of his meta-theory, and give rise to distinctive, and at times radical, features of his theory.

Wolterstorff presents control beliefs as those of our beliefs that prompt us to accept or reject theories and to devise the sorts of theories that we do. I outlined his notion of control beliefs, and the way that "the belief-content of authentic Christian commitment" ought to function as a control in a Christian scholar's devising and weighing of theories. Authentic Christian commitment was seen to be a selection from amongst the obligations which pertain to a particular Christian scholar: it is person- and situation-specific, as is its belief content. It operates as a control by means of the governing of our doxastic practices so as to accept and devise certain theories and reject others. However, the interaction between the belief content of authentic Christian commitment and particular bodies of theories is complex: at times a body of theory will alter what a Christian scholar takes to be the belief content of her authentic Christian commitment; at others, a theory may give way before it. I demonstrated that, according to Wolterstorff, which of these happens on a given occasion does, and should, depend upon person- and situation-specific factors. Thus in Wolterstorff's meta-theory a Christian scholar's control beliefs were seen to be person- and situation-specific, as are her devising and weighing of theories: there is no algorithm of rationality.

Nor, for Wolterstorff, is there a heuristic algorithm. I noted his rejection of the commonly held view that heuristics, or what he calls the direction-governance of doxastic practices, focuses on the quest for truth: that, he believes, is the domain of what he calls acceptance-governance. Instead heuristics, the decisions a scholar makes about which research tradition she ought to pursue, is to be governed by the quest for *shalom*. I noted Wolterstorff's discussion of how this differs from heuristic principles in classical Christian traditions, contemporary science, and liberation theologies. Wolterstorff believes that justice-in-*shalom* is the ultimate *telos* of human life. The primary obligation of Christians is to foster the quest for justice-in-*shalom*, and so it should govern their scholarly practice. Knowledge is itself an aspect of *shalom*, and can also contribute to the quest for liberation. Thus both pure and praxis-oriented theory may be justified in the heuristics of *shalom*. Which particular research tradition a scholar pursues is a context-specific decision. Such decisions, Wolterstorff contends, must take account of the operation of sinful doxastic practices, which give rise to and sustain research traditions that foster the vested interests of individuals or powerful elites. Christian scholars should faithfully and openly listen to the Word of God and the cries of the oppressed in order to unmask their operation. This notion of the heuristics-of-*shalom*, and the distinction he draws between the contexts of direction- and acceptance-governance of doxastic practices, is important in my articulation of his meta-theory.

In Part Three I critically appraised his meta-theory. In Chapter 6 I articulated and defended his meta-theory in light of criticisms that have been levelled against it. This involved placing it in the context of his theory of rationality, and demonstrating that it shares its empirical and situated nature. In doing so I argued that its situation- and person-specificity entails neither historicism nor the violation of the "naturalised" nature of the natural sciences. I proceeded to develop a criterion of rational theory acceptance and rejection on the basis of his criterion of rationality, drawing out the implications of Wolterstorff's theory of rationality for the practice of scholarship. I also noted the important relationships that obtain between a theory and its associated research tradition. Two lines of argument that indicate that Wolterstorff's is not a relativist meta-theory, despite its person- and situation-specificity were noted. The first is his adoption of a (critical) realist ontology and epistemology. This asserts that we can know not only our conceptual schemes, but the reality to which they apply, despite the theory-ladenness of the concepts that act as bridges between us and the world. I articulated this notion, demonstrated that it is a reasonable one for a Christian scholar to hold, and indicated how it allows Wolterstorff to avoid relativism. The second is his separation of heuristics and theory-choice. I noted here the conceptual and empirical problems associated with their conflation, and showed that Wolterstorff's notion avoids them. I argued that this, in turn, provides good reasons in favour of his meta-theory's being non-relativist.

In Chapter 6 I outlined the epistemological structure of Wolterstorff's meta-theory. I demonstrated that he believes his theories of rationality and

Wissenschaft to be non-foundationalist ones. The nature and function of control beliefs in his meta-theory were seen as central to its non-foundationalist structure. Plantinga's broad foundationalism was outlined. I argued that Wolterstorff's notion of control beliefs and his more dynamic model of rationality avoid certain crucial problems and infelicities inherent in Plantinga's theory. The contention that such a non-foundationalist theory is incompatible with Christian faith was shown to be unjustified. I proceeded to note the similarities and differences between Wolterstorff's and other non-foundationalist meta-theories, in so doing indicating reasons for the greater cogency of his meta-theory.

I then suggested a dynamic epistemological model which attempted to do justice to Wolterstorff's meta-theory and the nature of human believings. As a clue for the further articulation of this model I presented an organic epistemological metaphor in which beliefs, particularly control beliefs, function in a manner analogous to biological systems. Belief systems, in turn, relate to their intellectual environment as organisms do to their physical environment, growing and evolving in response to the challenges they encounter. While this model and its associated metaphor need to be developed in detail, they provide a serious alternative to their foundationalist and coherentist rivals. I conclude that Wolterstorff's meta-theory is rationally acceptable, and indeed is superior to those of its rivals I assessed.

Thus, in this work I have indicated the need for the kind of person- and situation-specific rationality and meta-theory that Wolterstorff has developed. I expounded, critiqued, defended and articulated it. In so doing I sought to defeat the main arguments that have been used to justify its rejection. Where appropriate, I have modified Wolterstorff's meta-theory, in order to extend its scope so as to include the corroborated content of alternative meta-theories, and defeat or modify and incorporate potential challenges to it. One important area in which this was done was the outlining of a dynamic conceptual model and governing metaphor alternative to traditional static foundationalist and coherentist ones. In light of these findings, I conclude that Wolterstorff's meta-theory provides a cogent explanation of the social practice of scholarship, and fruitful and challenging guidelines for the appraisal of theories by a Christian scholar.

Bibliography

Abbreviations follow the JBL conventions for theological publications, except for the following works:

"Can Theologians Recover from Kant?"
        "Is it Possible and Desirable for Theologians to Recover from Kant?", *Modern Theology* 14/1; Wolterstorff, 1998
C&T   "Commitment and Theory", *Christian Higher Education: The Contemporary Challenge*; Wolterstorff, 1976
CBGR? "Can Belief in God be Rational If It Has No Foundations?", *Faith and Rationality: Reason and Belief in God*; Wolterstorff, 1983
EB&G   "Evidence, Entitled Belief and the Gospels", *Faith and Philosophy* 6/4; Wolterstorff, 1989
H&R   "Hume and Reid", *The Monist* 70/4; Wolterstorff, 1987
IFS   "Integration of Faith and Science – The Very Idea", *Journal of Psychology and Christianity* 3/2; Wolterstorff, 1984
J&P   *Until Justice and Peace Embrace*; Wolterstorff, 1983
MSRP "Falsification and the Methodology of Scientific Research Programmes", *Criticism and the Growth of Knowledge*; Lakatos, 1970
New Critique (I)
        A New Critique of Theoretical Reason, vol 1; Dooyeweerd, 1953
New Critique (II)
        A New Critique of Theoretical Reason, vol 2; Dooyeweerd, 1955
R&BG *Reason and Belief in God*; Wolterstorff, 1983
Reid   *Thomas Reid and the Story of Epistemology*; Wolterstorff, 2001
RWBR *Reason Within the Bounds of Religion*; Wolterstorff, 1984
SSR   *The Structure of Scientific Revolutions*; Kuhn, 1970
TRR   "Thomas Reid on Rationality", *Rationality in the Calvinian Tradition*; Wolterstorff, 1983

Primary Sources: Nicholas Wolterstorff

Wolterstorff, N.; "Are Properties Meanings?" *Journal of Philosophy* 57/8 (April 1960) 277–281.
— "Faith and Philosophy", *Faith and Philosophy: Philosophical Studies in Religion and Ethics*, ed. A. Plantinga (Grand Rapids: Eerdmans, 1964) 3–33.
— "Qualities", *Philosophical Review* 69 (1964) 183–200.
— "On God Speaking", *The Reformed Journal* 19/7&8 (Jul–Aug 1969) 7–11.
— "How God Speaks", *The Reformed Journal* 19/9 (Sept 1969) 16–20.
— "Canon and Criterion", *The Reformed Journal* 19/10 (Oct 1969) 10–15.
— *On Universals: An Essay in Ontology* (Chicago: University of Chicago Press, 1970)
— "Commitment and Theory", *Christian Higher Education: The Contemporary Challenge* (Potchesfstroom: Institute for the Advancement of Calvinism, 1976) 116–133.
— "Response to Dennis Casper", *Philosophical Studies* 30 (1976) 121–124.
— "On Avoiding Historicism", *Philosophia Reformata* 45/2 (1980) 178–185.

- "Theory and praxis", *Christian Scholar's Review* 9/4 (1980) 317–334.
- *Educating for Responsible Action* (Grand Rapids: Eerdmans, 1980)
- "Is Reason Enough? A review essay", *The Reformed Journal* 31/4 (April 1981) 20–24.
- *Until Justice and Peace Embrace* (Grand Rapids: Eerdmans, 1983)
- "The mission of the Christian college at the end of the 20th century", *The Reformed Journal* 33/6 (June 1983) 14–18.
- "Thomas Reid on Rationality", *Rationality in the Calvinian Tradition*, ed. H. Hart, et al (Boston: University Press of America, 1983) 49–69.
- "Can Belief in God be Rational If It Has No Foundations?", *Faith and Rationality: Reason and Belief in God*, ed. A. Plantinga and N. Wolterstorff (Notre Dame: University of Notre Dame Press, 1983) 135–186.
- "Introduction", *Faith and Rationality: Reason and Belief in God*, ed. A. Plantinga and N. Wolterstorff (Notre Dame: University of Notre Dame Press, 1983) 1–15.
- *Until Justice and Peace Embrace* (Grand Rapids: Eerdmans, 1983)
- "On keeping women out of office: the CRC committee on headship", *The Reformed Journal* 34/5 (May 1984) 8–14.
- *Reason Within the Bounds of Religion* (2nd ed; Grand Rapids: Eerdmans, 1984)
- "Integration of Faith and Science – The Very Idea", *Journal of Psychology and Christianity* 3/2 (Summer 1984) 12–19.
- "Realism vs Anti-Realism: How to Feel at Home in the World", *Proceedings of the American Catholic Philosophical Association* 54 (1985) 182–205.
- "Reply to Paul de Vries", *Christian Scholar's Review* 16/1 (1986) 53–58.
- "The Migration of the Theistic Arguments: From Natural Theology to Evidentialist Apologetics", *Rationality, Religious Belief, and Moral Commitment: New Essays in the Philosophy of Religion*, ed. R. Audi and W. J. Wainwright (London: Cornell University Press, 1986) 38–81.
- "On Christian Learning", *Worldview and Social Theory*, ed. P. Marshall, et al (University Press of America, 1986) 56–80.
- "Hearing the Cry", *Women, Authority and the Bible*, ed. A. Mickelsen (Downers Grove: IVP, 1986) 286–294.
- "Teaching for Justice", *Making Higher Education Christian*, ed. J. Carpenter and L. Shipps (Grand Rapids: Eerdmans, 1987) 201–216.
- "Are Concept-Users World-makers?" *Philosophical Perspectives* 1 (1987) 233–267.
- "Hume and Reid", *The Monist* 70/4 (Oct 1987) 398–417.
- "The Bible and Economics: The Hermeneutical Issues", *Transformation* 4/3&4 (June–Dec 1987) 11–19.
- "Once Again, Evidentialism – This Time, Social", *Philosophical Topics* 16/2 (Fall 1988) 53–74.
- "Evidence, Entitled Belief and the Gospels", *Faith and Philosophy* 6/4 (Oct 1989) 429–459.
- "Between the Times", *The Reformed Journal* 40/12 (Dec 1990) 16–20.
- "The Assurance of Faith", *Faith and Philosophy* 7/4 (Oct 1990) 396–417.
- "What Reformed Epistemology is Not", *Perspectives* 7/9 (Nov 1992) 14–16.
- "What is Cartesian Doubt?", *American Catholic Philosophical Quarterly* 67/4 (1993) 467–495.
- *Divine Discourse* (Cambridge: Cambridge University Press, 1995)
- "From Liberal to Plural", *Christian Philosophy at the close of the twentieth century*, ed. S. Griffioen and B. Balk (Kampen: Uitgeverij Kok, 1995) 201–215.

- "Will Narrativity Work as Linchpin? Reflections on the Hermeneutic of Hans Frei", *Relativism and Religion*, ed. C. M. Lewis (New York: St Martin's Press, 1995) 71–107.
- "Response to Quinn", *Relativism and Religion*, ed. C. M. Lewis (New York: St Martin's Press, 1995) 119–124.
- "Does the Truth Still Matter? Reflections on the Crisis of the Postmodern University", *Crux* 31/3 (Sept 1995) 17–28.
- *John Locke and the Ethics of Belief* (Cambridge: Cambridge University Press, 1996)
- "Should the Work of Our Hands Have Standing in the Christian College?", *Keeping Faith: Embracing Tensions in Christian Higher Education*, ed. R. A. Wells (Grand Rapids: Eerdmans, 1996) 133–151.
- "Theology and Science: Listening to Each Other", *Religion and Science: History, Method, Dialogue*, ed. W. M. Richardson and W. J. Wildman (New York: Routledge, 1996) 95–104.
- "Entitled Christian Belief", *Religion and Science: History, Method, Dialogue*, ed. W. M. Richardson and W. J. Wildman (New York: Routledge, 1996) 146–150.
- "The Travail of Theology in the Modern Academy", *The Future of Theology: Essays in Honour of Jürgen Moltmann*, ed. M. Volf, et al (Grand Rapids: Eerdmans, 1996) 35–46.
- "The reformed tradition", *A Companion to Philosophy of Religion*, ed. P. Quinn and C. Taliaferro (Oxford: Blackwell, 1997) 165–170.
- "The Importance of Hermeneutics for a Christian Worldview", *Disciplining Hermeneutics: Interpretation in Christian Perspective*, ed. R. Lundin (Grand Rapids: Eerdmans, 1997) 25–47.
- "Suffering, Power, and Privileged Cognitive Access: The Revenge of the Particular", *Christianity and Culture in the Crossfire*, ed. D. A. Hoekema and B. Fong (Grand Rapids: Eerdmans, 1997) 79–94.
- "Reply to Levine", *Religious Studies* 34 (1998) 17–23.
- "Is it Possible and Desirable for Theologians to Recover from Kant?", *Modern Theology* 14/1 (Jan 1998) 1–18.
- "Can Scholarship and Christian Conviction Mix? A New Look at the Integration of Knowledge", *Journal of Education and Christian Belief* 3/1 (1999) 35–50.
- *Thomas Reid and the Story of Epistemology* (Cambridge: Cambridge University Press, 2001)
- *From Presence to Practice: Mind, World and Entitlement to Believe*, The Gifford Lectures for 1994–1995 (forthcoming)

Audi, R, and Wolterstorff, N.; *Religion in the Public Square: The Place of Religious Convictions in Political Debate* (Lanham: Rowman & Littlefield, 1997)

Secondary Sources

Allaire, E. B.; "Wolterstorff and Bradley on Ontology", *Journal of Philosophy* 70/19 (Nov 1973) 727–733.

Alston, W. P.; "Christian Experience and Christian Belief", *Faith and Rationality: Reason and Belief in God*, ed. A. Plantinga and N. Wolterstorff (Notre Dame: University of Notre Dame Press, 1983) 103–134.

- "Plantinga's Epistemology of Religious Belief", *Alvin Plantinga*, ed. J. E. Tomberlin and P. van Inwagen (Dordrecht: Reidel, 1985) 289–311.
- *Epistemic Justification* (Ithaca: Cornell University Press, 1989)

Appleby, P. C.; "Reformed epistemology, rationality and belief in God", *International Journal for Philosophy of Religion* 24/3 (Nov 1988) 137–139.

Avgelis, N.; "Lakatos on the evaluation of scientific theories", *Imre Lakatos and Theories of Scientific Change*, ed. K. Gavroglu, *et al* (Dordrecht: Kluwer, 1989) 157–167.

Ayer, A. J.; "Verification and Experience", *Logical Positivism*, ed. A. J. Ayer (Glencoe: The Free Press, 1963) 228–243.

Banner, M. C.; *The Justification of Science and the Rationality of Religious Belief* (Oxford: Clarendon, 1990)

Beach, E.; "The paradox of cognitive relativism revisited: a reply to Jack W. Meiland", *Metaphilosophy* 15/3&4 (Jul/Oct 1984) 157–171.

Bearn, G. C. F.; "Nietzsche, Feyerabend, and the voices of relativism", *Metaphilosophy* 17/2&3 (Ap/Jul 1986) 135–152.

Birch, B. C.; *Let Justice Roll Down: The Old Testament, Ethics and Christian Life* (Westminster: Louisville, 1991)

Boer, H.; *Above the Bible? The Bible and its Critics* (Grand Rapids: Eerdmans, 1975)

Bosch, D. J.; *Transforming Mission: Paradigm Shifts in the Theology of Mission* (Maryknoll: Orbis, 1991)

Brandt, R. B.; *Ethical Theory: The Problems of Normative and Critical Ethics* (Englewood Cliffs: Prentice Hall, 1959)

Brett, M. G.; "Four or Five Things to do With Texts: A Taxonomy of Interpretative Interests", *The Bible in Three Dimensions*, ed. D. J. A. Clines, *et al* (Sheffield: JSOT, 1990) 357–377.

— "Motives & Intentions in Genesis 1", *Journal of Theological Studies* 42/1 (1991) 1–16.

— "The Future of Reader Criticisms?", *The Open Text: New Directions for Biblical Studies?*, ed. F. Watson (London: SCM, 1993) 13–31.

Bright, J.; *Early Israel in Recent History Writing* (London: SCM, 1956)

Brownstein, D.; "Wolterstorff on Qualities", *Philosophical Studies* 23 (1972) 98–104.

Brueggemann, W.; *Living Toward a Vision: Biblical Reflections on Shalom* (United Church Press: New York, 1976)

Brunner, E.; *The Christian Doctrine of God: Dogmatics: vol 1* (Philadelphia: Westminster, 1950)

Calvin, J.; *Institutes of the Christian Religion* (Grand Rapids: Eerdmans, 1983)

— *The Gospel According to St. John, 1–10* (London: Oliver and Boyd, 1959)

— *Commentary on the Epistle to the Romans*, ed. H. Beveridge (Edinburgh: The Calvin Translation Society, 1884)

Carnap, R.; "The Elimination of Metaphysics Through Logical Analysis of Language", *Logical Positivism*, ed. A. J. Ayer (Glencoe: The Free Press, 1969) 60–81.

Carnell, E. J.; *An Introduction to Christian Apologetics: A Philosophical Defense of the Trinitarian-Theistic Faith* (5th ed; Grand Rapids: Eerdmans, 1956)

Carroll, R. P.; *Wolf in the Sheepfold: The Bible as a Problem for Christianity* (London: SPCK, 1991)

Casper, D.; "On Wolterstorff's Nominalistic Theory of Qualities", *Philosophical Studies* 30 (1976) 115–119.

Chalmers, A. F.; *What is this thing called science?* (St Lucia: University of Queensland Press, 1976)

Chisholm, R.; *The Problem of the Criterion* (Milwaukee: Marquette University Press, 1973)

— *Theory of Knowledge* (2nd ed; Englewood Cliffs: Prentice Hall, 1977)

— *Theory of Knowledge* (3rd ed; Englewood Cliffs: Prentice Hall, 1989)

Clark, K. J.; *Return to Reason* (Grand Rapids: Eerdmans, 1990)
Clayton, P., and Knapp, S.; "Rationality and Christian Self-Conceptions", *Religion and Science: History, Method, Dialogue*, ed. W. M. Richardson and W. J. Wildman (New York: Routledge, 1996) 131–142.
— "Is Holistic Justification Enough?", *Religion and Science: History, Method, Dialogue*, ed. W. M. Richardson and W. J. Wildman (New York: Routledge, 1996) 161–167.
Clines, D. J. A.; "Reading Esther From Left to Right: Contemporary Strategies for Reading a Biblical Text", *The Bible in Three Dimensions*, ed. D. J. A. Clines, *et al* (Sheffield: JSOT, 1990) 31–52.
— "Story and Poem: The Old Testament as Literature and as Scripture", *Beyond Form Criticism: Essays in Old Testament Literary Criticism*, ed. P. R. House (Winona Lake: Eisenbrauns, 1992) 25–38.
Conn, H. M.; "Normativity, Relevance and Relativism", *Inerrancy and Hermeneutic: A Tradition, A Challenge, A Debate*, ed. H. M. Conn (Grand Rapids: Baker, 1988) 185–209.
Cooke, V. M.; "Current Theology: The New Calvinist Epistemology", *Theological Studies* 47/2 (1986) 273–285.
Dancy, J.; *Introduction to Contemporary Epistemology* (Oxford: Basil Blackwell, 1985)
Davies, M.; "Reader-Response Criticism", *A Dictionary of Biblical Interpretation*, ed. R. J. Coggins and J. L. Houlden (London: SCM, 1990) 578–580.
Davies, P.; "Do Old Testament Studies Need a Dictionary?", *The Bible in Three Dimensions*, ed. D. J. A. Clines, *et al* (Sheffield: JSOT, 1990) 321–335.
Dooyeweerd, H.; *A New Critique of Theoretical Reason* (3 vol; Philadelphia: Presbyterian and Reformed, 1953; vol 1)
— *A New Critique of Theoretical Reason* (3 vol; Philadelphia: Presbyterian and Reformed, 1955; vol 2)
— *A New Critique of Theoretical Reason* (3 vol; Philadelphia: Presbyterian and Reformed, 1957; vol 3)
— *In the Twilight of Western Thought: Studies in the Pretended Autonomy of Philosophical Thought* (Nutley: Craig, 1975)
Doppelt, G.; "Kuhn's Epistemological Relativism: An Interpretation and Defence", *Relativism: Cognitive and Moral*, ed. J. W. Meiland and M. Kraus (Notre Dame: University of Notre Dame Press, 1982) 113–146.
Douma, J.; *Another Look at Dooyeweerd* (Winnipeg: Premier, 1976)
Dowey, E. A.; *The Knowledge of God in Calvin's Theology* (New York: Columbia University Press, 1952)
Duran, J.; "Reliabilism, Foundationalism, and Naturalized Epistemic Justification Theory", *Metaphilosophy* 19/2 (April 1988) 113–127.
Echeverria, E. J.; "Towards a Critique of the Subject", *Philosophia Reformata* 44/1 (1979) 86–105.
Edwards, D. L.; "The Authority of the Scriptures", *Essentials: A liberal-evangelical dialogue*, D. L. Edwards and J. Stott (London: Hodder and Stoughton, 1988) 41–82.
Erickson, M. J.; *Christian Theology* (Grand Rapids: Baker, 1987)
Evans, C. S.; *Philosophy of Religion* (Leicester: IVP, 1982)
Feigh, H.; "The origin and development of logical positivism" *The Legacy of Logical Positivism*, ed. P. Achinstein and S. F. Barker (Baltimore: John Hopkins, 1969) 3–23.

Feldman, R.; "Epistemic Obligations", *Philosophical Perspectives, no.2: Epistemology* (1988) 235–256.

Ferré, F.; *Basic Philosophy of Religion* (London: Allen and Unwin, 1967)

Feyerabend, P. K.; "Consolations for the Specialist", *Criticism and the Growth of Knowledge*, ed. I. Lakatos and A. Musgrave (Cambridge: Cambridge University Press, 1970) 197–230.

— "Philosophy of Science: A Subject with a Great Past", *Historical and Philosophical Perspectives on Science*, ed. H. Stuewer (Minnesota Studies in the Philosophy of Science, vol V; Minneapolis: University of Minnesota Press, 1970) 172–183.

— *Science in a Free Society* (London: New Left Books, 1978)

— *Against Method* (rev. ed; London: Verso, 1988)

Fiddes, V. H.; *Science & the Gospel* (Edinburgh: Scottish Academic Press, 1987)

Fowl, S. E.; "The Ethics of Interpretation: or What's Left After the Elimination of Meaning", *The Bible in Three Dimensions*, ed. D. J. A. Clines, *et al* (Sheffield: JSOT, 1990) 379–398.

Gavroglu, K., Goudaroulis, Y., and Nicolacopoulos, P., (ed); *Imre Lakatos and Theories of Scientific Change* (Dordrecht: Kluwer, 1989)

Gibson, R. F.; *Enlightened Empiricism: An Examination of W. V. Quine's Theory of Knowledge* (Tampa: University of South Florida Press, 1988)

Goetz, S. C.; "Belief in God is not Properly Basic", *Religious Studies* 19/4 (Dec 1983) 475–484.

Goldingay, J.; "How far do readers make sense? Interpreting biblical narrative", *Themelios* 18/2 (Jan 1993) 5–10.

Goodman, N.; "The Fabrication of Facts", *Relativism: Cognitive and Moral*, ed. J. W. Meiland and M. Kraus (Notre Dame: University of Notre Dame Press, 1982) 18–29.

Gowan, J.; "Foundationalism and the Justification of Religious Belief", *Religious Studies* 19/3 (Sept 1983) 391–406.

Grenz, S.; and Franke, J.; *Beyond Foundationalism: Shaping Theology in a Postmodern Context* (Louisville: Westminster John Knox, 2001)

Grigg, R.; "Theism and Proper Basicality: A Response to Plantinga" *International Journal for Philosophy of Religion* 14 (1983) 123–127.

— "The Crucial Disanalogies between Properly Basic Belief and Belief in God", *Religious Studies* 26/3 (Sept 1990) 389–401.

Grudem, W. A., "Scripture's Self-Attestation and the Problem of Formulating a Doctrine of Scripture", *Scripture and Truth*, ed. D. A. Carson and J. D. Woodhouse (Grand Rapids: Zondervan, 1983) 19–59.

Gruenler, R. G.; *Meaning and Understanding: The philosophical framework for understanding biblical interpretation* (Grand Rapids: Zondervan, 1991)

Gunn, D. G.; "Reading Right: Reliable and Omniscient Narrator, Omniscient God, and Foolproof Composition in the Hebrew Bible", *The Bible in Three Dimensions*, ed. D. J. A. Clines, *et al* (Sheffield: JSOT, 1990) 53–64.

Gutenson, C.; "An Examination of Nicholas Wolterstorff's *Divine Discourse* – Review Essay", *Christian Scholar's Review* 28/1 (Fall 1998) 140–154.

Gutting, G.; "Review of *Reason Within the Bounds of Religion* (2nd ed)", *Faith and Philosophy* 4/2 (April 1987) 225–228.

— *Religious Belief and Religious Skepticism* (Notre Dame: University of Notre Dame Press, 1982)

Hart, H.; "The Articulation of Belief: A Link Between Rationality and Commitment", *Rationality in the Calvinian Tradition*, ed. H. Hart, *et al* (Boston: University Press of America, 1983) 209–243.
— "A Theme from the Philosophy of Herman Dooyeweerd", *Faith and Philosophy* 5/3 (Jul 1988) 268–282.
Hasel, G. F.; *Old Testament Theology: Basic Issues in the Current Debate* (4th ed; Grand Rapids: Eerdmans, 1991)
Hasker, W.; "Review of *Rationality in the Calvinian Tradition*", *Christian Scholar's Review* 14/3 (1985) 259–260.
— "Faith-Learning Integration: An Overview", *Christian Scholar's Review* 21/3 (Mar 1992) 234–248.
Hatcher, D.; "Plantinga and Reformed Epistemology: A Critique", *Philosophy and Theology* 1/1 (Fall 1986) 84–95.
Heal, J.; "Pragmatism and Choosing to Believe", *Reading Rorty*, ed. A. R. Malachowski (Oxford: Basil Blackwell, 1990) 101–114.
Helm, P.; "Why be Objective?", *Objective Knowledge*, ed. P. Helm (Leicester: IVP, 1987) 29–40.
— "Understanding Scholarly Presuppositions: A Crucial Tool for Research?", *Tyndale Bulletin* 44/1 (1993) 143–154.
Hempel, C. G.; "The Empiricist Criterion of Meaning", *Logical Positivism*, ed. A. J. Ayer (Glencoe: The Free Press, 1969) 108–129.
Henry, C. F. H.; *God, Revelation and Authority* (6 vol; Waco: Word, 1976; vol 1)
— *God, Revelation and Authority* (6 vol; Waco:Word, 1979; vol 3)
— *God, Revelation and Authority* (6 vol; Waco: Word, 1979; vol 4)
Hester, M.; "Foundationalism and Peter's Confession", *Religious Studies* 26/3 (Sept 1990) 403–413.
Hodge, C.; *Systematic Theology* (ed. E. N. Gross; Grand Rapids: Baker, 1992)
Holmes, A. F.; "Commitment and Rationality", *Rationality in the Calvinian Tradition*, ed. H. Hart, *et al* (Boston: University Press of America, 1983) 191–208.
Hookway, C.; *Quine: Language, Experience and Reality* (Cambridge: Polity, 1988)
Hume, D.; *A Treatise on Human Nature* (Oxford: The Clarendon Press, 1888)
Jacob E.; *Theology of the Old Testament* (London: Hodder and Stoughton, 1964)
Kalsbeek, L.; *Contours of a Christian philosophy: An introduction to Herman Dooyeweerd's thought* (ed. B. and J. Zylstra; Toronto: Wedge, 1975)
Kaufman, G. D.; *In Face of Mystery: A Constructive Theology* (Cambridge, Ma: Harvard University Press, 1993)
Kennedy, G.; "'Truth' and 'Rhetoric' in the Pauline Epistles", *The Bible as Rhetoric: Studies in Biblical Persuasion and Credibility*, ed. M. Warner (Routledge: London, 1990) 195–202.
Klapwijk, J.; "Rationality in the Dutch Neo-Calvinist Tradition", *Rationality in the Calvinian Tradition*, ed. H. Hart, *et al* (Boston: University Press of America, 1983) 93–111.
Knox, D. B.; "Propositional Revelation the only Revelation", *Reformed Theological Review* 19/1 (Feb 1960) 1–9.
Knudsen, R. D.; "The Idea of Christian Scientific Endeavour in the thought of Herman Dooyeweerd", *Philosophia Reformanda: Reflections on the Philosophy of Herman Dooyeweerd* (R. Knudsen; 1971) 1–8.

— "Dooyeweerd's Philosophical Method", *Philosophia Reformanda: Reflections on the Philosophy of Herman Dooyeweerd* (R. Knudsen; 1971) 9–19.
Kolakowski, L.; *Positivist Philosophy* (Harmondsworth: Penguin, 1972)
Kourany, J. A.; "Towards an Empirically Adequate Theory of Science", *Philosophy of Science* 48 (1982) 526–548.
Kroger, J.; "Prophetic-Critical and Strategic Tasks of Theology: Habermas and Liberation Theology", *Theological Studies* 46/1 (Mar 1985) 3–20.
Kuhn, T. S.; *The Structure of Scientific Revolutions* (2nd ed; Chicago: The University of Chicago Press, 1970)
— "Reflections on my Critics", *Criticism and the Growth of Knowledge*, ed. I. Lakatos and A. Musgrave (Cambridge: Cambridge University Press, 1970) 231–278.
— "Logic of Discovery or Psychology of Research?" *Criticism and the Growth of Knowledge*, ed. I. Lakatos and A. Musgrave (Cambridge: Cambridge University Press, 1970) 1–22.
— "Objectivity, Value Judgement, and Theory Choice" *The Essential Tension* (Chicago: University of Chicago Press, 1977) 320–339.
Kuyper, A.; *Lectures on Calvinism* (Grand Rapids: Eerdmans, 1931)
— *Principles of Sacred Theology* (Grand Rapids: Baker, 1980)
Lakatos, I.; "Falsification and the Methodology of Scientific Research Programmes", *Criticism and the Growth of Knowledge*, ed. I. Lakatos and A. Musgrave (Cambridge: Cambridge University Press, 1970) 91–196.
— "Introduction: Science and Pseudoscience", *Philosophical Papers, vol 1: The methodology of scientific research programmes*, ed. J. Worrall and G. Currie (Cambridge: Cambridge University Press, 1978) 1–7.
— "History of Science and its Rational Reconstructions", *Philosophical Papers, vol 1: The methodology of scientific research programmes*, ed. J. Worrall and G. Currie (Cambridge: Cambridge University Press, 1978) 102–138.
— "The problem of appraising scientific theories: three approaches", *Philosophical Papers: vol 2; Mathematics, Science and Epistemology*, ed. J. Worrall and G. Currie (Cambridge: Cambridge University Press, 1978) 107–120.
Laudan, L.; *Progress and its Problems: Towards a Theory of Scientific Growth* (Berkley: University of California Press, 1977)
Layman, C. S.; *The Shape of the Good: Christian Reflections on the Foundations of Ethics* (Notre Dame: University of Notre Dame Press, 1991)
Lehrer, K.; "Beyond Impressions and Ideas: Hume vs Reid", *The Monist* 70/4 (Oct 1987) 383–397.
Levine, M.; "God Speak", *Religious Studies* 34 (1998) 1–16.
Lewis, G. R. and Demarest, B. A.; *Integrative Theology* (3 vol; Grand Rapids: Academie, 1987; vol 1)
Lindbeck, G.; *The Nature of Doctrine: Religion and Theology in a Postliberal Age* (London: SPCK, 1984)
— "Postcritical Canonical Interpretation: Three Modes of Retrieval", *Theological Exegesis: Essays in Honor of Brevard S. Childs*, ed. C. Seitz and K. Greene-McCreight (Grand Rapids: Eerdmans, 1999) 26–51.
Livingstone, D. N.; "Science and Society: Reflections on the Radical Critique of Science", *Faith and Thought* 113/1 (April 1987) 17–32;

— "Farewell to Arms: Reflections on the Encounter between Science and Faith", *Christian Faith and Practice in the Modern World: Theology from an Evangelical Point of View*, ed. M. A. Noll and D. F. Wells (Grand Rapids: Eerdmans, 1988) 239–262.

Locke, J,; *An Essay Concerning Human Understanding* (2 vol; ed. A. C. Fraser; New York: Dover, 1959; vol 2)

Louthan, S.; "On Religion: A Discussion with Richard Rorty, Alvin Plantinga and Nicholas Wolterstorff", *Christian Scholar's Review* 26/2 (Wint 1996) 177–183.

Loux, M. J.; "Recent Work in Ontology", *American Philosophical Quarterly* 9/2 (April 1972) 119–138.

McFague, S.; *Metaphorical Theology* (London: SCM, 1982)

— *Models of God* (Philadelphia: Fortress, 1987)

McGrath, A.; "The Challenge of Pluralism for the Contemporary Christian Church", *Journal of the Evangelical Theological Society* 35/3 (Sept 1992) 361–373.

— "The Christian Church's Response to Pluralism" *Journal of the Evangelical Theological Society* 35/4 (Dec 1992) 487–501.

MacKay, D. M.; "Objectivity as a Christian Value", *Objective Knowledge*, ed. P. Helm (Leicester: IVP, 1987) 15–27.

McKim, R.; "Theism and Proper Basicality", *International Journal for Philosophy of Religion* 22 (1989) 29–55.

McKnight, E. V.; *Post-Modern Use of the Bible: The Emergence of Reader-Oriented Criticism* (Nashville: Abingdon, 1988)

McInerny, R.; "Thoughts on Wolterstorff's 'Theory and Praxis'", *Christian Scholar's Review* 9/4 (1980) 335–336.

MacIntyre, A.; *After Virtue: A Study in Moral Theory* (2nd ed; Notre Dame: University of Notre Dame Press, 1984)

— *Whose Justice? Which Rationality?* (London: Duckworth, 1987)

McLeod, M. S.; "Can Belief in God be Confirmed?", *Religious Studies* 24 (1988) 311–323.

— "Making God Dance: Postmodern Theorizing and the Christian College", *Christian Scholar's Review* 21/3 (Mar 1992) 275–292.

Macquarrie, J.; *Principles of Christian Theology* (rev ed; London: SCM, 1977)

Madden, E. H.; "Did Reid's Metaphilosophy survive Kant, Hamilton and Mill?", *Metaphilosophy* 18/1 (Jan 1987) 31–48.

Malino, J.; "Comments on Quinn", *Faith and Philosophy* 2/4 (Oct 1985) 487–491.

Marsden, G.; "The Collapse of American Evangelical Academia", *Faith and Rationality: Reason and Belief in God*, ed. A. Plantinga and N. Wolterstorff (Notre Dame: University of Notre Dame Press, 1983) 219–264.

Marshall, B.; *Trinity and Truth* (Cambridge: Cambridge University Press, 2000)

Marshall, I. H.; "Using the Bible in Ethics", *Essays in Evangelical Social Ethics*, ed. D. F. Wright (Witlon: Moorehouse-Barlow, 1979) 39–55.

— "'To Find Out What God is Saying': Reflections on the Authorizing of Scripture", *Disciplining Hermeneutics: Interpretation in Christian Perspective*, ed. R. Lundin (Grand Rapids: Eerdmans, 1997) 49–55.

Masterman, M.; "The Nature of a Paradigm", *Criticism and the Growth of Knowledge*, ed. I. Lakatos and A. Musgrave (Cambridge: Cambridge University Press, 1970) 59–89.

Matteo, A. M.; "Can Belief in God be Basic?" *Horizons* 15/2 (1988) 262–282.

Mavrodes, G.; "Jerusalem and Athens Revisited", *Faith and Rationality: Reason and Belief in God*, ed. A. Plantinga and N. Wolterstorff (Notre Dame: University of Notre Dame Press, 1983) 192–218.

Meiland, J. W.; "On the paradox of cognitive relativism", *Metaphilosophy* 11/2 (April 1980) 115–126.

Meiland, J. W. and Kraus, M.; "Introduction to the 'Fabrication of Facts'", *Relativism: Cognitive and Moral* ed. J. W. Meiland and M. Kraus (Notre Dame: University of Notre Dame Press, 1982) 13–17.

Meyer, B. F.; "The Challenge of Text and Reader to the Historical-Critical Method", *The Bible and its Readers*, ed. W. Beuken, *et al* (Concilium 1991/1; London: SCM, 1991) 3–12.

Miguez-Bonino, J.; "Theology as Critical Reflection and Liberating Praxis", *The Vocation of the Theologian*, ed. T. W. Jennings (Philadelphia: Fortress, 1985) 37–48.

Mitchell, B.; "Two Approaches to the Philosophy of Religion", *For God and Clarity: New Essays in Honour of Austen Farrer*, ed. J. C. Eaton and A. Loades (Allison Park: Pickwick: 1983) 177–190.

— "Reason and Commitment in the Academic Vocation", *How to Play Theological Ping-Pong: And Other Essays on Faith and Reason*, ed. W. J. Abraham and R. W. Prevost (London: Hodder and Stoughton, 1990) 98–112.

— "Neutrality and Commitment", *How to Play Theological Ping-Pong: And Other Essays on Faith and Reason*, ed. W. J. Abraham and R. W. Prevost (London: Hodder and Stoughton, 1990) 113–131.

— "Faith and Reason: A False Antithesis?", *How to Play Theological Ping-Pong: And Other Essays on Faith and Reason*, ed. W. J. Abraham and R. W. Prevost (London: Hodder and Stoughton, 1990) 132–150.

— "How to Play Theological Ping-Pong", *How to Play Theological Ping-Pong: And Other Essays on Faith and Reason*, ed. W. J. Abraham and R. W. Prevost (London: Hodder and Stoughton, 1990) 166–183.

Montgomery, J. W.; "The Place of Reason in Christian Witness", *Faith Founded on Fact* (Nashville: Thomas Nelson, 1978) 27–42.

— "Once upon an A Priori: Van Til in Light of Three Fables", *Faith Founded on Fact* (Nashville: Thomas Nelson, 1978) 107–127.

Moroney, S.; "How Sin Affects Scholarship: A New Model", *Christian Scholar's Review* 28/3 (Spring 1999) 432–451.

Morris, L.; *I Believe in Revelation* (London: Hodder and Stoughton, 1976)

Mouw, R. J.; "Dutch Calvinist Philosophical Influences in North America", *Calvin Theological Journal* 24/1 (April 1989) 93–120.

Murphy, N. C.; "Acceptability Criteria for Work in Theology and Science", *Zygon* 22/3 (Sept 1987) 279–297.

— "From Critical Realism to a Methodological Approach: Response to Robbins, Van Huyssteen, and Hefner", *Zygon* 23/3 (Sept 1988) 287–290.

— *Theology in the Age of Scientific Reasoning* (Ithaca: Cornell University Press, 1990)

— *Beyond Liberalism and Fundamentalism: How Modern and Postmodern Philosophy Set the Theological Agenda* (Valley Forge, Pennsylvania: Trinity, 1996)

— "Postmodern Apologetics: Or Why Theologians *Must* Pay Attention to Science", *Religion and Science: History, Method, Dialogue*, ed. W. M. Richardson and W. J. Wildman (New York: Routledge, 1996) 105–120.

— "On the Nature of Theology", *Religion and Science: History, Method, Dialogue*, ed. W. M. Richardson and W. J. Wildman (New York: Routledge, 1996) 151–159.
— *Anglo-American Postmodernity: Philosophical Perspectives on Science, Religion, and Ethics* (Boulder, Colorado: Westview, 1997)
Nelson, R. R.; "Faith-Discipline Integration: Compatibilist, Reconstructionalist and Transformationalist Strategies", *The Reality of Christian Learning: Strategies for Faith-Discipline Integration*, H. Heie and D. L. Wolfe (Grand Rapids: Eerdmans, 1987) 317–339.
Netland, H. A.; "Review of *Faith and Rationality: Reason and Belief in God*", *Journal of the Evangelical Theological Society* 29/1 (Mar 1986) 91–93.
— *Dissonant Voices: Religious Pluralism and the Question of Truth* (Leicester: Apollos, 1991)
Newton-Smith, W. H.; *The Rationality of Science* (Boston: Routledge and Keagan Paul, 1981)
Niesel, W.; *The Theology of John Calvin* (Philadelphia: Westminster Press, 1956)
Noth, N.; *The History of Israel* (2nd ed; London: SCM, 1960)
— "The Laws in the Pentateuch: Their Assumptions and Meaning", *The Laws in the Pentateuch and Other Essays* (Edinburgh: Oliver and Boyd, 1966) 1–107.
— *Numbers* (London: SCM, 1968)
O'Donovan, O.; *Resurrection and Moral Order: An Outline for Evangelical Ethics* (Leicester: IVP, 1986)
Osborne, G. R.; *The Hermeneutical Spiral: A Comprehensive Introduction to Biblical Interpretation* (Downers Grove: IVP, 1991)
Padilla, C. R.; "The Fruit of Justice will be Peace", *Transformation* 2/1 (Jan/Mar 1985) 2–4.
Pannenberg, W.; *Systematic Theology* (3 vol; Edinburgh: T&T Clark, 1991; vol 1)
Patrick, D. and Scult, A.; *Rhetoric and Biblical Interpretation* (Sheffield: Almond, 1990)
Pera, M.; "Methodological Sophisticationism: A Degenerating Project", *Imre Lakatos and Theories of Scientific Change*, ed. K. Gavroglu, *et al* (Dordrecht: Kluwer, 1989) 169–187.
Phillips, T. R.; and Okholm, D. L.; *The Nature of Confession: Evangelicals and Postliberals in Conversation* (Downers Grove: IVP, 1996)
Pinnock, C.; "Response by Clark Pinnock", *The Reformed Journal* 31/4 (April 1981) 25–26.
Plantinga, A.; "The Reformed Objection to Natural Theology", *Christian Scholar's Review* 11/3 (1982) 187–198.
— "Reason and Belief in God", *Faith and Rationality: Reason and Belief in God*, ed. A. Plantinga and N. Wolterstorff (Notre Dame: University of Notre Dame Press, 1983) 16–93.
— "Replies to my Colleagues", *Alvin Plantinga*, ed. J. E. Tomberlin and P. van Ingwagen (Dordrecht: Reidel, 1985) 313–396.
— "The Foundations of Theism: A Reply", *Faith and Philosophy* 3/3 (July 1986) 306–312.
— "Coherentism and the Evidentialist Objection to Belief in God", *Rationality, Religious Belief, and Moral Commitment: New Essays in the Philosophy of Religion* ed. R Audi and W. J. Wainwright (London: Cornell University Press, 1986) 109–138.
— Positive Epistemic Status and Proper Function", *Philosophical Perspectives, no.2: Epistemology* (1988) 1–50.
— *Warrant: The Current Debate* (New York: Oxford University Press, 1993)
— *Warrant and Proper Function* (New York: Oxford University Press, 1993)

— "Reformed Epistemology", *A Companion to Philosophy of Religion*, ed. P. Quinn and C. Taliaferro (Oxford: Blackwell, 1997) 383–389.
— *Warranted Christian Belief* (New York: Oxford University Press, 2000)
Polanyi, M.; *Science, Faith and Society* (2nd ed; Chicago: University of Chicago Press, 1964)
— *Personal Knowledge: Towards a Post-critical Philosophy* (London: Routledge and Keagan Paul, 1962)
Polkinghorne, J.; *Science and Creation* (London: SPCK, 1988)
— *Reason and Reality* (London: SPCK, 1991)
— "Science and Providence: How God Works in the World" (Sydney: Morling College Annual Lecture, 1993)
Popper, K. R.; *Objective Knowledge: An Evolutionary Approach* (Oxford: Clarendon, 1972)
— *Conjectures and Refutations* (London: Routledge and Keagan Paul, 1974)
— *The Logic of Scientific Discovery* (rev. ed; London: Hutchinson, 1980)
— "Normal Science and its Dangers", *Criticism and the Growth of Knowledge*, ed. I. Lakatos and A. Musgrave (Cambridge: Cambridge University Press, 1970) 51–58.
Postema, G. J.; "Calvin's alleged rejection of Natural Theology", *Scottish Journal of Theology* 24/4 (Nov 1971) 423–434.
Poythress, V. S.; *Science and Hermeneutics* (Leicester: Apollos, 1987)
Quine, W. V.; "Two Dogmas of Empiricism", *From a Logical Point of View* (Cambridge Mass: Harvard University Press, 1964) 20–46.
— "Posits and Reality", *The Ways of Paradox and Other Essays* (New York: Random House, 1966) 233–241.
— "On Simple Theories of a Complex World", *The Ways of Paradox and Other Essays* (New York: Random House, 1966) 242–245.
— "Comments on Lauener", *Perspectives on Quine*, ed. R. B. Barrett and R. F. Gibson (Oxford: Basil Blackwell, 1990) 229.
— *Pursuit of Truth* (Cambridge: Cambridge University Press, 1990)
Quine, W. V. and Ullian, J. S.; *The Web of Belief* (New York: Random House, 1970)
Quinn, P.; "In Search of the Foundations of Theism", *Faith and Philosophy* 2/4 (Oct 1985) 468–486.
Ratsch, D.; *Philosophy of Science* (Downers Grove: IVP, 1986)
Reid, T.; *Essays on the Intellectual Powers of Man* (Glasgow: Richmond Griffin, 1854)
— *An Inquiry into the Human Mind*, ed. T. Duggan (Chicago: University of Chicago Press, 1970)
Remelts, G. A.; "The Christian Reformed Church and Science, 1900–1930: An Evangelical Alternative to the Fundamentalist and Modernist Responses to Science", *Fides et Historia* 21/1 (Jan 1989) 61–80.
Rienstra, M. H.; "History, Objectivity and the Christian Scholar", *History and Historical Understanding*, ed. C. T. McIntire and R. A. Wells (Grand Rapids: Eerdmans, 1984) 69–82.
Riggs, P. J.; *Whys and Ways of Science* (Carlton: Melbourne University Press, 1992)
Robbins, J. W.; "Is Belief in God Properly Basic?" *International Journal of the Philosophy of Religion* 14/4 (1983) 246–247.
Rorty, R.; *Philosophy and the Mirror of Nature* (Oxford: Basil Blackwell, 1979)
— "Pragmatism, Relativism and Irrationalism", *Consequences of Pragmatism* (Minneapolis: University of Minnesota Press, 1982) 160–175.

— "Introduction: Antirepresentationalism, ethnocentrism and liberalism", *Objectivity, relativism and truth: Philosophical Papers, Vol One* (Cambridge: Cambridge University Press, 1991) 1–17.
— "Is Natural Science and Natural Kind?", *Objectivity, relativism and truth: Philosophical Papers, Vol One* (Cambridge: Cambridge University Press, 1991) 46–62.
— "Introduction", *Essays on Heidegger and others: Philosophical Papers, Vol Two* (Cambridge: Cambridge University Press, 1991) 1–6.
— "Introduction", *Philosophical Papers, vol 3: Truth and Progress*, (Cambridge: Cambridge University Press, 1998) 1–15.
— "Is Truth a Goal of Inquiry? Donald Davidson versus Crispin Wright", *Philosophical Papers, vol 3: Truth and Progress*, (Cambridge: Cambridge University Press, 1998) 19–42.
Rosenbaum, S. E.; "Rortian Rationality", *Metaphilosophy* 17/2&3 (Ap/Jul 1986) 93–101.
Ross, M.; "Who is Telling the Myth?", *Objective Knowledge*, ed. P. Helm (Leicester: IVP, 1987) 129–143.
Runzo, J.; "World-views and the Epistemic Foundations of Theism", *Religious Studies* 25/1 (March 1989) 31–51.
Russman, T. A.; "'Reformed' Epistemology", *Thomistic Papers IV*, ed. L. A. Kennedy (Houston: University of St Thomas, 1988) 185–205.
Schaeffer, F. A.; *He is There and He is not Silent* (London: Hodder and Stoughton, 1972)
Schleiermacher, F.; *The Christian Faith* (2nd ed; Edinburgh: T&T Clark, 1928)
Schlick, M.; "The Foundation of Knowledge", *Logical Positivism*, ed. A. J. Ayer (Glencoe: The Free Press, 1963) 209–227.
Schlossberg, H.; "A Response to Nicholas Wolterstorff", *Transformation* 4/3&4 (Jun–Dec 1987) 20–25.
Siegel, H.; *Relativism Refuted: A Critique of Contemporary Epistemological Relativism* (Dordrecht: D. Reidel, 1987)
Shapere, D., "The Structure of Scientific Revolutions", *Reason and the Search for Knowledge* (Dordrecht: D. Reidel, 1984) 37–48.
— "The Paradigm Concept", *Reason and the Search for Knowledge* (Dordrecht: D. Reidel, 1984) 49–57.
— "Modern Science and the Philosophical Tradition", *Reason and the Search for Knowledge* (Dordrecht: D. Reidel, 1984) 408–417.
Somerville, J.; "Reid's Conception of Common Sense", *The Monist* 70/4 (Oct 1987) 418–429.
Sproul, R. C., Gerstener, J., and Lindsley, A.; *Classical Apologetics* (Grand Rapids: Academie, 1984)
Stenmark, M.; *Rationality in Science, Religion and Everyday Life: A Critical Evaluation of Four Models of Rationality* (Notre Dame: University of Notre Dame Press, 1995)
Stiver, D. R.; "Much Ado About Athens and Jerusalem: The Implications of Postmodernism for Faith", *Review and Expositor* 91 (1994) 83–102.
Stott, J; *The Lausanne Covenant: An Exposition and Commentary* (London: Scripture Union, 1975)
— "John Stott's Response to Chapter 2", *Essentials: A liberal-evangelical dialogue*, D. L. Edwards and J. Stott (London: Hodder and Stoughton, 1988) 82–106.
Suppe, F.; "Critical Introduction", *The Structure of Scientific Theories*, ed. F. Suppe (Urbana: University of Illinois Press, 1974) 120–221.

Sweetman, R.; "Christian Scholarship: Two Reformed Perspectives", *Perspectives* 16/6 (June/July 2001) 14–19.
Taylor, J.; "Science, Christianity and the Post-Modern Agenda", *Science and Christian Belief* 10 (1998) 163–178.
Thiselton, A. C.; "On Models and Methods: A Conversation with Robert Morgan", *The Bible in Three Dimensions*, ed. D. J. A. Clines, *et al* (Sheffield: JSOT, 1990) 337–356.
— *New Horizons in Hermeneutics: The Theory and Practice of Transforming Biblical Reading* (Grand Rapids: Zondervan, 1992)
— "Essay Review – Speech-Act Theory and the Claim that God Speaks: Nicholas Wolterstorff's *Divine Discourse*", *Scottish Journal of Theology* 50/1 (1997) 97–110.
Thomas Aquinas, *The Summa Theologica* (2 vol; Chicago: Chicago University Press, 1952; vol 1 & 2)
Thomson, A.; *Tradition and Authority in Science and Theology* (Edinburgh: Scottish Academic Press, 1987)
Thorson, W. R.; "Scientific Objectivity and the Listening Attitude", *Objective Knowledge*, ed. P. Helm (Leicester: IVP, 1987) 59–83.
Tillich, P.; *Systematic Theology* (Welwyn, Herts: Nisbet, 1968)
Topping, R. R.; "The Anti-Foundationalist Challenge to Evangelical Apologetics", *Evangelical Quarterly* 63/1 (1991) 45–60.
Torrance, T. F.; *Theology in Reconstruction* (Grand Rapids: Eerdmans, 1965)
Toulmin, S.; "Does the Distinction Between Normal and Revolutionary Science Hold Water?", *Criticism and the Growth of Knowledge*, ed. I. Lakatos and A. Musgrave (Cambridge: Cambridge University Press, 1970) 39–47.
Triplett, T.; "Recent Work on Foundationalism", *American Philosophical Quarterly* 27/2 (April 1990) 93–116.
Troeltsch, E.; "Religion and the Science of Religion", *Ernst Troeltsch: Writings on Theology and Religion*, ed. R. Morgan and M. Pye (London: Duckworth, 1977) 82–123.
— "Historical and Dogmatic Method in Theology", *Religion in History*, ed. J. L. Adams and W. F. Bense (Edinburgh: T&T Clark, 1991) 11–32.
Van Huyssteen, J. W.; "Is the Postmodernist Always a Postfoundationalist?", *Theology Today* 50/3 (Oct 1993) 373–386.
Veatch, H. B.; "Preliminary Statement of Apology, Analysis, and Critique", *Thomistic Papers IV*, ed. L. A. Kennedy (Houston: University of St Thomas, 1988) 5–63.
Vision, G.; "Veritable Reflections", *Reading Rorty*, ed. A. R. Malachowski (Oxford: Basil Blackwell, 1990) 74–100.
de Vries, P.; "Naturalism in the Natural Sciences: A Christian Perspective", *Christian Scholar's Review* 15/4 (1986) 388–396.
— "Multifaceted Perspective: A Rejoinder to Nicholas Wolterstorff", *Christian Scholar's Review* 16/1 (1986) 59–65.
Wainwright, W. J.; "Meiland and the coherence of cognitive relativism", *Metaphilosophy* 17/1 (Jan 1986) 61–69.
Watkins, J.; "Against 'Normal Science'", *Criticism and the Growth of Knowledge*, ed. I. Lakatos and A. Musgrave (Cambridge: Cambridge University Press, 1970) 25–37.
Watson, F.; "Introduction: The Open Text", *The Open Text: New Directions for Biblical Studies?*, ed. F. Watson (London: SCM, 1993) 1–12.
Westphal, M.; "Taking St. Paul Seriously: Sin as an Epistemological Category", *Christian Philosophy*, ed. T. P. Flint (Notre Dame: University of Notre Dame Press, 1990) 220–226.

— "A Reader's Guide to 'Reformed Epistemology'", *Perspectives* 7/9 (Nov 1992) 10–13.
— "Post-Kantian Reflections on the Importance of Hermeneutics", *Disciplining Hermeneutics: Interpretation in Christian Perspective*, ed. R. Lundin (Grand Rapids: Eerdmans, 1997) 57–66.
— "Review Essay: Theology as Talking About a God Who Talks", *Modern Theology* 13/4 (Oct 1997) 525–536.
— "Taking Plantinga Seriously: Advice to Christian Philosophers", *Faith and Philosophy* 16/2 (Apr 1999) 173–181.
Wiles, M.; "Review of *Divine Discourse*", *Journal of Theological Studies* 47/2 (1996) 802–804.
Williams, B.; "Auto-da-Fé: Consequences of Pragmatism", *Reading Rorty*, ed. A. R. Malachowski (Oxford: Basil Blackwell, 1990) 26–37.
Wogaman, J. P.; "Toward a Christian Definition of Justice", *Transformation* 7/2 (April/June 1990) 18–23.
Wood, W. J.; *Epistemology: Becoming Intellectually Virtuous* (Downers Grove: IVP, 1998)
Wolfe, D. L.; *Epistemology: The Justification of Belief* (Downers Grove: IVP, 1982)
— "The Line of Demarcation between Integration and Pseudointegration", *The Reality of Christian Learning: Strategies for Faith-Discipline Integration*, H. Heie and D. L. Wolfe (Grand Rapids: Eerdmans, 1987) 3–11.
Wright, C. J. H.; *Living as the People of God* (Leicester: IVP, 1983)
— "The Ethical Authority of the Old Testament: A Survey of Approaches. Part II", *Tyndale Bulletin* 43/2 (1992) 203–231.
Yoder, P. B.; *Shalom: The Bible's Word for Salvation, Justice and Peace* (Faith and Life Press: Newton, 1987)
Zeis, J.; "A critique of Plantinga's theological foundationalism", *International Journal for Philosophy of Religion* 28 (1990) 173–189.

Index

Absolutism and non-absolutism; 4, 44, 46n, 73, 97, 98, 102–110, 168–169, 250–254.

Authentic Christian commitment; 5, 132–148, 168, 173–177, 180, 193n, 219–220, 222, 236–240, 242, 244, 248–249, 252.

Belief-dispositions (belief forming mechanisms); 36, 80, 81, 82n, 86, 89–102, 103n, 109, 125, 136, 150, 158–159, 167, 181–182, 208, 216, 245n, 251.

Calvin, J; 90–91, 105n.
Consensus rationality; 1, 12, 107, 108n, 111–113, 116, 132–133, 139, 183, 195, 210, 250.
Control beliefs; 5–6, 102n, 105n, 112, 126n, 128–148, 165n, 167–168, 174–177, 182, 186–187, 189–191, 204n, 205–210, 212, 216–219, 222–229, 235–250, 252–254.

de Vries, P.; see 'V'.
Dooyeweerd, H.; 113, 114n, 117n, 118–126, 128n, 145n, 146n, 178n, 251.
Doxastic practices; 82, 88–89, 95–96, 102, 190, 251–253.

Echeverria, E. J.; 166n, 168n, 173–174, 176n, 178–179.
Entitlement (see also Rationality; Justification); 5, 46n, 82, 95–97, 102–103, 106, 146n, 176n, 180–191, 202, 204n, 212, 249–250, 251.
Evidentialism; 37–38, 73n, 79–80, 93n, 97, 183, 206n, 209n.

Faithful scholarship (see also control beliefs); 123–126, 176, 245–246n, 252.
Feyerabend, P. K.; 3, 32n, 47n, 58–59, 69n, 71n, 115n, 148n, 192, 201, 212, 217n.

Foundationalism, Broad; 13n, 15n, 25n, 38n, 39n, 97–98, 99n, 102n, 191n, 203–214, 223, 232, 254.
Foundationalism, Classical; 4–6, 9, 11–41, 43–44, 97–98, 111–113, 116n, 203–204, 204n, 212, 250–251.

Goodman, N.; 44–47, 192.

Hermeneutics (biblical interpretation); 1, 19–20, 44, 47, 64n, 65n, 67n, 120n, 123n, 144n, 169, 197–109, 214, 221n, 235–250.
Heuristics; 5–6, 112n, 128n, 146–147, 148–160, 181n, 186–187, 191–192, 200–202, 217–218, 246, 252–253.
Historicism; 46n, 109, 166n, 171–174, 192, 200–202, 253.

Incommensurability; 51–53, 57–59, 66–73, 116n, 124n, 199, 211–212, 250–251.
Integration; 150–151, 174–179.

Justification (see also Entitlement; Rationality); 5, 12–14, 17–19, 20–27, 34–37, 43, 45, 60, 79–97, 104–105, 107–108, 116, 125, 183–190, 198–199, 201–203, 204–208, 211–212, 244, 247–250, 251.

Kuhn, T. S.; 3–5, 9–10, 32n, 33n, 44–73, 77n, 99n, 115n, 117, 124n, 127n, 128n, 131n, 115, 165, 166n, 170n, 185, 187, 191–192, 198n, 211n, 217, 221n, 230n, 231n, 232, 250–251.
Kuyper, A.; 90–94, 113–118, 120–122, 125, 126n, 138n, 158–159, 251–252.

Lakatos, I.; 23n, 24n, 25n, 26n, 27n, 117n, 128n, 143, 144n, 146n, 147, 165–166, 167n, 180n, 185, 187, 200–201, 215, 217–222, 224, 231–232.

Laudan, L.; 167n, 185, 185n, 187, 193, 200n, 216n, 217n, 219n, 221–222, 224, 231–232.
Locke, J.; 13n, 14n, 83–84, 99n.
Logical Positivism; 9, 11–18, 23–24, 35–41, 70, 107n.

MacIntyre, A.; 170–172, 185n, 186n, 192n, 232n.
Meta-theory (see Table of Contents).

Neo-Calvinism; 5, 19, 91n, 93n, 111–126, 140n, 142, 144n, 150n, 157n, 158, 176, 178, 179n, 211n, 251–252.
Neutrality; 4, 11n, 19, 25n, 52–53, 59, 68, 70, 107n, 111–112, 174, 194n, 250–252.
Noetic effects of sin; 81n, 90–94, 109–110, 113n, 114–116, 118, 122n, 124–125, 158–160, 251, 253.
Noetic faculties; 34–37, 81, 88–95, 104n, 109, 113–114, 118, 124–125, 145, 158–159, 160, 181n, 197n.
Noetic Obligations; 35, 80n, 81, 82n, 83–89, 94–96, 103–108, 116, 124–125, 132, 135–136, 150–151, 152n, 157, 159, 167–168, 172, 182–184, 188–189, 192n, 205n, 219, 220n, 227n, 251, 252, 253.

Objectivism and subjectivism; 9, 17, 34, 40, 46n, 54–56, 58, 61–63, 65, 72n, 73, 107n, 111–112, 144, 168–169, 172, 194n, 196, 199, 201, 211, 214n, 220, 227n, 250.
Ontology; 62, 131, 191, 194–198, 199n, 221–222, 236, 246n, 253.

Paradigms; 2, 9, 49–60, 64n, 65–70, 72–73, 77, 106n, 117n, 124n, 127n, 230n, 250.
Philosophy of Science; 2, 4, 9, 20, 23, 31–34, 40–41, 60–70, 73, 127, 131, 165–167, 187–188, 217–222, 233, 250.
Plantinga, A.; 6, 13n, 15n, 35n, 36, 37–39, 90n, 91n, 96n, 102n, 146n, 191n, 193n, 203–212, 213n, 224, 225n, 254.

Pluralism; 1–6, 12, 46, 63n, 71n, 107, 108n, 111–118, 121–123, 133, 139–140, 168, 171, 172n, 177, 197–199, 235, 240n, 241n, 243n, 250.
Quine, W. V. O.; 15n, 31n, 40n, 167n, 187n, 192–193, 194n, 205n, 215–217, 224, 232.

Rationality (see also entitlement, justification)
  algorithmic; 5, 50, 55, 60n, 69, 70, 106–107, 148, 168, 177, 187, 190, 191n, 201, 230n, 258.
  and criterion (of theory choice); 5–6, 14–15, 20, 22, 24–25, 38–39, 53–55, 68–69, 81–82, 85–88, 96–97, 145–148, 171n, 168, 180–191, 199, 200n, 201–202, 204–206, 210–212, 219, 229n, 233, 236, 241, 249, 251.
  and doxastic practices (see Doxastic Practices).
  and obligations (see Noetic Obligations).
  and truth; 1, 3, 14, 21, 35, 39, 43, 45–47, 55–56, 63, 71, 83–84, 95, 104–106, 108, 144–146, 148, 160n, 166–169, 171–172n, 183–184, 192–193n, 196n, 197–199, 202, 213n, 214n, 221n, 227n, 247–248, 250–252.
  defeasible; 4–5, 10, 70, 108, 140, 143, 168–169, 175, 191, 193, 195, 199n, 201, 210n, 220, 250–251.
  innocent until proven guilty; 79–83, 89n, 90–94, 103, 180–191, 195n, 198n, 251.
  non-foundationalist; 6, 43, 147, 203–233, 254.
  situated; 4–6, 10, 21n, 73, 82, 85, 97–98, 102–109, 136n, 141, 156, 165–191, 193, 199–201, 219, 233, 239, 250–254.
Realism and anti-realism; 3–4, 6, 16, 43, 45–47, 51–52, 56, 62n, 63, 70n, 83–84, 89–92, 98, 110, 139n, 159, 167, 183–186, 187n, 192–199, 201–202, 225, 246n, 251, 253.
Reformed Epistemology; 2, 9, 15n, 35, 203, 209n, 211n, 219, 247n.

Index 273

Reid, T.; 5, 34–37, 71n, 80n, 81n, 88n, 90, 93, 95–102, 109, 208.
Relativism; 3–6, 9–10, 18, 41, 43–73, 85n, 97–98, 108n, 109–110, 146, 150n, 171, 171n, 173n, 185n, 191–202, 206, 210n, 211, 219n, 233, 235, 241n, 242, 246n, 250–251, 253.
Rorty, R.; 3, 44–48, 62n, 98n, 167n, 192, 212.
Russman, T. A.; 203n, 204n, 212–214.

Scientific method(s); 2–3, 17, 19, 23–24, 26n, 40, 49, 51–52, 58n, 62n, 65, 111, 127–128n, 140, 143, 165–179, 200–201, 215n, 218–222.
Shalom; 5, 105–107, 135, 148–160, 172–174, 186, 191, 200–202, 252–253.
Social practices; 82n, 126, 169–172, 254.

Theological Scholarship; 1–4, 6, 16, 19, 44, 64n, 65n, 66n, 79, 92n, 109n, 113n, 128n, 129n, 141n, 144, 163, 169, 174n, 180n, 187–188, 203, 220n, 214, 227n, 233, 235–250.

Theories, devising and weighing (see Contents).
Traditions in scholarship; 58n, 65n, 107, 122, 170–172, 183n, 185–188, 192n, 201n, 210, 220–222, 224, 231–233, 235n, 238, 241n, 244–250, 252–254.
Truth and Rationality (see Rationality and Truth).

de Vries, P.; 174–179.

Wissenschaft (*Scientia*); 2–6, 9–29, 77n, 92, 93, 110, 112–113, 115–116, 122, 124, 126, 127, 138–145, 151, 163, 165n, 168, 171n, 172, 175, 178–180, 183–184, 187n, 221n, 233, 243, 247, 250–251, 254.
Wolterstorff, N. P. (see Contents for major topics).
Wolterstorff's epistemology (see Contents).
Wolterstorff's meta-theory (see Contents).
World-view (*Weltanshauung*); 46n, 66–69, 71, 107, 118–121, 137n, 185, 192n, 212n.

Paternoster Biblical Monographs

(All titles uniform with this volume)
Dates in bold are of projected publication

Joseph Abraham
Eve: Accused or Acquitted?
A Reconsideration of Feminist Readings of the Creation Narrative Texts in Genesis 1–3
Two contrary views dominate contemporary feminist biblical scholarship. One finds in the Bible an unequivocal equality between the sexes from the very creation of humanity, whilst the other sees the biblical text as irredeemably patriarchal and androcentric. Dr Abraham enters into dialogue with both camps as well as introducing his own method of approach. An invaluable tool for any one who is interested in this contemporary debate.
2002 / 0-85364-971-5 / xxiv + 272pp

Octavian D. Baban
Mimesis and Luke's On the Road Encounters in Luke-Acts
Luke's Theology of the Way and its Literary Representation
The book argues on theological and literary (mimetic) grounds that Luke's on-the-road encounters, especially those belonging to the post-Easter period, are part of his complex theology of the Way. Jesus' teaching and that of the apostles is presented by Luke as a challenging answer to the Hellenistic reader's thirst for adventure, good literature, and existential paradigms.
2005 */ 1-84227253-5 / approx. 374pp*

Paul Barker
The Triumph of Grace in Deuteronomy
This book is a textual and theological analysis of the interaction between the sin and faithlessness of Israel and the grace of Yahweh in response, looking especially at Deuteronomy chapters 1–3, 8–10 and 29–30. The author argues that the grace of Yahweh is determinative for the ongoing relationship between Yahweh and Israel and that Deuteronomy anticipates and fully expects Israel to be faithless.
2004 / 1-84227-226-8 / xxii + 270pp

Jonathan F. Bayes
The Weakness of the Law
God's Law and the Christian in New Testament Perspective
A study of the four New Testament books which refer to the law as weak (Acts, Romans, Galatians, Hebrews) leads to a defence of the third use in the Reformed debate about the law in the life of the believer.
2000 / 0-85364-957-X / xii + 244pp

Mark Bonnington
The Antioch Episode of Galatians 2:11-14 in Historical and Cultural Context

The Galatians 2 'incident' in Antioch over table-fellowship suggests significant disagreement between the leading apostles. This book analyses the background to the disagreement by locating the incident within the dynamics of social interaction between Jews and Gentiles. It proposes a new way of understanding the relationship between the individuals and issues involved.

2005 / 1-84227-050-8 / approx. 350pp

David Bostock
A Portrayal of Trust
The Theme of Faith in the Hezekiah Narratives

This study provides detailed and sensitive readings of the Hezekiah narratives (2 Kings 18–20 and Isaiah 36–39) from a theological perspective. It concentrates on the theme of faith, using narrative criticism as its methodology. Attention is paid especially to setting, plot, point of view and characterization within the narratives. A largely positive portrayal of Hezekiah emerges that underlines the importance and relevance of scripture.

2005 / 1-84227-314-0 / approx. 300pp

Mark Bredin
Jesus, Revolutionary of Peace
A Non-violent Christology in the Book of Revelation

This book aims to demonstrate that the figure of Jesus in the Book of Revelation can best be understood as an active non-violent revolutionary.

2003 / 1-84227-153-9 / xviii + 262pp

Robinson Butarbutar
Resolving a Dispute, Past and Present
An Exegetical Study of Paul's Apostolic Paradigm in 1 Corinthians 9

The author sees the apostolic paradigm in 1 Corinthians 9 as part of Paul's unified arguments in 1 Corinthians 8–10 in which he seeks to mediate in the dispute over the issue of food offered to idols. The book also sees its relevance for dispute-resolution today, taking the conflict within the author's church as an example.

2005 / 1-84227315-9 / approx. 280pp

Daniel J-S Chae
Paul as Apostle to the Gentiles
His Apostolic Self-awareness and its Influence on the Soteriological Argument in Romans
Opposing 'the post-Holocaust interpretation of Romans', Daniel Chae competently demonstrates that Paul argues for the equality of Jew and Gentile in Romans. Chae's fresh exegetical interpretation is academically outstanding and spiritually encouraging.
1997 / 0-85364-829-8 / xiv + 378pp

Luke L. Cheung
The Genre, Composition and Hermeneutics of the Epistle of James
The present work examines the employment of the wisdom genre with a certain compositional structure and the interpretation of the law through the Jesus tradition of the double love command by the author of the Epistle of James to serve his purpose in promoting perfection and warning against doubleness among the eschatologically renewed people of God in the Diaspora.
2003 / 1-84227-062-1 / xvi + 372pp

Youngmo Cho
Spirit and Kingdom in the Writings of Luke and Paul
The relationship between Spirit and Kingdom is a relatively unexplored area in Lukan and Pauline studies. This book offers a fresh perspective of two biblical writers on the subject. It explores the difference between Luke's and Paul's understanding of the Spirit by examining the specific question of the relationship of the concept of the Spirit to the concept of the Kingdom of God in each writer.
2005 / 1-84227-316-7 / approx. 270pp

Andrew C. Clark
Parallel Lives
The Relation of Paul to the Apostles in the Lucan Perspective
This study of the Peter-Paul parallels in Acts argues that their purpose was to emphasize the themes of continuity in salvation history and the unity of the Jewish and Gentile missions. New light is shed on Luke's literary techniques, partly through a comparison with Plutarch.
2001 / 1-84227-035-4 / xviii + 386pp

Andrew D. Clarke
Secular and Christian Leadership in Corinth
A Socio-Historical and Exegetical Study of 1 Corinthians 1–6
This volume is an investigation into the leadership structures and dynamics of first-century Roman Corinth. These are compared with the practice of leadership in the Corinthian Christian community which are reflected in 1 Corinthians 1–6, and contrasted with Paul's own principles of Christian leadership
2005 / 1-84227-229-2 / 200pp

Stephen Finamore
God, Order and Chaos
René Girard and the Apocalypse
Readers are often disturbed by the images of destruction in the book of Revelation and unsure why they are unleashed after the exaltation of Jesus. This book examines past approaches to these texts and uses René Girard's theories to revive some old ideas and propose some new ones.
2005 / 1-84227-197-0 / approx. 344pp

Scott J. Hafemann
Suffering and Ministry in the Spirit
Paul's Defence of His Ministry in II Corinthians 2:14–3:3
Shedding new light on the way Paul defended his apostleship, the author offers a careful, detailed study of 2 Corinthians 2:14–3:3 linked with other key passages throughout 1 and 2 Corinthians. Demonstrating the unity and coherence of Paul's argument in this passage, the author shows that Paul's suffering served as the vehicle for revealing God's power and glory through the Spirit.
2000 / 0-85364-967-7 / xiv + 262pp

Scott J. Hafemann
Paul, Moses and the History of Israel
The Letter/Spirit Contrast and the Argument from Scripture in 2 Corinthians 3
An exegetical study of the call of Moses, the second giving of the Law (Exodus 32–34), the new covenant, and the prophetic understanding of the history of Israel in 2 Corinthians 3. Hafemann's work demonstrates Paul's contextual use of the Old Testament and the essential unity between the Law and the Gospel within the context of the distinctive ministries of Moses and Paul.
2005 / 1-84227-317-5 / 498pp

Douglas S. McComiskey
Lukan Theology in the Light of the Gospel's Literary Structure
Luke's Gospel was purposefully written with theology embedded in its patterned literary structure. A critical analysis of this cyclical structure provides new windows into Luke's interpretation of the individual pericopes comprising the Gospel and illuminates several of his theological interests.
2004 / 1-84227-148-2 / approx. 400pp

Stephen Motyer
Your Father the Devil?
A New Approach to John and 'The Jews'
Who are 'the Jews' in John's Gospel? Defending John against the charge of antisemitism, Motyer argues that, far from demonising the Jews, the Gospel seeks to present Jesus as 'Good News for Jews' in a late first century setting.
1997 / 0-85364-832-8 / xiv + 260pp

Esther Ng
Reconstructing Christian Origins?
The Feminist Theology of Elizabeth Schüssler Fiorenza: An Evaluation
In a detailed evaluation, the author challenges Elizabeth Schüssler Fiorenza's reconstruction of early Christian origins and her underlying presuppositions. The author also presents her own views on women's roles both then and now.
2002 / 1-84227-055-9 / xxiv + 468pp

Robin Parry
Old Testament Story and Christian Ethics
The Rape of Dinah as a Case Study
What is the role of story in ethics and, more particularly, what is the role of Old Testament story in Christian ethics? This book, drawing on the work of contemporary philosophers, argues that narrative is crucial in the ethical shaping of people and, drawing on the work of contemporary Old Testament scholars, that story plays a key role in Old Testament ethics. Parry then argues that when situated in canonical context Old Testament stories can be reappropriated by Christian readers in their own ethical formation. The shocking story of the rape of Dinah and the massacre of the Shechemites provides a fascinating case study for exploring the parameters within which Christian ethical appropriations of Old Testament stories can live.
2004 / 1-84227-210-1 / xx + 350pp

Ian Paul
Power to See the World Anew
The Value of Paul Ricoeur's Hermeneutic of Metaphor in Interpreting the Symbolism of Revelation 12 and 13

This book is a study of the hermeneutics of metaphor of Paul Ricoeur, one of the most important writers on hermeneutics and metaphor of the last century. It sets out the key points of his theory, important criticisms of his work, and how his approach, modified in the light of these criticisms, offers a methodological framework for reading apocalyptic texts.

2005 / 1-84227-056-7 / approx. 350pp

Robert L. Plummer
Paul's Understanding of the Church's Mission
Did the Apostle Paul Expect the Early Christian Communities to Evangelize?

This book engages in a careful study of Paul's letters to determine if the apostle expected the communities to which he wrote to engage in missionary activity. It helpfully summarizes the discussion on this debated issue, judiciously handling contested texts, and provides a way forward in addressing this critical question. While admitting that Paul rarely explicitly commands the communities he founded to evangelize, Plummer amasses significant incidental data to provide a convincing case that Paul did indeed expect his churches to engage in mission activity. Throughout the study, Plummer progressively builds a theological basis for the church's mission that is both distinctively Pauline and compelling.

2005 / 0-85364-333-7 / approx. 324pp

David Powys
'Hell': A Hard Look at a Hard Question
The Fate of the Unrighteous in New Testament Thought

This comprehensive treatment seeks to unlock the original meaning of terms and phrases long thought to support the traditional doctrine of hell. It concludes that there is an alternative—one which is more biblical, and which can positively revive the rationale for Christian mission.

1997 / 0-85364-831-X / xxii + 478pp

Sorin Sabou
Between Horror and Hope
Paul's Metaphorical Language of Death in Romans 6.1-11

This book argues that Paul's metaphorical language of death in Romans 6.1-11 conveys two aspects: horror and hope. The 'horror' aspect is conveyed by the 'crucifixion' language, and the 'hope' aspect by 'burial' language. The life of the Christian believer is understood, as relationship with sin is concerned ('death to sin'), between these two realities: horror and hope.

2005 / 1-84227-322-1 / approx. 224pp

Rosalind Selby
The Comical Doctrine
Mark and Hermeneutics
This book argues that the gospel breaks through postmodernity's critique of truth and the referential possibilities of textuality with its gift of grace. With a rigorous, philosophical challenge to modernist and postmodernist assumptions, Selby offers an alternative epistemology to all who would still read with faith *and* with academic credibility.
2005 / 1-84227-212-8 / approx. 350pp

Kevin Walton
Thou Traveller Unknown
The Presence and Absence of God in the Jacob Narrative
The author offers a fresh reading of the story of Jacob in the book of Genesis through the paradox of divine presence and absence. The work also seeks to make a contribution to Pentateuchal studies by bringing together a close reading of the final text with historical critical insights, doing justice to the text's historical depth, final form and canonical status.
2003 / 1-84227-059-1 / xvi + 238pp

George M. Wieland
The Significance of Salvation
A Study of Salvation Language in the Pastoral Epistles
The language and ideas of salvation pervade the three Pastoral Epistles. This study offers a close examination of their soteriological statements. In all three letters the idea of salvation is found to play a vital paraenetic role, but each also exhibits distinctive soteriological emphases. The results challenge common assumptions about the Pastoral Epistles as a corpus.
2005 / 1-84227257-8 / approx. 324pp

Alistair Wilson
When Will These Things Happen?
A Study of Jesus as Judge in Matthew 21–25
This study seeks to allow Matthew's carefully constructed presentation of Jesus to be given full weight in the modern evaluation of Jesus' eschatology. Careful analysis of the text of Matthew 21–25 reveals Jesus to be standing firmly in the Jewish prophetic and wisdom traditions as he proclaims and enacts imminent judgement on the Jewish authorities then boldly claims the central role in the final and universal judgement.
2004 / 1-84227-146-6 / xxii + 272pp

Lindsay Wilson
Joseph Wise and Otherwise
The Intersection of Covenant and Wisdom in Genesis 37–50
This book offers a careful literary reading of Genesis 37–50 that argues that the Joseph story contains both strong covenant themes and many wisdom-like elements. The connections between the two helps to explore how covenant and wisdom might intersect in an integrated biblical theology.
2004 / 1-84227-140-7 / xvi + 340pp

Stephen I. Wright
The Voice of Jesus
Studies in the Interpretation of Six Gospel Parables
This literary study considers how the 'voice' of Jesus has been heard in different periods of parable interpretation, and how the categories of figure and trope may help us towards a sensitive reading of the parables today.
2000 / 0-85364-975-8 / xiv + 280pp

Paternoster
9 Holdom Avenue
Bletchley
Milton Keynes MK1 1QR
United Kingdom

Web: www.authenticmedia.co.uk/paternoster

November 2004

Paternoster Theological Monographs
(All titles uniform with this volume)
Dates in bold are of projected publication

Emil Bartos
Deification in Eastern Orthodox Theology
An Evaluation and Critique of the Theology of Dumitru Staniloae
Bartos studies a fundamental yet neglected aspect of Orthodox theology: deification. By examining the doctrines of anthropology, christology, soteriology and ecclesiology as they relate to deification, he provides an important contribution to contemporary dialogue between Eastern and Western theologians.
1999 / 0-85364-956-1 / xii + 370pp

Iain D. Campbell
Fixing the Indemnity
The Life and Work of George Adam Smith
When Old Testament scholar George Adam Smith (1856–1942) delivered the Lyman Beecher lectures at Yale University in 1899, he confidently declared that 'modern criticism has won its war against traditional theories. It only remains to fix the amount of the indemnity.' In this biography, Iain D. Campbell assesses Smith's critical approach to the Old Testament and evaluates its consequences, showing that Smith's life and work still raises questions about the relationship between biblical scholarship and evangelical faith.
2004 / 1-84227-228-4 / xx + 256pp

Tim Chester
Mission and the Coming of God
Eschatology, the Trinity and Mission in the Theology of Jürgen Moltmann
This book explores the theology and missiology of the influential contemporary theologian, Jürgen Moltmann. It highlights the important contribution Moltmann has made while offering a critique of his thought from an evangelical perspective. In so doing, it touches on pertinent issues for evangelical missiology. The conclusion takes Calvin as a starting point, proposing 'an eschatology of the cross' which offers a critique of the over-realised eschatologies in liberation theology and certain forms of evangelicalism.
2005 / 1-84227-320-5 / approx. 224pp

November 2004

Sylvia Wilkey Collinson
Making Disciples
The Significance of Jesus' Educational Strategy for Today's Church
This study examines the biblical practice of discipling, formulates a definition, and makes comparisons with modern models of education. A recommendation is made for greater attention to its practice today.
2004 / 1-84227-116-4 / xiv + 278pp

Darrell Cosden
A Theology of Work
Work and the New Creation
Through dialogue with Moltmann, Pope John Paul II and others, this book develops a genitive 'theology of work', presenting a theological definition of work and a model for a theological ethics of work that shows work's nature, value and meaning now and eschatologically. Work is shown to be a transformative activity consisting of three dynamically inter-related dimensions: the instrumental, relational and ontological.
2004 / 1-84227-332-9 / xvi + 208pp

Stephen M. Dunning
The Crisis and the Quest
A Kierkegaardian Reading of Charles Williams
Employing Kierkegaardian categories and analysis, this study investigates both the central crisis in Charles Williams's authorship between hermetism and Christianity (Kierkegaard's Religions A and B), and the quest to resolve this crisis, a quest that ultimately presses the bounds of orthodoxy.
2000 / 0-85364-985-5 / xxiv + 254pp

Keith Ferdinando
The Triumph of Christ in African Perspective
A Study of Demonology and Redemption in the African Context
The book explores the implications of the gospel for traditional African fears of occult aggression. It analyses such traditional approaches to suffering and biblical responses to fears of demonic evil, concluding with an evaluation of African beliefs from the perspective of the gospel.
1999 / 0-85364-830-1 / xviii + 450pp

November 2004

Andrew Goddard
Living the Word, Resisting the World
The Life and Thought of Jacques Ellul
This work offers a definitive study of both the life and thought of the French Reformed thinker Jacques Ellul (1912-1994). It will prove an indispensable resource for those interested in this influential theologian and sociologist and for Christian ethics and political thought generally.
2002 / 1-84227-053-2 / xxiv + 378pp

David Hilborn
The Words of our Lips
Language-Use in Free Church Worship
Studies of liturgical language have tended to focus on the written canons of Roman Catholic and Anglican communities. By contrast, David Hilborn analyses the more extemporary approach of English Nonconformity. Drawing on recent developments in linguistic pragmatics, he explores similarities and differences between 'fixed' and 'free' worship, and argues for the interdependence of each.
2005 / 0-85364-977-4

Roger Hitching
The Church and Deaf People
A Study of Identity, Communication and Relationships with Special Reference to the Ecclesiology of Jürgen Moltmann
In *The Church and Deaf People* Roger Hitching sensitively examines the history and present experience of deaf people and finds similarities between aspects of sign language and Moltmann's theological method that 'open up' new ways of understanding theological concepts.
2003 / 1-84227-222-5 / xxii + 236pp

John G. Kelly
One God, One People
The Differentiated Unity of the People of God in the Theology of Jürgen Moltmann
The author expounds and critiques Moltmann's doctrine of God and highlights the systematic connections between it and Moltmann's influential discussion of Israel. He then proposes a fresh approach to Jewish-Christian relations building on Moltmann's work using insights from Habermas and Rawls.
2005 / 0-85346-969-3 / approx. 350pp

Mark F.W. Lovatt
Confronting the Will-to-Power
A Reconsideration of the Theology of Reinhold Niebuhr
Confronting the Will-to-Power is an analysis of the theology of Reinhold Niebuhr, arguing that his work is an attempt to identify, and provide a practical theological answer to, the existence and nature of human evil.
2001 / 1-84227-054-0 / xviii + 216pp

Neil B. MacDonald
Karl Barth and the Strange New World within the Bible
Barth, Wittgenstein, and the Metadilemmas of the Enlightenment
Barth's discovery of the strange new world within the Bible is examined in the context of Kant, Hume, Overbeck, and, most importantly, Wittgenstein. MacDonald covers some fundamental issues in theology today: epistemology, the final form of the text and biblical truth-claims.
2000 / 0-85364-970-7 / xxvi + 374pp

Keith Mascord
No Challenge Unfaced
Alvin Plantinga's Contribution to Christian Apologetics
This book draws together the contributions of the philosopher, Alvin Plantinga, to the major contemporary challenges to Christian belief, highlighting in particular his ground-breaking work in epistemology and the problem of evil. Plantinga's theory that both theistic and Christian belief is warrantedly basic is explored and critiqued, and an assessment offered as to the significance of his work for apologetic theory and practice.
2005 / 1-84227-256-X / approx. 304pp

Gillian McCulloch
The Deconstruction of Dualism in Theology
With Reference to Ecofeminist Theology and New Age Spirituality
This book challenges eco-theological anti-dualism in Christian theology, arguing that dualism has a twofold function in Christian religious discourse. Firstly, it enables us to express the discontinuities and divisions that are part of the process of reality. Secondly, dualistic language allows us to express the mysteries of divine transcendence/immanence and the survival of the soul without collapsing into monism and materialism, both of which are problematic for Christian epistemology.
2002 / 1-84227-044-3 / xii + 282pp

Leslie McCurdy
Attributes and Atonement
The Holy Love of God in the Theology of P.T. Forsyth
Attributes and Atonement is an intriguing full-length study of P.T. Forsyth's doctrine of the cross as it relates particularly to God's holy love. It includes an unparalleled bibliography of both primary and secondary material relating to Forsyth.
1999 / 0-85364-833-6 / xiv + 328pp

Nozomu Miyahira
Towards a Theology of the Concord of God
A Japanese Perspective on the Trinity
This book introduces a new Japanese theology and a unique Trinitarian formula based on the Japanese intellectual climate: three betweennesses and one concord. It also presents a new interpretation of the Trinity, a co-subordinationism, which is in line with orthodox Trinitarianism; each single person of the Trinity is eternally and equally subordinate (or serviceable) to the other persons, so that they retain the mutual dynamic equality.
2000 / 0-85364-863-8 / xiv + 256pp

Eddy José Muskus
The Origins and Early Development of Liberation Theology in Latin America
With Particular Reference to Gustavo Gutiérrez
This work challenges the fundamental premise of Liberation Theology, 'opting for the poor', and its claim that Christ is found in them. It also argues that Liberation Theology emerged as a direct result of the failure of the Roman Catholic Church in Latin America.
2002 / 0-85364-974-X / xiv + 296pp

Jim Purves
The Triune God and the Charismatic Movement
A Critical Appraisal from a Scottish Perspective
All emotion and no theology? Or a fundamental challenge to reappraise and realign our trinitarian theology in the light of Christian experience? This study of charismatic renewal as it found expression within Scotland at the end of the twentieth century evaluates the use of Patristic, Reformed and contemporary models of the Trinity in explaining the workings of the Holy Spirit.
2004 / 1-84227-321-3 / xxiv + 246pp

Anna Robbins
Methods in the Madness
Diversity in Twentieth-Century Christian Social Ethics
The author compares the ethical methods of Walter Rauschenbusch, Reinhold Niebuhr and others. She argues that unless Christians are clear about the ways that theology and philosophy are expressed practically they may lose the ability to discuss social ethics across contexts, let alone reach effective agreements.
2004 / 1-84227-211-X / xx + 294pp

Ed Rybarczyk
Beyond Salvation
Eastern Orthodoxy and Classical Pentecostalism on becoming like Christ
At first glance eastern Orthodoxy and classical Pentecostalism seem quite distinct. This ground-breaking study shows they share much in common, especially as it concerns the experiential elements of following Christ. Both traditions assert that authentic Christianity transcends the wooden categories of modernism.
2004 / 1-84227-144-X / xii + 356pp

Signe Sandsmark
Is World View Neutral Education Possible and Desirable?
A Christian Response to Liberal Arguments
(Published jointly with The Stapleford Centre)
This book discusses reasons for belief in world view neutrality, and argues that 'neutral' education will have a hidden, but strong world view influence. It discusses the place for Christian education in the common school.
2000 / 0-85364-973-1 / xiv + 182pp

Hazel Sherman
Reading Zechariah
The Allegorical Tradition of Biblical Interpretation through the Commentary of Didymus the Blind and Theodore of Mopsuestia
A close reading of the commentary on Zechariah by Didymus the Blind alongside that of Theodore of Mopsuestia suggests that popular categorising of Antiochene and Alexandrian biblical exegesis as 'historical' or 'allegorical' is inadequate and misleading.
2005 / 1-84227-213-6 / approx. 280pp

Andrew Sloane
On Being a Christian in the Academy
Nicholas Wolterstorff and the Practice of Christian Scholarship
An exposition and critical appraisal of Nicholas Wolterstorff's epistemology in the light of the philosophy of science, and an application of his thought to the practice of Christian scholarship.
2003 / 1-84227-058-3 / xvi + 274pp

Damon So
Jesus' Revelation of His Father
A Narrative-Conceptual Study of the Trinity with Special Reference to Karl Barth
This book explores the trinitarian dynamics in the context of Jesus' revelation of his Father in his earthly ministry with references to key passages in Matthew's Gospel. It develops from the exegeses of these passages a non-linear concept of revelation which links Jesus' communion with his Father to his revelatory words and actions through a nuanced understanding of the Holy Spirit, with references to K. Barth, G.W.H. Lampe, J.D.G. Dunn and E. Irving.
2005 / 1-84227-323-X / approx. 380pp

Daniel Strange
The Possibility of Salvation Among the Unevangelised
An Analysis of Inclusivism in Recent Evangelical Theology
For evangelical theologians the 'fate of the unevangelised' impinges upon fundamental tenets of evangelical identity. The position known as 'inclusivism', defined by the belief that the unevangelised can be ontologically saved by Christ whilst being epistemologically unaware of him, has been defended most vigorously by the Canadian evangelical Clark H. Pinnock. Through a detailed analysis and critique of Pinnock's work, this book examines a cluster of issues surrounding the unevangelised and its implications for christology, soteriology and the doctrine of revelation.
2002 / 1-84227-047-8 / xviii + 362pp

Scott Swain
God according to the Gospel
Biblical Narrative and the Identity of God in the Theology of Robert W. Jenson
Robert W. Jenson is one of the leading voices in contemporary Trinitarian theology. His boldest contribution in this area concerns his use of biblical narrative both to ground and explicate the Christian doctrine of God. *God according to the Gospel* critically examines Jenson's proposal and suggests an alternative way of reading the biblical portrayal of the triune God.
2006 / 1-84227-258-7 / approx. 180pp

November 2004

Graham Tomlin
The Power of the Cross
Theology and the Death of Christ in Paul, Luther and Pascal
This book explores the theology of the cross in St Paul, Luther and Pascal. It offers new perspectives on the theology of each, and some implications for the nature of power, apologetics, theology and church life in a postmodern context.
1999 / 0-85364-984-7 / xiv + 344pp

Graham J. Watts
Revelation and the Spirit
A Comparative Study of the Relationship between the Doctrine of Revelation and Pneumatology in the Theology of Eberhard Jüngel and of Wolfhart Pannenberg
The relationship between Revelation and pneumatology is relatively unexplored. This approach offers a fresh angle on two important twentieth century theologians and raises pneumatological questions which are theologically crucial and relevant to mission in a postmodern culture.
2005 / 1-84227-104-0 / xxii + 232pp

Nigel G. Wright
Disavowing Constantine
Mission, Church and the Social Order in the Theologies of John Howard Yoder and Jürgen Moltmann
This book is a timely restatement of a radical theology of church and state in the Anabaptist and Baptist tradition. Dr Wright constructs his argument in dialogue and debate with Yoder and Moltmann, major contributors to a free church perspective.
2000 / 0-85364-978-2 / xvi + 252pp

Paternoster
9 Holdom Avenue
Bletchley
Milton Keynes MK1 1QR
United Kingdom

Web: www.authenticmedia.co.uk/paternoster

November 2004

www.ingramcontent.com/pod-product-compliance
Lightning Source LLC
Chambersburg PA
CBHW050337230426
43663CB00010B/1893